D1569726

The Medieval European Religious Lyric

THE MEDIEVAL EUROPEAN
RELIGIOUS LYRIC

AN ARS POETICA

PATRICK S. DIEHL

UNIVERSITY OF CALIFORNIA PRESS
Berkeley · Los Angeles · London

University of California Press
Berkeley and Los Angeles, California
University of California Press, Ltd.
London, England
© 1985 by
The Regents of the University of California

Library of Congress Cataloging in Publication Data
Diehl, Patrick S.
The medieval European religious lyric.
Includes indexes.
1. Poetry, Medieval—History and criticism.
2. Christian poetry, European—History and criticism.
3. Lyric poetry—History and criticism.   I. Title.
PN691.D53   1984   809.1′4   83-6557
ISBN 0-520-04673-0

Printed in the United States of America

1   2   3   4   5   6   7   8   9

Les faits sont pleins d'idées
M. D. Chenu

CONTENTS

ABBREVIATIONS

Adam of St. Victor = Adam of St. Victor, *Sämtliche Sequenzen*, ed. F. Wellner (Munich, 1955).

AH = *Analecta hymnica Medii Aevi*, ed. Guido Dreves, Clemens Blume, and Henry Bannister, 55 vols. (Leipzig, 1886–1922).

Annalen = Josef Szoevérffy, *Die Annalen der lateinischen Hymnendichtung*, 2 vols. (Berlin, 1964–65).

Bianco da Siena, ed. Bini = *Laudi spirituali del Bianco da Siena*, ed. Telesforo Bini (Lucca, 1851).

Brown XIII = *English Lyrics of the Thirteenth Century*, ed. Carleton Brown (Oxford, 1932).

Brown XIV = *Religious Lyrics of the Fourteenth Century*, ed. Carleton Brown, rev. G. Smithers, 2d ed. (Oxford, 1952).

Brown XV = *Religious Lyrics of the Fifteenth Century*, ed. Carleton Brown (Oxford, 1939).

Cançons nadalenques = *Cançons nadalenques del segle xv*, ed. José Romeu i Figueras, (Barcelona, 1949).

Cantigas = Alfonso X, o Sabio, *Cantigas de Santa Maria*, ed. Walter Mettmann, 4 vols. (Coimbra, 1959–72).

CC = *Cancionero castellano del siglo XV*, ed. Raymond Foulché-Delbosc, 2 vols., Nueva Biblioteca de Autores Españoles, vols. 19 and 22 (Madrid, 1912–15).

CG = *Cancionero general de Hernando del Castillo según la edición de 1511, con un apéndice de lo añadido en las de 1527, 1540 y 1557*, ed. José de Balenchana, 2 vols., Sociedad de bibliófilos españoles, vol. 21, pts. 1 and 2 (Madrid, 1882).

Chenu = Marie-Dominique Chenu, *La théologie au douzième siècle*, Etudes de philosophie médiévale 45 (Paris, 1957).

CM = José Romeu i Figueras, ed., *La música en la Corte de los Reyes Católicos*, vol. 4, pt. 2: *Cancionero musical de Palacio (siglos XV y XVI)* (Barcelona, 1967).

Davies = *Medieval English Lyrics: A Critical Anthology*, ed. Reginald T. Davies (London, 1963).

EETS = Early English Text Society

Galletti = Gustavo Galletti, ed., *Laude spirituali di Feo Belcari, di Lorenzo de' Medici, di Francesco d'Albizzo, di Castellano Castellani, e di altri comprese nelle quattro più antiche raccolte con alcune inedite e con nuove illustrazioni* (Florence, 1863).

Gattungen = *Gattungen der Musik in Einzeldarstellungen: Gedenkschrift Leo Schrade*, vol. 1, ed. Wulf Arlt, Ernst Lichtenhahn, and Hans Oesch (Bern/Munich, 1973).

Gautier de Coincy, ed. Koenig = Gautier de Coincy, *Les miracles de Notre Dame*, ed. Vernon Koenig, 4 vols. (Geneva/Lille/Paris, 1955–70).

Gautier de Coincy, ed. Långfors = Artur Långfors, "Mélanges de poésie lyrique française: Gautier de Coinci," *Romania* 53 (1927): 474–538.

Giustinian = Leonardo Giustinian, *Laude devotissime e sanctissime composte per el nobile e magnifico Misser Leonardo Justiniano di Venetia* (Venice, 1506).

Grajales = Francisco Martí Grajales, *Les Trobes en lahors de la Verge Maria* (Valencia, 1894).

Helgason = Jón Helgason, *Islenzk Miðaldakvæði*, 2 vols. (Copenhagen, 1936–38) (= vols. 1.2 and 2; no more issued).

Iberian Hymnody = Josef Szoevérffy, *Iberian Hymnody: Survey and Problems* (Wetteren, Belgium, 1971).

Jacopone = Jacopone da Todi, *Laude*, ed. Franco Mancini, Scrittori d'Italia, no. 257 (Rome/Bari, 1974).

Jeanroy, *Joies* = Alfred Jeanroy, *Les Joies du gai savoir*, Bibliothèque méridionale, sér. 1, t. 16 (Toulouse, 1914).

Jeffrey = David Jeffrey, *The Early English Lyric and Franciscan Spirituality* (Lincoln, Neb., 1975).

Jonsson, *Tropes* = Ritva Jonsson, ed., *Corpus troporum I: Tropes du propre de la messe 1, Cycle de Noël*, Studia latina stockholmiensia, vol. 21 (Stockholm, 1975).

Le Gentil = Pierre Le Gentil, *La poésie lyrique espagnole et portugaise à la fin du moyen âge*, 2 vols. (Rennes, 1949–52).

Lotman, *Structure* = Juri Lotman, *The Structure of the Artistic Text*, trans. Ronald and Gail Vroon (Ann Arbor, 1977).

Lydgate = *The Minor Poems of John Lydgate*, ed. Henry McCracken, vol. 1, EETS, orig. ser. 107 (London, 1911 for 1910).

Mahn, *Werke* = Carl Mahn, ed., *Die Werke der Troubadours*, vol. 4 (Berlin, 1853) (contains S. Pfaff's edition of Guiraut Riquier's poems).

Meerssemann, *Akathistos* = Gérard Meerssemann, *Der Hymnos Akathistos im Abendland*, 2 vols., Spicilegium Friburgense 2 and 3 (Freiburg in der Schweiz, 1958).

Meerssemann, *Etudes* = Gérard Meerssemann, "Etudes sur les anciennes confréries dominicaines," parts 1–3, *Archivum fratrum praedicatorum*, 20–22 (1950–52): 5–113, 51–196 and 5–176.

Menéndez y Pelayo = Marcelino Menéndez y Pelayo, eds., *Antología de poetas líricos castellanos desde la formación del idioma hasta nuestras días*, 10 vols. (Madrid, 1914–22).

NM = *Neuphilologische Mitteilungen*.

Noulet/Chabaneau = Jean-Baptiste Noulet and Camille Chabaneau, eds., *Deux manuscrits provençaux du xive siècle contenant des poésies de Raimon de Cornet de Peire de Ladils et d'autres poètes de l'école toulousaine* (Montpellier/Paris, 1888).

Pero Martines = Pero Martines, *Obras*, ed. Martín de Riquer (Barcelona, 1946).

PG = *Patrologiae cursus completus: Series graeca*, ed. Jacques P. Migne, 161 vols. in 166 (Paris, 1857–99).

PL = *Patrologiae cursus completus: Series latina*, ed. Jacques P. Migne, 221 vols. in 222 (Paris, 1844–1902).

PLAC = Ernst Duemmler, Ludwig Traube, Paul von Winterfeld, and Karl Strecker, eds., *Poetae latini aevi carolini/Medii Aevi*, 6 vols., Monumenta Germaniae historica (Berlin, 1881–1951).

Raby, *Oxford* = Frederic J. Raby, ed., *The Oxford Book of Medieval Latin Verse* (Oxford, 1959).

Recueil = Edward Jaernstroem and Artur Långfors, eds., *Recueil de chansons pieuses du 13ᵉ siècle*, 2 vols., Suomalaisen Tiedeakatemian Toimituksia, Helsinki, Annales Academiae Scientiarum Fennicae, B.III.1 and B.V.20 (1910–27).

Reinmar = *Die Gedichte Reinmars von Zweter*, ed. Gustav Roethe (Leipzig, 1887; reprint, Amsterdam, 1967).

Riquier, ed. Pfaff = Mahn, *Werke* (q.v.).

SATF = Société des anciens textes français.

Schroeder = Mary Schroeder, "Mary-Verse in Meistergesang" (Ph.D. diss., Catholic University, 1942).

Skjaldedigtning = Finnur Jónsson, ed. *Den norsk-islandske Skjaldedigtning B*, 2 vols. (Copenhagen/Kristiania, 1912–15).

Spanke, *Beziehungen* = Hans Spanke, *Beziehungen zwischen romanischer und mittellateinischer Lyrik, mit besonderer Berücksichtigung der Metrik und Musik*, in Gesellschaft der Wissenschaft, Göttingen, philologisch-historische Klasse, Abhandlungen, 3d ser. 18 (1936).

Stroppel = Robert Stroppel, *Liturgie und geistliche Dichtung zwischen 1050 und 1300* (Frankfurt, 1927).

Suchier = Hermann Suchier, *Denkmaeler provenzalischer Literatur und Sprache*, vol. 1 (Halle, 1883).

Vicente = *Lyrics of Gil Vicente*, ed. Aubrey Bell (Oxford, 1914).

Wack. = Philipp Wackernagel, *Das deutsche Kirchenlied von der aeltesten Zeit bis zum Anfang des XVII. Jahrhunderts*, vol. 2 (Leipzig, 1867).

Zumthor, *Essai* = Paul Zumthor, *Essai de poétique médiévale* (Paris, 1972).

Zumthor, *Histoire* = Paul Zumthor, *Histoire littéraire de la France médiévale, viᵉ–xivᵉ siècles* (Paris, 1954).

Zumthor, *Langue* = Paul Zumthor, *Langue, texte, énigme* (Paris, 1975).

Zumthor, *Masque* = Paul Zumthor, *Le masque et la lumière* (Paris, 1978).

INTRODUCTION

i

The title of this book claims as its province "the medieval European religious lyric," suggesting boundaries of time, space, and genre while leaving their precise location vague. My first task is to dispel this uncertainty.

Every word of the title demands scrutiny, even its definite article, which suggests a unity and homogeneity in the subject matter that do not exist, and a comprehensiveness that the book indeed aims at but which it does not wholly achieve. Certain European languages of which I am largely or entirely innocent are consequently not covered here: Dutch, Rumanian, Basque, Finnish, the Celtic and the Slavic groups. But the reader will find the liturgical and learned languages, namely, Latin and Greek; and the major and some minor vernaculars, namely, Catalan, Old and Middle High German, Italian, Old and Middle English, Old French, Old Norse, Portuguese, Provençal, and Spanish.

The meaning of "medieval" varies with the language in question. The Christian Latin poetic tradition, both liturgical and nonliturgical, came into being in the later fourth century A.D., and it cannot be understood without recourse to certain of its earliest texts. The chronological limitations implicit in normal usage of the term *medieval* must be transgressed therefore at their early boundary. Medieval Latin religious poetry continues its career, in some parts of Europe and in the hands of some writers, down to the sixteenth century, when humanist tastes brought a rejection within the Catholic Church of medieval poetic values, but it is neither very creative nor very interesting after the end of the thirteenth century. So little heed will be paid here to late medieval Latin poetry.

The first extant Greek religious poetry that forms part of the medieval (or Byzantine) tradition may be as old as the fifth century A.D. Liturgically, the tradition was most productive in the early period, that is, up to about 800 A.D.; the most important nonliturgical religious verse belongs to the ensuing three or four centuries; after 1200 there is little of note. Again, the boundaries of the "Middle Ages" and of a poetic tradition as treated here do not entirely coincide.

The vernaculars raise chronological problems of their own. None pro-

duced any religious lyric extant today till well after the beginning of the medieval period. The birthdates vary widely: Old English, ca. 700; Old High
German, ca. 800; Old Norse, eleventh century; Middle High German,
twelfth century; Italian, Middle English, Old French, and Provençal, ca.
1200; (Galician-) Portuguese, Catalan (in the isolated case of Ramon Llull),
and Spanish, thirteenth century. (In many cases, utilitarian religious poetry
appears some time before religious lyrics begin to be composed, and in languages such as Old High German, Old English, and Old Norse before the
fourteenth century, the lyric is a marginal or fragmentary feature at best.) So
long as one bears these chronological disjunctions in mind, they will cause
little difficulty—though one cannot but be haunted by the thought of the
silent generations that lie beyond the dates at which our records begin, silent
to us but surely vocal, and songful, enough in their day. More vexing is the
question of where the medieval ends and the Renaissance, or at least the
nonmedieval, begins. On the level of folk tradition, medieval poetry, and
sometimes medieval poems, have survived down to our own times in certain
areas of Europe. On the level of the art-lyric, one may find, as in the case of
Italian lyric, "medieval" and "Renaissance" poetries existing side by side,
differing in audience and function but not in time or place of composition.
And on the northern European periphery, as in Iceland, the Reformation
came late, and medieval culture persisted till 1550 or even later. However, in
all cases, a date of roughly 1500 A.D. will serve as a provisional limit, to be
ignored when appropriate.

"European" appears in the title to acknowledge "medieval" periods figuring in the history of other cultures besides our own (e.g., Arabic, Chinese,
Japanese, Cambodian) and to indicate the linguistic and geographic ambitions of this book. By "religious," "Christian" as well as "nonsecular" is
meant. I regret this acquiescence to the usual practice of ignoring Arabic
and Hebrew poetry when discussing European medieval literature (except in
connection with the origins of certain Romance forms and themes), but I
am not in a position to deviate from it. The term *religious* has the additional
function of excluding fundamentally moral or sapiential verse, even though
such work has the excellent warrant in religious tradition of several books,
canonical and apocryphal, of the Old Testament itself. Only poetry in some
sense concerned with the beliefs and historical material specific to the Christian faith and with their intellectual and affective consequences plays a part
in this investigation.

Further exclusions are implied by the word *lyric*. The difficulties it raises
when applied to medieval poetry will receive extensive discussion later on.
For the moment, I shall simply state that *lyric* here means nonnarrative poetry, generally of modest dimensions, not predominantly doctrinal or didactic in mode and aim. By way of exception, a longer poem that is thoroughly

"lyrical" in nature may enter into the discussion, but such cases will be few.

Put briefly, the scope of this book encompasses the roughly twelve centuries between ca. 300 A.D. and ca. 1500 A.D., an equal number of languages, and the untold thousands of poems that fall within the limits of "religious lyric" as defined and that have appeared in print to date. Ideally, more might have been included, but nets cast wider and a larger draught of verse might imperil even the best-found venture.

ii

As the codicil to the title states, I am offering an *ars poetica* of (Christian) medieval European religious lyric, not a literary history of the subject. The focus is on the form and presentation of content, not the content itself. However, the pervasive influence of historical change, in poetry, in liturgy, in piety, in the religious institutions of clergy and laity, and the persistent differentiation of religious material into a number of "genres" and "subgenres" distinguished by theme must not and will not be ignored. To do so would be to perpetuate the still-powerful notion of the Middle Ages as a time of stasis and stagnation and to cheat ourselves of the rich experience of grasping the complex interplay between change and continuity over a span of more than a millennium.

For much the same reasons, I chose not to call the book a "poetics" of its subject, preferring the obsolete phrase *ars poetica* instead. There is no single model to fit these diverse poems, no "generative grammar" to which they answer or by which they might be reproduced, only certain aesthetic and ideological principles (so far as they can be isolated from each other) that are prior not only to religious poetry but to very nearly all medieval artistic expression. Such principles are well worth discussing and will be discussed below, but they do not truly constitute a poetics, or part of a poetics. In addition to paying homage to the diachronic realities of medieval religious poetry, the phrase also beckons the reader to look back to the *artes* of the twelfth and thirteenth centuries, and to Horace's letter to Piso in the Augustan long ago. Horace's document is something of a conundrum, but it does shed much light on ancient ideas about literature; the medieval *artes* serve mainly as a course of bad advice concerning the writing of secular Latin verse. In a sense, I am setting out to do the job that the authors of the *artes* failed to do. That is, I seek to construct an accurate account of the nature of medieval religious lyric in as many languages and aspects as possible, one that might in fact serve as a guide to aspiring authors of neomedieval Christian lyric, though that is scarcely its intent.

To this end, and to the further end of destroying the false sense of inevitability into which one easily falls in dealing with a single tradition or with a number of traditions separately, I follow a comparative approach. In particular, a comparison with Byzantine religious lyric reveals the originality and individuality (in other words, the quirkiness and oddity) of Latin lyric—both were languages of liturgy, and of Christian liturgy, but they pursued very different courses, and in form and ethos they lie poles apart. But when they are compared to the vernacular traditions, certain consequences arising from their liturgical and learned status, and shared by both, suddenly appear in sharp relief. By the same token, the vernacular traditions share certain features that Greek and Latin lyric do not share. But when compared among themselves, they lose any appearance of homogeneity and reveal a fascinating diversity, analogous at any single point in time to the internal diversity of each tradition when its development is traced along the line of history.

Such are the major goals of this book. It is also my hope that it will serve two additional purposes that grow out of the pursuit of these goals. First, one may view it as a test of the ubiquity of formal "rhetoric" and of Ernst Curtius's *topoi* in medieval literature, a test that in this particular (but extensive) area yields mainly negative results. Second, it is intended as a contribution to a worldwide, cross-cultural study of religious literature and to the study of literature in general. For this last reason, as well as out of consideration for the reader who is also a European medievalist but whose repertory of languages and areas of literary study may not entirely coincide with those of the author, I offer translations of all quoted passages and a concluding section of "Orientations" (q.v.) that contains historical sketches and select bibliographies, primary and secondary, for all the linguistic traditions of religious lyric that figure in these pages.

But in the end, my ultimate goal is to provide a vade mecum for students of our own Middle Ages. If it achieves its purpose, it will simultaneously serve as a stimulus to read further in the area of religious lyric; as a guide for researchers who would like to venture into or inform themselves about unfamiliar terrain; and as a basis for subsequent investigations and interpretation of its subject. In part, it is a selective synthesis of the historical and critical scholarship of the past 150 years; in equal or larger part, it is a new presentation of new conclusions reached by direct experience with the primary sources over a period of 7 years. The reader will judge how far I have succeeded in either regard.

iii

Before one can proceed to an analysis of the medieval religious lyric, however, certain cultural obstacles and theoretical issues have still to be faced, a task to which this introduction will now devote itself, taking them up in the order stated.

The obstacles that impede appreciation and understanding of this poetry reside both in the poetry itself and in us as readers whose assumptions about poetry are so deeply ingrained as to be largely unconscious and which have been produced by a period and culture that differ in many self-evident and yet also quite subtle ways from any of the various phases of medieval culture. In order to cleanse the doors of our literary perceptions, I propose to bring the most important of these assumptions into the open and to offer an explanation for the ways in which the Middle Ages and its literature do not conform to our own notions of beauty, truth, and goodness. With historical explanation may come historical understanding, which in turn may beget sympathy and even delight.

Whatever our personal religion or irreligion, few of us are likely to warm instinctively to religious poetry. Those who do probably think of it as a privileged category not subject to the demands and expectations placed upon other sorts of poetry. The majority simply avoid it as an unappealing contradiction in terms. Both groups are in fact operating within the same set of rules that include the following precepts: (1) poetry should be the expression of individual not institutional opinion; (2) poetry should offer experiential not doctrinal truth; (3) poetry should have no "palpable design" (Keats's phrase) upon the reader. So far as poetry having to do with religious matters conforms to these rules (as it does in the cases of Donne, Herbert, or Hopkins), it will be treated like other poetry, though at the cost of becoming merely an expression of one person's religious experience and no longer part of an ongoing colloquy of mutual aid within the enduring community of believers. So far as it does not—and most medieval religious lyric does not— it will be subject to rejection or segregation.

Nor is this the only form taken by the challenge that the concept "religious poetry" must face. Auden for instance seems to have felt that a genuinely religious and a genuinely poetic impulse were antagonistic. The first should issue in action, either public (between man and man) or private (between man and God); the second must inevitably reduce whatever it deals with to an object of aesthetic comprehension, so that one has "poetry about religious feelings" and not "religious poetry." The assumptions already sketched out clearly underlie this position, which is in fact no more than a variant from within the faith of the position held by those without.

Objections of this kind apply equally to all poetry that presents itself as "religious." The religious poetry studied in this book evokes other sorts of resistance that are specific to it and our culture. First, the Christian faith that it expresses is very much a living issue today. Large sections of the Western population may view it as an atavism, but its language, institutions, and adherents are part of the fabric of our daily lives. In consequence, a poem about the Crucifixion cannot be viewed with the same detachment as a poem about Thammuz or Isis or Zeus, which has long had only a historical and aesthetic existence without any answering belief to stir at its words. Despite its historical distance, it is difficult to respond to medieval religious poetry without one's sentiments or opinions about Christianity coming into play.

Second, the shifts in piety that characterized the development of Christianity from the outset did not cease with the passing of the Middle Ages. The Catholicism of today is far in tone and outlook from the tone and outlook of fifteenth- much less fifth-century Catholicism, and modern Protestantism is farther removed still. And both are allied in their unawareness of the degree to which piety has changed, their lack of historical sense or imagination, and their inability to understand or accept earlier forms of piety. Most twentieth-century believers feel far more at home with other twentieth-century believers of whatever doctrinal or institutional persuasion than they do with the Christians belonging to the past of their own faith. This would be a matter of little moment, given the fact that we are primarily concerned with religious literature rather than the development of popular spirituality, were it not that a secularized form of Christian values and attitudes pervades Western culture. Therefore, all readers are likely to share the sense of violation that modern-day believers feel (as if the sunlight had suddenly changed its cast) when confronted with medieval religious poetry. Those who are out of sympathy with our age may welcome this alteration; those who share its values, whether or not they think them realized in actual life, will find it little to their taste; few of us are likely to remain emotionally neutral.

Taking these two sources of resistance together, one can see that paradoxically both our continuity with the Middle Ages and our differences act as impediments to understanding. Somehow, we feel that in our grandparents, however many generations lie between, we are entitled to find ourselves, and when we do not, we have been wronged. Equally, their dead hands should not rest too heavily upon the present we call ours, for we like to think we have left them far behind. On both accounts, the Christian civilization of the European Middle Ages is a very uncomfortable ancestor.

Our differences extend to far more than piety past and present, however, and require detailed statement and examination so that medieval literature may seem not an isolated aberration but a coherent part of a culture all of whose levels show strong relationships of analogy one to the other. Most of what I will say holds true more or less for the entire Middle Ages and the entire geographical zone that they involve: more, that is, in the earlier period (sometimes called "Romanesque," by extension of a term from art history), and less in the later (sometimes called "Gothic").

Medieval culture was centripetal, theocentric, and ecclesiological. Modern culture is centrifugal, anthropocentric, and sociological. In self-conception, medieval culture was normative and paradigmatic; modern culture is pluralistic and paradigm-breaking. Temporally and spatially, the medieval universe was bounded and closed; its contents were elaborately interconnected, but the principle of their organization reposed in the vertical relationship of each entity, event, or object to the Creator and not in a horizontal relationship on the plane of history or material causation. By contrast, the modern universe is open and indeterminate; its contents are interconnected, but the principle of their organization is material, mechanical, and horizontal in orientation. Further, for the medieval mind, the universe was a cosmos (in the ancient senses of both order and ornament) whose elements had a qualitative meaning expressive of the will and activity of God which had once been legible to man but now, due to the Fall, could be traced out only through a painful process of spiritual restoration and only, at most, in some small part. For the modern mind, the universe (now merely "cosmic") is a mystery whose sense we are gradually discovering by the exercise of human reason and our powers of quantification; this sense promises to yield no human or qualitative meaning, and the growing suspicion confronts us that it is not the universe that makes sense but we that are making sense of the universe; if so, the results bear the stamp of their makers and are suitable for domestic consumption only. Even if we posit the objective validity of our scientific models, we are still concerned with processes in which states are fictions created by an imaginary cancellation of time's arrow, rather than the medieval view of reality in which process is a temporary erosion of being within the parentheses of time. A stronger opposition could scarcely be imagined.

With such a metaphysics, it is understandable that at all levels medieval culture resisted process by pretending that it was changeless, or that its changes represented a closer approximation to some prior, better state of things. (In this illusion, medieval minds were greatly assisted by the lack of adequate means for measuring and recording reality; without mensuration and general contact with accurate records, it is difficult to perceive change as anything but a bad smell hanging in the air of a *mundus senescens*, a world growing old). The constant citation of precedent and authority served to justify both views or practices that genuinely perpetuated the past and those that by deviating from it stood in even greater need of the cloak of continuity—a mode of proceeding one may observe today especially in our politics.

The desire to return to a better past has not left us, but our dominant mode is still the appeal to a better future, and change is a fact of life we no longer hope to exorcize (outside of politics) with mere talk. Chronometry, comparative statistics, newsreels, old phonograph recordings, all conspire to make us overestimate the force of change perhaps as grossly as the Middle Ages underestimated it.

Out of medieval metaphysics grows an alien sense of the human individual as well as of society and history. For the Middle Ages, what matters finally is the eternal fate of the individual, and yet the individual remains an abstract, empty, pointlike concept, defined by social status perhaps, but with even those rags of difference stripped away by Death and the Judge: every man as Everyman. If man is conceived of as anima (i.e., as soul or essence), and anima is ultimately a space closed upon one everlasting choice, then what room is left for personality? Again, the modern view of the individual reverses the medieval. We tend to think in terms of large groups of humanity, of impersonal forces, of collective destinies, with selfhood as a refuge from the "real world," a refuge where a freedom to be and a powerlessness to affect what really "matters" seem to go hand in hand. For us, there may be considerable doubt whether individuals are in possession of an essence, but we generally agree in setting a high valuation upon the structure of personality in all its wealth of accidental particulars. And so we seek a happy life in which the self can flower, not a saved soul from which the self must fall away.

Understandably then, we look to experience, or representations of experience, for guidance in our lives, not to prescriptive texts. It is hard for us to imagine a world in which books were few, experience narrow, and the human voice spoke and passed away like the wind. We must adjudicate among a babble of texts, integrate an overwhelming flux of experience direct and vicarious, endure the recording of words without end. Yet not so many centuries ago it was all quite different. From the end of antiquity until some decades even after the advent of printing, books were generally rare and expensive. What is more, until late in the Middle Ages, it took special training to read them, since they were not written in one's mother tongue—and even then, it was largely, from the medieval viewpoint, texts of lower status and lesser importance that appeared in the vernacular. Christian literature was by and large homogeneous and harmonious, though it is true family quarrels were often perceived as involving far greater disagreements than they actually did. There was some uneasiness about the presence of pagan literature (authors such as Vergil, Ovid, or Juvenal, in the West, and Homer or the tragedians in the East) within medieval curricula and culture, but it was easy enough to aestheticize or allegorize these texts, treating them as *gradus ad Parnassum* to be mined by poetasters or as sources of wisdom concurring with Christian ideas when interpreted properly. In the early Middle Ages, a library of two hundred books was quite a large one and was to be found (in the West) primarily in monasteries; private libraries did not become a factor until the thirteenth century. This scarcity of texts made it so much easier to direct all study toward and to found all thought upon a single authoritative text, the Bible, out of which all other texts flowed and from which they derived such lesser authority as they possessed. Significantly, the Latin West sometimes calls the Bible *bibliotheca*, which is not only a pun upon the Greek meaning of its name (*biblos* [book]) and a reference to the fact that it houses several score "books" within it but also a way of expressing its function for educated medieval man. Beside it, the *classici* or classics (a concept appearing in the second century A.D.) were no more than light reading.

The most important text that the Bible gave birth to was not, strictly speaking, "literature" at all. In medieval eyes, it was much more. Directly and indirectly (through their borrowings from Jewish synagogue services or Syrian hymnody), the Greek and the Latin liturgy owe nearly everything to the Scriptures. In part, liturgy cites or paraphrases the words of the Bible; for the rest, it adopts its phrases or phraseology, recombining and elaborating them but never being emancipated, or seeking to emancipate itself, from their example. The life of the only or the most highly educated segment of the population, that is, the clergy—the regular clergy from the first, and increasingly, in the later Middle Ages, the secular clergy as well—revolved around what was called the *opus Dei*, "the work of God," and their written works are permeated with the words and spirit of the liturgical work in which they participated day in, day out. The Psalter in particular was at the heart of the Jewish service and retained its role in Christian hands, and the influence of its words should never be forgotten when reading medieval literature. In short, culturally and literarily, the dominant organizing factors, both in terms of their actual effect on people's lives and of their prestige, were the Bible and its liturgical daughters in West and East. For some, they still have great power today, though even this is a diminished thing; for most, they are rapidly passing from direct experience and even from memory. A hierarchy of more and more abstract structures has seized the center of life, and language mutters confusedly in the *quartiers*.

Yet the coherence of medieval culture, based upon Scripture and liturgy, coexisted in the West with a degree of localism and diversity we would think anarchic today. Certainly this was not because the Middle Ages esteemed diversity. In fact, the Church (like all churches) had an innate drive toward uniformity, whether of rite, of canon law, of custom, or of any other aspect of religious life. In the East, a strong central political organization closely allied with the church hierarchy did succeed, though not without setbacks, in imposing a high degree of uniformity and centralized control. Yet even in the Byzantine Empire, secessionist movements had their impact, the Moslem conquest liberated local forms of Christianity from Constantinople's control, and within the shrunken Hellenic sphere of later centuries the distribution of hymnic poetry still remained far from homogeneous. In the West, for most of the Middle Ages, strong political organization was the rare exception, and in most cases its relationship to the Church was an ambivalent or even hostile one. Latin was never the speech of the Germanic or Celtic areas, and in the Romance zone it lapsed to the state of learned language by Carolingian times, whereas Greek, whatever the differences between demotic and written forms, remained the common tongue of the Eastern Empire. In addition, the latter was for the better part of the Middle Ages a relatively small and ethnically homogeneous domain, and the Mediterranean and Black Seas offered relatively easy access to many of its major centers. Travel in Western Europe, though less infrequent than is thought today, was primarily overland and therefore slow and difficult. Political, linguistic, and ethnic diversity, coupled with an extreme depression of commercial activity in the early Middle Ages, did nothing to encourage the traveler to set out or to speed him on his way. The result was a proliferation of local jurisdictions, each with its own ways, loosely grouped into larger units in some cases (cf. for example, in the case of liturgy, the Gallican or Mozarabic rites, which embraced with infinite local variations large areas of Gaul and of Iberia until Rome succeeded in imposing its own rite over popular resistance). Until the late Middle Ages, even in theory, control was something to be exercized by each diocese over its own territory, with Rome as a court of last (and mostly infrequent) resort. In fact, diocesan governance was often very loose, so that individual churches could go their own way so long as they caused no scandal. The most striking example of this situation was perhaps the city of Rome itself, where each church had its own traditions and its own liturgical books, and no one felt obliged to fall into line behind the gonfalon of the papal chapel. Under the circumstances, one sees why one of the best writers on the subject, Dom Gregory Dix, called his magnum opus *The Shape of the Liturgy*, for it would be a falsehood to claim that medieval Christianity observed much more than that shape in its almost indefinitely local liturgical habits. In our own time, existing means for the recording, replication, and diffusion of information and for exerting close inspection and control make such a situation inconceivable. Local custom is tolerated, but only on the periphery of the liturgy, in the worship of saints or supererogatory devotions and the like. And yet the recent Church decision to impose worship in the vernacular introduces a degree of involuntary variation into the liturgy the results of which remain to be seen.

All these features of medieval culture, whether ideological or pragmatic, had their impact upon medieval literature and more particularly upon the medieval religious lyric, deriving as it did from the central regions of its culture and serving their ends. This culture's centripetal, theocentric, and paradigmatic nature makes it no more than logical that its literary expressions should reflect an "aesthetic of identity" rather than our own "aesthetic of opposition," as one contemporary theoretician puts the dichotomy.[1] That is to say, rather than finding its raison d'être in its difference from foregoing texts and therefore stressing the ways in which it surpasses what has been written, the medieval poem seeks to reconfirm a set of thematic, formal, and rhetorical norms, disguising its divergences from those norms or presenting itself as a permissible variation within the limits they set.[2] Such a description is truest for poetry dealing with matters most central to its culture and most subject to its culture's control, in short, religious matters. It applies less well to matters that medieval culture officially deemed of less moment, such as erotic love, politics, or narrative fiction, but even here, the "aesthetic of identity" usually triumphs (cf. the domestication of early Provençal love poetry by later troubadours and by the northern French trouvères, as well as the stereotyped treatment of its themes throughout Europe in the fourteenth and fifteenth centuries).[3]

As a way of giving a name and hence a warrant to the major fundamental difference between modern "serious" literature, on the one hand, and popular, folk, and medieval literature, on the other, I believe that the concept of an "aesthetic of identity" has general validity and value both. However, its generality is also, and inevitably, its limitation. Covering a multitude of different phenomena, it naturally has little to say about any single phenomenon taken by itself, except that it was not created nor should it be judged according to the "aesthetic of opposition" under which we live and read. To define more precisely the particular form that the "aesthetic of identity" takes in the Middle Ages, I offer the further concept of the "gloss."

In the area of religious literature and art, at least, it is possible to view all "texts" as a direct or indirect "gloss" upon the Scriptures, which themselves offer many internal examples of "glossing," the chief of them involving the interplay between the Old and the New Testaments in which each can be seen, depending on which eye one uses, as the other's commentary. (The analogy between this sort of intertextuality and the vertical relationship between God above and created world, man, and history below is of course no accident; as proof, we have the common medieval metaphor that makes the latter God's book, i.e., the collected utterances of the Supreme Author, with each a comment on His nature.)[4] The ability to gloss the Scriptures, known technically as *sacra pagina*, was the supreme goal of education, challenged perhaps in the scholastic period, but not really overthrown until the nineteenth century. The commentaries, abridgments of commentaries, compilations of commentaries, and commentaries upon commentaries this activity produced made up the bulk of medieval libraries and exercized (outside of the utilitarian area of legal documents and the like) a near-monopoly on the use of parchment up to the twelfth century.[5]

One of the few varieties of text that could compete with *sacra pagina* was the liturgy in its many divisions. No monastery or church or chapel could dispense with copies of missals, lectionaries, antiphonals, and the like. But of course the liturgy is itself another sort of gloss, one that grew luxuriantly until the sixteenth century pruned back its branches. Moreover, not only is the liturgy as a whole a gloss upon the Bible, but like the Bible it involves glossing relationships governing its own internal economy. Details of the birth and career of liturgical forms must wait until chapter 2. Suffice it to say here that the forms take shape within the interstices or upon the margins of existing liturgy and themselves create further interstices and margins where new forms can grow. The glossing relationship is sometimes explicit, sometimes implicit, but it is never absent.

Nonliturgical religious poetry may also be viewed as a gloss, either of the Bible directly or (more usually) of the Bible as already glossed by the liturgy. There are even cases of poems expanding upon scriptural commentaries, and there are innumerable instances in which religious poetry draws upon material deriving ultimately from patristics and their medieval progeny.[6] And again, the process of glossing proceeds within religious poetry as well as between it and other sorts of text. It may take the form of allusions to well-known hymns or of outright imitation of the stanzaic scheme or melody or both of an earlier poem, in a practice known as *contrafactura*. It can even involve juxtaposition of the existing poem and the gloss, or an intermingling of the two. In every such case, one is dealing with no more than a further extension of a principle underlying all of medieval culture.

In support of this proposition, one may venture outside religious lyric. Consider for example the medieval manuscript, with its literal gloss in the margins, its frame of ornament, its miniatures, all supported by the text they surround, and even in their seeming sometime irrelevance asserting a vital connection between text and world beyond.[7] Consider the medieval religious drama, in which each unit grows out of a passage from Scripture or the liturgy, with (in the case of bilingual plays) the vernacular dialogue acting as a gloss upon the traditional text.[8] Consider the medieval Church and its decorative program, which serves to bring home to the viewer the full meaning, on a spiritual level, of "door," of "window," of "right" and "left," of "high" and "low," each detail glossing a larger structure that is itself a symbolic gloss upon the Christian faith.[9] Consider the medieval *organum*, in which the "tenor" is a piece of plainchant which the other voice or voices rhapsodically gloss. To be sure, one may object that in each of the artistic areas I have mentioned it is the fresh creation that matters, and in a sense that is so. But it was the structure and security the gloss-relationship provided that allowed the medieval creative artist the freedom to take his liberties and make a success of them in medieval terms.

Another concept that is useful in understanding medieval poetry is "translation." Like the idea of "gloss," it lays the necessary stress upon the indefinite derivativeness of the mainstream of medieval culture, and it too is no mere metaphor but an accurate literal description of a significant fraction of the literature the Middle Ages produced. Translation played a crucial role in the early development of all the European vernaculars, and it was also the means by which some important Greek religious poems entered the Latin tradition. Examples range from the purely utilitarian, such as interlinear glosses of hymns of the Psalter and close versions of texts basic to the Christian faith like the Pater noster or the Creed, to the largely artistic, such as free scriptural narrative paraphrase or late medieval expansions upon the seven penitential psalms.

In a metaphorical sense, "translation" also fits a number of other characteristically medieval intertextual relations. Texts migrate not only from language to language, but from prose to verse and verse to prose, from one stylistic level to another, from secular to religious and religious to secular domains. The fundamental symbolic operation involved in typology itself is a translation of the events and figures of (scriptural) history into their New Testament or subsequent fulfillments, so that one text becomes another's sign. (Note the analogy with *contrafactura*, in which a form hitherto put to secular use is filled with spiritual content and meaning, or a religious form has conferred upon it an additional spiritual function.)

Over and above the literal and metaphorical presence of acts of translation throughout medieval literature, I believe that it is the title of translator, not poet, that comes closest to describing the role of the medieval writer of verse. He and the postmedieval verse translator share certain important traits: a submission to givens, a devoted and serviceable desire to "get it right," a concentration on finding a way to render something already said into words that a new audience will understand, an overall function of representing the original to that audience. This kinship would go some way in accounting for the interesting fact that when medieval religious verse fails it is "bad" not in the way common to modern religious verse (i.e., it is neither mawkish, vulgar, nor maudlin) but is simply flat and dead, like a cautious, respectable, literal, academic translation of someone else's poem. In addition, both verse translations and medieval religious lyric produce the sensation that the poem is still half-embedded in its matrix, half-emergent, haunted, or inhabited by its origin. Neither the verse translation nor the medieval religious lyric seeks to become fully independent; indeed, both actually stress their derivation. But in the case of the religious lyric, the ultimate reference is not simply to another preexistent text but to a highly coherent textual tradition that is itself only one link in a chain of textual traditions leading back to the Word.

At some point, particularly in medieval practice, "gloss" and "transla-tion" become indistinguishable. Many poems combine them or practice both simultaneously. Together, they define the particular direction that the "aesthetic of identity" took in medieval European religious lyric, and the reader should always bear them in mind when reading this poetry.

Not only was medieval culture centripetal and paradigmatic, but its uni-verse was closed and its contents vertically ordered. These features of the medieval world view relate directly, by analogy or as partial cause, to im-portant features of medieval texts. To spatial and temporal closure answer the strict limitations of content and vocabulary of most early medieval liter-ature. As "second causes" gain more respectability in the course of the twelfth century, there is a corresponding expansion in the range of words, objects, and ideas available to authors. This expansion applied to religious lyric as well as to other sorts of writing, but in all of them it brought only an enlargement not a demolition of the old confines. Cases such as Dante (in a long narrative poem, be it noted) or the German sequence tradition that seems to extend from Notker Balbulus down to Henrich von Meissen (known as "Frauenlob") remained isolated exceptions.

The vertical organization of medieval reality, with coherence and mean-ing conferred upon the universe by its multitudinous relationship to a super-reality outside it, likewise has its analogue or reflex in medieval texts. I am referring here to their typically paratactic, discontinuous, anacoluthic struc-ture. In this structure, ideas and phrases have the air of fragments washed down from higher and older regions, their angles pointing out from the text to some external point at which they will meet and marry into meaning, if the reader has the qualifications for ascending to that focus. Little or noth-ing is primal in these texts, except perhaps for the juxtaposition into which their elements enter. In this regard too, medieval culture and literature start to move toward a more modern world view beginning in the twelfth century, so that horizontal relationships figure increasingly in the generation of meaning, but this shift has little effect on the specifically religious text. In particular, the religious lyric resisted any complication of the old simplici-ties, for if anything is more conservative than religion, it is lyric poetry.

The most important case of paratactic structure, and one that has re-mained unchanged down to the present, involves the liturgy. Given the cen-trality of the liturgy, of which much has already been said here, one might expect that the subject of liturgical structure would by now have received exhaustive treatment. In fact, it has been almost totally neglected. Some decades ago, however, the Italian scholar A. Viscardi did devote a number of pages to the subject, taking up first the relationship among readings (*lectiones*), psalms, antiphons, and responses in the typical case of the liturgical observance of Maundy Thursday, the day of the Lord's Supper.[10] The individual elements are fragments or mere motifs. Events are alluded to without regard for chronological order. The imagery is highly discontinuous. As a whole, Viscardi describes this composite liturgical "text" as "patient mosaic-work." The other text that he scrutinizes, the Corpus Christi office, shows much the same traits. In it, the effort to indicate connections by juxtaposition is the central feature, and one notes that it is impossible to grasp the full significance of these connections without some knowledge of Scripture and the long tradition of its interpretation. Without implying any causal link between liturgical parataxis and the parataxis that characterizes much medieval literature, the homology between them is strong enough to suggest a common underlying source. In all such cases, the vertical referentiality of the medieval cosmos seems both to foster and to justify the horizontal incoherencies of the medieval text.

Vertical referentiality may also have a good deal to do with the variations in the number and order of elements in poems that appear in multiple manuscripts. (The important literary historian and theoretician Paul Zumthor uses the phrase "mouvance du texte" for this phenomenon.)[11] These variations are too pervasive and too considerable to be dismissed as merely the result of scribal inattention or indolence; rather, they seem to be the result of active intervention by scribes who felt no inhibitions about altering nonauthoritative texts as they saw fit. They are certainly not the result of oral tradition, which is rarely a factor in the transmission of religious lyric, even lyrics in the vernacular. The explanation that lies closest to hand, I believe, is the structure of the typical medieval religious lyric. Nearly always it is stanzaic, and nearly always, its stanzas are autonomous units that occur without any clear logical or rhetorical order to specify their proper sequence. This paratactic relationship means that stanzas may be omitted, inserted, or rearranged without materially injuring the coherence and meaning of the text, since after all the latter derive from a preexistent and enduring "reality" to which the text and its stanzas severally refer. In a sense, the medieval religious lyric, like the liturgy, has neither beginning nor end. It is all middle, and as such can be freely altered. Its existence too is in a middle state, between eternity and eternity, a passing and fragmentary expression of the ancient relationship between mankind and God. No wonder it was easy prey to the copyist's fancies: what city can stand without walls, and what text without boundaries?

Since a true vision of the inherent significance of the cosmos and its history can only be recovered not created by man, and since medieval man saw himself and his fellows, on the level of ideology though scarcely of daily life, as faceless anima beset by equally faceless body, it is not surprising that the wisdom the medieval religious lyric offers and the authorial activity it implies contrast sharply with what one finds in the postmedieval lyric. Experience cannot generate knowledge, it can only confirm it. In fact, in a fallen world and a fallen subject, it is as likely to lead astray as to lead aright. Therefore, the medieval religious lyric admits life only as a gloss (to use the term again) upon a truth that transcends individual experience.

Similarly, the author one senses behind the text remains fundamentally anonymous and without personality whether or not he names himself. Moreover, as I have already argued, he is more like a translator, that is, a craftsman-middleman given over to the service of his audience and a text not his own, than a poet. This is a crucial point, because from the Renaissance onward "serious" Western poetry has so consistently adhered to a certain myth of the author that we are likely to fault poems of another age from which it is absent without even realizing why they fail to satisfy us. The myth to which I refer is implicit in the extraordinary intensity of metaphorical activity in poetry since the Middle Ages. The power to make new and revelatory connections that has become the sine qua non of the "true" poet brings with it a new conception of the poetic author, both on his own part and on the part of his audience. He no longer transcribes the patterns that God impressed upon matter and history: he makes the patterns. In a sense, he creates, or at least re-creates, the universe; no matter what his personal ideology might be, as practitioner of the art magick of novel metaphor, he cannot help but "be as gods." (I take this to be the major factor behind the practice that reappears in the later Middle Ages, notably in Dante, of invoking the muses, the pagan pantheon, or God Himself; by doing so, the poet lays claim to the possession and use of quasi-divine powers while cloaking that claim in the form of a prayer.) This new (or recovered) role of the poet-author offers the audience the opportunity to participate in a total if temporary mastery over a usually recalcitrant reality. We too can be as gods. Undoubtedly, the supreme example of what I am describing remains Shakespeare. Beyond any other poet, he offers us the heady vicarious experience of all-mastering consciousness. In this respect, his lack of definable "personality" is an incalculable asset, for the reach and depth of his re-ordering of reality remains unattached to and unconfined by any limitations of a specific selfhood. He (though perhaps "it" would be the more accurate pronoun) is for us the pure power to connect and to express connection in the closest approach to the nature of God, seen as pure act, that one can imagine. The very fact that he remains within normal human notions of what counts and what can be properly connected plays a vital part in his effectiveness. No particular views or idiosyncracies of perspective, or very nearly none, exist for a Western audience to exclude the possibility of a given reader's free enjoyment of Shakespeare's recasting of the world as metaphorical word.

In our own century, this myth of the poet-author has perhaps reached its culmination, or perhaps the general audience has reached the limits of its willingness to participate in the ultimate results of the myth. Certainly much contemporary theoretical thinking, particularly of a structuralist, semiotic, deconstructionist persuasion, seems to spring from a revulsion against the centuries-, even millennia-old belief in the poet as heroic seer or creator, seeking to replace these figures with a mouth through which the shadows of language and society speak. Despite the polemic atmosphere created by the rise of such schools of thought, they have probably made it easier for us to consider revaluing medieval lyric, with its (for the most part) far humbler placing of the poet-author in the economy of the text.

The literary position of the medieval poet was largely reflected in his social position and also in the anonymity of most medieval poetry. True, a few individuals began to make a career of writing beginning in the twelfth century (cf. Peter of Poitiers or, somewhat later, Frauenlob), much as Venantius Fortunatus had still been able to do during the sixth century in the last twilight of antiquity. But they are the exception until the Renaissance and even beyond. Most major poets who enjoyed high social status had it by advantage of birth or obtained it by filling important social functions that made no direct use of their poetic gifts (cf. the diplomatic activities of a Chaucer or a Dante—the tradition of the poet-diplomat in fact remains very much alive even today in the countries where Romance languages are spoken.) Of course, this lack of status for poets as poets can partly be accounted for by the fact that the world of letters, though it existed, was not the going commercial concern it has since become. (Surely it is no coincidence that the appearance of mass printing and marketing of books in the eighteenth century closely preceded a dramatic increase in the social, literary, even religious pretensions of poets. It is hard to stand fully erect without a solid economic base on which to stand.) On the other hand, a culture that saw poets as quasi-divine in their function would confer high status on them and find ways of directly rewarding them for their poetry (cf. archaic Greece in the sixth and early fifth centuries). The economic base can be created, it need not already exist.

For reasons involving both the nature of the poetry and the position of the poet, then, the Middle Ages clearly did not share what I have characterized as the modern myth of the poet-author. As corollary, the *audience* for medieval poetry, particularly religious poetry, lacks the heroic character of comrades in a journey of poetic discovery and transformation. In fact, the audience implied by the medieval poetic text is usually a very abstract entity, wanting in personality and internal differentiation. Where close-knit literary circles existed (as in Provençe, for a time), one finds exceptions to this rule. But in the main, the audience remains a nearly featureless point upon which the lines of the poem converge.

The same lack of differentiation applies in other matters, and for the same reasons. If the poet is a self-effacing mediator of a preexistent truth, to whose patterns he must conform his work, then the basis for a clear distinction beween poetic and unpoetic, between fictive and nonfictive, between literature and nonliterature, between art and utility necessarily vanishes.[12] The Middle Ages seem to have preserved a confidence in the monistic nature of value, even when its expressions have a very dualistic look to us, and monisms notoriously annihilate the careful discriminations to which pluralism is compelled. It is this underlying situation that explains the further absence of a separation of religious poetry into distinctively "narrative," "didactic," and "lyric" varieties, indeed, the apparent licence with which poems will move from one domain to another without any sense of impropriety. The extended meditation continues to interfuse these elements today (cf. texts as different as "Howl" or the "Four Quartets"), but the modern poem has behind it the unifying force of an explicitly developed and central authorial consciousness which has the full sanction of our myth of the poet-author. There is no such force acting to unify the medieval poem, only the impersonal and omnipresent forces of the coherence of its culture.

What differentiations do exist are of a character the modern reader will find alien. First, they are formalistic. Particularly in the later Middle Ages, poets and readers focus their attention upon the external features of the poetic text (its rhyme scheme, the structure of its stanzas, the length of its lines), and it is upon this basis that medieval treatises usually define poetic genre, whereas our notions of genre (and poetic value), while paying some heed to form, put the emphasis upon the nature of content. Second, medieval differentiations are linguistic. Indeed, there is no real expectation that an author will write in his mother tongue; rather (in some areas and periods), he will write in that dialect or language which is appropriate to the genre he has chosen. For example, no matter what part of the peninsula they came from, Iberian poets wrote their lyrics in Galician-Portuguese, a literary form of western and northwestern dialects, during the thirteenth and most of the fourteenth centuries; thereafter, the situation was reversed, and Portuguese poets wrote their lyrics in Castilian from the later fourteenth through the later fifteenth centuries (Camões, in the sixteenth century, is still poetically bilingual). Yet religious poetry (cf. Gonzalo de Berceo) and popular epic (cf. the *Cid*) were composed during the thirteenth century in their authors' native Spanish, not in Galician-Portuguese. In northern Italy during the same century, one finds a still more complex picture (one reflected in Dante's treatise *De vulgari eloquentia*). In the early decades, the language of lyric is Provençal; didactic poetry is written in Old French; and a peculiar amalgam called Franco-Venetian served for a number of narrative poems that derived more or less directly from France. Examples of poets writing irrespective of genre in a language other than their birth-tongue (cf. Catalonia before 1400 and after 1475) or in an alien or artificial dialect (cf. the role of Icelandic as a literary language in the North) or in a highly archaic form of their birth tongue (cf. written Byzantine Greek up to the twelfth century and for that matter, intermittently down to the present) are numerous, even usual; they should be borne in mind when one reads misleading statements about the artificiality of *Latin* as a language of medieval literary expression, particularly if one reflects on the oral use of Latin, often from childhood on, in monastic and cathedral schools. This habit of requiring the poet's alienation from the language he was born into runs completely counter to our own expectations, but it is entirely consistent with the medieval view of the function of the mediatory, nontransformative role of poet, language, and text. One of the great projects of our century has been to eliminate the distance between literary language and common language; it has been a shared faith, or fiction, that such a project could succeed. By contrast, with what most today will consider a remarkable perversity, the Middle Ages sought to make that distance as great as possible, going so far as to magnify differences of stylistic level or subject matter into actual differences of natural language. This means that the "aliveness" or "precision" we especially seek in poetic discourse is a rarity in medieval poetry. It was a value, and readers responded to it, but there were other values (e.g., magnificence of ornament, elevation from life, observation of generic decorum) that generally took precedence—quite properly, given the medieval outlook. *Autres pays, autres moeurs*—and other poetics too.

iv

At this point, one may be inclined to ask whether, if the foregoing characterization of medieval poetry is reasonably accurate, medieval religious lyric can have any but a purely historical interest in the twentieth century.

Undeniably, the original purpose of all but a few medieval religious lyrics was not primarily aesthetic. Nonetheless, I believe that the means of achieving the central religious purpose of this poetry were aesthetic in nature and that therefore (as with a great deal else that we now call literature but that had other concerns originally) medieval religious lyric can properly be read for its aesthetic value.

First, one ought not to overlook or discount the fact that these texts are in verse simply because it is obvious. Whatever the aims of the writer or user, verse brings with it a number of aesthetic demands. Prosodic requirements must be met, ideally with meter and the "natural" gait of the words interacting to produce an interesting verse rhythm. The words themselves must be selected according to certain notions about what the diction of a poem of this or that kind should be. Decisions must be made about the shape and length of the poem as a whole and about the internal ordering of its elements. And, for most medieval religious lyrics, there is (or was) the additional factor of musical setting, which introduces another, stubbornly nonideological level undergirding the text and interacting with it in ways that require still more choices of a fundamentally aesthetic character. In theory, all these features are doubtless supposed to remain merely instrumental; in fact, they each have a material existence of their own, and this survives even the most profound changes in the beliefs of the hearer-reader.

In this regard, then, the medieval religious lyric shares the aesthetic features common to poetry of any kind. Fortunately, that is not the end of the matter. Medieval religious lyric also has the indispensable aesthetic trait of indefinite repeatability. Some of it may have been written for liturgical occasions or the like, but that does not render it occasional—the occasions of liturgy are themselves indefinitely repeatable, year in, year out. Further, as we are told all art should, these lyrics lay claim to universal significance. In intent at least, their audience encompasses all mankind, their usefulness all of time. Tested stringently, very few poems entirely live up to this claim; certainly medieval religious lyric never did and does not now. What matters is that the claim is made and that the possibility of suspending disbelief (in a stricter sense than usual) and experiencing these texts aesthetically as valid expressions of an alien culture remains in consequence open to us. In addition, medieval religious lyric was meant to move. It shares the affective purpose that we associate with aesthetically valuable poetry or prose. A good deal of it seeks to commemorate moments of great emotional power vividly enough that the reader will enter into an intense contemplation of their reality. In this fashion, though not in all cases, these lyrics seek just as more modern poetry does to make the imaginative object of the poem as intensely present as possible to the reader and to communicate an attitude toward it that the reader is to accept as his own.

There are also aspects of the medieval religious lyric that, though scarcely identical, are nonetheless analogous to aspects of modern lyric, aspects in which one might suspect the latter is the cultural successor to the former. One of these involves the clear intent of medieval poets that their religious verse serve as a means of entering into, or restoring, a proper relationship with the divine. Put more abstractly, this means that the user was to seek a new or fuller contact with the ordering truth behind appearances, in a sense, with "what counts" in or beyond our universe. Modern "secular" lyric has the analogous function of persuading or reminding the reader of "what counts" in life, whether it is the striking of a fashionable attitude to the chaos of modern urban life or an awareness of human historical continuity or a quasi-religious communion with the natural world or (to come full circle) an ideology that purports to make sense of it all.

The other aspect involves the sense of solidarity with a community (of belief, in this case) that the medieval religious lyric offered its users. To read or recite or sing a text of this kind, or to hear it read or recited or sung, was to participate, at least in imagination, quite often in physical fact, in a group with similar values, views, and goals. I believe that the modern audience for lyric poetry comes to it for analogous reasons. Aside from closely meditating upon a text, an activity in which the medieval and the modern hearer-reader both share, the latter is affirming his or her solidarity with a community that feels it is in touch with what is "fully human" (our form of the sacred). This sense of inclusion may or may not bring with it the exclusion of present-day analogues to Saracens or Philistines, though such is usually the case. The ideal group that defines itself by this corporate involvement with lyric poetry can and does (like the medieval audience for religious lyric, though less frequently) physically assemble together to share its experience of the texts it prizes. Poetry readings have become an important feature of the contemporary literary scene, restoring us to something more like the historically normal contact between mankind and art. The celebrants perform the service, and the congregation joins with them, lending their presence and support to the proceedings but participating little if at all (a description that also fits the medieval Church congregation, as it happens). There is one major flaw in the analogy however: the audiences at poetry readings today resemble the early Church meeting secretly in the atria of wealthier converts and surrounded by a majority of pagan Romans much more than the medieval Church in its splendor and security.

I hope that the citation of these shared aesthetic features and these analogies of function will help readers make the transition from poetry as they expect it to be to the medieval religious lyric. One further source of pleasure in the latter has so far gone unmentioned, not because it is unimportant, but because it has no real counterpart in modern "serious" poetry. This is the pleasure that variation within fixed limits, and the ability to respond to it, can give. The "aesthetic of opposition" that I alluded to earlier and that dominates modern art and literature in its higher forms excludes a relationship among texts that could make this appeal. The "aesthetic of identity" characteristic of medieval poetry favors precisely the intertextual relationship that does. Cultures that value ornament highly offer visual analogies to this relationship, with their repertory of inherited patterns that can be infinitely inflected but that nonetheless retain their basic shape and structure.[13] Our own music has been largely built upon the auditory analogue of "variation," whether in the obvious form of "theme and variations" or in the subtler form of the inflection or "development" of melody or motifs in motet, fugue, or sonata movements (or, for that matter, in medieval songs).[14] Medieval religious lyric, read appreciatively, produces a similar "formal" pleasure. Its patterns and "genres" soon become familiar to the reader, and one may learn to enjoy the perception of restatement of the traditional qualified by a number of features that deviate from the expected or go beyond what is strictly necessary in terms of the tradition; the latter can of course serve an expressive purpose (like ornament in music) but may be there simply for the sake of their own beauty or interest. Our own standards of poetic economy (which have their interesting parallels in our notions of the ideal functioning of commerce, industry, administration, transportation, and social relations) do not apply here. In a way, medieval religious texts form a close community much like the community of believers they were meant to help support; within this community, everyone knows what the important things are and takes comfort in their restatement, but there is also room and time for the inessential precisely because the great questions have been settled (or so most medieval people apparently liked to think most of the time). This situation accounts for the surprising marriage of a basic unpretentiousness and a love for ornamental detail in this "serious" poetry. Whether through music, the visual arts, or popular culture (jokes, jazz, genre fiction), readers should already be familiar with the workings of variation and in particular just such a combination of humble foundation and elaborate superstructure. The avenue of approach matters little, so long as one succeeds in entering by it into the spirit of medieval art.

v

Medieval religious lyric challenges not only our sensibilities but our literary methodologies and theories as well. Therefore, this closing section of the Introduction will be concerned with the problems one encounters in trying to "place" this particular object of study in terms of customary literary categories, in characterizing its workings, and in creating a critical approach within which accurate understanding and interpretation become possible. It ends with a description of the approach followed in the remainder of this book.

The question of the sense in which medieval religious lyric is genuinely "lyric" arose earlier, only to be dismissed. It is time to confront the question more squarely.

In certain respects, medieval lyric was more like canonical lyric (e.g., archaic Greek examples, or nonnarrative folk songs) than modern lyric is. It was commonly sung or even danced, although rarely the latter in the case of religious lyric. It was normally attached to some sort of social or communal occasion or gathering, whether church worship, procession, or entertainment in hall, courtyard, or street. Its character was impersonal and objective, with the author in effect playing ventriloquist to a publicly accepted poetic role (storyteller, suitor to Mary, homilist, grateful Christian, repentant sinner, Christ on the cross, and so forth). As others have remarked, it is often closer to modern song *lyrics* than to what we mean by *lyric*.

The root of the problem here is the very loose definition of lyric under which we operate (quite properly, I think). Like other equally capacious concepts of genre (cf. *satire* or *epic*), the concept of *lyric* can only stand so much scrutiny. As one examines it more and more closely, contradictions begin to emerge as details become more sharply visible, and the fine figure lyric had cut at a distance threatens to fall apart into a collection of smaller and smaller pieces, which in turn lose their appearance of coherence and homogeneity as one continues to look into the matter. Nonetheless, at the level of large, loose, and baggy concepts, lyric has a validity and usefulness one should not dismiss. In this case, if one considers not just modern lyric (whose differences from medieval lyric were developed at length in section ii of this introduction) but the full historical and cultural variety of lyric, the appropriateness of the term to the subject matter of this book becomes more evident. At the same time, one must try to bear in mind that each historical corpus of lyric poetry that goes to make up the far larger corpus of world lyric will show peculiarities that fall outside the scheme of family resemblances into which it otherwise fits. For medieval religious lyric, these include not only its unusual blending of narrative (or "epic"), panegyric, and (in the conventional modern acceptance) lyric traits, but also a significant number of thematic, formal, structural, and rhetorical details that will emerge in the chapters to come, as well as historical and regional and linguistic and institutionally based differences within medieval religious lyric itself.

Yet even if one accepts the term *lyric* for this poetry, one must still ask how far existing approaches to medieval lyric will serve us in dealing with religious lyric of the period.

Despite some recent attempts to demonstrate the contrary, literary criticism (as opposed to rudimentary theories about the nature or function of texts, or exegetical techniques for making texts serve predetermined meanings) did not exist in the Middle Ages. This should hardly be surprising— after all, English literary criticism can hardly be said to exist, as a traditional, collective activity, until the later seventeenth century. The extant corpus of rhetorical treatises in Latin, Greek, or the vernaculars written or commonly used during the Middle Ages is primarily valuable as a means by which one can reconstruct medieval attitudes, especially on the part of the practitioners of the more derivative and pretentious forms of literature, toward what they thought they were doing. Except in extreme moderation, their use impedes rather than assists understanding of most medieval poetry, providing a set of reductive categories to which atomistically treated elements of the text can be assigned and so dismissed. Conscious rhetoric is fundamental to medieval religious lyric (cf. chapter 3 of this book), but there is no reason for us to use intellectual tools that were often already antiquated in the twelfth century to analyze its rhetoric when we can devise better instruments ourselves.

The approach to medieval religious lyrics through the ultimate or even proximate sources of its thematic materials has similarly deleterious effects. Rarely is it the case that the medieval poet reaches for anything that is not "in the air" or the *poetic* tradition.[15] The "source" of his poem is other poetry, not patristics or scholastics, and studies of medieval religious lyric that focus on the antecedents in commentary and homily of a given poetic tradition belong more properly to the field of intellectual history than to that of literary history or criticism. In addition, even if the passages cited in such studies were actually the sources of the poems they analyze, the direction of their approach would be no less misguided, for it leads out of the text into a tangle of supposed causes that could never in reality account for or elucidate what is literarily valuable in the text. What is in front of one, that is, a physically existent ordering of words with determinate, internally generated meanings, dissolves into an abstract historical construction without any apparent or potential aesthetic interest. In fact, to practice such an approach under the guise of literary analysis is to make the tacit assertion (so to speak) that the texts one thus treats are not literature but documents and nothing more.

A number of recent scholar-critics have adopted approaches that honor the literary nature of the poetry with which they concern themselves. Each approach, however, has defects or limitations that render it partly or wholly unsuitable for the study of medieval religious lyric. (It should be noted that a large number of valuable articles and books deal with the general religious and literary contexts of this poetry, particularly in connection with Middle English, but that these provide data rather than a model for the critic; what critical commentary they engage in normally involves the unspoken agreement between author and reader that the problems discussed in this introduction can be safely ignored. Obviously, I do not agree.) Perhaps the most notable figure in Anglophone discussion of shorter medieval poetry during the past fifteen years has been Peter Dronke of the University of Cambridge. His approach, which remains consistent in all his published work, including the fine general book *The Medieval Lyric* and the more specialized studies such as *Medieval Latin and the Rise of the European Love-Lyric*, or *Poetic Individuality in the Middle Ages*, exemplifies the possibilities and the drawbacks of a method of interpretation growing out of conventional study of the high lyric tradition in postmedieval English. The more modern in character the text under discussion (i.e., the denser and darker its imagery, the greater its individuality) turns out to be, the more rewarding is Dronke's approach. That this approach entails the exclusion from consideration of all but the most unmedieval of medieval lyric does not immediately strike the reader, unless he is familiar with medieval lyric in its natural state and therefore can measure the eccentricity of Dronke's choices with respect to medieval poetry. The wide influence of his work can be easily accounted for: its outlook and its selection of texts for analysis flatter our unexamined preconceptions about what poetry ought to be, and its critical approach genuinely, even excitingly illuminates the texts he presents. One feels a certain compassion for readers who first discover medieval poetry in Dronke's *The Medieval Lyric* and hurry forth all aglow to experience the wonders of this new world of poetry in which the natives are much like the people back home apart from a few pleasantly exotic differences, only to find that the real country and its inhabitants are not like that at all.

Two further Anglophone scholars demand attention here, though less for their influence than for the intrinsic interest of their ideas. The first is Robert M. Jordan, who argues in his *Chaucer and the Shape of Creation: The Aesthetic Possibilities of Inorganic Structure* against the application of the modern dogma of "organic" unity, as laid down by Schlegel and Coleridge, to medieval poetry.[16] Since it is arguable whether medieval aesthetics as articulated in medieval documents or derived from authoritative antique texts known to the Middle Ages are another symptom of a deeper set of causes that also underlie medieval literature, rather than a direct influence on that literature, his attempt to ground medieval literary structure in medieval aesthetics is perhaps of limited value. What remains is his notion that paratactic, disjunctive, heterogeneous structures such as do in fact characterize medieval texts may have an aesthetic value comparable to though different from that of classical or "modern" texts. To put it metaphorically, plants and animals are beautiful, but so can buildings be. Jordan's application of this hypothesis to Chaucer's "Merchant's Tale" seems fruitful to me, and I believe that it can be generalized to shed light on smaller literary structures, including lyric, in the Middle Ages. However, it does not constitute a critical approach in itself, only a needed *caveat* against trying to shoehorn premodern literature into modern aesthetic schemata or damning it when it does not fit. (William W. Ryding's more recent *Structure in Medieval Narrative* [1971] performs much the same valuable but limited function for longer narrative texts and Aristotelian critical concepts.)

The second scholar writing in English I wish to discuss at this point is Jonathan Saville. In his *The Medieval Erotic Alba: Structure As Meaning*, he claims to present "a theoretical framework that I believe could be profitably applied to many other literary works—lyrics and non-lyrics, medieval and nonmedieval." [17] In my opinion, this claim is justified. However, his framework encompasses only some aspects of medieval poetry, and its derivation from a secular genre that existed only in certain languages and and areas of Europe naturally means that it is less well adapted to other, more widely distributed and thematically less well defined medieval poetic genres. He concentrates on an exposition of the symbolic elements and their interrelationship within the lyric plot that characterize examples of the *aube*. In order to deepen our sense of the *aube*'s significance and meaning for its culture (and therefore, perhaps, for us), he also develops at some length certain analogies in medieval thought or life to the *aube*'s symbolic mode of operation. In this aspect of the book, his method, though constantly interesting, threatens to replace the poem with its analogies, much as source studies replace the poem with its sources. The values of the *aube*, its handling of characters and of time and space, and its complex relationship to the far more frequent *chanson d'amour* all receive their due, but there is little extended analysis of actual texts (even though this is a monograph on a relatively small corpus), and one is left with the impression that the ideas mediated by the *aube* are its chief claim to attention, rather than the direct experience of the verses in which the *aube* variously embodies its ideal self. This result is due not only to Saville's understandable desire to improve the present standing of this genre but also to the bias inherent in a method that lays so much stress upon abstractions and so little upon the language through which one reaches them.

To my mind, the best though imperfect paradigm for a study of medieval religious lyric remains Paul Zumthor's *Essai de poétique médiévale*, in its relevant sections. It is less the details of his methodology of analysis than the principles implicit in it that seem of general value to me, but since it would be difficult to appreciate the latter without some knowledge of the former, I feel that the contents of the *Essai* and related articles or works must receive a degree of attention.

Zumthor's critical methodology revolves around a term closely related in meaning to the concept of *genre* but differing in its internal articulation, which derives from structural linguistics, and in its connotations, which are frankly mechanistic, like much of the nomenclature of structuralism and semiotics. The term is *register*, and Zumthor's most accessible exposition of its meaning for the English-speaking reader can be found in *Literary Style: A Symposium* under the title "Style and Expressive Register in Medieval Poetry." [18]

In his *Essai*, Zumthor defines register as "a network of preestablished relationships among elements at their several levels of formalization as well as
among these levels themselves—this network constitutes a global prefigura-
tion of the song [i.e., the *chanson d'amour*]." [19] In this definition (which
most readers will probably feel stands in great need of glossing), there are
certain salient features. First, the elements of a register preexist any particular poem in which they appear. (There may in fact have been a text in which
these elements first appeared, but one cannot generally point to a specific
text representing a medieval genre and say that it was the one from which all
others sprang.) Second, their interrelationships also preexist any particular
embodiment. Third, the text may be analyzed into different formal levels.
Fourth, the interrelationships among these levels are also part of the register.

Such a definition has several major implications. Some of these concern
the conditions under which the poet had to write; some concern the way in
which the poet's audience would have perceived his poem; others concern
the analytic method that the critic should adopt.

To begin with the poet: one can see that he or she would have a great deal
less latitude of choice, about form, content, or treatment of content, than a
modern poet enjoys (or endures). Of all possible medieval cases, this is perhaps truest of the *chanson d'amour*, the northern French tradition of love-
poetry dating from the later twelfth century and deriving by a process of
purification, or etiolation, from the troubadour poetry of the south; it is
next truest, but far less so, of the religious lyric. As a general characterization of medieval poetry in contrast to modern poetry, Zumthor's is valid,
but as one examines particular cases within the Middle Ages, it requires frequent and significant qualification. Of this Zumthor is well aware; for instance, he admits that registers are mainly a feature of the Romanesque period (the vernacular poetry that now exists mainly in imagination rather
than in manuscript, making it very convenient for theoretical manipulation)
and that the Gothic period shows constant use of registers, but registers reduced to the state of fragments and the role of constituent parts of more
comprehensive and heterogeneous literary structures. Still, one understands
why, in view of the radical terms in which he states the concept, Zumthor
focuses his demonstration of its value upon the *chanson d'amour*.

For Zumthor, the audience for the *chanson d'amour* (and for other types
of medieval poetry as well) is interested not in new ideas, values, or terms
but in a refined celebration of the shared ideology, ethics, and vocabulary of
their society or social class. The least threatening variability would then,
logically, affect form, and it is in fact novelty of stanza form (and of rhyme
in Provence and Germany) that acted as the major distinguishing feature of
different poems, particularly in the early period of each tradition, and that
poet and audience especially prized. In this aspect, too, the implications of

Zumthor's definition are largely valid, but they must again be increasingly qualified the closer one gets to the end of the Middle Ages and the further one strays from aristocratic or official literary types.

The chief importance of Zumthor's concept of register for this book lies less in its effect on our view of medieval poets or audiences, however, than in its possible usefulness as a basis for critical methodology. Zumthor's implementation of the concept in connection with the *chanson d'amour* takes the form of a carefully compiled statistical inventory of first the sounds and syntactical features of the poems in the corpus, then of their diction (including the use of pronouns), and finally of their motifs. This inventory allows him to state with confidence what is invariant in the corpus and what constitutes a deviation from the norm in each text. It also allows him to draw the conclusion that the *chanson d'amour* is ultimately self-referential in function— in fact, one could even call it liturgical, since in both the medieval love-poem and in the liturgy, the text is itself a ritual action that is fully consummated within its own limits.[20]

The statistical inventory that Zumthor has chosen to impose upon himself is a cumbersome proceeding. In a sense, it is redundant, overdetermining what a sensitive, properly trained medievalist has already intuited in the texts; certainly it assumes an antecedent judgment about what texts constitute a corpus sufficiently coherent to repay such a form of analysis, that is, one must have perceived the existence of what Zumthor calls "register" and must in fact have identified, *grosso modo*, its salient features before one switches on the statistical sausage-grinder and sets to work. Even though it is a superb form of insurance against subjective errors or oversights, one would hesitate to advocate its general use.

Nevertheless, Zumthor's critical methods incorporate certain assumptions and attitudes that I believe to be indispensable to the study of medieval religious lyric. First, and most important, he explicitly takes the existence of a "register" (i.e., a set of clearly defined norms constituting a poetic genre or subgenre) to be a source not of constriction or monotony but of "a powerful dynamism" to which the medieval audience clearly responded and in which the modern reader can still find value.[21] Second, he bases his interpretation of medieval lyric texts upon an intensive examination of their various corpuses, letting their individual and collective significance emerge from their poetic relations, not from their relations of content or analogy to extrapoetic domains of discourse or culture. Third, he perceives the nature of medieval lyric intertextuality, with the medieval text normally remaining so closely tied to its fellows that it can scarcely be said to exist apart from them.

These three ideas—namely, the creative power of convention, the use of poetry to explain poetry, and the quasi-collective nature of the medieval lyric poem—will act as guiding principles throughout this book. There is nothing revolutionary about any of them, except possibly the third, but few critical studies of medieval poetry observe them, and many, in practice if not always in theory, reject them outright. To demonstrate their validity in the case of medieval religious lyric would be a sufficient goal in itself.

In other respects, however, my approach and methods will differ considerably from those of Zumthor. As I have already said, historical change as well as the differences between the various linguistic traditions represented, will remain in the foreground here. I have no intention of trying to set up a self-sufficient synchronic model in an ideal atemporal space. Rather, I wish to describe the range of variety in the medieval religious lyric and to identify the lines of continuity and the reasons for their existence within its development. The heterogeneity of the material; the lack of sharp generic distinctions; the impurity (in aesthetic terms) of this poetry's appeal, in particular, the impossibility of pure self-referentiality in a religious poem; the predetermination of its "plot," not by poetic, much less experiential, considerations, but by what medieval people believed to be "reality"; its function for its culture as means, never in any degree as an end—all these ways in which medieval religious lyric does not resemble the *chanson d'amour* or the other, lesser genres that Zumthor examines would make it impossible to imitate Zumthor's approach at all closely even if I were to concentrate on the later Middle Ages and a single language as Zumthor does.

In consequence, I will offer, instead of internal quantitative analyses of "registers," comparisons within certain large poetic types that cut across linguistic boundaries. I will seek to identify, instead of the general "constitutive" function for the courtly class that Zumthor hypothetically attributes to the *chanson d'amour*, the less abstract, more provable functions that medieval religious lyric served in different times, places, and languages. Finally, I will not remain silent on the issue of evaluation (a side of literary criticism that some varieties of modern literary theory ignore or explicitly reject) but will work toward the creation of a basis for judging the relative aesthetic value of separate religious lyrics, though it should be said at the outset that most examples within a given thematic type are of much the same quality, with few poems achieving either signal failure or signal success relative to the others.

The body of this book is divided into three unequal chapters: one on the functions of medieval religious lyric, one on its genres, forms, and structures, and one on its rhetoric. Throughout, content will remain a strictly subordinate issue, entering into the discussion only as necessary. The order of topics moves from the most general and abstract to the most particular and concrete; it is in the latter that medieval religious lyric best reveals its individuality, both in medieval and in modern terms, and it is there that this study will culminate. As ancilla to these three chapters, there follow the "Orientations" promised near the beginning of this introductory essay. Readers should refer to them and to the index whenever they desire information concerning the major figures and overall development of religious lyric in a given language. The only watchword of these "Orientations" is, "Ich dien'."

I

FUNCTIONS

Oro vel honoro

Hermannus Josephus

Scitis ista, neque vos doceo
Sed quod scitis, facere moneo.

The Archpoet

Given the number of centuries, countries, and languages with which this study deals, it is impossible to offer a single, comprehensive statement that would cover the multitude of uses to which medieval religious lyric was put. Nonetheless, the texts in themselves consistently pursue three large goals: praise, prayer, and instruction or, more accurately, anamnesis. As the authors of the epigraphs to this chapter say of themselves and their hearers, "I pray or praise," and "You know all that, and I'm not your teacher, / I'm telling you to do what you [already] know about."

All three of these goals have ample precedent in Scripture and in the general practice of religion. The Psalter and certain lyric passages from the Old and New Testaments called the *cantica* acted as the principal models for praise; the many supplications of scriptural figures, particularly in the Psalter, played the same role for prayer; and the Old Testament prophets and sapiential books and the teachings of Christ and the Epistles in the New Testament showed the way to the pulpit of didacticism. In addition, Greco-Roman religious language, both in its cultic form and in literary stylizations, had a profound effect on Christian liturgy and on Christian religious verse.[1] One need only examine the prayer style of the early Roman rite or the praise style of the Greek Akathistos hymn to grasp the extent of this influence.[2] But there were also strong influences from Semitic rites, notably the Jewish synagogue service out of which Christian worship sprang and the early Syriac hymnody, which left its stamp upon liturgical practices at Jerusalem (the trendsetter for the late antique Church) and especially upon the Byzantine liturgical form, the *kontakion*, and since these were themselves derived from Scripture, they served to reinforce the central place of the language and style of Scripture in the development of Latin and Greek religious literature.

Of these three goals of religious discourse, prayer is no doubt the primordial one. Human beings are born to dependency, and the cry for help upon which survival hangs precedes language, individually by many months, collectively by many species and many score million years. Praise arises as a means of identifying the addressee of prayer securely and of obtaining its, his, or her goodwill. These original motives for religious praise persist, sometimes only vestigially, sometimes quite transparently, even explicitly, in medieval Christian lyric. The goal of (anamnetic) instruction is logically and probably historically posterior to both prayer and praise. In primitive cultures, it takes the form of myth, narratives that teach paradigmatically. In more "advanced" cultures, where the faculty for abstract thought has seen

some development, it turns into precept and dogma—a form that an organized church finds far easier to control and transmit than the ambiguous
riches of myth. (With its movement from the narratives of Genesis to the
tribal regulations of Deuteronomy, the Pentateuch may serve as an exemplary case of this evolutionary pattern.) Yet the old use of story as a teaching
device does not entirely die out. It is too effective a way of winning an audience's attention, holding it, and impressing one's message upon its memory
for any Church (or other organization) to give it up. In fact, the amount of
narrative content to which a medieval writer resorts increases in direct proportion to his desire to reach the "people," with the result that, in many late
medieval texts, story reasserts its old primacy and leaves precept hanging on
by the fingernails.

In Christian terms, prayer is one aspect of any believer's participation in
the ongoing dialogue that God initiated at the Creation.[3] If this is true for
the layman, it is even truer for those who dedicate themselves fully to the
religious life, which Origen in the third century described as $\mu i\alpha\ \mu\epsilon\gamma\dot{\alpha}\lambda\eta$
$\sigma\nu\nu\alpha\pi\tau o\mu\epsilon\nu\dot{\eta}\ \epsilon\dot{\upsilon}\chi\eta$, "one great unbroken prayer."[4] Praise is the other aspect of the human role in this dialogue, and the hymn was defined by Au-
gustine (and therefore by the Middle Ages, in so many respects his corporate
epigone) as *laus Dei cum cantico* (praise of God in song).[5] Furthermore,
prayer and praise were seen as ultimately the same action, a notion with
strong support from the history of religious language, from Christian metaphysics, and from the realities of Christian religious poetry, in which praise
and prayer go hand in hand, dancing their pas de deux through most texts.[6]
Even confession, the mainstay of penitential poetry, was felt to be still another way of praising God, since it acknowledges his power and his rights
and our human weakness and our human duties.[7] (The famous *confiteor*
with which Augustine opens his spiritual autobiography has this larger
sense, as the complex interfusion of confession, praise, and prayer that follows clearly shows.)

Yet to characterize medieval religious texts as fundamentally man's response to God and no more would be seriously misleading. It is perfectly
proper for liturgiologists to confine themselves to such a definition, since
they are concerned with the ideal purpose of liturgy and other religious expression. But a student of religious language and literature who is concerned
to see and account for his subject in human as well as creedal terms must
step back far enough to take in its actual as well as its ostensible functions.
Perhaps this seems too obvious to need stating. But in fact, what is perhaps
the most valuable series of articles and monographs concerned with religious literature and appearing in the last twenty years, namely the work of
Hennig Brinkmann and his students, has reiterated the creedal view of the
functions of religious texts without any sense of its inadequacies.[8]

Aphoristically speaking, religious texts are theocentric but anthropo-tropic. That is to say, they are consistently concerned with God and the history of God's past actions and prospect of God's future actions (either direct or mediated by God's ally-delegates), yet even when they are ostensibly addressed to God or his saints, the *actual* addressee is mankind or some particular part of it, and not the citizenry of heaven. This is particularly true for ritual (i.e., liturgical) texts that are repeated from day to day or year to year ad infinitum. Such texts are an act of communion, or community, rather than communication.

The places of their intended use, whether secular church, minster, chapel, or eremitic cell, contain not presence but absence—absence of the quotidian, the not-holy, the ungodly, all that the word *saeculum* sums up. Their walls force back the world to make a space in which a sense of divine presence can be created by and for the worshipper. The means by which this presence can be created range from the exclusion of furnishings one would expect to find in such a building to a lavish surplus of objects far exceeding one's expectations. In each case, every article present (or excluded) acts as a symbolic statement evoking the sacred in the beholder's mind. Yet all the appeals of ornament, incense, music, and lighting that the Church evolved remained secondary to language. It was the presence of the liturgy that guaranteed the presence of God to worshippers, and its words could of themselves make any room or roadside, however briefly, a holy place. From a purely human, noncreedal viewpoint, one could say that it was out of language, publicly reiterated and elaborated, that God was made.

Whatever the case may be today, few in the Middle Ages would have claimed any experience of the divine outside of the act of worship. Even those who participated in the popular mystical movements of the later Middle Ages both advocated and practiced the use of symbolic means, linguistic or visual or a combination, to achieve the sense of direct contact with God. The spontaneous seers of visions were rare, and they were celebrated (or execrated) for their extraordinary gift. Of all this, the Church, like any other form of institutionalized religion, was perfectly well aware. It knew that the act of worship had to seem authentic if the worshipper was to feel that his participation was efficacious, that is, that God was present and listening. It sensed that it was essential both that the details of worship remain largely familiar, lest the atmosphere of worship be violated, and that there also be a degree of openness to new texts and practices, lest the spirit of the liturgy and the spirit of the worshipping community lose all contact with one another. This is why, on the one hand, garments that were originally nothing more than the garb of secular officials of the Roman Empire survive today as ecclesiastical vestments (a conservative phenomenon that has repeated itself in long-established Protestant denominations).[9] What began as a metaphor of authority became an indispensable feature of decor. On the other hand, the crucial openness, within limits, of the liturgy to changes emanating from below as well as from within the Church hierarchy meant that it was in a constant state of expansion. Indeed, it has been said that theology followed in liturgy's footsteps, busily justifying its changing emphases after they had already appeared.

The development of the liturgy will receive fuller treatment later on. What immediately concerns us is that it both changed and resisted change, and that both aspects of its history have everything to do with the needs of mankind and nothing to do with the needs of God (the latter concept is of course theologically meaningless in any case). Were liturgy entirely theocentric in fact as well as in theory, rather than fundamentally anthropotropic, one would be hard put to explain the existence, much less the precise pattern, of its development.

It is time now to begin to distinguish between liturgical and nonliturgical religious lyric, for what is true of the functions of one may often be untrue of the functions of the other. Such a distinction may be impossible to sustain in some cases, particularly where a text has begun its existence in one category and migrated at some point into the other (cf. the famous Latin sequences, the Stabat mater and the Dies irae, both of which began life outside the liturgy and innocent of the sequence-style musical setting they subsequently received). Nevertheless, in most cases one is dealing with a poem that is clearly either liturgical or not, and it is safe to say that in principle no vernacular text achieved fully liturgical status until after the end of the Middle Ages (in fact, within the Catholic Church, until the recent decision to impose worship in the vernacular worldwide). In addition, with almost no exceptions, the forms Byzantine liturgical poetry uses are entirely distinct from those of nonliturgical religious poetry in Greek. One must only keep in mind that such distinctions are relative—changes in status and complex reciprocal influence between poems in both categories did in fact occur from time to time.

Within the initial division into liturgical and nonliturgical, further distinctions are needed. Traditionally, scholars speak of "paraliturgical," "extraliturgical" and "nonliturgical" poems, thereby introducing two intermediate zones (or stages) between the two extremes. These terms reflect the degree of control the Church exercised over a given text. Paraliturgical poems proliferated in Latin in the later Middle Ages (from ca. 1100 on) and figured in "optional" or "occasional" religious celebrations or as ornamental additions on the margins of the liturgy. The music books preserve the distinction between liturgy and paraliturgy, but one doubts that it was always very clear to the congregation. Extraliturgical poems would include such examples as vernacular songs sung during processions or in parallel with the celebration of the liturgy. The line between para- and extraliturgical texts is often a very faint one, but one should be aware of its existence. The Church, or its clergy, or its composers took a very active interest in paraliturgical forms; the extraliturgical it could be said to have tolerated, as little as possible, as a concession to the unlettered. Finally, there is the vast territory of the entirely nonliturgical text. This includes a host of forms meant for private meditation or for conventual use by lay groups, and for other purposes. Poetry of this sort most readily responded to changes in popular piety and makes up almost the entirety of the vernacular corpus of religious lyric.

One should note that there is no possibility of fitting any of these categories into an opposition between "public" and "nonpublic." The public mode dominates in the first three categories (liturgical, paraliturgical, and extraliturgical), but it is also important in the last, the nonliturgical. Conversely, the private mode is usual only in nonliturgical texts, but it was always possible in principle to use texts in the other categories for private religious contemplation. Indeed, one finds the desire expressed that the clergy should reflect privately on the worship it performed publicly, so that both modes would exist concurrently in the same person. Such being the case, one can understand why the boundaries between the various categories would be indistinct and why changes in one might easily lead to, or attend, changes in another.

Whatever classification scheme is adopted, any account of the specific, historically determined functions of medieval religious lyric must begin with an account of the liturgy and work out from there. Since we are concerned with both Latin and Greek here, the following discussion will consider the development of liturgy in first one then the other language.

In Christianity's infancy, Christians viewed themselves, and were viewed, as a Jewish sect, one of many that existed in the first century A.D. As such, they naturally continued, so far as it was permitted, to worship in Jewish synagogues and in the Jewish fashion. This meant that readings (cyclically organized), psalmody (involving the congregation), prayers, sermons, and the performance of songs, nonscriptural as well as scriptural in nature, were all constituent parts of the Christian service from its very beginnings. As the faith spread and its membership ceased to be composed mainly of Jewish "converts," Christians naturally stopped looking upon themselves as a Jewish sect (a fact that caused tensions within the new Church that surface here and there in the New Testament). The language of Christian worship came to be Greek, thanks to its origins in the eastern Mediterranean and the ethnic and social origins of most of the early Christians. In addition, the proliferation of "heretical" (that is, different) Christian sects in the early centuries, many of which produced nonscriptural song texts advancing their own divergent views, led to a rejection of nonscriptural inclusions in worship by the Christian factions that held a more conservative, antispeculative view of the faith and succeeded in the end in defining their view as "orthodox." In consequence, the hymnic element that had been inherited from the synagogue service went into eclipse, while the other elements remained in place.

This exclusion of nonscriptural hymnody was not to endure, however. In the fourth century—by which time early "Italic" translations of the Bible were in circulation and Latin had largely replaced Greek as the language of the Western liturgy—Hilary of Poitiers, who had come into contact with heretical use of hymns while in exile in Asia Minor, and Ambrose, who faced the threat of the state-supported Arian heresy as bishop of Milan, both wrote hymns to instruct and strengthen the orthodox faithful. Hilary's syntactically complex prosy and cerebral efforts found little favor, but Ambrose's lucid, shapely quatrains became the heart of Western hymnody and the pattern for the majority of its texts up till the eighth century. His hymns met the need not only of his beleaguered flock for a way to express and confirm their solidarity, but also of the new cenobitic movement that was replacing the heroic eremitism of a Saint Anthony and whose members desperately needed texts to give voice to their piety, to fill up the empty spaces in the community's day, and to establish liturgical ties binding the many disparate groups within the movement together.[10] The monks principally supported the new hymnody in the late antique and early medieval period, and one can see the vital role hymns played for them in the pages of the Rule of St. Benedict, which contain guidelines for their use and the incipits of recommended texts.

The secular clergy took a much dimmer view of the nonscriptural hymn. In 361, a quarter century prior to the birth of the *ambrosiani*, the Council of Laodicea expressly forbade its use, giving an official expression to what had in fact been long-standing orthodox practice. This prohibition and later conciliar statements to the same effect reveal that popular (including monastic) pressure for the use of hymns was intense enough that the Church hierarchy felt steps had to be taken. As usual, these steps were in reality if not in their language stages in one of those slow retreats in good order the Church early learned to conduct so well. By the Council of Tours (561), nonscriptural hymns were acceptable so long as the author's name appeared in manuscript to guarantee the orthodoxy of the text it preceded, and Toledo IV (633) gave its approval to their use, alluding in particular to the work of Hilary and Ambrose, which the passage of nearly three centuries had given the prestige of age and (in Ambrose's case) familiarity. However, if prohibitions are evidence of the existence of what they forbid, it is no less true that official stamps of approval imply that some may still be resisting what is being approved of. So one should not be surprised to learn that the Papal Chapel, as chief bastion of conservatism, did not accept nonscriptural hymnody until the twelfth century.

There was more to this pattern of resistance than simply a distrust of freely composed texts that might deviate, even unawares, into heresy. At a more visceral level, churchmen feared the uncontrolled, aesthetic element in sacred *song*—feared, that is, the intensity and irrationality of their response to melody, to rhythm, to the pure sensuousness of sound. In the tenth book of the *Confessions*, chapter 33, Augustine expresses this ambivalence with his usual eloquence and honesty. His mentor Ambrose uses the ambiguous phrase *grande carmen, quo nihil potentius est* (a great charm/spell/song/ lyric poem, than which nothing is more potent) of his own hymns.[11] Much later, in the thirteenth century, Aquinas devotes a passage of the *Summa theologiae* (2.2.91.2) to the proper liturgical role of poetry and music. In his view, song should serve to awaken devotion in men, especially in the weak; it is not in itself a way of honoring God (a de jure statement of a de facto truth). One should not seek a primarily aesthetic effect, and instrumental music is particularly to be avoided—that is, instrumental music had become particularly popular in the period. Properly used, singing can move the worshipper to contemplate each word as it is sung. Melodies should therefore be simple and, if possible, borrowed in order not to distract from comprehension and contemplation of the text—that is, elaborate melodies and complex polyphony were now the dominant musical forms. In writing hymns, one should adopt sermons as one's principal model, with instruction rather than the excitement of devout feelings as the ultimate goal. (Here Aquinas, himself a Dominican, is responding to the emotionalism of the new piety that the fraternal orders, especially the Franciscan, were spreading or at least fostering throughout Europe.)[12]

No mere reflection of a narrowly scholastic outlook, Aquinas's views are entirely consistent with the attitude of the higher clergy throughout history. Meaningful liturgical change (as opposed to tinkerings with prosody and diction) has always come from below, from the laity, the monks, the musicians, or the lower clergy. It was from the monasteries that the new liturgical forms of the sequence and the trope (see chapter 2) emerged in the ninth century, and monks, lower clergy, and professional church musicians combined forces in the late eleventh and twelfth centuries to create the *conductus* and other forms of the *cantio* or religious "song" that have an irrepressibly popular vitality. The same largely holds true for the new feasts, or the changes in the importance of old feasts, which provided fresh opportunities throughout the Middle Ages for the creation of new texts in which contemporary piety could find a voice.

Both as background to the discussion of religious lyrical "genres" in the next chapter and as the most graphic way possible of conveying the fact that the liturgy has been in a constant state of significant evolution from the beginning, a selective account of the evolution of the most important church feasts is necessary. The medieval liturgy was not only quite different from modern-day Catholic liturgy, any given period of the Middle Ages shows significant differences in its liturgy from any other period.

Christmas seems a good place to begin, particularly since it acted as the beginning of the "church-year" (to use a sixteenth-century phrase) at Rome until the tenth century and in Germany until much later, a status that it still enjoys today in Papal Bulls.[13] The celebration of Christmas had appeared in the West by the fourth century, and the apocryphal gospels which take such an interest in Christ's birth and infancy followed, in translation from Greek, between 400 and 600, attended by Papal condemnations. Popular piety seems to have centered on the Nativity from an early date; there is evidence of early use of crèches in France and Germany, and vernacular poems on Christ's childhood proliferated in the late Middle Ages.[14]

The other feasts of the Christmas season did not spring full-blown into existence with all their retinue of extraliturgical practices any more than did Christmas itself. For instance, Epiphany may date back to St. Clement (second century A.D.), but it was at that time identical with the Nativity feast celebrated on 6 January. In addition, it did extra duty as the occasion for commemorating such events as the baptism of Christ, the miracle at Cana, and (later) other proofs of Christ's divine powers, with Augustine playing a leading role in making it primarily the feast of the Magi (whose number ranged, in the East, as high as twelve!).[15] One can document its appearance in the West in the course of the fourth century, but Rome began to celebrate it only much later. Like Christmas, it collected a rich folklore around it in the course of the Middle Ages.

The Advent season, with which the church-year now begins, arose as a side effect of Christmas, in the process of "glossing" and expansion usual to the Middle Ages. The first clear reference to its observance belongs to the late sixth century, though the Gallican church seems to have designated the weeks leading up to Christmas as a time of fasting even earlier on. Gregory I took it up at Rome; Cluny (tenth century) and the Franciscans (thirteenth century) lent it their support; it was promulgated in the present form in 1570.[16]

Though of the greatest antiquity, the celebration of Eastertide also saw important changes. The Palm Sunday procession apparently originated in the eighth century in the Carolingian sphere, but it did not enter the Roman-German pontifical till 950 and the Roman missal till even later.[17] The Good Friday ritual derives from Byzantine practice and was introduced in the West during the seventh century in the Gallican church.[18] Easter vigil

(Saturday night) lost its original character as the occasion for the baptism of adult catechumens as mass conversions of adult heathens ceased to be common, and like a great deal else in the liturgy its details acquired a symbolic interpretation with the loss of their original purpose.

Later on in the church-year, Trinity Sunday now occupies a prominent place, with the Sundays between it and Advent dated relative to it. It was not until the tenth century, however, that it entered observance, and this observance was not general till the following century. For official promulgation by Rome, it had to wait till John XXII and the year 1334.[19]

Most other medieval feasts show the same pattern of early observance and tardy recognition. The feast of Corpus Christi is an interesting example of an inversion of this pattern. Upon a papal commission, Aquinas himself composed the principal poetic texts for its liturgy, and a papal bull of 1264 proclaimed the feast, responding to the intense interest of the period in the Eucharist (particularly at a theological level) and the need to expound the official orthodox position on the issue of transubstantiation. But this attempt to impose a feast from the top down enjoyed little immediate success. Clement V had to promulgate the feast again in 1311, with a subsequent reconfirmation coming in 1323.[20] And one finds passages in vernacular religious poetry referring to Corpus Christi as a "new" feast on through the fourteenth and fifteenth centuries, that is, for something like two hundred years after it was first "instituted."[21]

The persistent localism and loose-knit organization of the medieval Church, together with an initial absence of strong popular support, accounts for the lagging pace at which the feast of Corpus Christi was adopted. The same pace governs the spread of other liturgical innovations in the Middle Ages. And the same localism leads to a situation in which local feasts proliferate almost without restraint. In Bohemia, for instance, by 1350, there were approximately 150 feast days and "holidays" (i.e., holy days) in the course of a year, and the liturgical and extraliturgical accretions which all these celebrations occasioned kept some twelve hundred singers busy in the churches of Prague.[22] Much of this activity concerned saints' days, calendars of which are still permitted a great deal of variation in the Church today.

Easily the largest contributor to the late medieval proliferation of feasts was the cult of Mary. Since it was also the largest single contributor to late medieval religious lyric, its evolution requires separate and special treatment here.

The worship of Mary has its roots deep in the Gospels and in human psychology. The Council of Ephesus (431) officially recognized Mary's special status, granting her the title of *theotokos*, or "Mother of God"; the practice of dedicating churches to her dates back to the preceding century. By the seventh century in Rome and the end of the eighth century in the area under Carolingian influence, the four great Marian feasts were being observed. These are Purification (2 February), Annunciation (25 March), Assumption (15 August), and Nativity of Mary (8 September).[23] The first two began as Christological feasts, that is, as the Presentation at the Temple and as the Conception of Christ. Indeed, the history of the medieval development of Marian cult is one of a progressive annexation of days, attributes, and functions that had originally all belonged to Christ—the most striking example is Christmas, which in popular late medieval piety and vernacular lyric comes to focus much more on the Mother than on the Child.[24]

This process did not proceed at a uniform rate, however. In hymns from roughly A.D. 600 to 1100, Mary is merely a peer of the other saints,[25] though Saturday apparently became "Mary's Day" in the ninth century, and certainly no later than the eleventh.[26] Around 1050, her status began to improve rapidly, and Marian literature flowered in the following centuries. Greek influence was important both in the early phase (before 600) and in the late phase (after 1050), for the cult of Mary developed much more quickly in the East, stabilizing at a point far short of the extravagant forms Western development was to take at the end of the Middle Ages and in the centuries since.[27] The most significant fact to note is that though Greek Marianism was a constant presence to the East, its effect on the Latin West was anything but constant. Some combination of forces that escapes secure identification kept it in a dormant state for very nearly five hundred years, despite intermittent political and cultural contacts and the great prestige of the Byzantine Empire.

In the twelfth and thirteenth centuries, the creation of new Marian feasts got under way and has yet to run its course. With Franciscan backing, the Visitation (2 July) appeared in 1263 and was extended to the whole church in 1389 and reconfirmed, along with its date in the church-year, in 1441. The doctrine of the Immaculate Conception, deriving from Greek tradition and known in the later Middle Ages as *dos Mariae* (Mary's dowry), spread from southern Italy via the Normans to northwestern France and Anglo-Norman England.[28] It produced a feast of the same name, occurring on 8 December (i.e., the date of Mary's Nativity, 8 September, minus nine months), which after early reversal won a gradual general acceptance, though the official promulgation came only in 1854. The doctrine became a major subject of scholastic debate and of German and northern French poetry in the fourteenth and fifteenth centuries.

Most of the lesser Marian feasts that appear in the same period derive from the apocrypha or popular devotional practices (cf. the Presentation of Mary, 21 November, mentioned in the East in 1166, adopted at Avignon in 1371, promulgated in 1585 after a temporary Papal suppression, and the

Feast of the Rosary, 7 October, promoted by Alain de la Roche, a Domini-can, at the end of the fifteenth century and promulgated in 1721).[29] They all have their reflexes in religious lyric, which in its turn reflects the shifts in piety that led to the creation of the various feasts. Some have still not re-ceived offical recognition, and there are also Marian roles, frequently asso-ciated with these "unofficial" feasts, that have not been promulgated as dogma. In short, in the Marian cult as in other areas, religious feeling and expression continue to lead the way, with the theologians and the Church hierarchy following circumspectly behind, amending, certifying, or rejecting with all deliberate speed what comes into their hands.

Finally, the evolution of the medieval Western liturgy involved large-scale changes that had nothing directly to do with the institution of new feasts or alterations in the character of old ones. Some of these will be discussed in the middle section of chapter 2. Others include such important extrapoetic developments as the multiplication of votive masses, which form a lengthy appendix to the results of Alcuin's work on the liturgy commissioned by Charlemagne and grow into an elaborate system that breaks down under its own weight from the thirteenth century on, or the massive introduction starting in Gaul of hagiographical readings into the office from the seventh century onward.[30] The most important and pervasive change, however, is in the relationship between the lay congregation and divine service. The Mid-dle Ages, especially in their latter half, saw an increasing sequestration of ritual from the worshippers, who consequently fell into a more and more passive role, first of audience to a spectacle, then of petitioners relegated to the antechamber of a secret negotiation between the qualified and God. This was a far cry from the original informality and openness of the services of the early Church, in which the faithful participated actively and to which they brought their own bread to be consecrated for use in the communion. In the later Middle Ages, the Eucharist became a matter of so much mystery and spiritual consequence that the average Christian understandably par-took of it as seldom as possible. (This was so much the case that the Lateran Council of 1215 replaced the traditional expectation that a Christian would take communion at least thrice a year with the rock-bottom requirement of a single annual reception. And in fact regular lay Catholic communion is a development that belongs to the last century or so.) Ordinary bread no longer sufficed, and special wafers were created.[31] The miracle of the con-secration of the host received the awe-inspiring emphasis of the "great ele-vation" (twelfth century), which in Dominican churches of the thirteenth century became the only moment at which the window of the chancel was opened to let the lay congregation see what was going on behind the rood screen.[32] Indeed, late medieval Western worship became surprisingly like the Byzantine rite, with its barrier of the iconostasis set between congregation and celebrants, a window or door occasionally opening to disclose a glimpse of magnificence.

The late medieval exclusion of worshippers from the actions of worship, which led ultimately to not only invisible but inaudible performance of the Mass (cf. the "silent," sotto voce performance of the canon by the priest in the late Middle Ages), was the end result of a process that began before the end of antiquity. This process had major effects on medieval religious lyric, creating a stillness in which lay piety, and the vernacular, could speak.

Already in the fourth century, the training of singers for the performance of liturgy began.[33] The schools that trained them grew out of the schools for lectors, and their members were recruited from the monasteries, orginally to be specialists in psalmody. The *schola*, as it was called in Latin, came in time to absorb all the old functions of the congregation. The existence of these trained choirs provided an opportunity for composers, who used them in the performance of the remarkable and often very difficult sacred poly-phony of the later Middle Ages (twelfth century on). But this nightingale had proved a cuckoo to the laity, who lost their place in the nest.

The language of the liturgy early became an even greater obstacle to lay participation in worship. Originally, it had been the language of the people, just as the priest's garments had been nothing more than the contemporary uniform of officials of the state. Ambrose's hymns, for instance, could be easily understood by the congregation, and in their quatrains they nimbly trod the line between traditional learned quantitative and popular accentual meter. Indeed, they represented a superb resolution of the problem of bal-ancing the liturgical need for dignity, the doctrinal need for precision, and the pastoral need for comprehensibility. But like the priest's garments, the language of Western liturgy remained essentially the same while the world changed around it. And the Carolingian reform put an end to what conces-sions it had made to the proto-Romance forms spoken Latin had assumed in the Merovingian period. The Carolingian decree of 813 that sermons should be preached in German (*theotisca*) and Romance (*lingua rustica*) as well as Latin tells us both that most bishops (or their deputies) were not preaching in the vernacular and that their sermons were consequently not being understood.[34] In the German-speaking areas such as Anglo-Saxon Eng-land, this had of course always been the case (which perhaps acted as a stimulus leading to the development and recording of a vigorous Old Eng-lish vernacular literature). But in the Romance countries, the drift of Latin into superannuation, archaism, and finally incomprehensibility must have come slowly and almost stealthily.[35]

The Carolingian fusion of Roman and Gallican liturgical traditions and its revival of a correct, often painfully correct, Latinity had effects on Euro-pean culture that have endured down to our own day. The concomitant concern on the part of Charlemagne and his cultural aides for lay piety and lay comprehension of the liturgy (as well as the projected collection of traditional oral literature) died almost a-borning.[36]

There was a fundamental contradiction between the imperial urge to control and standardize and the imperial curiosity about a culture, or collection of cultures, that the state was attempting to submerge under administrative, legal, and linguistic forms taken from a dream of old Rome. And there was never any doubt about which would triumph.

The liturgical role of the laity shrank to almost nothing. It had its pilgrimage songs, its processional songs, its ditties for Christmas and Easter, and perhaps a hymn translation to sing at the end of Vespers or the end of Mass. Even the sermon moved out of Church into the streets—it was only by shedding its liturgical status that it could speak the language of its audience—and before and after it the people might also sing.[37]

Clearly, this is a picture of extreme deprivation. No doubt the gap it reveals between clergy and laity, a gap that physically as well as linguistically existed during worship, played an important part in producing the climate of pervasive and often virulent anticlericalism. So great was the gap that the monks and priests and secular canons of the twelfth century entirely failed to meet the challenge of a vigorous lay piety that was spreading to fill the spiritual territory the clergy had abandoned, even though the papacy tried desperately to rouse them to begin teaching the people lest its energies take strange paths.[38] It required the creation of the fraternal orders to reestablish some sort of communication between the Church and its flock, and the fraternal orders, especially the Franciscan, exercised a dominant influence on late religious poetry in the vernaculars and even in Latin from the thirteenth century onwards.

In fact, as it turned out, the laity's loss of its ancient liturgical role was also an opportunity. Driven back on its own resources, but with the assistance of the friars, the laity began to develop means for the practice of piety *outside* the confines of the official liturgy. Those whom the clergy had ceased to treat as its children came to act more and more like its rivals.

The Church attempted to control lay piety by various means, including the creation of "mass prayers" meant to be said silently by individuals during the service—apparently the music and the liturgical gestures enabled the worshipper to keep track of where he or she was.[39] This at least gave the laity something to do at Mass beside stand there and watch. But lay demand also led to the creation of other sorts of vernacular religious texts, notably the books of hours, which served as a layman's equivalent to the Breviary that priests and monks used when abroad from church or cloister. There was also a large production of vernacular verse prayers, to be used individually, or in the domestic devotions pious households now practised, or at the meetings of lay religious groups. In particular, the devotion of the rosary, which can be traced back to the thirteenth century and had a chapel in every church in Europe by the sixteenth century, stimulated the writing of "Mary-Psalters," Latin and vernacular poetic texts built upon multiples of fifty (stanzas, lines, words, even letters).[40]

Most of this poetic activity produced little of poetic value. However, the institutional forms in which lay piety—especially *urban* lay piety—expressed itself often led to more significant results.

In Germany and the Low Countries, the *devotio moderna* movement took shape in the thirteenth century, reacting against contemporary scholasticism and the abstractions of theology in favor of a personal relationship with God (which, not coincidentally, bypassed the need for Latin). Great mystics like Eckhart, Tauler, Suso, and Mechthild of Magdeburg all contributed, consciously or not, to this movement, and its literature has the directness and warmth of the spirituality of mystics but also its frequent esotericism and its reiterated aporia, in which failure to find the words becomes a virtue. Still, the lyrics the movement produced often have great charm, and its wider influence on northern European religious lyric in the fourteenth and fifteenth centuries was a revivifying one.

One can scarcely say as much for the guilds of Meistersingers that first took official shape around 1450. Their exclusivity, conservatism, and exaggerated concern for form made for verse that is often a travesty of the tradition of *Spruchdichtung* (sapiential poetry) out of which it grew. Most of their output lies outside the chronological limits of this book—an accident of fate few acquainted with *Meistersang* will regret.

These guilds had their analogues in the Romance countries. In northern France, they were called *puys* (probably from "podium," in reference to the platform where poems were read—the derivation from *puits* or "well" is folk etymology); in southern France and Iberia, *consistori* or *joyas*. Examples of the former existed, for example, in the towns of Amiens, Abbéville, Caen, Dieppe, and Rouen; they were mostly dedicated to the Immaculate Conception and organized (like the Meistersingers' guilds) in the second half of the fifteenth century or even later—none seems to have existed in a poetry-fostering capacity before the end of the fourteenth century. Examples of the latter include the *consistori* at Toulouse (1323–1484) and the *joyas* convoked from time to time in the south (e.g., at Valencia in 1474). In all these cases, competition provided the motive for writing poetry, and prizes, originally of nominal value, were awarded. Since most of the authors were poetic amateurs, aristocrats or of the professional classes and the verse forms demanded were often (except in Iberia) rather difficult, even the prize-winning entries that have come down to us from these contests are usually very bad. One must say that however interesting the *puys* and their kindred may be for their connection with municipal life at the end of the Middle Ages and thereafter (a rather neglected side of European cultural history, considering how many major creative figures emerged from these towns with their poetic academies and learned societies), they have little to offer to the student, not to mention the reader, of poetry.

Happily, the history of Italian lay religious institutions and their role in the creation of religious lyric is another matter altogether. They grew out of the pious confraternities dating back to the eighth century that drew their membership from clergy or laity and aimed at the personal salvation of the members and the provision of assistance to the poor.[41] Lay examples were organized and supervised by members of the clergy, and the lay *confratres* enjoyed participation in the spiritual benefits of the monastery to which their *charité* was attached in return for their support of the monastery. However, as early as the twelfth century, one can see the *confratres* beginning to rebel against clerical tutelage, especially in fiscal matters, in the selection of their leaders, and in the determination of bylaws. In time, the clergy became no more than hired chaplains, and laymen set up confraternities without any attachment to a church, a saint, or clerical administration.

This sort of conflict between laity and clergy is typical of the late Middle Ages. It would be of little concern to us here, were it not for the significant change in the nature of Italian lay confraternities that took place in the second half of the thirteenth century.

Unlike their counterparts in the rest of Europe, these bodies undertook the regular corporate performance in a systematic fashion of religious texts in the vernacular that are not merely devotional but celebrate to a greater or lesser extent the various occasions of the church-year. In effect, the Italian confraternities created or caused to be written an abbreviated vernacular equivalent to the monastic office for collective lay celebration, much as the books of hours provided the individual layman the opportunity of performing a private vernacular equivalent to the office. The texts the confraternity sang or (more often) had a paid choir sing for them (note the imitation of contemporary liturgical custom!) were called *laude* or *laudi*, a term that derives from the Latin word *laudes* used by the Church for certain texts in praise of God and includes the closing of Matins or Nocturns, the last three Psalms of the Psalter, the Alleluia, and the expanded or "troped" Gloria; extraliturgically, it covers certain songs of the *scholae cantorum*—cf. also St. Francis's famous *Laudes creaturarum*.[42] Over two hundred different *laudari*, or manuscripts containing the *laude* used by a confraternity, are extant today, many of them as yet unpublished. The vast majority of *laude* are in the form of a *ballata*, a dance-song (cf. *ballare* [to dance]) consisting of a refrain that opens the poem, recurs after each strophe until the poem ends and contributes a rhyme to each of these strophes (e.g., aaX/ /cccX/dddX/

eeeX . . .).[43] The texts themselves concern in particular the Christmas season, the Easter season, and the various Marian feasts—precisely those areas
of the church-year that most interested the pious laity.

What gave the impulse to this massive creation of religious poetry in the
vernacular seems to have been the flagellant movement of 1260, the most
impressive of several popular religious movements that agitated Italy period-
ically in the later Middle Ages (others include the "Alleluia" movement of
1233, fostered by the Church, and the "Bianchi" movement of 1399, which
apparently began in southwestern Provence or Catalonia; the 1260 movement affected Germany as well, but north of the Alps neither it nor the
flagellant movement of 1349 produced anything of poetic interest). The
movement began in Perugia, spread thence throughout Umbria, and soon
involved most of the peninsula. Its active phase was relatively brief; its lasting
importance is in the galvanizing impact it had on existing confraternities.[44]

Confraternities known as *laudesi* and dedicated to the Virgin may have
predated the 1260 movement, and some of the few early texts in the vernacular of a *lauda*-like character, thought not in the *ballata* form, probably
also belong to the period before 1260. In fact, the question of the ultimate
origins of the *lauda* is of little importance. The very paucity of evidence
from the first half of the thirteenth century shows that a major change took
place: before 1260, no sign of collections of *laude*, and no proof of religious
use of the *ballata* form (aside from a Lombard account of the Passion);[45]
after 1260, collections form rapidly (though few can be dated securely to
1300 or earlier), and nearly all of the *laude* in the first generation or two of
laudari are *ballate*.

In any event, after 1260, existing lay confraternities in some cases re-
organized themselves to incorporate the penitential spirit of the flagellants
or *disciplinati*. In addition, entirely new confraternities of *disciplinati* mate-
rialized. Even those confraternities that continued to hew to the traditional
devotional line responded by creating or commissioning *laudari*. (Only the
purely charitable confraternities failed to follow suit.) The *disciplinati*, on
the one hand, and the *laudesi*, on the other, produced *laudari* that are distinct in several respects. First, though both groups are known to have sung
laude, the *laudari* of the *disciplinati* contain no music. Second, the *laudari*
of the *laudesi* are much more lyrical in character, while it was the *disciplinati*
whose most dramatic *laude* led ultimately to the creation of *sacra rappre-
sentazione* or religious drama in fourteenth-century Italy. Third, the *disciplinati* stressed the Passion, since they sought to excite themselves to feelings
of penitence (one of the "genres" most characteristic of their *laudari* is the
planctus Mariae, Mary's lament for her sufferings from the news of Christ's
arrest until his death); the *laudesi* pay much greater heed to Mary, and their
laude are less closely associated with the cycle of the church-year.[46]

The construction and use of *laudari* continued on into the Renaissance. Some of the most important contributions to this literature, however, were the work not of anonymous clergymen supplying texts for confraternal use but of various poets who wrote for personal or literary rather than (primarily, at least) institutional reasons. These include the leading poet of the generation before Cavalcanti and Dante, Guittone d'Arezzo (five *laude* in *ballata* form in a unique manuscript); Iacopone da Todi (whose highly idiosyncratic *laudario* had a huge success and great influence, though in fact few of his poems turn up in the numerous "popular" *laudari*); Bianco da Siena, a follower of the fourteenth-century St. Colombine (his 100-odd *laude* are mostly prolix and facile to the point of unendurability); and a number of fourteenth- and fifteenth-century writers, several of whom in quality if not in quantity far surpassed Bianco (e.g., Ugo Panziera, Neri Pagliaresi, and the notorious Savonarola). Overall, however, as the confraternities lost their old vigor, even anonymous *laude* become more and more subjective and private—more "poetic," in fact, but poorer as poetry. The old public and corporate spirit survived, intensified, in the religious drama of the later fourteenth and fifteenth centuries, but the dissolution of the initial fusion of dramatic expression and lyric feeling in the early *laudari* had unfortunate consequences for the *lauda*.

In this whole poetic tradition, which completely dominated Italian vernacular religious lyric save for the occasional sonnet or *canzone* or literary exercise in *terza rima*, one should neither under- nor overestimate the role of the friars. To the Dominicans goes the credit for conceiving of the *lauda*-singing confraternity, and the Franciscans and other orders participated intensively in the constitution of these confraternities and their *laudari*.[47] Nonetheless, it was the urban laity who provided the energy and the opportunity upon which the friars capitalized, and it was the desire of the laity to have a surrogate liturgy that they could understand and participate in that sustained the *lauda* movement for so many years. What competition failed to produce in the case of the *puys*, the cooperative impulse to worship succeeded in producing in the case of the Italian confraternities of *laudesi* and *disciplinati*: a vigorous, "popular," and poetically valuable religious lyric.[48]

In the course of the foregoing discussion of the development of the liturgy, of lay piety, and of lay religious institutions, much has already been said concerning the authorship and the audience of religious lyric in the West. The next pages will collect these scattered remarks and provide a somewhat fuller treatment of this important subject.

As one would expect given the need for special training in the language, the authors of medieval Latin religious lyric were almost entirely ecclesiastical. So long as Latin remained one's birthright, a layman like Prudentius might be found (ca. 400 A.D.) contributing to the tradition. But with the shift of Latin from partly native to entirely learned language, such exceptions disappear. Yet to say that a writer was a member of the clergy is only a first step toward understanding his position. It mattered a good deal whether a writer was of the higher or the lower clergy, of a traditional monastic or a fraternal order (after 1200), of a community of regular canons (after 1108) or a chapter of secular canons; it mattered whether he lived in a house frequented by royalty or a house frequented by no one, and so on. Roughly speaking, one can say that most authors of Latin religious lyric up to the twelfth century were monks of a settled mode of life; thereafter, the picture becomes more complex, and includes the contributions of rootless clergymen at court because they had no parish position, distinguished figures at the universities, and later on the friars.

The usual audience for medieval Latin religious lyric was local, perhaps no more than one's own monastic community or church. Being a member of a famous monastery or an important functionary in the Church hierarchy or a noted saint or great teacher all helped—it might at least attract false attributions to your name—but by and large a new poem had to make its own way in life, generally clothed in an honest anonymity. Under medieval conditions, few poems got very far, but parchment is durable and religious orders are tenacious of their manuscripts, and enough has survived to fill the fifty-five volumes of the *Analecta hymnica* and still leave a good deal for future editors to bring to light. At the same time, a certain number of religious lyrics, primarily hymns, caught on and became universally known and used. In this process, the formation of a canon of hymns by a monastic order (cf. the Benedictine hymnary or the Cistercian hymnary) played a major role. Whatever texts were admitted into the canon became an integral part of the celebration of the Office in all the houses of the order. In a less official way, lyrics (*pia dictamina*) for devotional and meditative use circulated among the clergy in the later Middle Ages, satisfying the apparently universal desire for a more personal, private, and direct form of religious experience. Whatever the diffusion or the particular use made of a given Latin religious lyric, its language limited its audience as strictly as its authorship.

The authors of vernacular religious lyric were a much more varied lot, though there is no question that the friars held a plurality. This fraternal authorship is particularly prevalent in Middle English religious lyric, where (it has been estimated on good grounds) anywhere from two-thirds to 90 percent of pre-1350 texts are not only by friars but by Franciscans.[49] After the Plague of 1349, the friars lost their dominance of the religious lyric just as they lost their leadership in spirituality (a fact that is obvious enough from the figure they cut in Chaucer and in contemporary literature). Laymen and monks claim a place among the creators of religious lyric, and

Franciscan authorship drops to a mere 25 percent, a change that may have something to do with the markedly cooler, more formal tone of fifteenth-century English religious poetry.

The authors of early Middle High German religious literature belonged to the secular clergy rather than to the monasteries (1050–1200); since they produced virtually no lyric, in any sense, this fact is of only peripheral interest here. Laymen contributed most of the considerable amount of non-anonymous religious lyric dating between 1200 and 1350, though one should know that the bulk of it, being part of the tradition of *Spruchdichtung*, is not very lyrical in its tonality. Aristocratic, later replaced by bourgeois, support created a situation in these centuries that permitted one to make a career as a vernacular poet—and in view of the strength of lay piety, it is not surprising that poets produced a good deal of religious as well as secular poetry. Indeed, as aristocratic support declined and bourgeois interest grew, the balance tilted away from the secular toward the religious, and it remained in that position in the urban middle class that supplied the members of the Meistersingers' guilds. A number of ecclesiastics (e.g., the "Monk of Salzburg") also contributed by name, and more (including friars no doubt) may be hidden behind the large anonymous output of Middle High German religious verse. Nonetheless, the history of its authorship contrasts sharply with the history of the Middle English religious lyric, thereby showing what effect the existence of a confident vernacular poetic tradition created by laymen and the enjoyment of full social standing by a language can have even on religious literature.

Much the same can be said of Provençal and Iberian poetry. For all practical purposes, religious lyric emerged in Provence only with the beginning of the thirteenth century. Nonetheless, its authors came from the ranks of the troubadours, and even the anonymous later poetry of the decline is probably the work of the urban bourgeoisie (cf. the *joyas* of Toulouse, where the authors are a mixed urban bag, with lawyers the most common species).[50]

Due to the eclipse of the language as far as art-lyric is concerned between 1350 and 1450, Portuguese religious poetry is rather a special case. From the early period, with insignificant exceptions, there is only the huge collection of Marian miracles and lyrics, supervised and partly written, it would seem, by King Alfonso the Wise. His son Denis is reputed to have written a religious *cancioneiro*, but it has not survived. The poets contributing to the *Cantigas de Santa Maria* were probably drawn from the ecclesiastics at Alfonso's court. In the fifteenth century, with the revival of Portuguese for lyric use, aristocratic poets (who dominate the major collection, Garcia de Resende's *Cancioneiro Geral* of 1516) entirely ignored religious poetry. One finds only the humblest sorts of prayers and paraphrases, the work of a friar here and a pious noblewoman there. In point of fact, Portuguese religious lyric had become subliterary.

The authors of Spanish religious lyric are partly aristocratic and middle-class professionals, partly clerical (usually friars). There are very few among them who view themselves primarily as poets. Since Spanish poetry eschewed the elaborate formal games of Romance poetry to the north, non-professionals were in fact able to do good work on occasion. However, this tradition (somewhat like the German) tends to the abstract and conceptual, with thought much stronger than feeling in most cases.

In Catalonia, before Catalan attained literary status for a few score decades in the fifteenth century, native troubadours wrote their religious poems, when they wrote them, in Provençal. Later anonymous lyrics, in Catalan, and of a "popular" character, seem to have been written mostly by friars or by secular clergy for the use of their parishioners. Educated laymen also contributed, though it is quite clear that they considered normal devotional poetry to be beneath them. Instead, one has the intensely personal ruminations of an Ausias March, which are often religious, but never religious lyric. The same is true even of Pero Martines, a Dominican friar hideously executed in 1463, and that precocious thirteenth-century phenomenon Ramon Llull, both of whose bodies of religious poems are thoroughly idiosyncratic and literary (Llull expresses his feelings about popular piety in a dialogue among several figures, one of whom is a learned hermit who praises Mary and shows up an ignorant hermit, whose Marianism is of a more popular kind, for the vulgarian he is).[51]

Among the major figures in the early history of Old French religious lyric, one finds both a king (cf. Alfonso the Wise) and a monk: namely, Thibaut de Champagne, king of Navarre, and Gautier de Coincy. Most thirteenth-century Old French religious lyric—in particular the religious chansons—was the work of laymen and was diffused by jongleurs and minstrels.[52] Some part of the oeuvre of most noted lay poets is religious, including the professional court poets of the end of the Middle Ages known rather loosely as the *grands rhétoriqueurs*. Ecclesiastics may have been responsible for most of the anonymous, entirely utilitarian production of verse prayers and devotional pieces for books of hours and the like. But aside from Gautier de Coincy, whose work is probably the most interesting of all the medieval French religious lyricists, the clergy seems to have been responsible for virtually nothing of artistic value.

Because of the peculiar nature of its poetic history, Italy has already received more than its share of attention. Most of the *laude* were probably written by friars, but there was also a considerable production of "literary" *laude* by laymen (cf. Feo Belcari or the Medici clan) in the later period. The presence of one "Garzo" as author of four *laude* in the famous, and largely thirteenth-century, Cortona 91 collection indicates that perhaps more *laude* than one suspects were also the work of laymen even in the first century of their existence. Nor should one forget the lay brother like Guittone d'Arezzo or the member of a saint's following like Bianco de Siena, neither of whom was really clerical in the slightest. Meanwhile, the greatest poets, those who were most aware of their gifts and the nature of their calling, avoided the writing of *laude* and popular religious lyric as assiduously as ambitious Catalan or Portuguese poets (or Chaucer) avoided the equivalent sorts of poetry in their own traditions. Dante wrote no religious lyric at all, and Petrarch wrote only his canzone to the Virgin, a calculated, nostalgic, and magnificent pastiche of traditional Marian poetry under the aegis of *Paradiso* 33. In their attitude toward religious lyric, these poets foreshadowed the ruling attitude of all the centuries of poets since.

Finally, there is Iceland, which came late to Christianity (1000 A.D.) and still clings to its native poetic traditions even today. Its early Christian poetry survives only as fragments embedded in prose texts (narratives and treatises on grammar or poetry); since monks and secular clergy were slow to appear in Iceland, authorship was the province of the laity, whose doctrinal notions are often very curious, till about 1150. Thenceforward, the clergy took over the reins, especially the regular clergy, though one also encounters the occasional layman who wrote both religious and secular verse. Most of the later work is anonymous, and after 1350 it becomes much like the religious poetry of the rest of Europe. One of the few authors whose name and occupation we know for certain in this later period was Eysteinn Ásgrímsson, an Austin canon whose *Lilja* is one of the finest in a distinguished company of late medieval Marian poems from all over Europe.

The audience for vernacular religious lyric can be described more succinctly than its authors. Throughout Western Europe, nuns, who were usually ignorant of Latin, formed an important element in its makeup. Many texts are addressed directly to women in religious orders, and still more seem thematically designed to suit their devotional needs. In particular, hymn translations allowed them to understand what they were singing. Another significant element was composed of the lay confraternities and religious societies already described that were so prominent a feature of middle-class life in the rising towns of Italy, Germany, France, and the Low Countries. At a higher social level, royal and local courts often cultivated religious lyric, particularly religious song, in its more fashionable and elegant forms. And the masses had their popular religious songs (to judge by medieval reports—few have come down to us), their pilgrimage songs, and the humble religious lyric written for them by the churchmen who dealt with them directly, mainly friars, but also some parish priests. Finally, pious and educated men and women, including even the clergy toward the end of the Middle Ages, provided a growing audience, not to say market, for reflective and devotional lyric suitable for domestic use. In each case, the nature of the intended hearers or users is an important factor in determining the nature of the poem.

Because of its enormous diversity in all aspects of culture, to describe the medieval West is to describe a world. Fortunately, the relative cultural homogeneity of the Byzantine East makes it far easier to handle. Even the various categories of religious lyric—liturgical, paraliturgical, extraliturgical, and nonliturgical—are more clearly distinguished thanks to an almost infinitely greater degree of centralized institutional control. In addition, though the Eastern Church made a mystery of the Eucharist long before the Western Church, the language of its liturgy remained accessible to the lay worshipper. Therefore, nothing like the Western situation that proved so favorable to the development of vernacular religious lyric arose in the East. (One should remember that this book does not cover Byzantine poetry or religious evolution after 1200; however, the situation is apparently no different in the later Greek Middle Ages—the folk songs that clearly date back to that period but that were recorded only in postmedieval times have their analogues all over Europe and arise out of an opposition not between languages but between literate and illiterate.)

The authors of the Byzantine liturgical lyrics were mostly monks, or a nun like the ninth-century aristocrat Kassia. Their audience was in principle the entire Greek church; in fact, as in the West, it might be only one's own monastery, as the irregular diffusion of Byzantine hymnody shows.[53] Even the greatest hymnodist of them all, Romanos (first half of the sixth century), putatively composed his *kontakia* for a single church in Constantinople, and a manuscript copy of his output was among that church's prized possessions. Of course, the quality of his hymns, as well as Church backing and the dominant influence of anything Constantinopolitan, soon won them wide reception all over the eastern Mediterranean.

Nonliturgical Byzantine religious lyric took various forms. Laymen were responsible for much of the poetry in classical (or quasi-classical) meters like the iambic trimeter, and their readers included not only the upper clergy but the large public of well-educated civil servants who staffed the imperial court—and from whose ranks the upper clergy was frequently drawn. Their tastes were highly literary and "humanistic," and the poems they created and read somewhat resemble the Latin poetry of the university-educated clergy of the later Western Middle Ages, even to the point of seeking by the use of sometimes extremely archaic morphology and diction as great a distance as possible from the everyday speech of the people, including themselves. Since quantity had ceased to function phonemically in Greek well before the end of antiquity, the use of (more or less) quantitative meters, rather than the syllabic meters of the liturgy and of popular poetry (cf. the so-called political verse of fifteen syllables), had the same distancing effect.

The first example of the political verse just mentioned that has come down to us is the poetry of Symeon the New Theologian (tenth century). Strictly speaking, his long polemic verse treatises do not belong to the history of religious lyric, but the lyrical power of certain passages makes them impossible to ignore here. As a rebel against traditional hierarchical and institutional religious forms, he resorted to an equally untraditional verse form, one that clearly had an appeal for the average monk, clergyman, or layman that classicizing verse lacked. But in itself the political verse is no better suited for lyric than (for instance) the Germanic alliterative long line is, and it receives mention at this point largely because its use by Symeon, and by later writers like Theodore Prodromos (twelfth century), indicates important divisions within the audience of Byzantine poetry, with the readers of quantitative verse constituting a distinct and privileged minority.

In sum, then, it is largely possible to consider Byzantine religious lyric, liturgical, paraliturgical (cf. paracletic kanons, chapter 2), or nonliturgical, without much reference to its context in "real life." This is consistent with the antihistorical, intensely hierarchical character of Byzantine religion and civilization that made the East far more effective in preventing or ignoring change than the West was.

By the ninth century, the practice of writing hymns to existing stanza forms and melodies had become general. The available niches in the liturgy filled up, and though monastic production continued into the eleventh and twelfth centuries and new saint's days or the like occasionally created a need for new texts, most of the material in Orthodox liturgical books dates back to the early Middle Ages. No important new forms appeared after the seventh century (cf. chapter 2, section 2), in complete contrast to the West, where liturgical or paraliturgical forms continued to come into being up into the thirteenth century. Instead, Byzantine creative energy turned to the elaboration of the musical settings of its hymns, and the repertory of hymns and their very texts were progressively abridged, in a sort of retaliation (one might imagine) against the impossibility of creatively altering or replacing them.[54] And it expressed itself in nonliturgical religious poetry, which in its own way also sought the transcendent, universal status of the liturgy. Life may have given birth to Byzantine literature, but it succeeds almost wholly in escaping life's control.

After sifting through what we know about scriptural and patristic injunctions, the evolution of the Greek and Latin liturgies, the development of lay piety, the rise of lay religious societies, and the authorship and audience for vernacular religious lyric, it becomes possible to identify and understand more completely a number of principles of function that characterize the role of medieval religious lyric for its age.

First, it served the needs of an expanding liturgy. New feasts, new processions, and the like required texts to fill the gaps of time they opened up. And the human urge to ornament and re-create what is traditional worked no less powerfully in favor of liturgical growth.

Second, it served the need for texts to mark important religious actions that did not form a part of the liturgy proper. Supplications, pilgrimages, and Christmastide celebrations were only a few of the occasions that created a place for poetry and song.

Third, it served the need for texts for private use. Both the clergy and (in the later Middle Ages) the laity sought ways to consecrate their hours that lay outside existing religious forms. As the official Church came more and more into disrepute in the West, this hunger grew; in view of comparable tendencies to the private and subjective in the East in the later Middle Ages, without the attendant alienation between laity and clergy, it may be that such a hunger is a natural result of the long continuance of an established formal religion.

Fourth, it served the need for texts for conventual use, mainly by lay groups, but perhaps even as refectory reading for Western monks.[55] As such, it acted as surrogate for a Latin liturgy that only a minority among the laity, and far from all those in religious orders, could any longer understand.

Fifth, it served the need for elementary instruction of the illiterate layman, monk, or nun in the faith.[56] Most translations or paraphrases of hymns and liturgical texts like the Creed or the Pater noster have this aim in view, as does the typical anonymous vernacular lyric on the Nativity or the Crucifixion or the Virgin.

Sixth, it served the need to provide the Church with an antidote, to be administered to its flock, against the blandishments of heresy or the world. By co-opting existing tunes, stanza forms, secular motifs, secular genres, or anything else that exerted a popular appeal, in a process known in Latin as *contrafactura*, the Church could spoil the Egyptians (to cite a typologically crucial passage in the Old Testament, Exodus 12:36) and make the devil's weapons rebound upon his own head. Aldhelm used *contrafactura* in his labors in seventh-century Anglo-Saxon England; it flourishes throughout Europe in vernacular religious lyric in the later Middle Ages; and it is a fixture of religious poetry in the centuries between.[57] The results of its application could of course meet any of the other needs listed above, and it was used in religious verse and music as well as secular—the preference of the age for glossing the old rather than replacing it with something wholly new is again apparent.

Seventh, and last, it met a host of further, rather ill-assorted needs, most related in some way to the larger general functions already identified. Religious lyrics appear in miscellanies that friars used in constructing their sermons, and they were cited in these sermons to drive a point home or as a text to elaborate upon. They appear in collections of exempla that often served the same homiletic purpose.[58] In the form of written paraphrases of major liturgical or meditational texts, they acted as rewards to those who made contributions to the aid of the friars.[59] Their rubrics sometimes speak of the time off from purgatory that daily use will bring. In poetic competitions, they might earn their authors recognition or even a valuable prize, and in general, they were an excellent pretext for the author to ask for prayers for his soul—which were far more expensive to obtain by regular means from a priest. In particular, Marian lyrics might win the Virgin's favor—if she intervenes so often on behalf of sinners who merely repeated texts in her praise by rote, what might she not do for someone who actually wrote such texts?[60] Finally, religious lyrics might serve no religious purpose whatever, treating a religious subject for its purely literary interest; this was certainly true of a good deal of Byzantine and of some twelfth-century Latin "religious" epigram.

All of this greatly complicates any attempt to explain the workings of medieval religious lyric. "Religion," it seems, covers a multitude—of things, of peoples, of social classes, of institutional forms, of historical periods, and of attitudes and tastes and individual quirks—and it is necessary to keep this multitude in view when discussing it. Yet a simpler subject would be a duller one. Besides, what else could one expect from an age in which belief and the Church occupied so central and preeminent a place?

2

GENRES, FORMS, AND STRUCTURES

With this chapter, the discussion turns from the historical context of medieval religious lyric to its actual shape and characteristic organizing features, whether of overall form or internal structure. It seems advisable, however, to begin with a brief survey of those features of theme, tonality, and intergeneric relationships that allow one to distinguish among different types of religious lyric, particularly since the nature of the content often affects the choice of form and structure.

GENRES

A lively debate is in progress among medievalists and general theoreticians of literature about the status and meaning of the concept of "genre."[1] I am using it, rather loosely, to refer to groups of poems, synchronic and diachronic, that medieval authors and audiences clearly perceived as distinct in some important way or ways from other groups of poems. Obviously, the more ways a given group is perceived as differing from another group, the stronger the sense of a difference in genre becomes. In consequence, the term *genre* has only a relative and fluctuating value and rarely implies anything like total insulation of literary kinds one from the other. Since the concept of the medieval religious lyric, even more than for most other sorts of medieval literature, was highly pragmatic—that is, aesthetic ends were secondary to practical ends—genres had only a provisional, instrumental value, and their "rules" could be disregarded for cause. Therefore, the genres of medieval religious lyric described below should not be viewed as a rigid system with prescriptive force for the period.

In fact, there are different bases from which one can speak of genres in this poetry. Three seem to me particularly meaningful, both to medieval contemporaries and for the purposes of this study. In the order in which they will be discussed, these three bases are (1) subject matter, (2) treatment of subject matter, and (3) relationship to existing secular genres. The three arrays of genres founded upon these different bases can serve as complementary, though not exhaustive, ways of defining the nature of any given medieval religious lyric. Indeed, I would argue that it is generally wisest to conceive of genre in concrete cases as a composite created by the intersection of independent systems or axes.

i

Classification by subject matter has a solid base in the doctrinal structure of medieval Christianity. On the other hand, the dependence of religious lyric on this extrapoetic structure means that it is subject to the same laws, in particular the law that all power and goodness is ultimately an expression of the reality of God. Thus, there is a vertical, metonymic relationship among all saints and sacred events—and therefore among all poetic texts concerning them—that allows distinctions only a contingent value, disappearing as one's gaze turns upward to their source.

Despite this caveat, certain religious subjects produced a large medieval poetic progeny that in its themes and motifs has the character of a "genre." One such group of subjects focuses on sacred persons, the other on sacred events involving these persons.

In the first, one finds poems to the persons of the Trinity, collectively or individually. Christ appears as a child at the Nativity, a man at the Crucifixion, a judge at the Last Day, or in other guises drawn from his leading function in redemptive history.[2] Different periods, and different linguistic traditions, emphasize different moments in Christ's career, and these emphases reflect important differences in cultural outlook (e.g., Western humanization versus Eastern transcendentalism) or changes in piety (e.g., Romanesque ethos versus Gothic pathos). The other two receive much less attention; God the Father appears regularly in association with the act of creation or celebration of the created world, and the Holy Spirit in association with Pentecost. Outside of the doxology, explicitly Trinitarian poetry is still less common, and examples of it often seem to be the reflex of a dogmatic controversy. Finally, God, who is so all-encompassing that description fails and leaves a sense of brilliant vacancy, who as the maker of history is without history, figures only as a word on which words converge.

Among the saints, from the beginning in the East and after 1100 in the West, Mary easily dominates. In fact, in some Western traditions after 1200 or so, she threatens to eclipse her son. One sees her again and again in the context of one of her feasts, at the Annunciation, at the Nativity (which she shares with Christ), at the Presentation, at the Passion, at Pentecost, at the Assumption, in heaven, at the Last Judgment. She is also the wonder-worker of the miracle collections of the later Middle Ages, and the intercessor for sinners with her angry Son. In the last two centuries, her preexistence in God's mind and her (immaculate) conception join the older Marian topics, so that poets had a rich panoply to choose from when writing of her.[3]

In the vernaculars, other saints are surprisingly underrepresented. Some traditions offer poems concerning only a few of the most important or en-

tirely neglect them except for an occasional author who decided to write a
small cycle of panegyrics in their honor (cf. Catalan, Middle English, Old
French, Provençal, and Spanish). Naturally, in the liturgical languages and
in the *lauda* tradition, where saint's feast days were celebrated as an integral
part of the church-year, the result was entirely different: hundreds of examples in Italian, and too many examples to count in Latin.[4] In Greek, the later
kontakion and *kanon* (see the second section of this chapter) were predominantly hagiographical, and saints are an important subject of both liturgical
and nonliturgical poetry from the beginning. Where no bond to the church-
year existed, as was true of all vernacular traditions but Italian, the governing principle seems to have been the desire to make religious lyrics as generally useful as possible. Since Mary clearly subsumed the powers of all the
other saints within her own, it was Mary whom the authors of religious
lyric concentrated on. Otherwise, the names of most other saints will turn
up only in verse calendars (called *cisiojanus* in the German tradition) or
litanies that list them.[5] The Archangel Michael (believed to come for believers at death), John the Evangelist (Christ's best friend), and Mary Magdalene (the best hope of the genuine sinner), along with a few others, have
their moments, but none can hold a candle to the Virgin.[6] It is really only
within Latin that one could reasonably speak of subgenres of saints' lyrics
such as Peter and Paul or Cross hymns (both canvassed by Josef Szoevérffy;
yes, the Cross was treated as the peer of holy men, women, and angels).[7]
(One should know, however, that the *prose* pieces in the prayer books that
are so common at the end of the Western Middle Ages do give the saints
their due, even to the point of including a prayer to a different saint for
every day of the year.[8] And of course narrative literature about the saints,
particularly about their sensational deaths if they were martyrs, reached
formidable proportions in the same period.)

The second group of religious subjects I will discuss is composed of
events. One can see from the account of poems focusing on sacred persons
that the events of Scripture and Church history figure there as well—it
would be hard to imagine any other situation. But in the Western and Eastern liturgies, and in the liturgically structured *laudari*, certain moments
from the Gospels receive repeated poetic treatment in themselves, with
Christ, Mary, or others constituting the cast of characters and not the poetic
subject. By far the most important of these, to judge by the amount of poetry concerning them, were Christmas and the Passion.

Lyrics for Christmas were demonstrably a "popular" genre in the vernaculars and largely even in Latin. At least, one finds a neglect of the subject
by the artistically ambitious that could scarcely have been accidental. One
of the largest bodies of Catalan lyric, for instance, is composed of anonymous Christmas poems meant to be sung by the laity (a sizable fraction

being so entirely Marian in nature that one would be hard put to guess their original function on merely internal evidence).[9] In Provence, the noël dates back to the late Middle Ages and survived them, thanks to popular support, whereas the art-lyrics of the *joyas* perished unlamented. Almost no Old French Christmas poems are nonpopular in character. As for Middle English, one need only remember the Christmas carols that were produced for if not by the people in large numbers during the fifteenth century. The German tradition is somewhat more complex in this regard. There is little Christmas lyric from the thirteenth century, probably because popular examples went unrecorded. Thereafter, one finds a strong tradition of folk poems that strongly resemble the Catalan *cançons nadalenques*. In addition, art-poets produced a highly learned and artifical version of Christmas poetry and, in a few exceptional cases, poetry that struck a happy balance between the "popular" and the "artistic." In Italy, the *laudari* pay rather little heed to Christmas compared to the Passion, for reasons having to do with the penitential nature of the 1260 movement that catalyzed their creation (see chapter 1). Fifteenth-century literary *laude* (such as Lucrezia Tornabuoni's) on the Nativity are clearly examples of pastiche of popular poetry, but their *faux naïf* style can sometimes be quite attractive. Traditions like Spanish or Old Norse (which strongly resisted popular religious lyric on standard subjects) or like Portuguese (where the evidence is very spotty) almost entirely lack lyrics having to do with Christmas.[10] In Greek, examples are in several cases very distinguished (for liturgy, cf. Romanos; for nonliturgical work, cf. John Mauropus), but they are not particularly numerous, nor do they (given the reigning Byzantine attitude toward the common people and their speech) reflect any obviously popular traits.[11] By contrast, the Latin tradition is very rich, ranging from the sobriety of the "classic" early hymn to the dancelike exuberance of the Christmas *conductus* of the twelfth and thirteenth centuries.[12]

It is far less usual for lyrics on the Passion to show a strongly popular character. Intrinsically, the subject of Christ's suffering and death was suitable for the most serious treatment; indeed, the subject demanded it. Popular feelings found expression less in poems focusing on Christ himself than on his mother, whose lamentations appear in all traditions considered here except for the Old Norse. The countries where the influence of the friars was greatest also produced the most examples of the *planctus Mariae*: Italy and England. It is well represented in Latin (which boasts the most famous of all *planctus*, the Stabat mater) and in German, where the *planctus* embedded in the *Rheinisches Marienlob* (vv. 897–1313) towers above its mediocre compatriots. Elsewhere, examples are far less plentiful and (except for one Catalan poem) of little interest.

Still another genre associated with the Passion was the *horae* poem. Its distinguishing feature is the linking of the major stages in Christ's sufferings on Good Friday to the canonical hours, whence the name. Absent from the Greek tradition, it appears first of all in Latin prose (PL, vol. 94, coll. 561–68). The earliest Latin poetic example is a series of eight hymns by Gottschalk (PLAC 6:97–104) written in the ninth century. The most striking of the other Latin examples, which were all written centuries later, is John Pecham's "Philomena," in which the "imitation of Christ" as preached by St. Francis takes the form of a "nightingale" (the believer) singing itself to death on a tree, its gradual weakening marked by the passage of the *horae*. Catalan and Spanish, as well as Old Norse, lack this genre; it is rare in Italian, where the putatively or actually public and conventual use of the *laude* favored a more direct dramatic or narrative treatment of the Passion. It forms a regular part of the Old French books of hours (where hours of the Virgin and the Holy Spirit also figure), and it is alluded to in a remarkable set of mystically colored Old French poems from Lorraine that will get repeated attention in this book.[13] The same Franciscan spirituality that lies behind Pecham's and other Latin *horae passionis* was responsible for the handful of Middle English examples. In German, a half dozen poems use the pattern from the fourteenth century onward. In Portuguese, lyric interludes relieve a prose example by Friar João Claro.[14] And finally, in Provençal, a powerful fourteenth-century contemplation of the Cross from the region of Toulouse organizes itself into seven sections with references to the seven canonical hours.[15]

Of course, most lyrics on the Passion are neither *planctus* nor *horae*. Like these last, many are meant for devotional use, conjuring up the *imago pietatis*, the heart-rending image of Christ hanging on the Cross. As such, they involve rhetorical features that will come in for scrutiny in chapter 3. Others concentrate on the five instruments of the Passion or the seven words. And still others eternize the crucifixion, making Christ speak reproachfully or angrily to the sinner who daily nails him to the bitter tree.[16] The numbers of Passion lyrics may be endless, but the variety is not.

Other feasts commemorating Gospel events have their families of poems, but they are as nothing next to the nations that swarm around Christmas and Eastertide. Only the Marian feasts command a really impressive following, and most of these are usually allotted no more than a single stanza within a poem listing Mary's joys.

As for the rest of Scripture and the complex history it relates, religious lyric is almost entirely silent. One has to go to didactic, narrative, or epigrammatic scriptural paraphrases to find anything but a select few moments from the Gospel story covered. The reason for this selectivity is very simple: the rest of Scripture appears only as readings that serve as a gloss on the occasions of the church-year. It lacks any direct celebration in its own right.

Therefore, it does not act as the primary subject matter of medieval religious lyric, whose dependence upon the choices made in the shaping of the liturgy could not be more graphically demonstrated. What further scriptural material does figure in the lyrics gets in upon the coattails of scriptural saints (John the Baptist, the disciples, the apostles) to whom piety had awarded a feast day of their own.

Purely utilitarian lyrics such as paraphrases of the fundamental texts of simple religion (Ave, Creed, Lord's Prayer, certain Marian anthems in the later centuries) or table blessings may act as a pendant to this section on genres as determined by subject matter. Their very lack of any poetic value is a reminder that most other religious lyrics include an unmistakably aesthetic element in their composition.

ii

Treatment of subject matter is a wholly different aspect of the medieval religious lyric. The categories of approach that its examination reveals cut directly across categories of subject matter as such. And these categories show differentiation not only by internal features but also by function and audience, so that one can feel confident of their validity for their period as well as their taxonomical utility today.

In the tradition of Christian religious lyric, the hymnic mode is primary, both in time and in prestige.[17] Antiquity resisted the hymn; the early Middle Ages refused to use it pedagogically or to cite it on a par with the poetry of the pagan and Christian *classici* (e.g., Vergil or Juvencus); but the later Western Middle Ages made it a part of elementary education, and of course it exercised a pervasive influence on every educated person through its use in the liturgy.[18] In both Latin and Greek, the rate of production varied widely from period to period but reached its peak in the West at the very end of the Middle Ages.[19] As a mode, it is characterized by a focus on praise and by a congregational "we." In Greek hymnody, the first person singular occurs as well, singling out the author, though not separating him from the community of worship. In Latin hymnody, the first person singular remains rare in the later Middle Ages (where it indicates that the poem where it appears probably began life outside the liturgy) and essentially unknown before the thirteenth century. In addition, both Greek and Latin hymnody practice a certain formality and solemnity of address. In the later Middle Ages in the West, this tonality increases and diminishes at the same time; that is, two varieties of hymn develop, one seeking to make praise as splendid as possible, the other seeking to communicate the intense human emotions of believers confronted with the human joys and sufferings of (particularly) Christ and Mary.

A second mode is that of prayer.[20] Originally, prayer was a function of prose sections of the liturgy, in the main. It is of course true that some of the earliest Latin hymns are couched in the form of prayers, but prayer was nonetheless secondary to praise in Latin hymnody of the first part of the Middle Ages. The fact that the balance tilts markedly toward prayer thereafter is an important indication of that major shift in piety alluded to several times already in the course of this book. Outside hymnody and the liturgy, prayer decidedly dominates. In the Greek tradition, which lacks the "low" elements so important in the West, literary prayers are nonetheless common in nonliturgical poetry, and as *parakletika* (supplicatory pieces) they form an appendix to Greek hymnic collections. In the vernaculars of the West, the prayer mode is extremely abundant, with Mary the usual addressee. Interestingly, those poetic traditions that resisted popular influence—Old Norse, Provençal, and Spanish—are quite poor in examples of this mode. In Old Norse, the skaldic tradition that Christian poets sought to perpetuate up to the mid-fourteenth century was a tradition of panegyric, and praise far outweighs prayer as a mode even after the stanzas and language of traditional European religious poetry took over in the second half of the fourteenth century. In effect, poets shifted from the skaldic to the hymnic mode, that is, from a native to an imported style of praise. In Provençal, prayers are far more often in prose than verse, partly because the *joyas* favored the composition of eulogies, partly because the prominence of the poet's persona in Provençal lyric did not lend itself to the humility and general usefulness of the prayer.[21] In Spanish, the aristocratic poets who composed and collected the poetry of the *cancioneros* seem also to have found little to attract them in the mode of prayer. However, their work, which is almost entirely fifteenth century (Berceo is of course a case apart in every respect), may have been affected by a turning away from the intimacies of entreaty to the high ceremony of formal panegyric that characterizes fifteenth-century religious poetry all over Europe and includes the Latin tradition. One suspects that this phenomenon was partly due to the vernaculars' at last finding their legs fully as literary languages and proving that they could don the high style and make it their own. But there was also a shift of feeling that expresses itself in aspects of medieval culture other than just the religious or the poetic, a shift that I am inclined to associate with the gradual annexation of the symbols and pleasures of the aristocracy by the rest of society as perceived from their inferior vantage point. This process of annexation forced the aristocracy to exaggerate its traditional habits in order to maintain a separate identity, which in turn obliged the middle classes to move even further away from the homely, commonplace, and creaturely toward the high social rhetoric of dress, gesture, and language. This process now seems almost to have run its course and may even be reversing itself, but it was already well under way in the fourteenth and fifteenth centuries.

A third mode, the didactic, has a long and rich medieval history in verse, but it is innately nonliturgical and nonlyrical and so can only be mentioned here.[22] Nonetheless, since the urge to instruct affects poems in other modes to the point that few religious lyrics escape its touch, it might be useful to supply a profile of its importance in the various linguistic traditions. As stated, it is foreign to the liturgical spirit, and even in liturgical poetry where instruction may have been the ultimate motive (as in Aquinas's Corpus Christi poems), didactic content ends by serving as the basis for praise. Outside the liturgy, it is extremely common in Latin (the *Analecta hymnica* collection, despite its title, includes innumerable examples) but rather scarce in Greek, except in the epigram, where literary "point" is the object, not edification. Its frequency varies widely in the vernaculars. Rare in Catalan and Old Norse (for quite different reasons), it is abundant in the *laude*, in Middle English, in Alfonso's *Cantigas*, in German (cf. *Spruchdichtung* and *Meistersang*), and in Spanish. In Old French, it is well represented, but the hymnic mode of praise and the mode of prayer vastly outweigh it. In general, except in German and Spanish, with their taste for theology for its own sake, exhortation dominates over exposition and creates a strong kinship between examples of the didactic and the next mode, the moral.[23]

Like the didactic, the moral mode lies outside the purview of this book. Often, its content is not in any meaningful sense even religious—but then, neither is a good deal of the Old Testament's "wisdom" books. Some of the dullest but also some of the most immediately readable of medieval poetry is in the moral mode, and it certainly deserves much more study than it has so far received. Here there is no justification for more than a preliminary comparative profile on the pattern of the one just given for its close cousin, the didactic mode. The moral mode bulks largest in German, Latin, and Middle English. In the two vernaculars, it seems to satisfy a popular, especially urban middle-class need for generous helpings of good solid "sentence." German *Spruchdichtung* and its progeny offered a steady supply of this commodity, much of it of good or excellent quality. The voluminous Vernon Manuscript of the later fourteenth century contains the most interesting corpus of Middle English moral poetry; many of the texts also appear elsewhere, and their substantial, heavy-footed stanzas pace confidently but slowly foward, stiff with a sense of their own dignity. With like gait a procession of burghers might have moved through the streets of the City of London. Latin examples often achieve great wit and vigor (cf. the thirteenth century Serlo of Wilton);[24] their clerical audience makes for a more sophisticated and subtle approach. The moral mode is also important in Catalan, Old French, and Spanish religious verse but quite secondary in Italian, Provençal, and Portuguese. The lack of full printed evidence for the last renders any conclusions provisional, but the quasi-liturgical function of the *lauda* accounts for the relative infrequency of moral poetry in Italian, and the inclination of the Provençal tradition toward self-expression rather than teaching for its infrequency there. Its role in Greek and Old Norse is insignificant. Some *kontakia* have a strongly doctrinal or moral cast due to their function as poetic substitutes for the sermon, but the spirit of liturgy is fundamentally as much opposed to the moral as to the doctrinal mode, and neither plays much part in Byzantine liturgy. In nonliturgical poetry, except for a set of moral epigrams to his monks by Theodore the Studite (a sort of verse gloss on their Rule), the mode had little appeal for poets except as it occasionally served their taste for epigram. Up to the Reformation, Old Norse remained too skaldic, and then hymnic, to adopt the European tradition of moral poetry. Its wisdom poetry remained that of the heathen, Eddic tradition, which expresses itself in the aphorisms of characters in the sagas (its continental analogue of course exists in abundance in Latin and vernacular proverbial literature, which similarly represents the voice or voices of experience and oral tradition and tacitly opposes the voice of official, religious culture).

A fifth mode, the epigrammatic, has already come in for repeated mention in connection with nonliturgical Byzantine religious poetry.[25] It is marginally lyric at best, but its importance in the East (where it perpetuates the tradition represented by the Greek Anthology and in fact contributes a "book" of Christian epigrams that is one of the fourteen in the Anthology) earns it treatment here. Since wit is in the ascendant in epigram, not only is it unlyrical in spirit, it is also unreligious. In the West, one finds it in Latin scriptural paraphrase (cf. the favorite twelfth-century practice of *abbreviatio*, that is, condensing a narrative into an epigrammatic structure, as practiced for instance by Hildebert of Lavardin)[26] or in *tituli*, captions that accompany manuscript or even architectural representations (cf. stained-glass windows) of scriptural scenes.[27] Otherwise, the medieval Latin tradition, at least in matters of religion and morals, preferred expansiveness to concision. In the vernaculars, some Italian sonnets on religious questions (cf. Savonarola's) have the effect of epigram, but it is precisely this, as well as their form, that makes one feel they already belong to the Renaissance, which brought a large-scale revival of Latin epigram and a considerable production of epigram in the vernaculars as well. In Old Norse, a number of brief poems cited in the Fourth Grammatical Treatise seem to reflect the Latin tradition of *tituli* and school-exercise epigram; one at least bears an uncanny resemblance not to any Latin analogues but to the tetrastichs of the twelfth-century Byzantine writer Theodore Prodromos on various events in the Bible[28]—the resemblance is strong enough to make one wonder about the possibility of direct influence, especially in view of the known Norse presence in "Mikligarðr," as they called Constantinople.[29] In Spanish, a number of epigrammatic religious lyrics testify to the intellectuality of that tradition. Finally, the German *Spruchdichtung* contains quite a few examples of doctrinal or moral epigram (cf. especially Heinrich von Muegeln), though like the Latin tradition it prefers more elbowroom for the elaboration of its ideas.

A sixth mode, the meditative, belongs particularly to the later Middle Ages, both in Latin (and Greek) and in the vernaculars.[30] In her *The English Religious Lyric in the Middle Ages*, Rosemary Woolf provides an excellent account of the origins, function, and nature of the Latin tradition of *pia dictamina*, to which I refer the reader. In essence, this mode, which originated in Latin and diffused outward into the vernaculars, stresses and seeks to evoke a strong personal response to divine deeds. The "meditation" it was meant to assist is not the highly organized meditative technique that one associates with the seventeenth century, for example, but simply the achievement of a certain affect or attitude believed to be of spiritual value both in itself and for the effects it had upon the meditator. Its focus on the Passion, and its assumption that the meditator should effectively reenact within himself the experiences of Christ, mark it as a fundamentally Franciscan mode, and the leading thirteenth-century Latin examples are by Franciscans such as Bonaventura, John of Howden, and John Pecham. The mode is extremely important to the *lauda*, where it could operate either conventually or privately, and where not only the Passion but also the Nativity appears as a frequent subject. Two of the finest examples are by Neri Pagliaresi (authorship disputed) and by St. Caterina di Tommaso Colombini of Siena, which respectively concern the Madonna and Child and (among other things) Mary at the Annunciation.[31] The Franciscan authors of most early Middle English religious lyric account for the prominence of the meditative mode in that tradition where it produced many of the best poems, beginning with the famous quatrain "Nou goth sonne under wod" that opens Carleton Brown's collection of thirteenth-century Middle English lyric.[32] Like the other vernaculars where the meditative mode exists, Middle English examples concentrate on the Passion but do not exclude Christ's nativity or childhood, and they frequently use the mirror of Mary to guide the reader to a proper response to Christ's deeds. Examples in Catalan, German, and Old French follow the same pattern; apparently, meditations on the Passion were especially popular in Anglo-Norman England in the mid-thirteenth century (that is, about twenty-five years after the arrival of the friars).[33] The meditative mode is unusual in Portuguese and Spanish, for the reasons usual with those traditions. Finally, Old Norse and Provençal lack the meditative mode altogether.

The seventh mode of treatment is penitential.[34] Here a sinner addresses God in self-accusation and prayer, often in response to the thought of the Passion, or simply out of a conviction of one's ingratitude to God or out of a fear of death and damnation. In the course of the poem, there is usually some sort of praise of God's glory and justice, and prayer often involves not merely forgiveness for the past but help in living a better life in the future. The concentration on self—even if only a typical "self"—that this mode entailed made it an important precursor of the subjective first-person-singular lyric of the later Western Middle Ages. It was innately open as well to genuinely personal expression, as in Gottschalk in Latin or John Mauropus in Greek (ninth and eleventh centuries, respectively). With its prominent and frightened ego, the Dies irae represents a later summit of the penitential tradition, and it should be interpreted in that light, rather than as the liturgical fixture it later became.[35] For the first-person-singular voice of the penitential mode effectively barred it from the Latin liturgy until the thirteenth century and permitted it only a subordinate place, mainly among the paraliturgical parakletika, in the Eastern liturgy. In the vernaculars, the late medieval emphasis on penitence, stimulated by Lateran IV's requirement (1215) of annual confession and fostered by the friars for religious, political, and finally commercial reasons, motivated a sizable production of lyrics in this mode. It is one of the major modes of the laude, as one would expect from their historical origins and authorship. It is also abundant in Middle English, where it has been studied by Frank A. Patterson in his The Middle English Penitential Lyric.[36] German examples considerably antedate Lateran IV; they are numerous and often unconventional, particularly in the atypical individualization of the penitent speaker—atypical for the penitential mode, but not for the Middle High German poetic tradition. It is common in Old French, but there is a tendency to use the nonlyrical form of the octosyllabic couplet (in fact, prayers of all kinds show the same tendency in Old French). One of the most popular late medieval poems in the language is Guillaume Alexis's (?) "Roÿne qui fustes mise," a penitential prayer to the Virgin that appears in as many versions as manuscripts.[37] In Provençal, the mode produces either subliterary couplets (as in Old French) or effective literary and personal poems (as in German) like the long series of penitential prayers by an ex-Albigensian in his old age that begins "Dona Sancta Maria, flors de virginitat," with parallels both in degree of autobiographical reference and in its scale in nonliturgical Latin poetry.[38] There is even one piece that turns a poem on the joys of Mary into a penitential lyric.[39] In Iberian and Old Norse religious lyric, one finds a few examples, but none is more than mediocre. Finally, one should be aware of the paraphrases of the seven Penitential Psalms (i.e., numbers 6, 31, 37, 50, 101, 129, and 142) that occur in various European traditions (e.g., Italian, English, Spanish) from the fifteenth through the seventeenth centuries and that hark back to the scriptural origins of the penitential mode in Christian religious prose and verse.[40]

The eighth and last mode for discussion here is the mystical.[41] It differs from both the meditative and the penitential by the fact that rather than a response to or imitation of the divine without further implication, it concerns the soul's union with God, that is, the ascent toward union, the joys it brings, or the sorrows of its loss. In consequence, though self-accusation for spiritual failings forms an important part of mystical poetry, especially the poetry of privation, neither self-accusation nor the simple desire for a life of Christian virtue can be central to the mystical as they are to the penitential mode. The mystical poem inhabits an upper atmosphere of purer air, purer light, and purer darkness. This atmosphere gives this mode its intoxicating allure and its peril, for the spirit that falls from its heights falls far and perhaps forever. The literary peril of the mode is in its incentives to incoherence, superlatives, mere exclamation in the place of expression, and to verbal tumult that must be maintained even when feeling and inspiration are not really equal to it, else one's subject would seem slighted.

The mystical mode is by definition unsuited to the collective spirit of the liturgy, which seeks what (in theory) all men may attain. As the mystics constantly warn, the mystical quest is only for the specially gifted individual. In Latin lyrics that lie outside the liturgy (cf. Gottschalk or John of Howden) or even upon its fringes (cf. Hildebert's "O Alpha et Omega" or Hildegard's prose poems, both from the twelfth century), the mystical spirit can be quite strong. And in Greek one has not only similar examples but also the explicitly mystical "Hymns of Divine Love" by Symeon the New Theologian (tenth century). Nonetheless, the true age of the mystical mode in poetry is the later Middle Ages, in the West and in the East. And its true language is the poet's birth tongue, for that is the truest voice of one's selfhood stripped of all worldly accidents until it becomes a naked intent seeking God.

Poems that practice this mode normally appear in association with a mystical tradition stemming from one extraordinary person or (less often) a group of mystics of kindred outlook associated by region, period, and language. From the mysticism of St. Francis and his follower Bonaventura, with additional input from Joachism and that grandfather of medieval mysticism, Dionysios the pseudo-Areopagite, come the mystical *laude* of the Franciscan tertiary Jacopone da Todi.[42] Some of these poems have a fairy-tale quality, making the speaker seem like Jack climbing a celestial beanstalk (no. 78) or Tom O'Bedlam (nos. 47 and 84), who in a wonderful old anonymous English poem declares in words that Jacopone might have written

> With a heart of furious fancies
> Whereof I am commander,
> With a burning spear and a horse of air,
> To the wilderness I wander.

> With a knight of ghosts and shadows
> I summoned am to tourney,
> Ten leagues beyond the wide world's end—
> Methinks it is no journey.

Beside the élan of Jacopone's *laude*, the mystical poems of Bianco da Siena seem static and nerveless, and their author seems like Jacopone's uninvited ape dancing at the end of a leash a century long. The mystical mode dominates much of Bianco's work, unfortunately, since it brings out the worst in him: his lack of proportion, ideas, and linguistic resources. Neri Pagliaresi, who was secretary to the active mystic Catherine of Siena, did much better. Fifteenth-century Italian examples largely imitate the highly imitable Bianco.

The mode is important in German from the early fourteenth century on because of the impact of the figures mentioned earlier (Tauler, Eckhart, Suso, Mechthild, and others) on religious feeling and life in Germany and the Low Countries (and East Anglia, for that matter). Even prose treatises on mysticism in German will abruptly rise into rhymed prose and verse. These texts are almost all quite artless, but they have the appeal of directness and strong feeling, and their colors tinge a good deal of Middle High German lyric in other modes. In Old French, one finds Beguine prayers, a number of poems to Christ from Lorraine (part of a small corpus already mentioned above), and a few scattered examples of other provenance. It is no accident that most of these come from the area of France closest to the Rhineland and the religious ferment out of which the great thirteenth- and fourteenth-century German and Dutch mystics, and the *devotio moderna* movement, sprang. Across the Channel, Richard Rolle (d. 1349) founded a school of mystical prose and poetry that continued to influence Middle English religious poetry on into the fifteenth century. The lyrics of Rolle and his followers (it is difficult to ascribe some of the texts with certainty to one or the other) lack artistic control, but there are isolated victories of phrase in them and a passionate involvement with the experience they struggle to express that can still move. In fact, however, the best Middle English mystical literature of the fourteenth century was in prose (the Lady Julian, Hilton, the *Cloud of Unknowing*).

The mystical mode is surprisingly absent from Spanish fifteenth-century religious lyric, since the sixteenth century produced the masterpieces of John of the Cross and many other examples of lesser stature. In Catalan, Llull (thirteenth century) represents it in his prose, and often splendidly, but not in his verse. Old Norse, Portuguese, and Provençal—as the reader will by now have expected—also leave the mode untouched in their lyrics.

The eight modes that have been identified and described in no sense constitute a "logical" system free of redundancies, gaps, or failures of hierarchical equivalence. They do however represent modes that had a real validity for poets and for their Christian audience in the Middle Ages. If nothing else, the extreme lack of uniformity in their distribution, which in most cases directly reflects the character of a given linguistic tradition of lyric, would support this claim. Enthusiasm or distaste for one mode of treatment as opposed to the others shows that such a mode had a distinct character of its own for contemporaries. Conversely, the comparative approach applied to this matter demonstrates that medieval religious lyric was anything but homogeneous in either time or space and that it responded sensitively to the needs (and limitations) of the various peoples and periods of the European Middle Ages.

It should also be emphasized that several of these modes produce poetry that no one would call "lyric" even in the broad definition used in this book. Indeed, I stated at the outset that in principle didactic and moral poetry were excluded from consideration. In addition, the epigrammatic mode is by inclination unlyrical in its tone, if in other respects it might pass muster. Finally, a great deal of poetry in the remaining five modes—hymnic, prayer, meditative, penitential, mystical—is without artistic ambitions, even if not entirely without aesthetic effect. This is particularly true of the mystical, penitential, and prayer modes, less true of the meditative mode, least true of the hymnic mode. So the interest even of these modes for a study concerned with religious lyric with some claim to poetic value is as little uniform as their historical distribution.

iii

The final basis I will present for discriminating among genres or genrelike categories of medieval religious lyric concerns religious co-optation of certain sorts of secular lyric poetry. Obviously, a taxonomy of this kind cannot achieve the same inclusiveness as the taxonomies already presented (most religious lyric in the West is quite independent of secular lyric, all of it in the East), but it puts the necessary emphasis upon what was an important aspect of the poetry we are investigating.

Certainly the poets speak loudly and clearly of the tensions between religious and secular poetry, and their practice reveals the ways in which the former may reject and yet transform features of the latter. The usual issue concerns the love of women as opposed to the love of Mary, or Christ, and the need to reject the first, and poems about it, in favor of the second. Reinmar der Zweter recommends the service of Mary instead of the conventional love-service of Minnesinger (ca. 1200).[43] Hugo von Montfort has a dream in which a priest tells him to stop writing *gebluemte wehe wort* (fine flowery words) about women, and he writes a poem in which he states and dates his decision to write them no more (early fifteenth century).[44] In the Urbino *laudario*, an anonymous poet confesses among his other sins that he has been guilty of "singing vain songs / night and day of vain loves" (fourteenth century?).[45] The noted love-poet and patrician of Venice, Leonardo Giustinian, writes twenty tercets on his turn from "false love" and its "verses" to "talking about God like a Christian" (second half of the fifteenth century)—the use of *terza rima* rather than the tripping stanzas of the late medieval secular dance-song is a statement in itself.[46] Lydgate begins a ballade to the Virgin by refusing to tell the stories of the love-poets of old (e.g., the Ovidian tales Chaucer uses in *The Legend of Good Women*) (first half of the fifteenth century).[47] Gautier de Coincy decries secular love and praises the love of Mary in several of the lyrics that cluster here and there in his *Miracles de Notre-Dame*; as he says in "Hui matin a l'ajornee": "Qui que chant de Mariete, / Je chant de Marie. / Chascun an li doi par dete / Une raverdie" (Whoever sings of Mariete, / I sing of Mary. / Each year I give her as her due / A reverdie, a lyric with a springtime opening; first quarter of the thirteenth century).[48] Alfonso the Wise, or one of the poets he set to work on his own collection of Marian miracles, the *Cantigas de Santa Maria*, scolds troubadours for not writing of Mary (no. 260) and describes himself as her troubadour (Prologue, st. 3; third quarter of the thirteenth century). Cerveri de Girona bids a *juglar* (jongleur) to leave "the false confraternity" of secular love-poets and sing the praises of Mary, and Guiraut Riquier points out that he sings of Mary regardless of the season, unaffected by the heat or cold other poets make so much of (second half of the thirteenth century).[49] In short, this particular polemic position recurs in nearly all the vernaculars, prefacing love-poems to Mary and occasionally figuring in other sorts of religious lyric (e.g., a Portuguese eulogy of St. Andrew with a pendant reproaching poets for praising tragic lovers instead),[50] allowing writers to transfer the language of *chanson d'amour* and *Minnesang* to the objects of religious desire.

Programmatic passages in or about religious lyric also sometimes concern the technical aspects of poetry. In the prose introduction to his "Cent Noms de Deu," Llull expresses the view, commonplace since late antiquity, that violations of prosodic rules (in this case, hypermetric verses) should be tolerated for the sake of the religious subject (thirteenth century).[51] Old Norse religious poets, faced with a public particularly sensitive to deviations from a well-established and highly esteemed tradition, take special pains to justify their work. The author of the "Petrsdrápa" (fourteenth century), who apparently lacks Llull's self-confidence, craves indulgence for the formal deficiencies of his attempt at a traditional skaldic genre, trusting that "God will be content."[52] Other poets in the same period take the offensive more or less openly.[53] Abbot Arngrímr Brandsson, adopting the *hrynhent*

stanza and untraditionally direct word order in his poem on Bishop Gud-
mund, states his position in no uncertain terms in stanza two:

> I have not laid out my plan according to the rules of the Edda; I have written
> in haste verses that I will not praise; the poem is not supple of neck; I have a
> stiff tongue for words; one cannot be blamed for this; I have no eagle's drop-
> pings to offer you; I am little noted among poets.[54]

In a *drápa* on the same saint, Abbot Arni Jónsson strikes a blow against the
traditional kenning, spelling out what Arngrímr had left to be inferred from
his contemptuous kenning "eagle's droppings":

> The great masters of the art of the Edda will think this poem very ill-made,
> those who are deep in the rules . . . it seems to me that the clear testimony of
> sweet writing befits the praise of a holy man; periphrases [i.e., kennings]
> strengthen no one but darken joy.[55]

And in the closing stanzas of his masterpiece *Lilja* (the lily, a traditional Marian symbol), Eysteinn Ásgrímmson speaks of the deliberate simplicity of his
poem, saying that it comes from the heart and attacking the archaic diction
and consequent obscurity of skaldic poetry, "the dark art of the men of old"
that must now yield to the new aesthetic of clarity and sincerity.[56] In religious lyric at least, the "dark art" did give up its old hold upon Norse poetry. Eysteinn's poem was so successful that the *hrynhent* stanza he used was
henceforward known as "liljulag," and its influence endured down to the
eighteenth century in Iceland. In all these passages from Old Norse, one can
see how artistically conscious medieval poets in at least one tradition could
be, even when writing religious lyric. Other traditions did not experience a
similar crisis of style, but it is clear that most medieval poets working at any
level above the lowest and most utilitarian were no less aware than the
Christian skalds of the rules of form and diction under which they wrote.

The strong sense of generic distinctions that went with this sense of the
importance of conventions gave a particular impact to any violation of normal generic boundaries. For religious lyric, there was the additional excitement (and meritoriousness) of consecrating the profane. So it is that in traditions where the "erotic alba" (as Saville calls it) exists, one finds religious
albas as well, signaling most often by no more than the mention of dawn in
some prominent, perhaps repeated position that the secular alba was being
superseded by the religious (cf. the German *Tagewîs* and a half-dozen religious albas in Provençal).[57] In German, the riddle appears as the religious
bîspel.[58] The fair maiden of the *chanson d'aventure* or *pastourelle* turns into
the Virgin Mary, with the secular framework of May morn and countryside
adventure usually reduced to an opening gesture that like the word *dawn* in
the religious alba sufficed to alert the reader to the transgression of bound-

aries being laudably committed (cf. German, Middle English, Old French, Italian and late medieval Provençal, though only Middle English and Old French, which had the Anglo-Norman kingdom in common, produced a significant number of religious *pastourelles*).[59] The lullabies of the folk become Mary's song to the Christ child, or even a miraculous dialogue between infant and mother in which the traditional roles are reversed and it is the infant who foretells his own future (cf. Catalan, lyrics from Spanish Nativity plays, and Middle English in the later fourteenth and fifteenth centuries).[60] May songs welcome Easter as well as spring (cf. Portuguese and Italian), and the reverdie lifts its eyes heavenward (cf. German, Old French, Latin, Provençal).[61] Dance-songs provide the form of the *lauda* (the *ballata*), the *conductus* (the *rondeau*), perhaps the carol, too.[62] Above all, courtly love-poetry (the *chanson d'éloge, de requête, de complainte*, and the *sirventes*)[63] yields up its rich repertory of motifs and attitudes for Marian lyrics, especially in Old French, Provençal, and the *Cantigas* (love-poems directed at Christ take their model primarily from the Song of Songs or other branches of the mystical tradition). The troubadours exploit the possibilities of teasing ambiguity to the utmost, with the result that in some poems one cannot be certain whether the lady is Mary or not (cf. Folquet de Lunel or Guiraut Riquier). Nor are the French behindhand; one of Jean Molinet's poems, according to its rubric, can be addressed either to the Virgin Mary or by a lover to his lady, and the text certainly lives up to this claim.[64] In his book on the alba, discussed in the Introduction, Saville argues at some length that the Middle Ages was characterized by a *sowohl-als-auch* mentality in which the irreconcilable claims of society and of religion were both acknowledged simply by granting each its own sphere.[65] If this is true, then one understands the special *frisson* it must have caused the medieval audience when the insulation was temporarily removed and the two spheres brought into direct contact.

This survey of the "genres" of medieval religious lyric reveals a certain number of significant general patterns. First, the range of subject matter is extremely restricted in comparison to the range of medieval religious tradition in prose. Very little of what one finds in Scripture or patristics or the medieval volumes of the *Patrologia Latina* or *Graeca* ever found its way into the medieval poetic tradition, except direct scriptural paraphrase; nor is much of the liturgy put to use. Second, the range of approaches to the subject matter is also restricted and conventionalized to a striking degree, though this restriction affects examples within each mode rather than the range of modes itself. Finally, certain important historical changes shape the frequency and character of the "genres" in the West: Marian lyric becomes vastly more abundant after 1100; religious lyric as a whole (until a sort of reaction sets in at the end of the Middle Ages) becomes much more subjective; what begins in the vernaculars as a way of filling those niches the liturgy has not preempted tends to become a way of replacing the liturgy; and all "genres" show a marked dependency on and responsiveness to changes in piety and institutional forms. It is well to be clear about these fundamental facts before we move from the long-range, relatively abstract view of the first half of this book to the close, even microscopic study of concrete particulars of its second half and the attendant citation of lyrics in part or in their entirety. I hope that sufficient background has been provided that the reader will not lose his or her way in the mazy paths we soon must travel.

FORMS

By forms, I mean those organizing schemes that control the overall shape of a poetic text by specifying matters like the meter, the length of lines, the rhyme scheme, the length of stanzas, the number of stanzas, and the grouping of stanzas into a unit that acts with other units to compose the text as a whole. Organizing schemes that function within forms but are not integral parts of forms will be discussed in the final section of this chapter.

In this section, the discussion of forms will fall into three parts: the first includes the centuries from late antiquity to ca. A.D. 800; the second, the period from the Carolingian age up to the rise of the vernaculars as literary languages in the twelfth century; the third, the remainder of the Middle Ages. So far as religious lyric is concerned, Latin and Greek stand alone in the first two periods. The first period saw the appearance of almost all the new forms the Eastern Empire was to create. By contrast, the Latin tradition, which gained a new lease on life thanks to the intended and accidental cultural effects of the Carolingian reform, continued to evolve important new forms until well into the twelfth century. Thereafter, as literary energies passed more and more into the vernaculars, the Latin tradition lost its generative powers to its competitors. Indeed, it is quite possible that from the first Latin had borrowed heavily and repeatedly from the forms of vernacular poetry, though transforming them to suit its own needs. It is certain that vernacular poetry was in turn influenced by Latin forms. Unfortunately, the question of the exact nature of the relationship between "popular" and "learned" medieval poetries (terms that in fact do not coincide at all points with the opposition between vernacular and Latin) has been the source of a protracted quarrel over precedence, one that the lack or ambiguity of existing evidence has helped keep alive. I would suggest that the proper model for their relationship is not native plant and alien parasite or wise master and admiring children, metaphors that reflect fairly accurately, I believe, the mental schemes underlying the positions the opposing sides adopt in this matter. Instead, one should imagine the relationship between Latin and vernacular poetries in the West as a coevolution conducted by men and women who lived mentally and physically in both linguistic domains at once. Even without knowledge of the Latin language, it would have been hard not to grasp the nature of Latin *forms* when examples were constantly being sung publicly as part of the liturgy; and knowledge of one's vernacular and its poetic forms came with the air one breathed. Such a coevolutionary conception finds particular support in the fact that the same period that saw the greatest production of Latin forms also saw the greatest production of vernacular forms. The medieval population was not divided into two species, *homo latinus* and *homo vernaculus*, who occasionally visited each other's habitats, nor was medieval culture divided into two foreign countries. Out of the countless villages and dialects of the Middle Ages came its people, and those individuals with creative gifts exercised their gifts according to their status and education and to the extent that the times helped or hindered them. When Latin culture and vernacular culture dwelt together in the same minds, what wonder that the same prosperity and the same blights usually affected both at once?

i

(ca. 350–ca. 800)

In the history of Latin religious lyric the first important "new" form is the Ambrosian hymn. As used by Ambrose in the 380s and by most of his imitators in the next few centuries and on through the Middle Ages, it consisted of eight quatrains of iambic dimeter.[66] In fact, however, melodies and syntax suggest that these quatrains ought to be analyzed as two sixteen-syllable-long lines with a strong break in the middle of each—similar uncertainties beset the perception of other Latin lyric stanzas.[67] Semantically, the stanzas often form pairs, suggesting antiphonal performance, which would provide a motive for an even number of stanzas (in this case eight). As to the meter, in the texts known to be by Ambrose most lines can be scanned either as quantitative or as accentual iambs, thereby meeting both the demands for classical prosody and the needs of the common people, whose poetry seems to have been accentual (at least to the point that natural word stress and metrical ictus coincided) from an early period. Furthermore, the disappearance of the phonemic function of quantity that affected both Latin and Greek in late antiquity meant that the people no longer had a natural "ear" for quantitative verse and that it was imperative that a new prosody be developed. Finally, one may see in Ambrose's choice of an extremely easy meter and a stanza that had not figured in classical lyric his way of expressing the marked opposition between the plain speaking of the New Testament (and so of Christianity) and the grandiloquence of pagan rhetoric. Even his skillful maintenance of classical quantitative prosody is typical of late antique Christian practice, which sought as it talked bravely of breaking with all things pagan to co-opt the familiar and aesthetically effective devices of pagan literature.

Unlike Ambrose, Hilary of Poitiers and Prudentius made few concessions to popular needs in their collections of religious poems. Both followed classical tradition for lyric collections in using a variety of meters and stanzas, and their meters are strictly quantitative, though it is significant that both chose or invented forms that do not seem to occur earlier in Latin (or at least Latin lyric) poetry. Hilary understandably had difficulties teaching his compositions to his flock; Prudentius escaped such problems by presenting his work as a purely literary contribution, meant for the delectation of the educated Christian. Ironically perhaps, but probably because Hilary was one of the poorer poets in late antiquity and Prudentius one of the best, Hilary's lyrics did not survive in the liturgy (despite a 633 Spanish conciliar pronouncement that singles him out with Ambrose as composer of hymns), while Prudentius's lyrics, though never meant for the liturgy, had a flourishing career in it once they were reduced by abridgment to more manageable dimensions.

Of the stanzas in Hilary and Prudentius, besides the Ambrosian stanza that the latter used several times, only the sapphic played an important role in later hymnody, especially the Mozarabic or early Iberian tradition.[68] Like other classical lyric stanzas, it appears during the Middle Ages both in its old quantitative guise and in an accentual transformation modeled upon the quantitative original. The same holds true of the trochaic septenarius, which figures in both Prudentius and in one of the great sixth-century hymnodists, Venantius Fortunatus.[69] Two further nonstanzaic verse forms used stichically, the elegiac couplet and the dactylic hexameter, also appear in liturgical and nonliturgical medieval Latin lyric,[70] but though both later acquired the frequent additional feature, quite unclassical, of internal ("leonine") and final rhyme, they maintain the quantitative prosody of their long classical history. In the liturgy, however, all these stanza and verse forms are of minor significance compared to the overwhelming early influence of the *hymnus ambrosianus*. Even outside the liturgy, classical lyric stanzas are uncommon in medieval practice, and the stichic verse forms were by nature ill-suited to lyric poetry.

One must look to poetry intended for the people, rather than for the educated or even for the monks who so strongly supported the growth of the hymn, for the metrical developments that laid the foundation for medieval Latin poetry of the high Middle Ages. Quantity's loss of phonemic function in actual speech opened the door both in West and East to two possible bases for prosody: syllabic or accentual. As we shall see, Greek liturgical poets opted for the former. In the West, however, despite early experiments in isosyllabic verse (cf. Augustine's psalm against the Donatists), it was accentual prosody that imposed itself. Ambrose's iambs already lean in that direction, and in the Merovingian period (ca. 600–ca. 750), some religious poetry that is accentual in nature seems to have been composed—hence the name *rhythmus*. Typically, these poems were meant to be used in processions where the laity was directly involved, probably singing the refrains that mark several surviving examples, and certainly taking part at least with their feet if not their voices. Quantity is entirely ignored, and the syllable count may vary slightly from line to line, so that there is no doubt that stress is functioning as the controlling principle. Even when, as Latin accentual meter develops and turns more regular in its parade of trochees or iambs, lines become isosyllabic as well as isotonic, it is still stress that rules, and the uniform syllable count is only a by-product of the new regularity.[71]

The initial resistance to this "popular" prosody, expressed most clearly in Spain in the seventh century (to the effect that hymns ought only to be written in dignified classical forms), was in vain.[72] In the Western liturgy, quantitative poetry became very much the exception after the Carolingian period, and even the Ambrosian hymn, which had by then become "classical" itself in medieval eyes, must have been commonly perceived as accentual.

In the East, liturgy, though not nonliturgical poetry, responded quite early to the same sort of linguistic change and popular needs. Out of all the hundreds of poems in the liturgical books spanning the church-year (i.e., the *Menaion*, the Lenten *Trisodion*, the *Pentekostarion*), only three, all by John Damascene, are in a classical quantitative meter, and even that is the plain iambic trimeter, the stichic verse form not of lyric but of dramatic dialogue in Greek.[73] Instead, liturgical poetry adopted a complex form of strophic responsion, in which the syllable count and the disposition of stresses are in principle the same in corresponding lines in each separate stanza (line one is structurally the same in all stanzas, as is line two, line three, and so forth, but all lines within the stanza can differ from each other).[74] The responsion is often imperfect, and there is a good deal of scholarly disagreement about how strict the rules affecting responsion really were, but there is no doubt about its reality. Its functioning recalls the strophic responsion of Greek choral lyric, though without the complications of strophe, antistrophe, and epode; in both cases, the repetition of the musical setting (plus choreography, in the Greek drama) necessitated the repetition of the stanza form. Only quantity no longer played any part.

The same structure of corresponding strophes governs all Byzantine liturgical forms, whether the greater forms of the *kontakion* and the *kanon* or the lesser forms of the *troparion* (also a term for stanza), the *sticheron* (of somewhat greater dimensions than the Ambrosian hymn), and similar forms (see the Orientation for Greek).

The *kontakion* owes many of its most characteristic features to Syrian hymnody, which had reached an early peak in the fourth century in the work of St. Ephraem.[75] Ephraem and his fellow hymnodists seem to have used existing popular melodies (as Ambrose may also have done, in an early example of *contrafactura*), competing both with heretical religious lyric and with the secular theater that still flourished in Damascus and elsewhere. These Syrian orthodox hymns were of the strongly didactic cast one might expect under such circumstances, with their major prose model being the homily. One of the Syrian hymnic genres, the *memrâ*, resembles the *kontakion* in themes and use of narration as a teaching device; in form, the *madraša* (instruction) is closer, since it was sung not read, sometimes contained an acrostic, and was composed of two alternating types of repeated stanzas whose lines varied in length from four to ten syllables, with the shorter of the two sometimes acting as a refrain, that is, the words as well as the form were repeated throughout the poem (cf. the elaborate layout of the "Akathistos" hymn, which may be fifth-century work). A subgenre of the *madraša*, the *sughitha* (canticle), had the additional feature of being mostly in dialogue, except for a brief introduction.

Certain isostichic hymns that may be the earliest extant products of Byzantine liturgy seem much like Western hymnody in their simplicity of form and handling of subject matter.[76] But with the writing of the "Akathistos" perhaps, and certainly with Romanos (first half of the sixth century), the complex liturgical strophe imposes itself. The greatest, and one of the earliest, of Byzantine poets, Romanos was born in Syria at Edessa to a converted Jewish family. He arrived in Constantinople before 518 and established the character of the *kontakion*, completely eclipsing any contemporary *melodoi* (hymn writers). In function, the *kontakion* acted as a sermon in verse during the centuries when the prose homily was out of favor. Any office that included a reading could in principle include a *kontakion* developing the meaning of the passage read. In form, it consists of a *prooimion* standing alone followed by a series of repeated stanzas or *oikoi* (cf. Syrian *baitho*, which also means either "stanza" or "house").[77] In length (in Romanos), it ranges from 11 to 40 stanzas, and 88 to 840 lines or *kola*. When time pressed, or in smaller churches, the longer *kontakia* could be sung or simply read in abridged form (hence their appearance in some medieval collections with most of the stanzas missing). In music, there was probably a close correspondence between the number of syllables and the number of notes; we also know that more than half of Romanos's melodies were original compositions, and in most of the rest at least the melody of the *prooemion* was new. Later, *contrafactura* became the rule rather than the exception; the number of model stanzas with their melodies in actual use dropped to 10 or so, and all *heirmoi*, as they were called, were conveniently collected in a liturgical book called the *heirmologion* for the guidance of singers, poets, and composers. Finally, in content and treatment of content, Romanos's *kontakia*—and hence the later *kontakion*, derived largely from his corpus of several score—show their derivation from the Syrian hymnody of his origins as strongly as they do in their form. Like the Syrian hymns, particularly the *memrâ* and the *sugitha*, they make heavy use of, respectively, narrative and dialogue; they are fundamentally homiletic or didactic (note that the homiletic tradition had itself been influenced at an early date by Syrian preaching, perhaps as far back as the second century A.D., and by a fourth-century Greek version of Ephraem's *mimrê*); and their appeal is strongly popular, even though their theology is carefully orthodox. But Romanos far outdid his antecedents in degree of artistic control, in dramatic sense, and also in his freer handling of much more complex verse forms; by contrast, the work of Ephraem or Narsai of Nisibis (d. ca. 507) is shapeless or stiff, not to say intolerably prolix in many cases.

   After 700, the *kontakion* continues to be productive but is no longer the major "great" liturgical form in the East. Instead, the much more lyrical, much less homiletic *kanon* assumes preeminence. It is uncertain whether this is because prose homilies began to return to fashion in the seventh century (thereby depriving the *kontakion* of its original function) or because a change in poetic taste favored the rise of the *kanon*, with the side effect that the now outmoded *kontakion* was replaced by prose homilies.[78] We do know for certain that while secular churches acted as the major theater for the development of the *kontakion*, the monks were the main force behind the *kanon*. In form, it consists of a series of eight or nine odes, each ode being a succession of (on the average) four repetitions of a model stanza or *heirmos* that changes from one ode to the next. Each ode was expected to allude in some fashion to one of a set of nine scriptural canticles, whose composition and order had been fixed by the sixth century. In fact, in the performance of the Psalter, these canticles figured, by way of appendix, as the last of twenty-one *kathismata* (sections at the end of which one would sit down again), and it was out of this liturgical phenomenon that the *kanon* apparently grew.[79] It took shape during the course of the seventh century, probably in Palestine; at least two of its major early authors came from Syria (i.e., Andrew of Crete and John of Damascus, who were both from the Syrian capital apparently), and there is also some possibility of Arabic influence, but it was Andrew's and John's and the others' activities in Jerusalem that most likely gave rise to the *kanon* form. In practice, the second ode of the *kanon* was usually omitted, since the canticle to which it corresponded (i.e., Deuteronomy 32:1–43, Moses' valedictory) was too somber for Sunday, at whose morning service (the *orthros*) the *kanon* was usually performed and which the Eastern Church saw as a metonym of Easter. In among the odes, other brief poetic forms (the *hypakoe*, the *katabasia*, the *exaposteilarion*, the *photagogikon*) act as interludes; one of these is called *kontakion*, which has become nothing more than a single stanza between odes 6 and 7 of the *kanon*. In general, the *kanon* is too diffuse to compete in poetic quality with the tauter, more unified *kontakion* that it engulfed and curtailed in this fashion. Nonetheless, it remained in favor among poets through the thirteenth century, and in the hands of a gifted writer like the eleventh-century John Mauropus, it attains moments of lyric beauty, even if its elaborate structure and great length imposed a burden on its authors none of them could fully sustain. Finally, it should be noted that its peculiar relation to the nine scriptural canticles makes it a signal example of the medieval inclination for "glossing" that received attention in the Introduction.

Outside the liturgy, and throughout the Middle Ages, the Byzantine form of choice for secular and religious shorter poems was the iambic trimeter.[80] In some writers, it generally meets the standards of classical quantitative poetry; in most, it only pretends to, fooling the eye but not the ear. Dactylic hexameter and elegiac couplet serve as the frequent choices for brief, epigrammatic poems in the manner of the Anthology, which took its final shape in the late Byzantine period.[81] No poem that was not meant for liturgical or paraliturgical use ever employs the form of isosyllabic, homotonic, nonquantitative strophic responsion. Indeed, nonliturgical texts are pervasively stichic, avoiding strophes of any kind. One may describe most Byzantine iambic trimeter as in fact syllabic verse with an iambic pulse, and the "popular" form, the political verse (i.e., the verse of the polis and its citizens) is also isosyllabic, counting the same fifteen syllables to the line as the old catalectic trochaic tetrameter (which is the same as the Latin trochaic septenarius, a fairly common medieval verse-line).[82] But overall, the contrast between the forms of the Greek liturgy and the forms used outside of it could hardly be clearer.

As I said at the outset of this section, the Greek tradition loses its formal creativity by 800 A.D., with the sole exception of the just-mentioned political verse. One of the last poets even to create new model stanzas (*heirmoi*) was the ninth-century poetess Kassia, and her work does not constitute the creation of a new form, only a variation upon the well-established liturgical tradition of correspondent nonquantitative stanzas. Religious-to-religious *contrafactura* takes over even earlier for the *kontakion*, so that one must begin to look to nonliturgical poetry for any innovations at a time when the Middle Ages were just finding their identity in the West under Charlemagne.

During the period when Byzantine poetry had the energy to influence Latin poetry, the West was too disordered to register its effects; and when the West got back on its feet again, and peaceful political contact with the East was reopened, that energy had already dissipated, and the West had more than enough new energy of its own. So one might hypothesize, at least.

ii

(ca. 800 to the rise of the vernaculars)

Henceforward, then, we will be concerned with Western contributions to the development of medieval poetic forms used in religious lyric. One knows perfectly well that vernacular verse forms and stanza forms existed in the period before the vernacular lyric begins to emerge from the shadows, but I prefer to ignore what may have been (an alluring but unproductive question, whose answer scholars usually bring with themselves to its study) in favor of the considerable body of texts that have survived. Consequently, these paragraphs on medieval forms between 800 and the rise of the vernaculars will confine themselves to Latin.

As it happens, one of the most remarkable of medieval formal creations belongs to Latin and this period, namely, the sequence.[83] As an innovation of revolutionary implications, it is on a par with the Greek *kontakion* or the fourteen-line sonnet. As a result, it has attracted a formidable amount of scholarly discussion, much of which is vitiated by a focus on speculation, based upon slender or nonexistent evidence, about the origins of the form. One would think that the sequences themselves were poor things, to judge by the apparent desire to avoid talking about them rather than their possible ancestors. Happily, this is not the case, as scholars like Wolfgang von den Steinen (*Notker der Dichter*), Peter Dronke (parts of *The Medieval Lyric*— his article, "The Beginning of the Sequence," belongs largely to the genre I am anathematizing), and Richard Crocker (from a poetic as well as musicological viewpoint) have recognized.[84]

Originally, the term *sequentia* referred to the extended string of notes that sometimes (by 830) replaced the repetition of the Alleluia and *iubilus* after the singing of the Verse in the section of the Mass between the reading of the epistle and of the gospel. Until about 950, the generic term for what we now call the sequence was *prosa*, which remains in frequent use in Latin and the vernaculars up through the end of the Middle Ages and gave the name of *prosarium* or "proser" to the liturgical books in which sequences came to be collected. It is important to be aware of these terms and their early usage because the commonly accepted hypothesis concerning the liturgical origins of the sequence has it that words were set to the music of existing *alleluia-iubilus* or *sequentiae*. In fact, as Crocker has been pointing out for the past fifteen years, texts actually set to such preexisting melismatic melodic material are quite different from "the new sequence" to which our use of the term refers (not to mention that the music of many sequences is prefaced by a title which suggests that a secular melody is being used). Instead,

> not only is there no documentary proof that these sequences existed as melismas before they were texted; but also, if we consider as a group the sequences that we know . . . to be of the ninth century, we find that about half of them show no clear relationship to a known alleluia.[85]

In addition, stylistically the *prosa* or sequence derives from late antique Latin art-prose, as studied by Eduard Norden in *Die antike Kunstprosa*, and from secular *laudes regiae* of the Frankish kingdom, rather than from scriptural or liturgical tradition. Both as music and text then, the ninth-century Carolingian sequence was a far more novel addition to the liturgy than most scholarship would lead one to believe. And this remains true even if one does not posit an unprovable though also undisprovable origin in vernacular song forms.

In structure, the "canonical" early sequence consists of an initial stanza standing by itself followed by a series of pairs of stanzas ending in another unpaired stanza (A/ /BB/CC/DD/ . . . / /X). The striking feature of this poetic form is that each "stanza" taken alone is merely a piece of prose printed in lines reflecting the phrasal structure of the music to which it is set— providing the editor has done his homework properly, that is. The repetition of each "stanza's" music means that in principle, though not always in detail, an isosyllabic and homotonic responsion bind each pair of stanzas together. In fact, some "proses" (to use the medieval term that so accurately reflects their origins) lack this organizing feature of responsion, so that they are verse only by courtesy, or by an anachronistic extension of the concept of *vers libre*. Others, by contrast, involve repetition not only within stanza-pairs, but of those pairs or whole series of those pairs (A/ /BB/CC/DD/EE/ BB/CC/DD/ /X, for example). Crocker feels that this "da capo" or double cursus sequence is in reality another ninth-century experiment and should not be seen as a variant upon the canonical sequence.[86] Finally, a sequence may lack either the initial or the final unpaired stanza, or both. The common denominator relating all of these ninth-century poetic structures is that they are a way of setting prose to music and that they are asymmetrical, to a greater or lesser degree. The first is simply an extension of the setting of Scripture to music, at least in Greek and Latin, where even the Psalter has been turned into prose. The second suggests a desire to replace the regularities of the Ambrosian hymn (or perhaps other sorts of strophic song, including the vernacular) with a structure closer to the structure of plainchant and art-prose (which was more "classical" in fact than hymnody was) and royal acclamations. In itself, the contrast between conventional Latin poetic forms and the new song of the sequence must have been an important source of artistic effect.

The reader will no doubt have noticed the similarities between the sequence and Byzantine forms like the *kontakion*. They include the prefatory unpaired stanza, the proselike character of the text (from a classical viewpoint), and the fundamental principle of strophic responsion. However, the differences are considerable and attempts to establish clear links have so far failed. (The prefatory stanza is usually far shorter in the sequence, and Byzantine liturgical forms involve not pairs but a whole series of stanzas on the same model.) It is possible that the West simply rediscovered, in its own terms, an artistic opportunity inherent in the common pagan and Christian literary tradition from which both medieval Latin and Byzantine culture derived. Under the circumstances, there is nothing improbable about a degree of polygenesis.

The finest creator of texts in the early sequence is by common consent Notker Balbulus, a monk at St. Gall in present-day Switzerland, who completed his *Liber hymnorum* (note the term chosen!) in A.D. 884. (The famous preface to that work is our most important direct witness to the early history and, by inference, prehistory of the sequence.) Though from the outset the sequence was performed as part of the Mass, most early examples do not seem to be firmly attached to specific liturgical occasions or therefore to constitute a part of the proper of a given Mass. Instead, they seem freely composed in response to the poet's particular interests; in their emphasis on Christmas and Eastertide, they remind one of the much-later emphasis given the same seasons in vernacular religious lyric, and in their strikingly poetic, even personal character, they resemble a poet's *laudario* such as Jacopone da Todi's rather than the anonymous *laudari* assembled for the quasi-liturgical use of a confraternity. It wasn't until the mid-tenth century that compilers began to try to assemble cycles of sequences numbering perhaps sixty or seventy items that assumed systematic correspondence to particular occasions in the course of the church-year. And it was perhaps only this activity that in turn stimulated poets to try to fill in the gaps that remained.[87]

The early sequence was eclipsed by the "regular" sequence, but it saw a revival as a result of the archaizing movement that characterized late fourteenth- and fifteenth-century medieval culture.[88] Indeed, the rate of production of both regular and "irregular" sequences became so great by the end of the Middle Ages that the Church officially forbade their further composition in 1568 and eliminated all but four from the liturgy. Unlike the hymn, whose birth came about five centuries earlier, the sequence never completely established itself in the liturgy (remember that the papal chapel did not accept even the hymn as liturgical until the twelfth century). It would seem that the Middle Ages ended too soon for the sequence to lose its alien aura. Another century or two and perhaps it would have been granted its naturalization papers . . .

Another liturgical form created in the ninth century, the trope, went out of fashion about the same time as the early sequence and shared its ultimate fate, for the same reasons.[89] Like the sequence, it involved prose rather than verse, set to music, and interpolated into the existing structure of the liturgy.[90] (However, the prose, like other medieval prose in some cases from the tenth century on, could be rhymed, and for Kyrie-, Gloria-, and Agnus Dei-tropes, the text is sometimes in verse, most frequently dactylic hexameter.) The Mass was the first part of the liturgy to be troped, and it is still an open question whether we should consider Introit-, Kyrie-, Gloria-, Offertory-, Sanctus-, Agnus-, and (Easter) Communion-tropes different genres or merely variants of the single genre trope—the fact that verse appears in only three of the Mass-tropes listed suggests that the former position has some basis.[91] Next, the readings at Matins (patristic homilies and saints' lives) began to be troped, and finally, the Office (tropes of which are called *verbeta*). It is noteworthy that in the end even sequences and paraliturgical *cantiones* succumbed, but never hymns or psalmody, presumably because the last two had a primeval, therefore sacrosanct quality for the medieval mind that the Ordinary of the Mass (which developed much later than the early hymn or, needless to say, the Psalter) or the Office (which was historically secondary to the synaxis and Eucharist) somehow lacked.

From the later eleventh century on, when disyllabic rhyme begins to become important in Latin, the brief, mainly prose interpolations of the trope begin to yield to independent, usually rhymed poems that are sometimes of considerable length—the leading example of this new development, the *conductus*, will be discussed later.[92] The texts of the trope consist mainly of citations or mosaics of phrases from Scripture, and their relation to the troped text is often syntactically discontinuous, so that they function as a comment interjected within it.[93] As the *Corpus Troporum* presently appearing under the editorship of Ritva Jonsson makes clear, the order and number of phrases constituting a trope was highly variable; indeed, one ought perhaps to speak of a pool of phrases out of which tropes could readily be constructed. In this respect, the trope illustrates especially well certain features of medieval literature and aesthetics raised in the Introduction, including not only "glossing" but also parataxis, anacoluthon, and the variability of the text.

The word *trope*, like the word *sequence*, began life as a musical term. It seems that musical embroidery upon existing melody preceded textual expansion. Indeed, the existence of the "extra" notes created room for the addition of words (form preceding content, in effect). According to a nineteenth-century book by Léon Gautier that remains fundamental for all its faults, 90 percent of extant tropers are of monastic provenance, and most date from the eleventh century.[94] Since the monks had the most time available into which to expand the liturgy, it is not surprising that even in the twelfth century one reads that, according to Jean Beleth, tropes "are wont to be sung mainly by the monks" (*cantari solent maxime quidem a monachis*).[95] The monastery of St. Martial at Limoges was a major center for the trope and sequence both, as well as for the *conductus*, though many of the texts that appear in its manuscripts need not have originated there. The major occasions for troping seem to have been Christmastide, followed by Easter and the Dedication of Churches (cf. the sequence).[96]

The trope was too unassuming a form to attract known poets or achieve much literary interest. It appears here for the light it sheds on liturgical evolution and for the part it played as structural antecedent to far more interesting forms of the twelfth and thirteenth centuries. Even in the manuscripts, it never achieved full integration as part of the liturgy, for many scribes used a different script or underlining to make certain that the trope remained distinct from the text it adorned.[97] Its separability left it an easy target for the liturgical reformers, who could find not even four just texts among the tropes to spare from their annihilation of the Sodom and Gomorrah of medieval liturgical liberties. Even L. Gautier, their leading modern student, sees in their fate the triumph of the liturgy over the threatening efflorescence of "these products of second-rate rhetoricians." And yet, as he notes, one might still hear the Kyrie-trope at Soissons and elsewhere in the eighteenth century—which proves yet again the tenacity of Church traditions and the localism of its churches.[98]

Another Latin form of some importance appears in the same period. Around the end of the ninth century, Hucbald of St. Amand (d. 930) introduced the notion of replacing the readings and antiphons of the Office with poems set to music.[99] The next step involved the construction of offices made up of a mosaic of antiphons in verse. Finally, in the thirteenth century, one encounters verse offices that show artistic control in both their plan and their details.[100] The form spread throughout Europe, particularly as a way of honoring newly canonized saints in a style that suited contemporary tastes for rhymed strophic poetry.[101] Even Iceland produced a *historia ritmica* (to use the Latin term) of St. Thorlac, which dates from about 1300 and is extant complete with music.[102] Since this form, like the Byzantine *kanon*, is in fact a form of forms, providing an organizing scheme that can include a number of poems, each with its own meter, stanza, and rhyme scheme, it does not require further detailed discussion here.

Finally, the Carolingian period also saw the brief revival of the figure-poem, used in late antique Greek and Latin for praises of the gods. In the hands of Carolingian court poets, it became the *carmen quadratum*, in which elaborate acrostics, mesostichs, and telestichs, as well as messages to be read diagonally, turned a set of laborious hexameters (as many lines as letters in a line) into a schematic picture of the Cross or other objects of sacred significance.[103] In such a poem, the message becomes a medium, taking to its logical conclusion the function of all religious discourse as a sign of the sacred. It was also the ultimate extension of the late antique delight in objectifying language and playing with its materials that lived on in the Celtic Latin tradition and reentered Continental tradition through natives of the British Isles who converged upon Charlemagne's court. Similar tendencies recur in late medieval vernacular poetry, where they reveal a sense of the unreality of poetic language brought on by the widening gap between its stasis and a rapidly changing reality and by the refusal to embrace change as a possibly constructive force. In the Carolingian period, these tendencies perhaps result from the attempt to replace the corrupt Latin of the Merovingian period with the linguistic and poetic forms of many centuries past. Their neoclassicism sits very ill upon Carolingian writers; in reading their work, one sometimes feels as one does when confronted with a nineteenth-century photograph of a Sioux Indian chief in a Victorian Sunday suit. In any event, one way of dealing with an alien language or style is to exploit, rather than to evade, one's alienation. But by far the better solution was the rhythmic poem and the sequence, both of which began to flower in the course of the ninth century, and both of which came to combine a relatively "correct" Latinity with a thoroughly "medieval" form.

In its later history, the figure-poem returned to its original nature. Though a Byzantine Greek edited a set of ancient examples as part of the Greek Anthology in the fourteenth century, no Byzantine writer revived the form.[104] Instead, it reappears at the end of the Middle Ages in the West. The Chantilly manuscript (late fifteenth-century Florence) includes two pieces by M. Baude Cordier that are written one "in the shape of a heart" and the other ("Tout par compas") "in a circular shape, a visual representation of the opening words of the text."[105] Slightly later, the English poet Stephen Hawes wrote a poem in the shape of "a pair of wings."[106] And since the Middle Ages, poets as disparate as Herbert ("Easter Wings") and Apollinaire (*Calligrammes*) have written *carmina figurata* of their own. But none of this approaches the elaborateness and difficulty of the Carolingian examples, which are the verbal equivalents of the intricately adorned yet also monumental miniature art of their age.

Reviewing this account of the centuries between Charlemagne and the first extant records of the lyric use of the vernaculars, one is struck by the remarkable fertility of the ninth century. Its patrimony of forms served Europe throughout these centuries and even beyond. Various students of the Carolingian age have suggested that it was the shock caused by the sudden confrontation of native Frankish (or Gallican) and officially imported Roman (both ancient and contemporary) culture that led, at a few generations' remove, to a new synthesis incorporating elements of both.[107] Such a hypothesis seems well founded.

On the other hand, one might also be struck by the slenderness of the repertory of stanza forms in Latin. Even with the addition of such important new forms as the Ambrosian "quatrain" and the sequence, it is a great deal less varied than it had been as late as Boethius, whose *Consolatio* is a remarkable display of hypermetry (some two dozen different verse forms in its brief compass). By contrast, the Eastern tradition evolved a great variety of stanza forms in its first centuries, then lived off a capital that it let slowly dwindle until most of its riches became unavailable.

In the next period, which begins in the twelfth century and closes out the Middle Ages, we will see dramatic changes. The repertory of stanza forms in Latin expands enormously. Disyllabic rhyme, in which the rhyme always includes a stressed as well as an unstressed syllable, suddenly (in medieval terms) ousts monosyllabic rhyme in Latin; monosyllabic rhyme was analogous, in its effect at least, to assonance in the modern languages and scarcely like what we mean by "rhyme" at all. Finally, in sequence and trope, irregular prose gives way to metrically regular verse, and the formal expectations that ruled European lyric until the twentieth century are born.

iii

(*ca. 1100–ca. 1500*)

Because one can see the impact of these changes in the most direct way possible, that is, by comparison of texts in a continuous tradition, the Latin regular sequence is perhaps the most striking demonstration of their magnitude.[108] The longitudinal asymmetry of the archaic sequence disappears, after a transitional period beginning in the later eleventh and ending in the early twelfth century. Many sequences now look exactly like hymns of the same period: a series of trimly rhymed trochaic stanzas of four, six, or eight lines of alternately eight and seven syllables that are all perfectly identical in form. Only the music (which is often borrowed) now identifies these texts as technically "sequences," since it retains the pair-wise progress of the sequence form (BB/CC/DD . . .). The best practitioners of the regular sequence, such as Adam of St. Victor (fl. 1130–1172/92) or Thomas Aquinas (d. 1274), sometimes exploit the possibilities of their form by altering the length of the stanza and even the line toward the end of a sequence, but this is not the usual practice.

However, the music to which the regular sequences were sung was anything but regular and metrical in structure. Instead, its flowing, phrasally stressed outlines contrast very pleasingly with the unremittingly trochaic pulse of the text. In addition, what is true of most musically set medieval lyric is true also of the regular sequence: the rhyme scheme is not reflected in any corresponding repetition of musical phrases (i.e., one does not find an aabccb rhyme scheme paralleled by an AABCCB musical structure). Instead, each element in the total economy of the sung poem goes its own way. Again, this asymmetry between text and music qualifies the apparent regularities of the text seen in isolation.

I stress these facts because the regular sequence has found little favor in recent decades. The same scholars who insist upon the need to study music and text together in the case of the archaic sequence then proceed to decry the supposed monotony of the regular sequence, completely ignoring the relationship between text and music in its case. To the argument that this relationship is inconsequential where most texts will fit the same melody and any given melody most texts, I would reply that this is only an extension of the habit of *contrafactura* (which characterizes the sequence itself at its very outset), that the formal effects described in the preceding paragraph exist no matter whether the fit between music and text is close or not in matters of detail, that word painting is in any case rare in medieval word setting (i.e., word-text relationships are usually rather abstract), and finally, that after all a good deal of Handel and Bach's vocal music also did service for more than one text.

Furthermore, I believe that the decided preference expressed by Peter Dronke or Stephen Ryle for the irregular over the regular sequence represents a projection of twentieth-century poetics onto the Middle Ages, exactly the sort of projection the Introduction of this book is intended to help the reader avoid.[109] It looks to me very much as if contemporary views about speech rhythm and organic form are being applied to the twelfth century and to Latin, where they have about as much business as the "bishop" of Chaucer's *Troilus and Criseyde* does in Troy, and a good deal less excuse. There was very little that was natural or speechlike or organic about any medieval poetry, including the archaic sequence, and it is deeply disappointing to see some of the most gifted readers of poetry among medievalists failing to escape the prejudices of their own age, praising a form that looks like what is considered good today and dispraising a form that looks like what the modernists of some generations ago rejected. And yet it is somehow typical of medievalists to be fighting an Edwardian battle in the latter part of the reign of Queen Elizabeth II.

In short, it is time to stop using one kind of medieval poetry as a stick to beat another kind with. In this case, both kinds produced masterpieces occasionally and mediocrity usually. Both have their particular appeals, and we should be glad of the opportunity to experience and appreciate each on is own merits. *Benedicamus domino.*

At the same time as the transition from archaic to regular sequence is taking place, the major new form of the *conductus* begins its development.[110] First attested in the Beauvais Play of Daniel and in the Codex Calixtinus (both from the second third of the twelfth century), the term itself indicates that the origin of the *conductus* was as an accompaniment to (new) processions.[111] Since in principle no procession could be permitted to take place in silence, particularly a festal one, there was a need for music and words to fill the freshly created gap in the continuity of the liturgy, or paraliturgy. For many centuries now, the processional lyric or *versus* had characteristically been "rhythmic," and it was out of the *versus* that the *conductus* apparently sprang. (However, the famous processional hymn *Salve festa dies, toto venerabilis aevo* [vv. 23ff. of Venantius Fortunatus's *Tempore florigero*] had also founded a well-represented tradition of pieces in elegiac couplets.) This accentual prosody, plus the rise of disyllabic rhyme (ca. 1075 on) and the clear contemporary bias in favor of the repetition of a single stanza form (cf. the regular sequence), determined the character of the *conductus* as text. Musically, the *conductus* was normally polyphonic (from two to four voices), though monodic examples also exist. All voices declaim the words together, so that they would be easily understood (contrast the somewhat later motet, or the *organum* so brilliantly cultivated in the second half of the twelfth century at Notre-Dame de Paris). Many *conductus* incorporate melodic flourishes or *caudae* (tails) into their music at structural joins or in connection with semantically important words; these may often have been drawn from secular songs or dance tunes.[112] The voice that acted as the foundation of the polyphonic structure in nonmonodic *conductus*, known as the *tenor*, was freely composed rather than borrowed from plainchant, as were the *organum* and motet. Apparently, the music could be performed without words, either by instruments or vocalise or a combination. In all these respects, one can see that the musical interest of the *conductus* was considerable, to such a point that the text might easily become a secondary matter. This impression receives support from the fact that manuscripts appear in the twelfth century in which material is organized not by liturgical function or textual subject matter, but by musical form. Indeed, the scribe often records only the first statement of a repeated musical unit (e.g., AABAAB), therefore omitting the second half of every stanza of the text.[113] This shift away from words to music is characteristic of the later Middle Ages in both the East and West, and it is reflected in the markedly greater emphasis on the aural qualities (elaborate rhyming, repetition of words, complex variations in line lengths) of the text by poets.

Though it began as an accompaniment to processions, the *conductus* soon became generalized to other functions; in the Codex Calixtinus, many *conductus* introduce lessons (i.e., readings), and a good deal of separate performance of *conductus* involving moral or political texts also occurred. (Interestingly, no "erotic" *conductus* exist.)[114] *Conductus* from ca. 1200 often incorporate refrains, internal or final or both, suggesting a style of performance in which a small group of soloists sang the polyphonically set stanzas and the chorus replied in unison at the refrains. As for the sequence and the trope, St. Martial's (Limoges) seems to have been the most important early center (ca. 1100), a role that Notre-Dame de Paris played in the later twelfth and earlier thirteenth century, for the *conductus* and for other musical forms as well. In northern France, the relationship between the Latin *conductus* and the vernacular lyric of the trouvères was fairly close; one finds analogues in Old French to the *conductus* (e.g., the preference for a length of three stanzas, the use of refrains, the festal dancelike rhythms),[115] and Gautier de Coincy composed the first *conductus* to Old French texts at the very beginning of the thirteenth century, when Notre-Dame was at the height of its influence and productivity.

Latin *conductus* include some of the most appealing of twelfth- and thirteenth-century lyrics. The prevailing gaiety of the many religious examples is partly due to their preference for Christmas, with its ceremonies and paraliturgical and popular observances, as their subject. Vernacular Christmas poems often share many of the *conductus*'s traits, without there being any suggestion of direct influence, so that one suspects a common popular spirit and poetic tradition underlying Latin and vernacular poems alike. Needless to say, the similarity is strongest in the case of the Christmas carol, which appears in Middle English toward the end of the fourteenth century.[116] Here, as Rossel H. Robbins has argued, there may in fact be a direct formal connection at work.[117] Even if this is so, however, and the carol grew out of the processional hymn, it is a mistake to pose the issue as a choice between popular or learned origins. As I have said before, and as is almost certainly the case with the *conductus*, popular and learned constantly cross-fertilize each other, with one side of medieval poetry often returning to the other, in altered shape, what it had borrowed in centuries past.

Finally, it is with the *conductus*, as represented in particular by the St.

Martial and the Notre-Dame repertories, that the Latin reserve of metrical stanza forms breaks out of its early medieval confines.[118] As in the ninth century, there are chronological and geographical links (not to say coincidences) between the centers of creative activity in Latin poetry and music and the creative centers for vernacular cultural development (i.e., southern, then northern France). As with the Carolingian flowering, this close association ought to seem natural, and it supports the unitive (but not monolithic) model of medieval culture that this book presumes.

The last form of importance to Latin religious poetry to receive attention in this chapter is the rhymed Psalter. Almost exclusively Marian, it appears in Latin in the twelfth century. As the Psalter of David contains 150 psalms, so the new Psalters of Mary number 150 stanzas, lines, or words—most usually the first.[119] The devotional practice of dividing the Psalter into decades grouped by fives (giving a total of 50 psalms per major section) led to Mary-Psalters based on the figure 50 or 100 as well.[120] According to Meerssemann, who is also the editor of the earliest Latin examples of the form, the use of Mary-Psalters belongs to northern Europe, where it plays a part in observances on the annual day of prayer for living and dead brothers belonging to a confraternity. (It was also used in funeral processions in the late Middle Ages.)[121] In France and the Low Countries, Beguine religious communities replaced the Psalter of David with a Mary-Psalter for the illiterate; at Gand, their rule went so far as to require the daily recitation of a Mary-Psalter (an extreme case of the degree to which the Marian cult could replace the traditional liturgical, Christological cult). Women wishing to enter the Beguines could pay for their entry with a Mary-Psalter recited on behalf of dead sisters. In consequence of these and other uses of the Mary-Psalter, it had established itself as a form of prayer (*forma orandi*) by the thirteenth century. However, it was not until the late fifteenth century that it began to replace the old system of prayer based on the seven *horae* in the statutes of Marian confraternities.

Except for a set of 100 Spanish tercets to Mary that might perhaps be considered a Mary-Psalter, vernacular examples are indeed confined to the north.[122] Of a handful of verse Psalters in Old French, one concerns Christ rather than Mary. Middle High German offers some two dozen printed examples of *Rosenkraenze* (i.e., rose wreaths for Mary) from ca. 1250 on, including a single Psalter to Christ. There are also a few fourteenth- and fifteenth-century Middle English examples (cf. two in the Vernon manuscript).[123] The Rosary movement of the last third of the fifteenth century stimulated production of Mary-Psalters to meet its devotional demands.[124]

Like most of Marian lyric, these Psalters are largely quite routine. Only a few German (especially the earliest) and Latin examples show the verbal and intellectual energy necessary to give the traditional phrases and symbols vitality and to fill the numerical limits of the form without flagging. However, the Mary-Psalter provides an interesting case of the ongoing late medieval interaction between piety, devotional practices, and poetry, and it also shows how a Latin form could relatively quickly diffuse outwards into the vernaculars when conditions were right.

In this period, the first important vernacular innovation in lyric form was the discovery, in the Provençal *canso*, of the tripartite (AA/B) stanza.[125] Even Hans Spanke, who was one of the strongest advocates of a strong influence on the vernaculars by the Latin lyric, believes that this discovery was entirely new.[126] Latin examples are later but abundant—half the extant *conductus* in fact use the *canso*-stanza (see especially the Notre-Dame repertory).[127] It is the basic structure for the stanzas of the art-lyric in Old French, Italian, and German, and therefore, so far as one is concerned with imitations of the secular chanson or with the tradition of the *Spruchdichtung*, it is frequent in vernacular religious lyric as well. Undoubtedly the most lucid and accessible "contemporary" discussion of the tripartite stanza is in the second book of Dante's incomplete *De vulgari eloquentia* (first decade of the fourteenth century). This structure encourages devices, both of rhyme scheme and line length, to articulate its parts and give each a well-defined shape. In consequence, at its higher levels, vernacular lyric moved quickly away from the mainly isolinear quatrains and hymn-stanzas of Latin to a subtle use of short lines and long-breathed stanzas oddly reminiscent in their effect of Byzantine hymnody (of precocious but prematurely arrested growth). Collateral developments, perhaps partly influenced by a desire to retain features of the now obsolete archaic sequence, appear in what one might call the "filigree" stanzas characteristic of a significant amount of liturgical and nonliturgical Latin lyric from the twelfth century onwards (cf. p. 101). Of course, the isolinear hymn-stanzas continue to dominate the bulk of the less ambitious Latin and vernacular religious lyric, with Old Norse pursuing its separate way, based upon skaldic stanza forms, till 1350 or so, when it too succumbs. In addition, even art-lyric shows a strong tendency to return to monolithic or modular stanzas, without the AA/B asymmetry of the tripartite form. According to Le Gentil, only the fixed forms remain genuinely tripartite at the end of the Middle Ages, at least in the Romance area.[128]

The *Spruch* (and so the *Meistersang*, in its conservatism) gave the common tripartite structure a particular German cast.[129] Like the *Minnesang*, it generated stanzas in which the contrast between line lengths is exaggerated to a point never reached in Romance lyric (one may perhaps compare the extremism of German to French Gothic art). Provençal may sometimes ad-mit one-syllable lines, but never the startlingly long lines of twenty or more syllables that mark some German stanzas. The use of such long lines makes for a weightiness and intellectuality that serves the reflective and discursive purposes of the *Spruchdichtung* tradition well.

In this whole development, which sooner or later affected almost all European poetry in a profound way (the sonnet itself is a development of the tripartite stanza, with the two quatrains and the sestet acting as the principal elements in the old AA/B structure), the role of music was crucial, and it may even have been primary. So long as there was a musical setting present to confirm the AA/B structure of the text by its use of the same structure, tripartition remained a stable feature of the art-lyric. As the poet ceased to compose (or at least, in cases of *contrafactura*, to select) his own melody, and as the music became the concern of a separate class of composers or declined to a merely optional and therefore often omitted ornament, poems could go their own way, free of the controlling force of that repetition of the first melodic paragraph (AA). And this is precisely what they did.

The other major feature of vernacular formal development affecting religious lyric was the flowering of refrain forms. The refrain itself is an immemorial part of folk poetry. It figures in classical epithalamia (cf. Catullus 61 or the Fates' wedding song that ends Catullus 64), occasionally in Latin elegy (cf. Ovid, *Amores* 1.6), and in the famous late-antique *Pervigilium Veneris*. In the early Middle Ages, it is a normal part of the *kontakion* in the East and of the processional hymn or *versus* in the West.[130] But its use is relatively limited, in recorded poetry at least, until the rise of the vernaculars.

One of the pioneers in the literary use of the refrain, in his Latin *Hymnary* for the use of Heloise's community of the Paraclete which was probably composed near the end of his life, was Abelard (d. 1142). The ninety-three hymns it includes span a rich range of stanza forms, many of them showing an intimate acquaintance with vernacular poetic development. These forms are marked by an unusual logicality and scrupulousness, repetition of forms serving to bind semantically and liturgically related hymns together into clearly defined groups. While Abelard justifiably seems to have felt that formal variety could be made to aid the reader or user to grasp the meaning of the texts, he preferred the old-fashioned austerity of monosyllabic rhyme for the most part, on the grounds perhaps that the fuller rhyme appealed too much to the ear and too little to the intellect. Nonetheless, in a number of hymns of a festal character, where the main object is to communicate joy rather than doctrine or morality, he uses either internal or final refrains, though never both at once. Thus, he approaches what Spanke calls "the Latin rondeau"[131] (which appears fully developed in the combined internal and final refrains of *conductus* in the Notre-Dame repertory) without ever quite writing anything that fits that description. All in all, his *Hymnary* rarely attains poetic heights, but it shows a remarkably intelligent control of formal means for primarily cognitive ends in its unique fusion of conservative austerity and progressive experiment.

One may think it odd that the first example of what has been called a vernacular formal development is in Latin. In fact, Latin examples of rondeaulike use of the refrain antedate most vernacular examples by several generations.[132] I am convinced, however, that Latin was turning formal devices that already existed in popular lyric to its own ends, rather than inventing them out of whole cloth. By contrast, the early authors of "artistic" vernacular lyric seem to have avoided direct use of popular forms, preferring instead to emphasize the radical novelty of their poetic ambitions by cultivating the unfolklike sophistication of the tripartite *canso*-stanza. In the various vernacular lyric traditions, it is usually only later on that poets begin to make significant use of popular vernacular lyric for "literary" purposes. Once a vernacular literary language was established, it was possible to assimilate features of oral tradition, but not before. In consequence, whatever simpler forms figured in early vernacular art-lyric were usually drawn from the Latin tradition, which had conferred literary status on them. (The glaring exception is of course the Galician-Portuguese *cantigas de amigo*, a poetically refined use of a parallelistic folk genre, and here one might suspect some influence from the sophisticated literary use made in the ninth and tenth centuries and thereafter by Arabic and Hebrew poets in Iberia of popular vernacular lyric.)

One should not be surprised, then, that literary use of the refrain in vernacular lyric does not become frequent until the thirteenth century. Outside of the Latin *conductus*, the rondeau (or *rondel*, to use the early term) has little significance for religious lyric.[133] It is another pattern in the use of the refrain, closely similar to the Spanish *zejel* and perhaps indebted to its Arabic antecedents, which cuts across linguistic lines and is responsible for the form of literally thousands of poems, religious and secular, in the later Middle Ages. This pattern may be represented, in an "ideal" schema, as follows: X/ /aax/ /X/ /bbx/ /X/ /ccx/ /X . . . / /X. Refrain and stanza may vary in length and rhyme scheme, even the rhyme shared between refrain and stanzas may be lacking (though this is uncommon)—so long as there is music, the last part or line of each stanza will be to the same melody as part or all of the refrain. The value of this repetition, especially when reinforced by a recurring rhyme as a signal to a chorus or congregation that their turn to answer the soloist(s) with the refrain has almost come, should be obvious. It makes sense then, irrespective of genetic cause and effect, that the *virelai* or *zejel* form turns up in so many different traditions. In Italian, as the *ballata*, it is the backbone and most of the skeleton of the *lauda*.[134] In Provençal, it is the *dansa*, one of the major Marian forms used in Catalan Provençal poetry (cf. the *goigs* genre) from the thirteenth century onward. In Portuguese, it is the form that 75 percent of Alfonso's *Cantigas de Santa Maria* (ca. 300 poems) follow. And in Spain, it yields the *villancico*, a popular form in which some of the most attractive religious lyrics from the end of the fifteenth century (especially songs from plays) are written.[135] In Middle English, it turns into Christmas carols. And in Catalan and French, it appears under its own name (so to speak) of *virolai* or *virelai*, a name that probably originated as nonsense syllables used as a refrain.

It is evident that variants of the *virelai* or *zejel* refrain form smacked unmistakably to contemporaries of the popular and the "low." That is why in several traditions the form is used earlier and more freely in religious than in secular lyric, which had higher artistic goals in those texts deemed worthy of recording in the *chansonniers* of the thirteenth and fourteenth centuries. When there is record that the Tripudiati danced in Italian streets and pilgrims danced at pilgrimage churches, what wonder that religious songs meant for the people took on the shape of their dances? [136]

In the later Middle Ages, as the religious lyric became more dignified and more middle-class, audiences and poets began to prefer less frolicsome poetic forms. Especially in Marian lyric, the refrain dwindles in France to a refrain-line closing each octave (or eleven-line stanza) and the envoi of the ballade and its more difficult variant the *chant royal* (which was de rigueur at the fifteenth-century *puys*).[137] The ballade penetrates English poetry in Chaucer's generation, and the refrain-line by itself becomes a frequent device (cf. the Vernon manuscript).[138] In Italy, too, some literary *laude* include a refrain-line as the last of each stanza as well as the traditional *ripresa*.[139] But the influence of this fashion for refrains, like the influence of the *virelai*, remains restricted to the Romance countries and to England, conquered by the French-speaking Normans.

A number of other vernacular forms have a certain importance for the religious lyric. This decidedly mixed bag contains the *lai* or *leich*, the *glosa*, the *pregunta* and *respuesta*, the *capitolo ternario*, the sonnet, and the octosyllabic couplet. The first is French and German; the second and third, Spanish; the fourth and fifth, Italian; the sixth, again French.

The *lai* (Old French) or *leich* (German) was a form of extraordinary complexity, in the latter tradition especially.[140] Its protean examples usually seem to bear some similarity to the sequence in their use of a degree of strophic responsion. In the Celtic tradition whence the *lai* arrived on the Continent ca. 1150, this relationship may have been clearer. In its German evolution (ca. 1200—ca. 1350), responsion can become elusive or nonexistent, to the point that one begins to believe that the object of this virtuosic form was to break all the usual formal rules. Of necessity, musical settings were through-composed; however, though 75 percent of free-standing French *lais* have notation in manuscript, only 20 percent of the German *leiche* do.[141] The effort that composing a *leich* cost poets may account for the fact that nearly all *leiche* are attached to a relatively or very well-known name, that few poets wrote more than one *leich*, and that no one wrote more than a handful. The baker's dozen of printed religious *leiche* date from Walther von der Vogelweide to the fourteenth century.[142] None is negligible, and several are extremely impressive. In particular, Heinrich von Meissen's, or "Frauenlob's," Marian *leich* (extant in five manuscripts), is one of the most difficult and the most dazzling of all medieval religious poems.[143] In its esoteric vocabulary, its use of unusual types, and its formal audacities, it is a fitting climax to a specifically German sequence tradition beginning with certain poems by Notker in the ninth century, continuing through Hermannus Contractus (eleventh century) and Hildegard of Bingen (twelfth century), and eventually deteriorating into the pretentious erudition of the Meistersinger. Not the least of Frauenlob's audacities was his decision to use a sermon by Alain de Lille on the Song of Songs as the basis of his poem. It is just this willingness to attempt to assimilate the full dimension of the Latin religious tradition by which religious poetry might have profited. Walter of Châtillon, besides the German sequence authors listed above, had taken steps in this direction during the twelfth century in some of his Latin Marian hymns, but without apparent issue. Frauenlob's great experiment had as little effect on subsequent poetry. But for its period, it was the equivalent of Milton's "Lycidas" or Hopkins's "Wreck of the Deutschland" or Crane's "The Bridge": a conscious try for a masterpiece, in the highest style and form available, that stretched the poet's powers to the utmost and consummated a subject and tradition central to the poet's age. In his degree of success, Frauenlob may have been closer to Crane than to Milton, but his *leich* still represents one of the ne plus ultras of medieval Marian poetry—and Mary was by then becoming virtually the only proper subject for religious art-lyric. Luckily for English readers—even for those with a good command of Middle High German, in view of the obscurity of the original—an effective nineteenth-century English translation of this poem exists under the title of *The Lay of Our Lady*.[144]

Outside German, the *lai* produced little important religious lyric. The two major exceptions are by Guillaume de Machaut, who dominated fourteenth-century French poetry and music.[145] In his hands, the *lai* became codified as twelve sections of two to four pairs of correspondent stanzas each; of the fifty-seven Old French *lais* of his century, nearly half are his work, and all but three have extant musical settings (generally monodic).[146] Later writers contented themselves with just the text, sometimes adorned with a few extra formal flourishes. Machaut's "Lay de nostre Dame" and "Lay de la fonteinne" are both elegant Marian poetry, the first more lyric, the second more theological in character, like Frauenlob's *Marienleich* and *Kreuzleich*. But except for the quality of their workmanship, they are entirely unremarkable. Finally, the Provençal *descort*, which may be related to the *lai*, produced only secular poems—understandably, since its very name testifies to its association with lovers' quarrels or "discords."

In Spain, *glosa a lo divino* was the technical term for *contrafactura* (cf. Juan Alvarez Gato and Ambrosio Montesino).[147] *Glosa* also designated a brief poem, often a single stanza, written as a pendant to, or perhaps incorporating the text of, an existing poem (a *cancion* or the like). In the fifteenth century, there was a vogue for this form, which made for a lively exchange among the members of Spanish literary circles. Most examples are secular, but religious subjects were also raised. The *pregunta* and *respuesta* are really no more than a variation on this intertextual relationship, with the added feature that the poet of the first poem actively seeks a reply to the question or conundrum he proposes, and the second poet obliges.[148] The popularity of such forms gives one a sense of the highly literary, self-conscious nature of the Spanish world that created the *cancioneros* and of the subordination of subject matter to the cultivation of personal poetic relations. It is understandable that in such an atmosphere religious poetry would usually offer the pleasure of intellectual play rather than deep feeling.

In Italy, poets after Dante applied his *terza rima* to a variety of religious subjects in what was called the *capitolo ternario* (chapter in tercets). Most of the dozen printed examples concern Mary, Marian texts (such as the Ave Maria or Salve Regina), or saints (such as Lucia or Margareta).[149] Bianco da Siena, who likes to salt his *laude* with Latin words or phrases, also has a weakness for this rather learned and discursive form, which he chooses not only for subjects like those mentioned but also for his paraphrases of the seven penitential psalms. Four *ternari* by Lorenzo de' Medici paraphrase texts by the so-called Hermes Trismegistos in an interesting display of Renaissance philosophical religion (Lorenzo, as well as other members of his clan, also wrote perfectly traditional Christian *laude* in the *ballata* form). A simplified form of the *ternario*, divided into tercets but without rhyme linking (i.e., abacdc . . . rather than ababcb . . .), appears in the later fifteenth century, easing the poet's task. Starting in the fifteenth century, *terza rima* began to penetrate into Iberia and France, with one result being a homily on Mary Magdalene by the sixteenth-century Portuguese poet Jorge da Silva that paraphrases John 20 : 11 – 15 in the shape of a *capitolo ternario*.[150] In all these cases, the nature of the form favors a reflective rather than a lyrical tone, reminding one of the obituary poems in couplets from England in the seventeenth century. Indeed, perhaps the most striking *ternario* was written for just such an occasion, in this case Neri Pagliaresi's strongly felt poem on the death of St. Catherine of Siena. As one can see, however, the *ternario* is of only peripheral concern to a study of religious lyric.

Still more modern in character than even the *terza rima* meditation is the sonnet. When Italian poets use this form for religious subjects, as they do occasionally, one feels as though one has been abruptly transported out of the Middle Ages into the Renaissance. The effect is particularly strong in reading a fifteenth-century poet like Leonardo Guistinian, whose religious lyrics mainly use the *ballata* form but include examples of the *ternario* and the sonnet, so that a traditional *lauda* may be directly succeeded by a radically different sort of poem. Diction thickens, word order coils back on itself, thoughts gather into a single complex thought organizing them all within its confines.[151] It is a fascinating example of the actual coexistence of two supposedly separate and successive historical and cultural periods. The very form of the sonnet, despite its thirteenth-century origins and its descent from the still earlier tripartite stanza (cf. the Italian *canzone* for the lineal heir to the same), seems emblematic of the Renaissance. Medieval forms are characteristically open, iterative, and strophic, based upon an accumulation of semiautonomous entities that gradually cover but cannot exhaust the subject, since (in religious poetry at least) the subject is ultimately God and all he has wrought. By contrast, the sonnet is closed and unrepeatable, a gestalt perception *uno ictu mentis* of a single idea encompassing all its parts at once. (Byzantine epigram lacks any equivalent form, but it gives one a similar sense of an underlying humanist or Renaissance mentality, in this case produced by a persistence of late antique culture rather than premonitions of a revival to come.) In the emergence of the sonnet from its original guise as a stanza within the iterative structure of the chanson, one can see the emergence of Renaissance from medieval literature.

Finally, one cannot ignore the octosyllabic couplet, which appears to have originated in France in the twelfth century and became the staple of narrative and didactic Romance and German poetry.[152] It plays a large part in the humbler or more prosaic sorts of French, Provençal, and Italian religious poetry. These occasionally rise to the intensity of lyric, but they really require little more here than an acknowledgment of their existence.

There are a number of important general observations to be made, or reiterated, concerning the development of late medieval poetic forms. First, a single impulse animated both Latin and vernacular poetry in the late eleventh and twelfth centuries, expressing itself in their joint production of a host of new stanzas and in their joint shift from (respectively) monosyllabic rhyme or assonance to true rhyme, involving in feminine cadences the last fully stressed as well as the last unstressed syllable in the line.[153] This shift was only the first step in an increasing emphasis on aural appeal, leading to

the intricate rhymes of French and German verse from the thirteenth century on, but already unmistakable in Provençal poetry of the second half of
the twelfth century (cf. especially Arnaut Daniel). It is notable that Iberian,
Middle English, and Italian poets all resisted this tendency, preferring less
virtuosic rhyming and stanza forms that put less strain on the poet's abilities.

Second, there was no distinction of a systematic character between either
the forms or the music of secular and religious poetry. This common ground
made *contrafactura* a natural and frequent practice. The major distinction
to be observed divides "popular" from art-lyric forms in both the religious
and the secular spheres, with assimilation of the former by the latter acceler-
ating toward the end of the Middle Ages.

Third, forms originating in the vernaculars have a widespread and profound impact on Latin religious lyric. This reverses the earlier situation, in
which the vernaculars (so far as existing records allow one to reach such a
conclusion) drew heavily upon the Latin stock of forms and motifs. The old
symbiotic relationship continues, but the dominant partner ceases to be
Latin.

Fourth, the Middle Ages as a whole are characterized by a significant acceleration in verse-tempo that late medieval poetic forms such as the sonnet,
the *ternario*, or the ballade seem to seek to counter. This application of the
brakes to a millennial gathering of momentum is a sign of a new sense of
the weight and dignity of poetry and therefore of the transition to the
Renaissance.

One can detect the beginnings of this quickening of verse-tempo in antiquity. Greek and Latin classical poetry had as its norm relatively long lines
and a deliberate pace, each syllable being allowed its due quantity; it also
tends to move in verse paragraphs, not in pairs of lines, single lines, or hemi-
stichs (Ovid's couplet style and its progeny, an important early exception to
this generalization, found ready imitation in medieval Latin poetry from the
twelfth century on). Often the thought will be distributed, in strophic
poems such as Horace's, over whole groups of stanzas, with the result that
parts of a sentence cannot be properly understood until well after their ut-
terance. Medieval verse contrasts sharply, and in the West, as the centuries
pass, the contrast becomes stronger. Short lines are its norm, a rapid pace,
and frequent cadences, emphasized in Western practice by assonance and
(even before the end of antiquity) by rhyme.[154] Its paratactic, end-stopped
structure permits a much quicker delivery and comprehension than the hypo-
tactic, enjambed structure of classical and most late antique verse. Even
quantitative verse shows a lower semantic density, a certain diffuseness and
facility and simplicity abetted by end stopping and parataxis. Movement in
itself became an important value, even at the expense of lexical meaning.
One sees this for instance in the late medieval proliferation of elaborate

rhymed stanza forms in Latin, which are quite a different matter from the seemingly ad hoc forms of the early sequence.[155]

By the thirteenth century, the choice of stanza types seems to have become limitless, and new variations are constantly being created. In them, what Northrop Frye terms the "musical" (enjambment, strong rhythmic clashes, violations of regular pattern) is rejected in favor of the melodious. This is particularly interesting since music itself was moving in the opposite direction, exploiting the possibilities of complex rhythmic interplay to their fullest and (except in Italy) reducing the old emphasis on melody. In the West, the poetic pursuit of the melodious leads to the development of those extraordinary filigree stanzas alluded to earlier (p. 93), long series of lines one or two words long threading their way through intricate rhyme schemes; compare this example of the archaic sequence, adorned with all the latest trappings and so combining the charms of both the antique and the modern:

Eburnea,
Nivea,
Lactea,

Liliata,		Alba, nitens
Margarita		Candens virgo
Fulgida		Maria.

Caelis admiranda		Cantica tuorum
Et saeclis praedicanda,		Suscipe famulorum
Quos pellicit falsitas,		Taeterrimis, sordidis
Perimit vanitas,		Vitiis implicat.

O mater Dei		Manna quae pluis
carens omni		Semper tuis
Macula		Servulis,
Lucida		Optima
Facula		Nobis da
Candens nubecula,		Iugiter gaudia.

(AH 48, no. 393, p. 424, stt. 1–5)

(Ivory, snowy, milky, lilied, glistening pearl, white, shining, glowing, Virgin Mary. Wondered at in heaven and proclaimed on earth, receive the songs of your servant, whom falseness entices, vanity destroys, tangles in vilest, filthy vices. O Mother of God, spotless luminous torch, glowing cloudlet, manna who always rain down upon your dear servants, give us highest joys forever.)

Among the artfully archaizing affectations of this text, one should note the frequent assonance on "-a" (characteristic of the West Frankish sequence from the earliest times), the grammatical rhyme (though this is common in contemporary vernacular poetry), the occasional omission of rhyme, and of course the irregularity of the "stanzas." But the rich play of sounds and the shortness of the lines are both characteristic of the late medieval fascination with aurality and the general medieval acceleration of verse-tempo.

In the vernaculars, the turn toward dance forms and heavy use of refrains in art-lyric is another manifestation of the same tendencies. It was against the background of an expectation that lines would be short and verse tempo rapid that the long lines of Middle High German lyric stanzas made their effect. And it is against this background that one should understand the choice by poets like Chaucer, Dante, and Petrarch (who announced the Renaissance in their conception of their art) of weightier stanza forms with no use, or limited use, of short lines, rather than the quick-moving couplets or dance-songs so typical of the closing centuries of the Middle Ages.

Even music participated in the acceleration of tempo. At least, notation moves from long to ever shorter notes as its basic unit, and the polyphony of both the *ars antiqua* and the *ars nova* makes heavy use of the effect of short-note lines running against the slow advance of a long-note tenor.[156] The deliberate, unceasing flow of plainchant consorts with or even yields to the nervous quicksilver dartings of the fourteenth century. At the same time, the growing complexity of music reduces the importance and interest of the text, which becomes merely an additional component in the aural texture. It is even possible that, conversely, the divorce of words from music (or growing estrangement) that one can trace from the twelfth century, when music was a support to the text in most cases, to the fifteenth, when music was no longer necessary to give a poem the status of lyric, may have been an important factor in causing poets to concentrate on the sound of their words, compensating internally for what had been lost with the passing of the old text-music interaction.

The subject of medieval music has by now arisen at a number of junctures, and the reader may perhaps be wondering why it has not played a more continuous role in this book—why, for example, there has been no attempt to discuss texts and music in tandem, where possible.

One reason is that, as Carl Appel put it, music is part not of the form but of the content of a poem.[157] As such, it is very resistant to abstraction and generalization. A second reason is that the analysis of music, particularly pure melody, is an extremely technical and yet subjective matter. Few scholars are really competent to discuss both text and music with equal confidence, and I am no exception to this rule. A third reason is that there seems to be little agreement on how to go about discussing the relationship between words and music. In fact, there is quite enough disagreement concerning the treatment of either by itself. To try to study language with language, as literary scholarship must, is like trying to catch water in water—only possible below the freezing point, when life stops or goes into hibernation. But to try to study *music* in language is like trying to catch a laugh or a cry in a butterfly net—the two occupy different domains of substance and function.

As a result, the brave maxim that music was an inseparable part of medieval poetry tends to lead to an appendix of half a dozen tunes that the reader is supposed to bring into some kind of relation to the words they accompany. I doubt the efficacy of such half-measures and the feasibility of full-measures in this dilemma. Also, the relationship between text and music in medieval lyric is neither uniform nor usually so very close, contrary to the implications of this maxim. A modern nostalgia for a lost lyric Eden that existed in a time before music and words fell out (or so it is thought) accounts for the impulse to find the lineaments of Eden in the high Middle Ages. In fact, the professional poets of the twelfth century were generally amateurs as composers, and few of their tunes equal their texts in interest. Later, the balance shifts, and the text becomes ancillary to the music, a makeshift construction of formulae that the audience will easily recognize (cf. most lyrics of popular songs, though not all, produced today). It was as rare in the Middle Ages as in the nineteenth-century *lied*, or perhaps rarer, for a perfect equilibrium to exist between text and music, each so illuminating the other that it seems they must have been born, hand in hand, from the same womb.

Nor should one forget the purely practical obstacles. Often, the music has been lost. Or its notation is indecipherable. Or its rhythmic interpretation cannot be securely determined. Or its details are as shifty, from manuscript to manuscript, as the details of any medieval poetic texts. Or the style of its performance, so crucial to the effect of a song, so sensitively felt by us when we are listening to a performance of modern material, eludes us, leaving us feeling that what we are hearing is no closer to the lost reality of medieval song than a foreigner's version based solely on the phonetic descriptions in a textbook would be to the actual sound of English. It is as if all the formidable difficulties one faces in reading medieval poetry "properly" had suddenly been magnified tenfold.

Finally, the demand that one study medieval song, that is, music and text together, rather than medieval poetry, is a tacit admission that medieval poetic texts cannot stand on their own merits, independent of their musical settings. The analogy to contemporary song lyrics, which even at their best will seem sloppy and diffuse or brittle and rhyme-obsessed until one hears rather than reads them, of course springs to mind, but I believe it should be disregarded. On the one hand, sung lyric was the norm in the high Middle Ages, not a paraliterary genre for which the rules were relaxed. The melody of secular as well as religious pieces strikes us as strangely asensual and unemotional; certainly there was no exploitation of natural spoken idioms or rhythms or phrasings in either texts or music such as one expects in contemporary songs. In consequence, where the text was not merely an adjunct to the music, it had the power to exist in its own right from the beginning. And on the other hand, it is an unavoidable fact of life that medieval poetry will continue, for the foreseeable future, to be judged as poetry not song, however unfair this may be in some cases. With the best will in the world, one cannot hope to reestablish the audience-performer relationship of the Middle Ages for this poetry. Such a goal would in fact be nothing more than a new mutation of that old chimera, the notion that it is possible for a modern consciousness to transform itself into the consciousness of an ideal reader or hearer of some past, dead age, and that only then will one's response to the artistic object be "correct." Instead, I believe that is is better to content oneself with "making allowances," as one does with anything that is strange to oneself but clearly has an inner law that gives it its integrity. For instance, it helps to be aware that medieval music, like some medieval lyric, may be a mosaic of formulae, or a close-knit development of a few cellular motifs.[158] It helps to know that musical and verbal structure do not usually coincide except in a general way in medieval songs and that in some periods and texts music was dominant and in others the words were. General propositions of this kind will not confer understanding, necessarily, but they will prevent gross misunderstanding and, above all, hasty rejection. If one is to spend time and effort on a subject, one needs principally some reason(s) to believe that it will eventually make sense, however incomprehensible it may seem at first. Then one can go forward with confidence, gradually developing a feeling for the inner nature of the subject that can be attained only by direct, personal experience. It is in this spirit that this book is written, and especially in this spirit that I make only such mention of medieval music as I believe might be helpful to the reader's conceptual grasp of medieval culture and poetry. For readers who desire intensive treatment of medieval melody in conjunction with medieval texts, I would recommend an excellent book mentioned earlier, Richard Crocker's *The Early Medieval Sequence*. It will amply demonstrate both the great promise of such investigations and the herculean efforts needed at this date to wrest a few firm conclusions from the tattered ghosts which are all that we moderns can summon back from the medieval grave.

STRUCTURES

This final section of chapter 2 will be concerned with all means of organizing the poetic text of medieval religious lyrics within the controlling form the poet chooses. These means may sometimes have their origin or their motive in utilitarian considerations, but in all cases they also have an aesthetic aspect.

The underlying abstraction that links all the structural devices to be discussed below is repetition. Indeed, as a modern theoretician like Lotman[159] and an ancient man of letters like the author of *Wen-hsin Tiao-lung*, Liu Hsieh,[160] have both recognized, the controlled use of repetition is fundamental to all artistic discourse. Self-evidently, it is indispensable to verse, which depends upon repetition for the existence of its meters, its rhythms, its lines, its stanzas. It is no less essential to the conferring of artistic significance upon words. The recognition of repeated sounds by the reader creates possibilities of association and opposition that assonance, consonance, alliteration, final or internal rhyme all exploit. In turn, these phonetic associations and oppositions lead the reader to perceive meanings that reinforce, complement, or even undercut the literal sense of the text in a fashion that is either absent from or no more than intermittent in nonartistic discourse. Repetitions of words or groups of words, of syntactic structures, of morphological features, even of graphic signs, all enter into the production of artistic meaning that the text and reader achieve in concert. Discourse without repetition, or whose repetitions are dismissed as meaningless (cf. "scientific" prose) can have no artistic function. Therefore, it is the concept of repetition and its consequences that the reader should bear in mind for the rest of this chapter.

i

We will begin with devices that have the structural function of articulating lines or stanzas. These may involve either the recurrence of an element or the recurrent contrast between elements of different kinds.

The commonest form of recurrence is anaphora (or epanaphora, to be more precise), initial repetition of a word. Its obvious origin is in the human habit of repeating a word to get a particular point across, especially when the speaker is excited. In poetry, the corresponding trope of anaphora has not only this "natural" effect, it also serves to mark the beginning of lines or stanzas of verse. As pure iteration, it is open-ended and anti-closural. There seems to be a special relationship of long standing between it and religious language; Martianus Capella (fifth century) calls the twenty-one repetitions of *sol* in a Latin poem an example of *hymnologein*, that is, of "writing in the style of a hymn,"[161] and cultic and literary religious texts provide abundant cross-cultural support for the association he makes between a high degree of repetitiveness and speaking to the gods. In medieval literature, the device is so common that it scarcely needs illustration. However, it is especially frequent in German and Italian, and in Marian literature in general

(an excellent example of Christian *hymnologein*), although it occurs notably less often in Iberian literature.[162] The intense emotions of Franciscan and
mystical poetry make constant resort to this device, the formal equivalent of
the instinctual response of the individual believer to a personal sense of God
that they seek to evoke. Finally, one should note that the rapid, striding motion it imparts to a poem is an important factor in that acceleration of verse
tempo discussed a few pages ago.

A related device, though it regularly figures at the end of lines and stanzas
rather than at their beginnings, is the motto-word. In the Provençal religious
aube, it will be the word for dawn, *alba*. Elsewhere, in the Italian *lauda* or
other traditions, it may be the name of Jesus, Mary, or a saint.[163] Like
anaphora, the motto-word serves the double function of marking out the
boundaries of formal units in the text and of emphasizing what is thematically central. Quasi-magical devotions, like the devotion of the Holy Name
(Jesus) or of the name Maria (there are many poems spanning the gamut of
European poetic traditions that take the actual letters of IESUS or MARIA
as their subject) are directly accountable for most late medieval cases of the
motto-word. In its stanza-ending function, it is nearly identical to the
refrain-line.

A third device usually involving simple recurrence of a word or phrase is
ring composition. In spite, or because, of the fact that it is a common phenomenon in oral poetry, where the repetition of the opening line of a poem
or section of a poem signals that the end has come, examples of the device
are not plentiful in medieval religious lyric, even if one includes borderline
cases in which a synonym or analogue of an opening word or motif appears
at the end of a poem. It seems to be commonest in the medieval form that,
due to its amorphousness, most needs it: the *lai*.[164] Examples of its religious
use in each tradition can usually be counted on the fingers of one hand, or at
most two hands. In Italian, the mostly Marian examples are by both anonymous and known authors. In German, a couple of mystical texts use it, and
a few elaborately literary pieces. In French, a translation of the Stabat mater
adds ring composition to its original. In Provençal, Guilhem d'Ieras ends a
verse prayer with it. In Portuguese, Gil Vicente uses it in a lyric from a
Nativity play. In Spanish, two of the very few examples I discovered come
from the *Cancionero musical* and are perhaps a reflex of musical structural
practices. In Catalan, a Marian poem ends with a reprise of its first stanza.
One of the "moral" lyrics in the Vernon manuscript ends by quoting its
opening as its penultimate line. In Latin and Greek, accomplished authors
like John of Howden or John Mauropus will occasionally resort to the device; in the liturgy, ring composition is possibly even rarer than outside it,
though one can point to subtle examples in Adam of St. Victor and Aquinas.
And Old Norse seems to lack any examples in religious poetry whatsoever.[165]

A quotation from the troubadour Folquet de Marseille (d. 1231) may serve to indicate both that medieval poets were well acquainted with ring composition and why they did not make more use of it (the standing of jongleurs was at best shaky):

> Farai o doncs aissi co'l joglars fai:
> Aissi com muoc mon lais lo finirai.[166]

(I'll do just as the jongleur does—I'll end my lay the same way it started.)

Whatever the reason, the significance of ring composition is how rarely medieval religious lyrics show it. Centuries later, in his *Also sprach Zarathustra*, Nietzsche beautifully described the aesthetic impulse behind ring composition: "Des Ringes Durst ist in euch: sich selber wieder zu erreichen, dazu ringt und dreht sich jeder Ring" (The ring's thirst is in you—every ring strives and turns to reach itself again).[167] It would seem that this thirst for wholeness and completion was satisfied by other means in the Middle Ages.

A recurrent contrast between elements of different kinds can take various forms. One is catechetical structure, which finds its place in the moral or doctrinal poem rather than in the religious lyric. Another, and one of the most important, is the refrain. This may be either a line ending each stanza (cf. the *ballade*), a separate stanza of its own (cf. the *ballata*), or a series of stanzas to a different melody than the principal stanza form that it alternates with and usually shorter than it (cf. the *chanson avec des refrains*). We have already been concerned with it as a feature of form, but it would be as well to examine it more closely in its structural function.[168]

In Catalan, most of the extant medieval Christmas songs have a separate refrain stanza. In German, most examples are post-1300 and in some way "popular" (mystical, Marian, dealing with Christmastide or Eastertide). In Greek, as noted, the refrain is common, under the name of *ephymnion*, as a refrain-line in the *kontakion*. In Italian, it appears as the *ripresa* in the *ballata* form in which virtually all *laude* were written, sometimes (especially in the fifteenth century) supplemented by a motto-word or refrain-line in the stanzas with which it alternates and shares a recurrent rhyme. In Latin, it appears first in paraliturgical *versus* (processional hymns) and later on in the liturgy (the earliest example is ninth century and Mozarabic, "Alleluia piis edite laudibus").[169] Despite Abelard's *Hymnary* (which had little influence), it remains characteristic of paraliturgical poems such as the *conductus* and not of the liturgy. In Middle English, it appears as the "burden" in Christmas carols, as the sententious refrain-lines of the Vernon manuscript and their like, and in formal Marian texts of the fifteenth century (cf. Lydgate's minor poems). In Old French, it appears occasionally as an internal refrain (17 of ca. 1000 examples in van den Boogard's index to Old French refrains) and in *rondeaux*, *ballades*, and *chants royaux*. Gautier's "Hui enfantez" (a translation of the famous *Laetabundus* sequence, which dates from the eleventh century) adorns its original with both internal and final refrain, to fine effect.[170] In Old Norse, it figures both as the *stef*, or refrain-line, used to bind together each section of the middle of a *drápa* and (after 1350) as a continental-style final refrain for strophic poems in either native or hymnic stanzas; one late poem even has both internal and final refrains.[171] In Portuguese, Alfonso's *Cantigas* display the full range of its possibilities in some 30 lyrics and 270 narrative poems. In Provençal, religious *aubes*, a Marian *planctus*, and several Marian panegyrics and prayers have a final refrain. In Spanish, the *estribillo* figures in religious lyrics in the *villancico* form; as Le Gentil points out, its semantic content increases as music becomes less important in the course of the fifteenth century, to the point that the stanzas become a gloss upon the refrain.[172] A similar situation exists for many French poems and also, to a degree, where a *contrafactura* is based upon an existing secular refrain, as in Italian *laude*.

The distribution of the refrain is wide and complex, and its structural uses are correspondingly various. Usually, it is syntactically independent, but it may be more or less closely integrated into the stanza it follows, interrupts, or ends (cf. the Byzantine *ephymnion* or the Vernon manuscript). Semantically, it will often sum up the main point of the poem, which may be either intellectual or emotional (the refrain is particularly effective as a collective cry of joy or sorrow). But it can also—though this is rare—clash with the apparent meaning of the rest of the poem, as in this striking use of the verse-and-response structure of the liturgy by Hildegard of Bingen:

> Rex noster promptus est
> suscipere sanguinem Innocentum.
> Unde Angeli concinunt et in laudibus sonant,
> sed nubes super eundem sanguinem
> plangunt.
>
> Tyrannus autem in gravi somno mortis
> propter malitiam suam suffocatus est.
> Sed nubes super eundem sanguinem
> plangunt.
>
> Gloria Patri et Filio et Spiritui Sancto.
> Sed nubes super eundem sanguinem
> plangunt.[173]

(Our king is quick to receive the blood of the Innocents. Wherefore the angels sing together and resound with praise, but the clouds lament over the same blood. Because of his wickedness, the tyrant has been suffocated in a heavy

sleep of death. But the clouds lament over the same blood. Glory to the Father
and the Son and the Holy Ghost. But the clouds lament over the same blood.)

Whatever its particular relation to the rest of the text, it will always establish a rhythm of alternation between two different orders of material, one
changing and one (usually) fixed. In this way, it helps create an open-ended,
typically medieval structure that pleasingly combines the predictable and
the unpredictable within a single form.

Such an alternation is also set up by lists.[174] Here a series of common or
proper nouns, typically, acts as the vertebral column on which the rest of the
poetic text hangs. The litany is the liturgical basis for religious examples,
involving a hierarchically ordered listing of sacred persons, beginning with
God and working down through Mary and the angels and finally the male
and female saints. The indefinite repetition of a single unit that the list en-
genders has its direct parallel in medieval music which consists of a "litany-
like" repetition of a single melodic line. Vernacular litanies appear in German, Italian, Old French, late Old Norse, and Provençal, but they are rarely
of any poetic value. One need only consider modern poetry, much of which
is structurally of the same additive or accumulative type (with Whitman the
most evident example), to realize that this structural device and excellent
poetry are not irreconcilable. Medieval authors simply perceived it as subliterary, fit for supplication in times of plague or the like, but not for other
religious purposes.

In a wider sense, however, the list is typical of Marian poetry, especially
of its cascades of epithets in which only the list and the structure of the line
or stanza survive to give the poem a shape. The aesthetic weakness of these
poems is precisely the lack of anything to resist and qualify the headlong but
predictable unfolding of their catalogues. One needs the contrast between
list and nonlist to create the possibility of surprise.

Other more specific versions of structural contrast include the *prosimetrum*, in which prose alternates with verse; *versus cum auctoritate*, in
which medieval Latin stanzas each end with a classical poetic quotation
contrasting its quantitative prosody with the rest of the stanza's accentual
prosody; citation of hymn lines at the start or end of the stanza, so that the
newly composed material in effect glosses the traditional phrase (cf. the
treatment of refrains in the late Middle Ages); and macaronic verse, in
which two or more languages alternate, usually in a systematic fashion.

The leading antique example of *prosimetrum* is Boethius's *Consolation*.
Various medieval Latin authors imitated its form, including Carolingian figures such as Audradus the Little and Sedulius Scottus.[175] In the vernaculars,
it is rare in religious literature. One could consider a mystical treatise like
the Middle High German translation of a Latin version of Mechthild of

Magdeburg's revelations to be a case of *prosimetrum*, though its rhapsodic ascents from prose to verse seem to owe nothing to the Boethian tradition. And there is João Claro's fifteenth-century Portuguese devotional *horae*, which mingles prose meditations and verse lyrics. In the main, the form seems to have been too literary for religious use.

The structural device of *versus cum auctoritate* seems to have originated in the twelfth century in certain Latin poems by Walter of Châtillon.[176] Its religious analogue is the citation of hymn incipits, which appears in the thirteenth century and spreads from Latin to the vernaculars.[177] One finds it here and there in German, Old French, and Spanish, for instance, and it is a minor but well-respected feature of late medieval Latin hymnody.

By far the most important of these devices based upon structural contrast is the macaronic combination of different languages. As one might expect in a tradition that resisted any concessions even to its own demotic, Greek shuns macaronics. Aside from decorative (often incorrect) use of Hebrew or Greek words, Latin shows no macaronic tendencies until the twelfth century, when an occasional French phrase begins to creep in for ironic or humorous effect.[178] Since France was the creative center for both Latin and the vernaculars at that time, it is not unnatural that French should be so favored when other languages were not. By the thirteenth century, macaronics have also penetrated the extra- or paraliturgical *cantio*.[179] But macaronic use of the vernaculars in Latin poetry remains rather insignificant, even if one includes secular as well as religious texts. After all, Latin, as the only language thought of as truly "literary," had nothing to gain by associating itself with its inferiors.

The situation was precisely reversed for the vernaculars, and it is to them one must look for the full development of the possibilities of macaronics. Normally, only two languages figure in a vernacular macaronic poem—the vernacular in question and Latin. To my knowledge, the record for number of languages used in a coherent fashion (or any fashion) in a religious poem goes without question to Bruder Hans von Cleve's *Marienlieder* of ca. 1400. In his prologue of 180 verses (15 times 12), Hans constructed a gloss on the Ave Maria (the favorite text for the late medieval gloss poem) in which each twelve-line stanza adheres to the following scheme: vv. 1, 5, and 10 are in German; vv. 2, 6, and 12 in French; vv. 3, 7, and 11 in Middle English; vv. 4, 8, and 9 in Latin. Since the rhyme scheme is aabcddbcceec, the rhyming sounds each involve different languages: a = German and French, b = English and French, c = Latin (thrice) and French (once), d = German and French, and e = German and English.[180] And the author manages to bring off this bravura display with fine effect.[181] As a quondam merchant from the area of Cologne, Bruder Hans took a justifiable pride in the languages he had mastered in his line of work. Most poets were content to seem less cosmopolitan.

The range of structural possibilities for macaronic verse is considerable, and each is represented in at least one of the linguistic traditions studied here:

1. The words in the "other" language (i.e., Latin, since I am disregarding the cases where Latin incorporates vernacular phrases) may be essential to understanding the poem, or they may be redundant. The former relationship is much the commoner, but in paraphrases of Latin hymns or glosses on Latin liturgical texts that include the original piecemeal, in whole or in part, sometimes the vernacular sections simply translate the Latin *currente calamo*. In one poem, written in prison, the Latin sections contradict the meaning of the Catalan sections—Pero Martines was using macaronics Aesopically to protest his plight.[182]

2. The position of the Latin words or phrases embedded in the vernacular poem may be partly or entirely random. This randomness is analogous to early medieval use in Latin of Greek or Hebrew words, and it occurs particularly in Spanish and in the Italian *laude* of Bianco da Siena.[183] It is also true of vernacular glosses that (like some Latin glosses on Latin texts) intersperse the Latin text throughout rather than assigning it a particular line or set of lines in each stanza.

3. The position of the Latin words or phrases may be systematic and regular. This is the usual case, with the syntactic relationship of vernacular and Latin ranging from complete mutual autonomy to closely woven interdependence. Within this case, there are several further alternatives:

   a. Latin words may occur in rhyme-position at the end of otherwise vernacular lines.[184] This seems not to occur by itself, without further use of macaronics, in religious lyric, but it is common in later burlesque poems of the modern period.

   b. Latin words may occur at the beginning of stanzas or lines. This is common practice in glosses on Latin religious texts such as the Ave Maria or the Salve Regina.

   c. Latin may fill entire lines in each stanza (e.g., the final line in Lydgate's "Regina celi letare"; or alternate lines, in "Dýrdarlegast dygða blóm"; or a more complex combination, say, vv. 2, 4, 5, and 7, in the septets of "De chanter m'est pris envie").[185] This is usually the case in Middle English macaronics.

   d. Latin may fill half of each stanza. Oddly, though this structure was sufficiently well established in Spanish to earn the name of *coblas meytatadas*, there seem to be no religious lyrics that use it. It is extremely unusual in any other tradition as well.

e. Latin may fill entire stanzas, either the refrain or stanzas alternating with, or followed by, a vernacular stanza or stanzas. Latin refrain stanzas occur in Middle English Christmas carols and in Spanish texts in the *Cancionero musical* (early sixteenth century). Lyrics in which Latin stanzas alternate with or precede vernacular stanzas are rarely truly macaronic, since the Latin will normally be nothing more than the original that the vernacular is translating or paraphrasing.

Occasionally, a religious macaronic lyric will involve two vernaculars rather than a vernacular and Latin.[186] And in the late fifteenth-century work of the *grands rhétoriqueurs*, Latin may lurk in the form of puns within the French text; Cretin's Ave Maria incorporates the Latin words *gratia* and *tui* as *grace y a* and *tu y*![187] But these are very much the exceptions. By and large, one is dealing with vernacular attempts at co-optation of the prestige of Latin that parallel contemporary attempts, via translation and paraphrase and imitation and substitution, at the construction of a public and private lay liturgy of devotion. For such attempts to have any meaning, there must be a certain degree of difference between Latin and the vernacular concerned. It is probably because of the absence of such a clear difference that macaronics are almost nonexistent in Italian religious lyric; one can easily overlook some of the Latin scattered through Bianco's *laude*, vocabulary and spelling in the two languages are so closely similar. It is perhaps the same reason that is behind the lack of systematic macaronics in Spanish religious verse, for Spanish also stayed closer to Latin than most Romance languages. In Provençal, macaronic religious verse is almost unknown (the early "Mei amic e miei fiel" is not a lyric, and it is virtually the only exception to this rule). Even in Portuguese, printed sources contain only a scant handful of examples, and one of these is unsystematic and another a *Te Deum* paraphrase and still another a *farciture* of a sequence.[188] One has to turn to the linguistically more highly evolved Old French to begin to encounter macaronic religious lyrics in significant numbers. And in the Germanic languages, where the contrast between Latin and the vernacular was most piquant, macaronic religious lyric flourishes. Discounting interlinear glosses, one can say that German examples begin with the St. Lambrecht and Muri sequences of the twelfth century. They continue to be popular up to the end of the Middle Ages and beyond, to the point that Hoffmann von Fallersleben concluded his still indispensable *Geschichte des deutschen Kirchenlieds* with a monograph on German-Latin "Mischpoesie," that is, macaronics. Macaronics abound in Middle English in the fifteenth century, and there are examples dating back as far as the thirteenth century (cf. "Of on þat is so fayr and bryght," a gem among Middle English lyrics).[189] Finally, in Old Norse after 1350, a half-dozen late medieval Marian texts (a significant number in what is a relatively small corpus) use macaronics in various forms (Latin as the refrain, in alternating lines, randomly distributed, as the rhyming words, as the final line).[190]

The association between macaronics and Mary is by no means peculiar to Old Norse. Poets in other traditions seem to have also felt that the use of Latin was appropriate in prayers and praise addressed to the Virgin, rather as one might have felt not so long ago that it was only polite to present one's hostess with a bouquet of flowers. In German and Middle English, in particular, there is also a strong association between macaronics and the festive spirit of Christmas (cf. the carols and a famous German song like "In dulci jubilo / Nun singet und seid froh"). In these lyrics, the Latin imparts a special glitter to the language. Since Christmas was one of the two points in the church-year when the liturgy of the church was less unaccommodating than usual, it seems logical that in the poems of that season too there should be a rapprochment between the language of the liturgy and the language of the people. French was the only tradition to use macaronics for the somberer subject of the Passion, which was the other season of concessions to popular piety (aside from a great Marian feast like the Assumption).[191] In general, French macaronics have a sobriety about them that is not characteristic of the Germanic examples—perhaps because the interlinguistic tension was so much lower in its case.

The entire subject of medieval macaronics deserves a full-scale, in-depth study.[192] It is filled with significance for medieval culture and medieval literature, of that one can be certain. In the sphere of religious lyric, it can signify either a reuniting of different levels of reality, with Latin standing for the heavenly and the vernacular for the earthly, or a carnival-like suspension of the normal rules of linguistic order which celebrates that reuniting. In this respect, it has important connections to the function of metaphor in religious lyric that will be discussed in the next chapter.

ii

All of the structural devices that have so far been discussed serve to articulate the structural units of the poems in which they occur but do not determine either the length of the poem or the order of stanzas within it. We will now turn to devices that have the latter functions, and sometimes the former as well.

The first usually goes under the sobriquet of "enumerative composition." Examples are extremely common in the later Western Middle Ages but infrequent in the East. Mary-Psalters, which use enumerative composition

(50, 100, and 150 elements), were dealt with earlier, and indeed enumerative composition is much more characteristic of Marian than of any other sort of religious poetry. It is particularly prominent in poems concerning the Joys (and by extension the Sorrows) of the Virgin. One can trace the devotional practice that led to this poetic genre back to the fifth or sixth century.[193] Originally, Mary's Joys were considered to be five in number (Annunciation, Nativity, Resurrection, Ascension, Assumption); in the thirteenth century, two more were added (the adoration of the Magi and Pentecost) to bring the total up to seven. This expansion of what were now called the *earthly* joys of Mary was perhaps prompted by the appearance in the twelfth-century of a collateral devotion of the seven *heavenly* joys, enshrined in a hymn by Thomas à Becket, "Gaude flore virginali," which became a regular item in the *livres d'heures*.[194] However, the expansion did not stop here. As one can see in the texts printed by Meerssemann, by Mone, and by Blume, later poems list as many as nine, ten, twelve, fourteen, or fifteen Joys, sometimes all earthly, sometimes a combination of both heavenly and earthly.[195] The precise composition of these lists varies (e.g., instead of Pentecost, the Purification will appear among the seven earthly Joys), and the wide choice of number of items introduces a degree of initial uncertainty for the reader about the length of the poem, compensated for by manuscript rubrics. The well-represented genre of the *gaudia Beatae Mariae Virginis* gave rise to generalized epanaphoric use of the injunction *gaude* (traceable to the *chaire* of the Akathistos hymn, which had an important impact on Latin Marian lyric through a ninth-century translation) and to another genre, the five or seven Sorrows of Mary, which derives its content though not its enumerative scheme from the tradition of the *planctus Mariae*.[196] Both the epanaphoric use of *gaude* (in its various vernacular equivalents) and the Sorrows, as well as the Joys, genre proved extremely productive in the vernaculars. In Catalan, the *goigs* (fixed at seven in number) became perhaps the chief genre of religious lyric from the fifteenth century on. Beginning in the early thirteenth century, the Sorrows and Joys of Mary became familiar subjects in German, with the Joys dominating by a wide margin. Both are common in fifteenth-century Middle English poetry. In Old French, Gautier de Coincy, Rutebeuf, Christine de Pisan, and Jean Molinet all wrote poems on the Joys, and anonymous examples abound, particularly in devotional books, in prose as well as in verse. In Provençal, there are several printed examples of the seven Joys (cf. Catalan); Guy Folquet ingeniously incorporated the Joys into a penitential lyric, and an anonymous poet translated the popular "Gaude flore virginali" as "Alegrat, verges sagrada!"[197] In Spanish, most of a dozen printed examples are the work of known authors and are written in the "higher" poetic forms, as is typical of formal fifteenth-century Marian lyric. The number of Joys reaches as many as twenty, and there are several non-Marian derivatives (such as the six gifts of John the Evangelist or a *gozos* on his birth, and the five Joys of the just in heaven).[198] The genres reach even Old Norse at the end of the Middle Ages (four examples of Joys, two of Sorrows).[199] For reasons that may have more to do with the choices of editors than with reality, I know of only one medieval Portuguese example of a Joys poem[200] and a mere handful of Italian Joys (two of them celestial). In the latter case, it is possible that Marian *laude*, lyric and dramatic, filled the devotional niche before the Joys and Sorrows genres could establish themselves.

To give the reader a clearer sense of the range of numbers in enumerative composition, I append a list with examples drawn primarily from Latin, in which this structural device sees the heaviest use:

Fives: cf. Meerssemann, *Akathistos* 2:190–95 and Brown XV, no. 30 (very common).

Sevens: cf. Meerssemann, *Akathistos* 2:195–205 and Brown XV, no. 28 (very common).

Nines: cf. AH 31, no. 180, p. 183ff.

Tens: cf. I. Sajdak, "Ioannis Kyriotis Geometri Hymni in ss. Deiparam," *Analecta byzantina* 1 (Posnen, 1931) (301 vv.: the poet states that the "perfect ten," i.e., the components of ten, three, and one, and the square of ten, are offered to Mary), AH 31, nos. 181–83, pp. 185ff., or Brown XIV, no. 102.

Elevens: cf. the Byzantine "exaposteilaria," by Emperors Leo and Constantine VII, in *Anthologia Graeca Carminum Christianorum*, Wilhelm von Christ and Matthaios K. Paranikas (Leipzig, 1871), pp. 105–12.

Twelves: cf. the "Akathistos" hymn, Sajdak, "Ioannis Kyriotis Geometri Hymni" (discussed in Meerssemann, *Akathistos* 1:97f.), and Meerssemann, *Akathistos* 1:188–90.

Fifteens: cf. Bernard's *Mariale* (AH 50, no. 323, pp. 424–56) or John Howden, *Poems*, ed. Frederic Raby (Durham, 1939), pp. 1–7 ("Quindecim Gaudia").

Twenties: cf. CC, vol. 2, no. 108, pp. 654–56, by Juan Tallante.

Twenty-fives: cf. Meerssemann, *Akathistos* 2:173.

Fifties: cf. John Howden, *Poems*, pp. 8–112 ("Quinquaginta Salutaciones").

Hundreds: cf. St. Edmund's "Grusspsalter" in Meerssemann, *Akathistos* 2:98–105 or the bizarre Marian "Centimomium," ibid., 2:174–77.

One Hundred Fifties: cf. AH 36, pp. 5–6, for a "Grusspsalter" in 150 words by Heinrich Egher von Kalkar (d. 1408) or John Howden,

Poems, pp. 118–75 ("Cythara"); the model for these last three choices of number is of course the Psalter, reinforced in the last case by the count of fifteen Joys sometimes used in the late Middle Ages.

In addition, a provisional expectation of a certain number of stanzas governs certain forms: three in the case of the *conductus*, eight in the case of the Ambrosian hymn. Medieval numerological symbolism may have played some part in the frequent reliance on enumerative composition, but with religious lyric I believe one should mainly look to the influence of numbers with scriptural prestige (e.g., 3, 7, 10, 12, 150) and to the requirements of liturgical or devotional practice (e.g., the even number of stanzas in the Ambrosian hymn, which lends itself to antiphonal performance, or Marian devotions based on fives and decades, for which the ultimate basis, far antedating Pater noster or Rosary beads, must have been the number of fingers on our hands). Numerology, like theology, follows behind, turning traditional or pragmatic features into sources of edification. Finally, the lack of any inherent reason in the subject matter of religious lyric for a poem to stop here rather than there created a need for some simple, arbitrary limit to the length of poems in which the audience would sense a certain "rightness." In its pure arithmetical abstraction, enumerative composition filled this need admirably.[201]

In the vernaculars, certain fixed forms, such as the *ballade* (three stanzas and envoi), the *chant royal* (five stanzas and envoi), the sonnet (fourteen lines), or the *rondeau* (thirteen lines, with variants) also predetermined the length of the poem.[202] However, they represent a small minority compared to the open-ended, strophic and stichic types, with or without refrain. Their increasing popularity in the late Middle Ages was a sign of a profound shift in the poetic currents.

Neither enumerative composition nor fixed forms can in themselves determine the order of elements within a poem. Several structural devices do have this effect, however, and it is these that now concern us.

So long as a scribe notices or respects them, acrostics will fix the order of lines or stanzas and often the length of the poem as well. This is particularly true of the acrostics, initial, internal, and final, of the *carmina quadrata* of the Carolingian period. Medieval manuscripts show that when the acrostic is of less central importance, it may simply be disregarded in order to omit stanzas or change their order to suit. The ABC acrostic using the letters of the alphabet is especially vulnerable to abridgment or rearrangement, because the acrostic is without semantic content.[203]

Historically, the acrostic appears in Greek and Latin poetry under Syriac and Hebrew influence (cf. the alphabetical acrostics of Psalm 119 and the Lamentations of Jeremiah).[204] In the fourth century, Hilary of Poitiers and then Augustine use it, among writers of religious poetry. Early Latin hymns from Ireland and the Visigothic kingdom of Iberia adopted in some cases, primarily processional, the ABC structure, and it continues to be the most popular form of acrostic throughout the Western Middle Ages.[205] In the East, however, the major use of acrostics in religious poetry affects the *kontakion* and to a lesser degree the *kanon*, taking the form not of an ABC but of a pious motto or supplication or signature, or combination of these functions.[206] The frequent inclusion of the poet's name served to authenticate the poem as an orthodox product, to call the attention of God, Mary, or a saint to the person responsible for the poem, to express a craftsman's satisfaction with his work (cf. the marks and signatures of medieval artisans), and also to provide some protection for the integrity of the text by indicating the proper number and order of stanzas. (Concerning the first of these four purposes, the reader may recall the demand of an early church council that poets sign their hymns.) Cases where a Western religious acrostic constitutes a coherent phrase or sentence are very rare.[207] More often, one finds the acrostic forms the name IESUS or MARIA or perhaps the name of a saint, rather like an embroidered monogram stitched into a hand-sewn gift.

Acrostics appear in the vernaculars beginning in the thirteenth century, a clear index to the new and growing reliance of vernacular culture on the written word, for the acrostic speaks to the eye and not the ear.[208] Scribes use illuminated or rubricated capitals to draw attention to its letters; these have the additional effect of clearly distinguishing the stanzas or lines of the text from each other. The distribution of acrostics, however, is far from uniform in the various vernacular traditions. To my knowledge, religious lyrics in Catalan, Provençal, and Old Norse contain no examples. Spanish uses acrostics in love-poetry but rarely in religious poems;[209] Juan de Padilla signs his name with an acrostic in the penultimate stanza of his long *Retablo de la vida de Christo*;[210] and there are poems on the letters of Mary's name, but no real cases of acrostics with religious lyrics. In Middle English, Chaucer paraphrased an Old French ABC to Mary by de Deguileville, producing an ABC of his own, and a number of fifteenth-century authors, including Lydgate, incorporated acrostics (ABC, MARIA, and so forth) into their religious poems.[211] Even in Old French, however, acrostics are relatively scarce. In Italian, they are almost nonexistent (though note an ABC and an AVE MARIA by Bianco da Siena, who had a penchant for the little elegancies of poetry).[212] Finally, Middle High German offers a number of ABC's, MARIA's, and IESUS's, as well as a few cases of the author's or dedicatee's name (cf. the so-called Monk of Salzburg or Friedrich von Zollern).[213]

The fact that no one vernacular tradition seems to have made heavy use of acrostics or influenced another tradition to do so suggests that late medieval Latin religious lyric was the common source. In general, there is a strong association between acrostics and the liturgical languages, and between acrostics and Marian literature. Only German produced any quantity of acrostics, and in its case the cause may have been the relatively high status of poets and poetry from an early period, the openness of the literary tradition to religious subjects (contrast Provence), and the pervasive German taste for the learned, whether in content or in form. Certainly, the greater the shift from oral to written in a vernacular culture, the greater the likelihood of an interest in acrostics. The regular presence of acrostics may attest then to a certain "bookishness" in a given tradition; it attests beyond a doubt to the existence of a religious art-lyric.

The association with Marian literature is partly an artifact of its dominance of late medieval religious poetry, partly a consequence of the late medieval image of Mary the Queen of Heaven. A queen requires the most sumptuous and elaborate of gifts, an interlayering of the most varied and costly materials. The textual equivalent is the construction of an interlayering of semantic and formal levels in which each achieves a maximum of saturation. Had the *carmina quadrata* of the Latin ninth century been written in the fourteenth, they would surely have borne the legend MARIA.

The device of stanza linking (also knows as *leixa-pren* or *coblas capfinidas*) plays an important part in the *laude* and a minor part in several other vernacular traditions. The Portuguese term *leixa-pren* designates the repetition of a whole line, with some variation permitted; it occurs in early Galician-Portuguese (the *cantigas de amigo*), in the medieval Latin rondeau, and in late French folk song.[214] In Provençal poetry, the device takes the form of *coblas capfinidas*, that is, the repetition of the last word or phrase in a stanza at the beginning of the first line of the next. Both devices have the same structural effect of fixing the order of stanzas by concatenation; in practice, the terms are often synonymous.

Latin examples are scarce; the *conductus* "In Domino confidite," the *cantio* "In ecclesia," and another paraliturgical text, "Prima mundi seducta subole" all involve *leixa-pren*, though in the second case the repetition affects the third line of each stanza, rather than the last, and there is the additional repetition of an internal and final refrain.[215] (All three texts date to ca. 1200.) No Greek poems use any sort of stanza linking. In the vernaculars, German and Old French seem as barren of religious examples as Greek. A single Old Norse poem, "Milska," uses concatenated lines.[216] Despite the frequency of *leixa-pren* in the *cantigas de amigo*, it is absent from Alfonso's *Cantigas de Santa Maria*, and I know of only one printed Portuguese religious lyric that contains the device.[217] In Catalan, an anonymous Christmas song begins each stanza with the final two lines of the last; a Marian poem by Johan Foguacot uses *coblas capfinidas*; Anthoni Vallmanya makes a fuss over the fact that his entry to the 1474 *joyas* at Valencia has *rims capfinits maridats encadonats e ab retronxa*, that is, that the last stressed syllable or word of a line begins the next.[218] The Middle English "God þat al þis myhtes may" virtually runs the gamut of stanza-linking patterns: repetition of several words, repetition of several verses, repetition of a single important word, alliteration, and semantic rather than lexical repetition.[219] A number of other Middle English lyrics make less complex and artistic use of stanza linking.[220] In Provençal, Guiraut Riquier seems particularly fond of stanza linking, whether through the repeated rhyme of *coblas capcaudadas* or through *coblas capfinidas*, and his "Kalenda de mes caut ni freg" involves the repetition of whole lines. (Two other Provençal religious lyrics also use *rims capcaudatz*.)[221] Where such devices occur, they usually reflect the general late Provençal tendency to formal complication for its own sake. In Spanish it is almost unknown in religious poetry, though stanza linking is frequent in the mid-fifteenth-century C ̄ionero de Baena (where it is confined to the Provençal-derived *maestria ̄ayor* or *media*, in which all, or at least one or two, rhymes are carried thro ̄ gh all stanzas).[222] In fact, it is only in the *laude* that one sees consistent use of stanza linking, in the form of *coblas capfinidas*. Jacopone's *laudario* shows it occasionally. The roughly contemporary Cortona 91 *laudario* has it in 15 percent or so of its texts, as does the Pisa *laudario*. It is a *tic* in Bianco, who resorts to it far more often than any other medieval religious poet. In the fifteenth-century literary *lauda*, it has become infrequent, despite Bianco's otherwise strong influence.[223]

It would appear that the origin of *leixa-pren*, *coblas capfinidas*, *rims capcaudatz*, and other forms of stanza linking is in the oral poetry of the folk. The (relatively early) Latin examples all belong to paraliturgical genres that were particularly open to popular influence. However, certain forms of it became attached fairly quickly to Provençal literary practice and were exported along with Provençal poetry to the other vernacular traditions. Even so, stanza linking met with a cool reception everywhere but in Italy. Perhaps it was felt to be too "oral" and popular a device, even with its Provençal accreditation; or perhaps the ruling medieval aesthetic, with its low valuation of horizontal coherence in texts, left poets uninterested in a device whose structural function was to specify a single order for otherwise autonomous stanzaic units.

iii

Quite a different way of determining the length or internal organization, or both, of a text was to use a preexisting structure. Gloss poems did this by incorporating words or phrases from a part of the liturgy that was well known to the audience.[224] The order of elements in the text being glossed imposed a linear order upon the gloss itself, and once the gloss reached the

last phrase or word of the glossed text, the poem ended. Translation, paraphrase, or *contrafactura* offered the same liberation from the need to create
a new structure; all three account for a significant amount of late medieval
religious lyric, especially in the vernaculars.

This process could also take a more abstract form. For instance, a prayer
could imitate the so-called narrative prayer or *commendatio animae* (cf. Roland's death for a famous vernacular example), evoking its structure by pre-
serving the order of motifs and saints invoked.[225] Far more frequently, a medieval verse prayer will be

> constructed after the fashion of medieval documents. In these documents,
> after the name and title of the sender comes an *inscriptio* or *salutatio* in which
> the person for whom the document is meant will be designated or greeted. The
> first major section, the *arenga*, follows. It voices a generality with particular
> reference to the content of the remainder of the document. Next is the *pro-
> mulgatio*, in which the sender says, "I determine," "I make known," etc. The
> second major section consists of the *expositio* or *dispositio*, which concerns
> the cause of the quarrel or the favor desired. The conclusion is the *cor-
> roboratio*, which formally closes the text of the document and precedes the
> signature and seal.[226]

Stefan Beissel goes on to point out the further parallel between references in
medieval documents to the backing of a highly placed person and references
in prayers to the intercession of the saints. The structural elements of verse
prayers analogous to the successive parts of a typical document as they were
recognized in medieval theory and practice include the initial laudatory address to God, Mary, or a saint (or a third-person allusion to a sacred person—cf. *salutatio*), the subsequent statement of the general proposition
that the person addressed has shown the ability to act in the past on behalf
of sinners and can reasonably be expected to do so again (this takes various
oblique forms, of course—cf. *arenga*), the statement of the speaker's problem (his undeserved sufferings, or, more often, his spiritual deficiencies—cf.
promulgatio), the nature of his request (relief or reform—cf. *expositio/
dispositio*), and a closing doxology or prayer for heaven (cf. *corroboratio*).
Similarity of function doubtless accounts for the prevailing similarity of
structure between petitions to the lords and ladies of heaven and of earth,
but given the frequent involvement of medieval men of letters in secretarial
or chancery or diplomatic positions that required the composition and handling of documents, as well as the impressive litigiousness of the age, one
should not ignore the possibility that Beissel is right, and that documents
had a direct influence on written medieval prayers, in prose and in verse.

Whether there was such influence or not, the existence of a conventional
documentary structure assured a context in which prayer structure would
seem particularly natural, not to say inevitable. The same applies a fortiori

to religious lyrics that imitate secular genres that possess an internal organization of motifs, such as the various sorts of love-poems. In sum, the importance of preexisting structures to medieval religious lyric is great enough that one should also ask oneself whether their invisible hand might not be determining the shape of the text one is studying.

iv

In a poetry written within a general cultural assumption that meaning arises from vertical relationships that the poet describes rather than discovers or creates, poetic closure becomes highly problematic.[227] Since the poem simply manifests one fold in the seamless cloak of Christian reality, its ending is fundamentally arbitrary. Of all medieval poetic modes, this is truest of lyric, from which narrative as the organizing principle is by definition excluded. In addition, the medieval suppression of the author's presence as a unique historical being means that the religious lyric cannot take its shape from the author's personal spiritual situation. A particular case might permit some sort of climactic resolution, but a general case must remain in suspension, so that all individuals can apply it to themselves. Medieval metaphysics and poetics work together to make closure look very much like an aberration or even a fault, at least in their terms.

I would suggest, then, that it is "philosophical" causes of this order that account both for the lack of closure in most medieval religious lyric and for the formal habits that in themselves would make closure difficult to achieve. Iterative strophic poetry, which is the dominant variety we are dealing with, gathers momentum as it proceeds, momentum that in modern terms needs to be dissipated if the poem is to conclude satisfactorily. But medieval poems rarely show any concern for this aesthetic requirement. Instead, one comes to feel that they are all part of some greater whole with respect to which they are at rest, for it moves as one, empyrean-like, while we must stand outside and see only the disconnected motions of its myriad expressions.[228] The same disinclination for closure, or lack of need for it, accounts for the relative infrequency with which medieval poets employ devices such as ring composition or stanza linking or "terminal modification,"[229] which would give their work a fixed shape. They seem entirely content with the weak closural effect of devices like enumerative composition or acrostics (whose arbitrariness may be their major virtue in medieval eyes), and with the singer's or composer's ability to indicate the ending of the text by musical means such as a cadence or a retard.

Closure is but one facet of a text's unity or coherence, though it is also the facet of which the reader is most likely to be aware—after all, the end of things, whether it be a movie or a symphony or an affair, has a particular importance by virtue of the silence or emptiness that follows it and from which one looks back, in joy or sorrow, over something gone to completion. In the case of medieval poetry, however, the same factors that favor weak or nonexistent closure prevent the achievement, or even the pursuit, of a poetic unity such as one may expect in classical or postmedieval work. The notion that "inorganic structure," or the analogy of architecture rather than the machine or the plant (to use the Enlightenment and romantic archmetaphors), characterizes medieval literature was raised in the Introduction to this book. I believe that the content of this chapter will have given it a good deal of credence, at least in the domain of the religious lyric. However, "inorganic structure" is still structure, and the religious lyric possesses a sufficient unity, given its cultural context and function, even if it must be said that this unity is conferred by the culture rather than achieved by the poem. Over and above this minimal coherence that a medieval poem has by right of birth and that is so striking to a modern reader, there are also means by which certain poems reach a degree of unity intermediate between the medieval norm and modern expectations.

Logical or pseudological argument is one of these means. Linguistically, it manifests itself in words that connect phrase to phrase, and sentence to sentence, in an active fashion, creating a forward, linear motion that counters the medieval tendency to simple juxtaposition of autonomous units, each looking upward to a controlling meaning somewhere above the level of the text.[230] English examples would include simple structures like if/then, then/now, when/then, not only/but also, as . . . so . . . so, either/or. In short, apodosis/protasis, coordination, and the like: what could be more ordinary? Yet it is a striking fact that in religious lyric, despite the nearly universal presence of prayer, such constructions, while frequent, are nonetheless absent from most poems. Where they occur, they seem to indicate a sense that argument is genuinely needed. In Marian poetry in particular, the sublimely elementary syntax of praise and of prayer to Christ twists into more complex patterns. One forgets now that Mary came to her position of eminence in the Christian cult of the West after the Middle Ages were half over. The poems remind us that her special power to act and her special obligation to her fellow humans had to be asserted and proven, over and over again, because it had not always been so. When poets cajole Mary or browbeat her, demanding their due of intercession, one is hearing the voice of a culture convincing itself that its prayers will avail. The same is true of the many vernacular poems that argue for the joys of serving Mary and the sorrows of serving an earthly woman—they trouble themselves to argue because there is need for argument. No wonder then that the *do ut des* (I do you a favor, you do me a favor) of primitive religion returns full-blown in

Marian poems.[231] Abelard puts it as bluntly as possible, ever the logician and rationalist, but also because Mary's new role was less than a century old in the West when he wrote:

> Opem quodam modo
> Toti debes mundo
> Quam velut ex iure
> Postulamus a te.
>
> Totum id honoris
> Nacta es pro nobis,
> Ut sis vitae porta
> Sicut mortis Eva.
>
> Ad hoc es creata,
> Ad hoc praeelecta,
> Causam recognosce
> Et effectum comple.
>
> Mundo debes opem,
> Mundus tibi laudem,
> Spes post Deum nostra,
> Nobis Deum placa.[232]

(In a way, you owe aid to the whole world—we demand it of you as if it were a legal right. For our sakes you obtained that honor, that you should be the door of life as Eve was of death. For this you were created, for this preselected—acknowledge the cause and carry out the effect. You owe aid to the world, the world owes praise to you—our hope next to God, reconcile God to us.)

In the contractual relationship Abelard describes, the hymn fulfills man's obligation of praise for the Virgin, at least in part. In return, the Virgin is to intercede for man with God. It should be noted that God remains the ultimate creditor in both cases.

Logical argument addressed to Mary can also take the form that because she has the power to act, she should do so. As Aeneas says to the Sibyl at *Aeneid* 6.117: *potes namque omnia* (after all, you can do it). A simple Middle English poem puts it neatly:

> Of vre sunnes make vs clene
>   & yef vs þat eche lyht,
> and to heouene vs alle i-mene
>   louerd, þu bryng, for wel þu Miht.[233]

(Cleanse us of our sins and give us everlasting light, and bring us all together to heaven, Lord, for you certainly have the power to.)

The argument is of immemorial currency, and there is no lack of examples in the liturgical languages or the vernaculars, though most of them prefer to soften the argument to a delicate hint.

Of course, logical argument does not provide a sustaining structure only for Marian poems. But Marian poetry is the only sort of religious lyric in the Middle Ages where it can claim a regular place. Therefore, as I said earlier, the motive for its use has a great deal more to do with theology and cult than with the needs of poetry. Nonetheless, its unifying effect remains and must be acknowledged.

Metaphor is perhaps the unifying force to which we are most accustomed. Full discussion of its use in medieval religious lyric must be reserved for the next chapter, but it can be said here that it rarely has a unifying function in this poetry. Like the lines and stanzas in which it occurs, metaphor functions atomistically by and large. It is rare for a series of metaphors to establish a continuity of vehicle, precisely because continuity of tenor is assured from the start (cf. the modus operandi of conventional Marian metaphors). As in other respects, the principle of vertical coherence militates against horizontal connections among elements, including metaphors. When part or all of a poem does base itself upon a central metaphor or a series of related metaphors, the effect is usually labored, because the genuinely metaphorical, associative habit of mind is alien to the medieval poet (with few exceptions). To put it briefly, one can say that the poet handles metaphor as if it were allegory. Adam of St. Victor, one of the most talented poets in the Latin tradition, achieves one of the more successful examples in medieval religious lyric of metaphorical unity, but it is sustained only through part of a sequence, and the passage suffers from an excess of prudence and calculation (the metaphor itself derives in its every detail from traditional typology):

> De radice flos ascendit,
> Quem prophetae praeostendit
> Evidens oraculum;
> Radix Jesse regem David,
> Virga matrem praesignavit
> Virginem, flos parvulum.
>
> Mira floris pulchritudo,
> Quem commendat plenitudo
> Septiformis gratiae.
> Recreemur in hoc flore,
> Qui nos gustu, nos odore,
> Nos invitat specie.

Iesu, puer immortalis,
Tuus nobis hic natalis
Pacem det et gaudia;
Flos et fructus virginalis,
Cuius odor est vitalis,
Tibi laus et gloria.[234]

(From the root the flower rises that the manifest oracle of the prophet foreshadowed; the root of Jesse foresignified king David, the rod the Virgin
Mother, the flower the little one.
Wonderful is the beauty of the flower that the fullness of sevenfold grace en-
hances; let us be refreshed in this flower that invites us with its taste, us with
its fragrance, us with its appearance [beauty].
Jesus, immortal child, may your birthday give us peace and joy here; virginal
flower and fruit, whose fragrance is life-giving, to you be praise and glory.)

In this careful working out of the relationship of root, stem, flower, and
fruit, easily the finest moment comes with the phrase *puer immortalis*,
which technically lies outside the metaphorical development but in fact cap-
tures admirably the implications of seeing Christ as a flower—childhood
and blossomtime are both brief, except in the Christ child, where they put
on immortality. Such sallies of esemplastic imagination are most unusual,
even in Adam, and still more so in Adam's lesser brethren. The handling of a
related metaphor in a Marian carol is more representative, and it will show
more clearly why one should perhaps not regret that medieval poets tried so
seldom to achieve metaphorical coherence in their religious lyrics:

burden = Of a rose, of a louely rose,
            Of a rose I syng a song.

Lyth and lystyn, both old and yyng,
How the rose begane to spryng;
A fayyrer rose to owr lekyng
    Sprong ther neurer in kynges lond.

v branchis of that rose ther ben,
The wych ben both feyer and chene;
Of a maydyn, Mary, hevyn quene,
    Ovght of hyr bosum the branch sprong.

The first branch was of gret honour;
That blyssed Mary shuld ber the flour,
Ther cam an angell ovght hevyn toure
    To breke the develes bond.

The secund branch was gret of myght,
That sprong vpon Christmes nyght;

> The sterre shone and lemeghd bryght,
>   That man schuld se it both day and nyght.
>
> The third branch gan spryng and spread;
> iii kynges than to branch gan led
> Tho to Owr Lady in hure chyldbed;
>   Into Bethlem that branch sprong ryght.
>
> The fourth branch, it sprong to hell,
> The deueles powr for to fell,
> That no sovle therin shuld dwell,
>   The branch so blessedfully sprong.
>
> The fifth branch, it was so swote,
> Yt sprong to hevyn, both croppe and rote,
> In euery ball to ben owr bott,
>   So blessedly yt sprong.[235]

(Heed and listen, both old and young, how the rose began to blossom; to our liking, a fairer rose never blossomed in king's land. There are five branches of that rose, which are both fair and lovely; of a maiden, Mary, heaven's queen, out of her bosom the branch arose. The first branch was of great honor, that blessed Mary should bear the flower; there came an angel from the tower of heaven to break the devil's bond. The second branch was great in might that grew on Christmas night; the star shone and gleamed bright so one could see it day and night. The third branch began to grow and spread; it led three kings to the branch, to Our Lady in her childbed; that branch grew straight into Bethlehem. The fourth branch grew down to hell to destroy the devil's power; so no soul should dwell therein, the branch grew so full of blessing. The fifth branch was so sweet it grew to heaven, both top and root, to be our salvation in every trial, so blessedly it grew.)

The (perhaps deliberately) naive charm of the poem notwithstanding, it is heavy-handed in its insistence on espaliering every branch into place on its grid of stanzas. And in that respect, it is typical of its age.

The carol just quoted verges on being an example of another means of unifying a poem, namely, miniature allegory. On the reduced scale at which it figures in lyric, allegory could be described as a static and verticalized form of metaphor, with each element reaffirming a single external sense, rather than dynamically questing forward after a sense that changes and grows with the searching. So far as medieval metaphors join forces in a lyric, they will tend to adopt the relationship of allegory.

Of all traditions, the highly conceptual *Spruchdichtung* makes the most frequent use of miniature allegory. Elsewhere—for instance, in Provençal poems for the Toulouse *consistori*—it is characteristic of the very end of the

Middle Ages, when little allegories and great were all the fashion, whether
as *blason* and *devise* or as the basis of a vast religious treatise. The Belgian
trouvère, Jacques de Baisieux (second half of the thirteenth century), produced one of the most interesting and original pieces of miniature allegory
in medieval religious lyric; he begins his poem with a *recusatio* of a full-
scale gloss on the Ave Maria, saying that he is capable of glossing only the
name "Maria," and a series of loosely connected mercantile metaphors
leads up to the following passage near the end:

> Si vos pri que me desloyés
> Et qu'amenuisiés la grant dete
> Ke j'ai envers vo duc fil faite,
> Si que por le marc prende malhe;
> Planez et l'escrit et le talhe,
> En quoi mes detes sont escrites,
> Si que jà mais ne soient lites;
> Car por payer ai pou monoie,
> Ma terre en tote ordure moie;
> Il n'y croist fors herbes savages,
> Chardons, orties, joins marages.
> Tant i a este en jussiere
> K'ele est devenue bruiere,
> Si n'i croist nus biens, n'i repaire
> Fors savagine deputaire,
> Ki mon cuer me vuet devorer,
> Cant j'i entre por laborer.
> Dame, si n'iert ja laboree
> Sans vos, car si est enborree
> K'entrer n'i puet hace ne bece,
> Et si est si dure et si sece
> Que on i pert quanc'on i same;
> S'arosee n'est de vos, dame,
> Laborage ai trop mal asiu.[236]

(And I ask you to unbind me and reduce the great debt that I have incurred
toward your son the duke, such that he will take a penny on the dollar; erase
the writing and the taxes in which my debts are written, so that they may
never be claimed; for I have little cash to pay with, my land is covered with
scrub—nothing grows there but weeds, thistles, nettles, rushes. It has been
briar and bush so long that it has turned into a heath, and nothing good grows
there, nothing lives there but vile-looking brambles, which gnaw at my heart
whenever I go to work it. Lady, it will never be worked without you, for it is so
neglected that neither hoe nor spade can penetrate, and so hard and dry is it
that one loses whatever one sows—unless it is watered by you, my Lady, I have
ill spent my toil.)

The agricultural comparison on which these lines are based has its roots in Scripture and the late medieval figure of the Plowman who holds center stage in Langland's great poem, in *Der Ackermann aus Boehmen*, and in many another text of the period. The energy with which Jacques de Baisieux develops the comparison threatens to bury the tenor in the swarming detail of the vehicle; one begins to attend to the description of the abandoned field for its own sake, and to forget that it is only a fancy and the real object here is the state of the author's soul. More striking still is what happens in a poem by Hugo von Montfort (1357–1423), unfortunately too long to quote here.[237] It begins as a prayer to an angry God, and one finds oneself in the familiar surroundings of the much-used ship-allegory of antiquity and the Middle Ages; but midway through what one had thought an imaginary voyage, the ship suddenly has become a real ship, the storm a real storm, and the allegorical problems with the tackle an actual incident in a voyage to Palestine. This encroachment of the concrete reality of the physical world upon the abstractions it is supposed to illustrate is an important phenomenon in the general use of metaphor in the Middle Ages, one we shall return to in the next chapter. In Jacques and in Hugo, because the metaphor has taken on the density and horizontal coherence of allegory, this pervasive effect is particularly spectacular.

In sum, two perils threaten the miniature allegory: an excessively mechanical relationship between tenor and vehicle, and a relationship in which the tenor becomes an excuse for gratuitous elaboration of the vehicle. Whether in Italian, German, Latin, French, Provençal, or Spanish, and whoever the poet, few poems founded on miniature allegory pass this Scylla and Charybdis safely.

Besides argument, metaphor, and allegory, authorial personality, expressed in attitude or tone, can work to give a text unity—in this case, the unity of the individual speaking voice. But as has been stated, medieval feelings about the proper function of poetry gave little encouragement to such a display; religious lyric in particular is very unaccommodating. Nonetheless, a Latin poet like Gottschalk of Orbais or Walter of Châtillon, a Greek poet like John Mauropus, an Italian poet like Jacopone da Todi, a German poet like Oswald von Wolkenstein, and French, Provençal, and Iberian poets like Gautier de Coincy, Peire Cardenal, and Alfonso el Sabio, will sometimes, perhaps even regularly, assert their particular personalities and situations strongly enough in their religious lyrics that they take on a nearly modern experiential unity. For just this reason, one warms to them today, and their work finds editors and a place in anthologies. But one must also remember that they are exceptions in this respect not just because they are more gifted (though that is certainly a factor) but more significantly because they were swimming against the current of their civilization. It is easy to forget this fact when the most mediocre poem and poet commonly strives today to create the illusion of personal presence. Besides, song favors objectification and the adoption of roles, and most medieval lyrics were either meant to be sung or conceived of in terms of a tradition that grew out of song and still retained its characteristics. For this and for other aspects of medieval literature the modern reader must make allowances.

Finally, a poem may achieve unity through the coherence of its theme or motifs. The verbal postures of prayer, praise, or instruction in themselves confer a degree of order upon a text. The "lyric plot" of the "we/thou" relationship of liturgy and the "I/thou" relationship of devotional poetry provides a situational outline within which the poem acts.[238] In turn, the very familiarity of Marian or Christological, penitential, mystical, meditative, hymnic, or supplicatory motifs guarantees a medieval religious lyric a degree of coherence. In this case, however, the difficulty lies not in the internal relationships of the text, but in its external, intertextual attachments. Not only does a lyric cohere with itself, it coheres so completely with poetic and religious tradition that it lacks a distinct identity. General unity makes particular unity almost impossible; it is as if one were trying to make out a white disc against a white wall—where are the edges? And if one tries to remove it from the wall to see it better, one discovers that it and the wall are all of a piece.

No doubt this description of the case overstates the truth; no doubt many poems do not fit the description. Still, it may serve to convey the surprising effects of an "aesthetic of identity" upon poetic unity and coherence. Without an understanding of these effects, one cannot hope to do medieval poetry even rough justice, either as reader or as critic.

3

RHETORIC

In the foregoing chapters, the discussion has moved from the widest and most abstract conceptual issues involved in the study of medieval religious lyric through its extrapoetic functions in medieval life to large-scale internal matters such as genre, form, and structure. In this final chapter, our eye will move closer to the subject, scrutinizing the small-scale phenomena of rhetoric as they determine the fine detail of these poems.

First, however, one must take note of the fact that the rhetoric of medieval religious lyrics is homogeneous in neither its composition nor its origins. Three major traditions entered into its creation: traditional religious language, which was itself a composite, created from a fusion of Semitic (scriptural and nonscriptural) and Greco-Roman habits of cultic diction and syntax; traditional poetic language, in the shape of the pagan and Christian "classics" studied at school and also in the shape of living poetic practice; and traditional rhetoric, inherited from antiquity and partially recast in the Middle Ages, in its own origins a formalization of the linguistic patterns of poets and orators. From their respective beginnings, each of these three traditions developed in anything but isolation; indeed, they were in a state of constant interaction from well before the beginning of the Middle Ages; but each tradition had its own canon of texts and thereby exercised a separate, if cooperative, effect on medieval authors.

Major contributions to the study of religious language have been made by Eduard Norden (*Agnostos Theos*), Friedrich Heiler (*Das Gebet*), several students of Hennig Brinkmann, and, most recently, Ricarda Liver, whose *Nachwirkung der antiken Sakralsprache im christlichen Gebet des lateinischen Mittelalters* unfortunately disregards liturgical prose prayers but does provide an exhaustive study of lexical, rhetorical, syntactic, and motival features that suggest a continuous tradition running from Greco-Roman religious language through medieval Latin religious lyric to the age and language of Dante.[1] There is also a considerable literature on aspects of liturgical prose style.[2] For reasons of space, it is impossible to reproduce the results of these scholarly investigations here; the interested reader who is equipped with a reading knowledge of German would be best advised to consult Liver's book and, with the help of its footnotes on earlier scholarship, work back from there. The skein is a tangled one, requiring the most scrupulous attention of anyone attempting to assign separate importance in any given case to one of the several major strands. For medieval religious lyric, the Latin and Greek translations of the Bible have a continuous and direct effect on writers; they also have an indirect effect through their shaping influence on the liturgy and on religious prose.³ Greco-Roman religious language is mediated in the Middle Ages by (again) the liturgy, especially its prose prayers, and by Christian-Latin poetry from late antiquity; but it was also available to the educated via their contact with pagan poetic stylizations (Vergil, Ovid, and others) such as those Liver and Norden have studied. In addition, Christian religious lyric of course created its own traditions, which acquired force with the passage of the centuries and the creation of authoritative poetic texts exemplifying the best in these traditions by authors like Ambrose and Venantius Fortunatus, in the West, or Romanos, in the East.

As we saw in the sections of chapter 2 that concern religious imitations of secular forms, genres, and motifs, the influence of secular poetry ought not be underestimated. The lack of formal and musical distinctions between secular and religious song, mentioned earlier, favored their interaction, and the activity of many poets in both areas, either concurrently or successively, made interaction of various sorts even more likely. So it is not surprising that poetry concerning secular love or friendship (the *chanson d'amour* or the Latin *amicitia* poem) played a major role in shaping the language and motifs of devotional and mystical poetry, indeed, in shaping the piety that lies behind both. Another secular, or partly secular, sort of poetry that affected religious lyric, especially in the hymnic mode, was panegyric, concerning which the arts of rhetoric had a good deal to say (see below). From the early Middle Ages on, verse and prose panegyric is richly represented in medieval Latin and has recently been studied by Annette Georgi (*Das lateinische und deutsche Preisgedicht des Mittelalters*); though there is less extant evidence, vernacular panegyric must also have had its impact—in Old Norse, for instance, the skaldic tradition of praise poetry leads directly into the religious *drápas* of the twelfth through fourteenth centuries. Panegyric became the dominant mode in the later development of the mainly hagiographical *kanon* and *kontakion* (ninth century on) and in the Marian poetry, Latin and vernacular, of the end of the Western Middle Ages. The degree of adherence to rhetorical rules varies widely, and in most cases these rules were probably mediated by poetic practice. One can say that the more formal the panegyric, the emptier and the colder it seems to us. The better medieval work in the mode maintains a warmth and informality that reflects a more truly Christian spirit.

As represented not only by Vergil and Homer but by late antique pagan and Christian poets as well (cf. Claudian, Prudentius, or Sedulius), the rhetoric of epic or epiclike narrative also left its imprint upon medieval religious lyric, particularly liturgical poetry. To it, and to panegyric, may be traced the high style of quasi-narrative hagiographical hymns and the medieval taste for abrupt apostrophes interrupting the course of a third-person exposition. In Greek and Latin, at least, I believe there is a pervasive influence of "epic" rhetoric on medieval poetry, perhaps traceable to the use of Vergil, Homer, and their imitators as the fundamental texts of education (for the sense of "epic" intended here, cf. the German phrase *epische Rede*). To modern ears, this presence of the "epic" in medieval religious poetry, constituting as it does a virtual antithesis to what we find appropriate to the lyric today, is especially disconcerting. One should understand that redemptive history is a constant background to this poetry, so that sacred persons, actions, and events never lose their participation in a culturally shared narrative, and that on this basis there is good warrant for the "epic" coloring of many an apparently "lyric" medieval religious poem.[4]

Finally, antique rhetorical treatises and medieval *artes poetriae* also figured in the education of the poets who wrote Latin, Greek, and most vernacular religious lyric. By and large, I believe scholars have overestimated the influence of these texts on medieval poetry. So far as I can see, their importance is close to negligible for vernacular texts and secondary to the other factors already covered here for texts in Greek and Latin, with the major exception being secular Latin school poetry and its closest Eastern relation, Byzantine epigram. In religious lyric, certainly, one rarely finds any but the simplest of "tropes," and these follow the model of earlier religious lyric rather than the precepts of the treatises. Such influence as the rhetorical tradition enjoyed was a highly mediated one, often in fact involving classical poems that themselves had strongly affected that tradition in antiquity. Still, even if aposiopoesis, hysteron proteron, chiasmus, and their ilk seem to have had little or no hold on medieval religious poets, some tropes they use do seem to owe a certain debt to formal rhetoric. For instance, Jacopone da Todi's unusual taste for the brevity formula is probably due to the rhetorical learning he acquired in the course of his education. Nonliturgical poems beginning or ending with an aphorism remind one of Geoffrey of Vinsauf's counsels on the uses of the *sententia*. The wide use of the *aporia* (which had good scriptural precedent too, of course) and the inadequacy topos (which seems more specifically "literary") may well derive in part from the experience of rhetorical as well as poetic texts, though even without knowledge of the rules of panegyric a Christian trying to do God or the saints justice would be likely to resort to such figures. In some Marian poetry, the *effictio* (derived from antique precepts concerning *ekphrasis*), mediated by love-poetry, shapes description of the Virgin, and it may be at work in poems on the *imago pietatis* as well. Notions about prologues and exordia may also have had a general effect on hymns. One can even try to apply the categories of the rhetorical treatises; for instance, one could say that medieval hymns often begin *a persona eius de quo loquemur* (i.e., focusing on the nature of the person under discussion), expressing a sense of personal or general *aporia* and our general obligation of praise.[5] But it seems rather a waste of energy to continue trying to force poetry into conceptions developed in connection with the training of orators, as antiquity, the Middle Ages, and the Renaissance did. For the most part, poetic practice continued, quite sensibly, to pursue its own course in accord with its own customs, little affected (except to its harm) by formal rhetoric. As this was especially true of medieval religious lyric, the rest of this chapter will pay little direct heed to rhetorical treatises, even though it appropriates some of their terms. Finally, I wish to express my complete concurrence with a position best expressed by Paul Zumthor at the start of the second section of his *Langue, texte, énigme*:[6] rather than a single medieval rhetoric, there are several medieval rhetorics, all deriving from an instrumental view of language. It is the antique tradition, encompassing a great deal more than formal rhetoric, rather than artificially separated aspects of that tradition that one should think of as influencing medieval literature. Medieval literature works within a general sense of the antique tradition rather than as a specific response to "source" passages in Cicero or the *Ad Herennium*. In such a model, rhetoric assumes its proper role as a subsidiary of literature and not its mistress.

i

The first group of rhetorical figures or practices I will discuss involves the handling of time and space in medieval religious lyric—that is, the annihilation of time and the collapsing of space. In one way, the medieval view of time is resolutely historical and linear, a continuum proceeding from Creation to eschaton. In other ways, it is throughly unlinear and ahistorical. The important events of sacred, redemptive history belong to the believer's present; Nativity, Crucifixion, and Resurrection are forever actual, and they are paradigms for the spiritual history of each individual Christian. In addition, the typological habit of mind severs the continuum of history and stacks the segments atop one another in a hierarchy of vertical correspondences that is fundamentally analogous to the poetic habit of mind and so lends itself with particular force to poetic treatment. Finally, the church-year converts the straight line into an infinitely repeatable cycle, symbolizing in its annual commemoration of the great events of sacred history, in the complex dedications of the Office (especially in the later Middle Ages),[7] and in the daily performance of the Eucharist the extratemporal reality of what it celebrates, and thereby inculcating by action what theology enjoins by precept—a simultaneous awareness and imitation of God's entire historical activity on mankind's behalf.

No wonder then that the language of medieval Christian religious lyric in Europe, like religious language in other periods and faiths, implies the insignificance of time. The only time that really matters is the time left in which to be saved or damned eternally. As for space, medieval notions of its nature were experiential rather than abstract and mensural. In any event, centuries of missionary work, as well as the breakdown in political and commercial links to the Near East, had converted the real Palestine into a country of the mind whose borders included all mankind. Only after several of the Crusades had come and gone, and then only very rarely, do we begin to find Palestine treated in poetry as the real place it still was for fourth-century Iberian pilgrims. Even in a world aware of its physical geography and knit together by excellent transportation, religious language resists recognizing the legitimacy of space. Space removes and limits; it compromises universality and presence. Therefore, place-names like Jerusalem, Bethlehem, or even Rome (city of the martyrs) remain connotative tokens that do not correspond in any important sense to the real places of the same name one finds on the map or on the ground. A fortiori, when conceptions of physical geography were vague and pragmatic, the antispatial tendencies native to religion could work unchecked. (Apropros of the late medieval rage for pilgrimages, one can say that, aside from the charms of tourism, it was not the place that mattered, but the relics that gave the place its significance, and these were eminently displaceable—in fact, frequently displaced, or "translated," as it was phrased.) As nongeographical as the meaning of place-names was in medieval religious lyric, it is still remarkable how seldom they are used, as if even the indirect acknowledgement of physical space constituted an erosion of the instant accessibility of the sacred. In this respect, Christian religious poetry contrasts sharply with the toponomastic habits of Greco-Roman religion—but, of course, pagan religion grew out of the convergence of a preexisting multitude of local cults into a syncretism, whereas Christianity began as a coherent collection of texts and thereafter ramified gradually outward and downward to produce its own equally numerous local cults (of the Virgin, the saints, and so forth). In its poetic expression, then, which like other poetic expressions seeks to unearth the *prima materia* of things, Christianity naturally looks back to the nonspatial, nonlocal singleness of its beginnings.

Apostrophe is perhaps the most ubiquitous and potent instrument for the destruction of temporal and spatial distance. Based as it is upon the pattern of face-to-face conversation in real life, it necessarily implies that the speaker (and hence the audience or congregation) is in the presence of what is being addressed, and that the latter can reply. Its use is too constant in medieval religious poetry to reward a tradition-by-tradition description. One should only note how often it serves as a means of handling narrative, often quite artificially according to our tastes; but it is precisely narrative that threatens to impose the barriers of history and geography between the believer and the story being told, and apostrophe that acts as an antidote. Also, as emotivity and subjectivity increase (e.g., in devotional and mystical poetry such as one finds in the group of Old French poems from Lorraine mentioned before), so does the incidence of apostrophe. Last, apostrophe can function as nothing more than a means of formal variation, as it does in classical epic catalogues, relieving the monotonous recurrence of third-person description.[8]

Most rhetorical figures can indeed function in medieval religious lyric without any peculiarly Christian or religious significance attaching to them; the mechanical use of poetic devices, in which they become merely devices and no longer poetic, has never been uncommon in literary traditions. But two particular sorts of apostrophe seem to me always to have the additional significance described above in medieval use.

As-if-there apostrophe involves a fictive attempt by the speaker to intervene in an event that is historically past but spiritually present. It appears especially in meditative poems on the Nativity or the Passion, which the Church and its poets sought above all to make present to believers. Byzantine Greek, German, Catalan, and Spanish poetry all make significant use of this sort of apostrophe, and there are a few examples in Italian; interestingly, it seems to be absent from the Latin tradition, at least up through the thirteenth century. In Middle English, occasional passages in lullabies sung by "man" treat Christ's career as still in the future, and the carols occasionally call on us to "go to Bethlehem" (in soul rather than body), but this is a relatively weak form of the figure.[9] It takes on much greater intensity in poems addressed to the Virgin, such as Jacopone da Todi's "O Vergen plu ca femena," in which the poet telescopes Annunciation and Nativity, apostrophizes Mary repeatedly and passionately, and calls on us to "run, run" to see "eternal life wrapped in swaddling clothes."[10] A Nativity poem by John Mauropus (eleventh century) makes a similar appeal, bidding us "run with the shepherds" and treating the Nativity story as if it were happening before our eyes and the icon on which the poem is based were not a painting but a window on Christmas.[11] Even more striking are certain poems that involve an apostrophe to Mary during the Passion. In his "Al rei Jesus donada la sentenca," Pero Martines tells how he was present at the Crucifixion and spoke to Christ and Mary (like dream figures, though, they do not respond), closing with a shift into the present tense that destroys the narrative distance and a prayer for exactly the sort of reception of the Passion that he has just acted out.[12] Most remarkable of all is a passage in the *Rheinisches Marienlob*, a long thirteenth-century Marian panegyric for devotional use, in which the speaker addresses Mary, assuming the messenger role traditionally assigned to the disciple John. Though this passage is one of the high points of medieval Passion-poetry, it is far too long to be given in its entirety (vv. 779–896);[13] the following excerpts may give some idea of the power it derives from the fiction of direct involvement on the speaker's part:

> Shoền muder, meʒig dine trene,
> bedwinc ein luetzel din trurich gedene!
> din trene wundent 's lîven herze,
> van in wirt me sins herzen smerze.   (781–84)

*   *   *

> Schonet, schonet, unmilde man,
> disen man, de nî schult 'n gewan!
> of schonet doch dit vroewelin,
> der dî slege machent groʒe pin!
> ir herze groʒe wunden entfeit,
> als ůr hant irn lîven sun sleit.   (827–32)

*   *   *

> Owi, dî galge si is so swar!
> kum, wir machen uns offenbar
> ind helpen im sin krueze dragen
> bit unsen trenen, bit unsen klagen!
> Vil schoene můder, beide min,
> laʒ mich dins růn gesselle sin!
> du bis snel, du loeufs so sere,
> so mich min tracheit so ser beswere.   (839–46)

*   *   *

> He wart nachet, dat he snel were,
> mich zu erloesen, min erloesere;
> he wart nachet, als he war,
> dů din magtdůn sin genas.
> nachet quam he in dit lant,
> he vůr ouch hin al an gewant.   (853–58)

*   *   *

> wî mach din herze disen strit liden!
> Leider ich bin dir alzů verre,
> dat ich sî al, dat dir werre.   (872–74)

*   *   *

> Wan gif uns self bit dinem munde
> dines herzen war urkunde!
> du versteis din herz aleine,

klag self din rüen, maget reine!
din klag mach alle herzen brechen.
ich wen, du moechtes alsus sprechen.   (891–96)

(Fair mother, moderate your tears, restrain your sad song a little! . . . Cruel
man, spare, spare this man, for sin never touched him. Or at least spare this
virgin, whom the blows cause great pain! Her heart takes great wounds as
your hand strikes her dear son. . . . Alas, the gallows, how dreadful they are!
Come, we'll show ourselves and help him carry his cross with our tears, with
our laments! Fairest mother, wait for me, let me be comrade to your grief! You
are quick, you run so fast, my indolence makes me so very heavy. . . . He is
naked, as if in a hurry to save me, my savior; he is naked, as he was when your
virginity enjoyed him. Naked came he into this land, he goes forth too without
a rag. . . . How can your heart bear this strife! Alas, I am too far from you to
see all that besets you. . . . Then give us yourself from your own lips the true
testimony of your heart! Only you understand your heart; lament your sorrow
yourself, pure maid! Your lament can break all hearts. I think you might speak
thus. [A *Marienklage* in lyric stanzas and almost four hundred lines long
follows.])

Here, as in Pero Martines's Passion poem, Mary makes no response, except
in the form of the *planctus* the poet puts in her mouth while pretending to
ask her to speak for herself. Besides the vivid imagination of direct participation in the events of Good Friday, the reader should note the expansion of the speaking "I" into the first person plural at vv. 840f.; it of course
reveals the ultimate goal of the text, which is to infect the readers or hearers
with the feelings the speaker expresses. Perhaps the finest achievement of
the passage is the complete naturalness with which spiritual meanings arise
out of physical details such as the speaker's lagging pace or his distance
from Mary; for instance, the sight of the gallows, one deduces from examining the poem's juxtapositions, slows the speaker down, and even his exhortation to his readers to help Christ carry the cross turns out to be in part an
evasion of his own duty to "keep up" and act personally. How subtly these
points are made, and how effectively in eight lines, when eight pages of sermon would be more typical of the age! In general, and particularly here, the
heavier the use of as-if-there apostrophe, the higher the poetic energy and
achievement.

Toward the end of the excerpts from the *Rheinisches Marienlob*, the poet
gives us an example of the second sort of apostrophe that I believe always
has a particularly religious significance: *do-as-you-did apostrophe*. This is
characterized by an injunction on the speaker's part that the addressee do
something that we in fact know, or believe, the person in question actually
did. In the case of the *Marienlob*, Mary is asked to lament her sorrows at
the foot of the cross when medieval tradition had already presented her as

doing precisely that, unrequested and spontaneously. In fact, however, this figure is quite unusual in any of the vernaculars, including German, and entirely absent, to my knowledge, from most of them. As in German, there are a handful of examples in Italian, in response to the Annunciation or as *compassio* with Mary and Mary Magdalene at the Crucifixion; two of the equally scarce German examples are translated from Latin, and most concern the Nativity. By contrast, the figure is not at all unusual in nonliturgical Latin poetry and in Greek. Josephus's apostrophe in a liturgical piece to the Magi is representative of its use in both traditions:

Φαιδρυνέσθω ἡ γῆ,
τὸν πρὶν αὐτὴν κοσμήσαντα
    δυναστείᾳ πολλῇ
πολυειδέσιν
ἄνθεσιν
ὑποδεχομένη
σπηλαίῳ τεχθέντα.
'Ανθρώπων γένος,
ἀνακαινίσθητι
καὶ σκίρτα καὶ χόρευε.
Σὺν δώροις, Μάγοι,
ἰδεῖν προφθάσατε
τὸν 'Εμμανουήλ. Βρέφος θεάσασθε,
ποιμένες, τοῦτο
μετὰ ἀγγέλων·
ὑμνολογήσατε ὁμοῦ·
Δόξα, βοῶντες, τῷ Θεῷ
ἐν ὑψίστοις, εἰρήνη
ἐπὶ γῆς, ὅτι
ἐτέχθη
    παιδίον νέον,
    ὁ πρὸ αἰώνων Θεός.[14]

(Let the earth be radiant, for it has received him who adorned it before with flowers of many sorts, with great power, born in a cave. Mankind, be made new, and leap and dance. Magi, hasten to see Emmanuel with gifts. Shepherds, behold the infant with angels; sing hymns together, crying, Glory to God in the highest, peace on earth, for the new child is born, God everlasting.)

The reader will probably feel that this figure has a particularly rhetorical, even oratorical flavor. If so, it would be with good reason. Its antecedents seem to lie in the *suasoria* of the Greco-Roman schools for orators under the Empire; one form the *suasoria* might take was advice to a historical or mythological person on their course of action, which would sometimes involve the speaker in persuading the addressee to do what the addressee was known to have done. In the learned languages, Latin and Greek, with their direct connection to late antique education, Christian writers turned the figure to poetic use, giving it the new significance of affirming their participation in and approval of God's plan of salvation. It was an exemplary form of yea-saying. But the vernaculars, resistant as usual to the more rhetorical figures, largely eschewed it.

They show no such inhibitions in their use of *prosopopoeia*. This figure summons up a sacred person and sets him or her speaking, thereby raising the effect normally achieved by apostrophe to a higher power. One is not confined to addressing God, Mary, or a saint; instead, they speak to us, annulling not only the distances of history and geography, but the spiritual distance between sinful earth and high heaven. In the process, the poem, or part of it, becomes fictionalized, since it is being treated as if it were an actual piece of speech, produced in a face-to-face experience of the sacred. Like apostrophe, prosopopoeia is a highly effective way of reducing the distance between audience and narrative, in this case by a sort of in-the-streets (of Heaven) interview. Since medieval Christians wanted particularly to get into touch with Christ and Mary, it is usually Christ or Mary who does the talking. But we also find Joseph speaking in Catalan, Paul in Middle High German, martyrs in Greek, one's good angel in Italian, David and Jephtha and other Old Testament figures in Abelard's Latin, Adam in Middle English, Judas in Old French, Andrew in Portuguese, God to Christ after the Crucifixion in Provençal, and the Magi in Spanish—as well as many other figures out of Scripture and hagiography.[15]

Prosopopoeia abounds in all traditions, but it seems especially common in Italian, where the *laude* showed a strongly dramatic bent from the beginning; the heaviest user is the fifteenth-century Feo Belcari, who was also the author of a sizable number of plays. Not because it is typical, but because it is inspired, I include the relevant passage from the Provençal poem mentioned above as an illustration of medieval religious lyric's use of prosopopoeia. (Technically speaking, the poem in question is a verse sermon on *Surgens Iesus mane* by Cerveri de Girona, but portions of it achieve great lyric power, particularly the stunning description of heaven in its sixth section—see p. 214.):

> E can lo viu sos Payres venir axi nafrats,
> Despullats e batuts, ferits e malmenats:
> "Ay Fill! Ta males gens so dis avets trobades
> e tan dures batalles sofertes e passades?
> Pauchs trobes qui·us aydesson a soffrir vostra guerra;
> be par que males gens estan la jus en terra.
> Mas be·m plats, pus avem nostres guerres vensuts

e conbrats tots aycells que aviem perduts,
  cuy may auran pausa."

(vv. 118–26)

(And when his Father saw him return so battered and maltreated, he said, "O Son! You found the people so evil, suffered and endured such bitter battles? Few you found to help you suffer your warring; clearly they must be bad people down there on earth. But it pleases me well, since you've won our wars and recovered all those we'd lost, who'll now rest forever.")

In fact, this is an example of a rare historical use of prosopopoeia, as one might have a character speak in a historical novel. What one normally finds is something like the following complaint of Christ to an errant soul written by Jacopone but like countless other Western derivatives from the (originally Byzantine) Improperia:

Omo, de te me lamento,
  che mme vai pur fugenno, et eo te voglio salvare![16]

(Man, I complain of you, that you keep on running from me, and I want to save you!)

Or perhaps Mary will suddenly appear, singing her own praises, as in this rondeau of pretty braggadocio by Guillaume Alexis (fifteenth century):

Vueillent ou non les maulditz envieux
Pucelle suis et demourray pucelle,
Et si m'a mis le laict en la mammelle
Le plus beau filz qu'on vit onc de deux yeulx.

Et se querez des dames en tous lieux
La plus bruyant, je dy je suis celle,
  Vueillent ou non.

D'un bel accueil courtois, sollatieux,
Simple en doulceur comme la turturelle,
Sage et prudente plus que femme mortelle,
Seulle sans si de maintien gratieux,
  Vueillent ou non.

Dont les amans qui seront curieux
Chanter de moy ceste chançon nouvelle,
Je leur dourray peult estre chose telle
Qu'en ce monde l'en ne trouveroit mieulx,
  Vueillent ou non.

Il est mon filz, mon pere et Dieu des Dieux,
Sa mere suis, sa fille et son ancelle.
Oultre je dy que sur toutes suis celle

Que par amours il ama jamais mieulx.
Vueillent ou non . . .[17]

(Whether or not the accursed envious like it, I am virgin and I'll stay virgin,
and the fairest son you've ever seen with two eyes has put the milk in my
breast. And if you're looking for the most brilliant of ladies anywhere, I say
that I am she, like it or not. Courtly and comfortable in my fair greeting, sweet
and simple as the turtledove, wise and prudent beyond mortal woman, alone
without reservation in gracious behavior, like it or not. As for the lovers who
will take the trouble to sing this new song about me, I may give them such a
thing that they'll never find better in this world, like it or not. He is my son, my
father, and God of Gods; I am his mother, his daughter, and his handmaiden.
Further, I say I above all others am she whom he always loved best in the way
of lovers. Like it or not . . .)

Besides illustrating how prosopopoeia can be turned to the ends of panegyric (and wit), this rondeau also shows how far late medieval poetry could
go in transforming Mary into a very earthly woman. To give examples of
other uses of prosopopoeia—say, for instructional ends, or as prayer—is
tempting but would be disproportionate; the use of the figure is as various
as the requirements of medieval religious lyric.

Put apostrophe and prosopopoeia together, and you will have *dialogue
between the speaker and a character* (or characters). Such dialogue lends itself to a question-and-answer format, with the questioner as our surrogate
and the informant a higher authority suitable for our instruction.[18] But it
can also serve for story telling, for praise, for prayer, eliciting a response
from, typically, the Virgin. In whatever form and for whatever purpose, this
sort of dialogue is quite rare in Old Norse, Middle English, Old French,
Provençal and Portuguese. In Catalan, it appears in popular Christmas
songs and here and there in Marian poetry. In German, it is infrequent and
normally has a didactic function involving Mary, Christ and a soul, body
and soul, or watchman and soul (where the soul acts as the speaker's self). It
is fairly common in Spanish (with Mary, with God, with death, and so
forth), common in Latin and Greek (particularly in scriptural epigram and
saints' calendars, neither of which is strictly lyric), and commonest of all in
the Italian *laude* (cf. Jacopone and Bianco), though some *laudari* lack any
examples. On the whole, this particular kind of dialogue seems less suitable
for lyric than for doctrinal or moral poetry. But there are a great many exceptions, among them this anonymous fifteenth-century *lauda* from the important Buonaccorsi *incunabulum* of 1485, *Laude fatte e composte da piu
persone spirituali*:

O vaghe di Gesu, o verginelle,
Dove n'andate si leggiadre e belle?

Dov'è'l vostro Gesu, ch'andar volete
Per suo amor cercando la suo luce?
Creature d'amor, se vo' 'l volete
Trovare: ed e' vi chiama ad alta voce,
Vedetelo confitto in su la croce,
Ch'ha sì il cor ferito ed esciene fiammelle.

O vaghe . . .

No' vegnam per trovar Gesu diletto,
Che 'n piccol loco l'abbiamo smarrito,
Per nostro male e per nostro difetto
L'abbiam lasciato, e s'è da noi partito:
Cercando noi n'andiam per questo lito
Per ritrovarlo, miser tapinelle.

O vaghe . . .

Ben si posson doler vostre bellezze,
Po' ch'n tanta viltà le dimostrate:
In voi non regnan piu le gentilezze,
Si come quando in grazia mostravate.
Ditemi un po', se voi vi contentate
Sequitar Cristo cosi poverelle.

O vaghe . . .

Più è dolente ciascuna di noi
E più ci lamentiam della sciagura
D'aver sì presto perduto colui
Che creò il cielo e l'umana natura.
Cercando vogliam gir nostra ventura
Di Gesu Cristo così poverelle.

O vaghe . . .

Ballata mia, s'i' fussi come fui,
E ritornassi agli anni piccolini,
Prima che i' dicessi mal d'altrui,
E dispiacer facessi a mie' vicini,
El prossimo amerei e Dio divino
E sempre i' amerei le suo fiammelle.

O vaghe . . .[19]

("O lovers of Jesus, O little virgins, where are you going so fine and fair?
Where is your Jesus, since you want to go for his love's sake looking for his
light? Creatures of love, if you wish to find him—and he calls you there with
loud voice—see him fixed high on the cross, for his heart is so stricken and

little flamelets come forth." "We come to find beloved Jesus, for in a lowly place we have lost him, in our sin and our weakness we have left him, and he has departed from us; we search along this shore to find him again, poor little things that we are." "Well might you mourn in your beauty, since you show yourselves to be in so bad a state; those charms no longer reign in you such as you displayed while in grace. Please, tell me, are you content to follow Christ in such wretchedness?" "Each of us feels more grief, and we mourn more for the disgrace of having so soon lost him who created heaven and mankind. We want to go seeking our fortune from Jesus Christ [even] in this wretchedness." "My *ballata*, if I were what I was and might return to those childhood years before I spoke evil of others and displeased my neighbors, I'd love my neighbor and God the divine and I would always love his little flamelets" [sung to the tune of "O vaghe montanine e pastorelle" ("O pretty mountain girls and shepherdesses")].)

This religious *ballata* is interesting on several counts. First, it shows how question-and-answer dialogue (in this case derived from the *stilnovo* poetry of Dante's youth) can be genuinely lyric. Second, it is a good example of fifteenth-century Italian *contrafactura*; notice how the opening line of this *lauda* alludes to yet varies the first line of its secular model. Third, it makes effective use of the situations and language of love-lyric for a religious purpose. Fourth, it shows the Italian capacity for sentimentality, which threatens the equilibrium of the Franciscan lyric from the beginning and becomes an acute problem by the fifteenth century, with its self-consciously naive poets. Fifth, it ends with an envoi (itself taken from secular lyrics) that contains a surprisingly early indication of an attitude to childhood that reaches full flower only in the modern period. In most of these respects, it is atypical. But then, so would any other single example illustrating dialogue between the speaker and a character be, if it had any claim to interest in itself.

Dialogue between (or among) characters in the poem, or genuine *dramatization*, fills similar functions and shows a similar distribution among the linguistic traditions. Edification is usually the primary purpose, sometimes narration (especially of the Annunciation, already a dialogue in Luke), very occasionally prayer, and almost never praise. As with dialogue between the speaker and a character, examples are the most plentiful in Italian, followed by Latin and Greek, and at a considerable distance by German, Spanish, and Middle English. In the Italian tradition, however, outside of the sacred drama, which grew out of the *laude*, and the *laudari* of Jacopone da Todi and of Urbino, dialogue between characters is surprisingly infrequent and therefore not to be viewed as simply a matter of course, particularly since we know that the Urbino *laudario* was itself especially indebted to Jacopone's influence. German cases cover a wide variety of subjects, such as the

Assumption, the approach of the Magi, the drama of divine anger, of Marian intercession, and of our prayer, the search for Christ, the need for repentance, debate among parts and faculties of the body, and purgatory and hell as discussed by God and Moses.[20] In Spanish, one finds a dialogue on the arrival of St. Vincent Ferrer in heaven, a Nativity playlet with speeches by the Instruments of the Passion, and a powerful exchange between St. Matthew and St. Dionysios (or Denis, *à la française*) by Lucas Hernandez (fifteenth century) in which the old story of Good Friday is imaginatively retold in the form of an *egloga* or staged dialogue.[21] As one would expect, in traditions where sacred drama had developed, dramatic dialogue constantly verges on or crosses over into outright drama. In Byzantine Greek, Romanos, working out of the Syrian hymnic tradition, makes brilliant use of dialogue in many of his *kontakia*. Much later, in the twelfth century, one finds dialogue enlivening the tetrastichs on the Bible by Theodore Prodromos. The following is a particularly amusing bit of Byzantine epigram, bringing one of the Egyptian plagues to vivid life with admirable economy:

> Τίς ποτ' ἔης; Ὅδ' ἐγώ. Ποῖ στείχομεν; Οὔτι
> [πω οἶδα.
> Ὤμοι ἐγώ, κατέαγα τὸ κρανίον. Ἐκ δὲ θυράων
> Τίς με λαβὼν ἀγάγῃσι; Χέρες ⟨προοδεύετ' ἀταρπόν.⟩
> Μωσῆς τήνδε κέδασσε μακρὴν καὶ ἀπείρονα νύκτα.[22]

("Who's that?" "It's me." "Where are we going?" "Haven't a clue." "Ouch, I've banged my head. Will somebody get hold of me and get me through this door?" "Put your hands out in front of you." Moses caused this long and limitless night.)

Latin examples are numerous and varied but rarely liturgical. Heart and Eye discourse, Mary and Cross, Christ and Mary, Mary and Gabriel, and so forth. Among a limited number of dialogues, Middle English happens to have the very best example of the subgenre of overheard conversations between Mary and the Christ child. Its main purpose is a fresh retelling of the life of Christ, which is contrived by making Mary ignorant of the future and letting Christ reveal it to her. Not least of the poem's virtues is that a lullaby is called for but never delivered—the Middle English audience would certainly have expected one after the vision opening in which the poet sees "A maiden child rokking" (v. 4, below)—and that the norm is instead turned on its head and the child tells its mother about its career-to-come. And there is a further inspiration, less major in its effects but still of unique delicacy in Middle English poetry: the unspecified "nith" (night) of stanza 1 is not revealed as "þis yolis-day" (this Christmas day) until the last stanza, when the story has been told and presumably absorbed. It is as though the author insists that the Birth of Christ must be grasped by the audience in all its implications, somber as well as glad, before it is possible truly to know the day of its celebration. I refer the reader to Brown XIV, no. 56, pp. 70–75 and quote selectively here:

  1. Als i lay vp-on a nith
   Alone in my longging,
   Me þouthe i sau a wonder sith,
   A maiden child rokking.

  2. þe maiden wolde with-outen song
   Hire child o slepe bringge;
   þe child pouhte sche dede him wrong,
   & bad his moder sengge.

  3. 'Sing nov, moder,' seide þat child,
   'wat me sal befalle
   Here after wan i cum to eld—
   So don modres alle. . . .

  6. 'Suete sone,' seyde sche,
   'Wer-offe suld i singge?
   Wist i neuere ʒet more of þe
   But gabrieles gretingge. . . .

  16. 'Moder,' seide þat suete þing,
   'To singen I sal þe lere
   Wat me fallet to suffring,
   & don wil i am here. . . .

  26. I sal ben so simple
   & to men so conning
   þat most partiʒe of þe puple
   Sal wiln maken me king.'

  27. 'Suete sone,' þan seyde sche,
   'No sorwe sulde me dere,
   Miht i ʒet þat day se
   A king þat þu were.'

  28. 'Do wey, moder,' seide þat suete,
   'þerfor kam i nouth
   But for to ben pore & bales bete,
   þat man was inne brouth . . .

  31. Samfuly for i sal deyʒe,
   Hangende on þe rode,
   For mannis ransoun sal i payʒe
   Myn owen herte blode.'

32. 'Allas! sone,' sayde þat may,
    'Siþen þat it is so,
    Worto sal i biden þat day,
    To beren þe to þis wo?'

33. 'Moder,' he seide, 'take et lithe,
    For liuen i sal a-ȝene,
    & in þi kinde þoru my mith,
    for elles i wroughte in weyne. . . .

37. Serteynly, þis sithte i say,
    þis song i herde singge,
    Alls i lay þis yolis-day
    Alone in my longingge.

(As I lay alone one night in my longing, I thought I saw a wonderful sight, a virgin rocking a child. 2. The virgin wanted to get her child to sleep without singing; the child felt she did him wrong and told his mother to sing. 3. "Sing now, mother," said that child, "about what will happen to me hereafter when I come of age—all mothers do this. . . ." 6. "Sweet son," said she, "What should I sing about? I've never known anything more of you than Gabriel's greeting. . . ." 16. "Mother," said that sweet thing, "I shall teach you to sing of what I will have to endure and to do while I am here. . . ." 26. "I shall be so simple and so cunning to men that the greater part of the people will want to make me king." 27. "Sweet son," then said she, "No sorrow could touch me, if only I could see the day you were king." 28. "Oh no, mother," said that sweeting, "I did not come for that, I came to be poor and remedy the disaster brought upon man . . . 31. For I shall die shamefully, hanging on the cross; I shall pay my own heart blood to ransom man." 32. "Alas! son," said that maiden, "Since it is so, why shall I await the day to bear you to this woe?" 33. "Mother," he said, "Take it lightly, for I shall live again, and as one of your own kind through my power, for otherwise I will have labored in vain. . . ." 37. Certainly I saw this sight, I heard this song sung, as I lay this Christmas day alone in my longing.)

Though no recorded examples exist from as early as this poem, various traits of its language suggest the existence of a ballad tradition, including the unusual ring closure, with its oral associations (see the end of chapter 2). The poem makes excellent use of this tradition, of the immemorial tradition of cradlesongs, and of the possibilities of dialogue between naive Virgin and miraculously prescient Infant. In sum, it has that fresh, popular quality that the late Italian *lauda* constantly seeks but rarely achieves.

The Middle English poem just quoted uses a *vision* as its framework. This and the *chanson d'aventure* opening provide a narrative setting for a number of Marian *planctus*, lullabies, panegyrics, and complaints in the later Middle Ages. The dramatic dialogue calls up a scene for the mind's eye; the religious vision or *pastourelle*, with its first-person narrator, not only creates or recreates a scene, it insists that the speaker saw it personally and that therefore so might we. The vision framework owes something to the religious tradition of dreams of the afterworld, but its principal derivation is from the secular dream vision so popular in the later Middle Ages; the *chanson d'aventure* frame that characterizes the *pastourelle* (from the twelfth century on in Provençal, Latin, Old French, then German) is entirely secular in its antecedents. As with the religious alba, there is a direct link between a significant presence of secular versions of the vision and of the *chanson d'aventure* and religious transformations. Consequently, neither the vision nor the *chanson d'aventure* figures in Latin or Greek religious lyric; the one exception I know of in Latin, a poem written in the twelfth century in the Anglo-Norman kingdom about Thomas à Becket, shows the influence of vernacular French love-poetry.[23] Vernacular traditions that lacked the *pastourelle* and made little or no use of the vision as a lyric frame, such as Catalan, Portuguese, Spanish, and Old Norse, similarly failed to produce religious analogues. In Provençal, where the *pastourelle* attained its greatest artistic heights, poets seem to have resisted converting it to religious ends. It is only in the late (fifteenth-century) poems entered in the contests sponsored by the Toulouse *consistori* that one occasionally finds a narrator telling how "recently, in Jerusalem, I saw the fairest woman in the world weep" (i.e., the Church, complaining of the Turk) or how "I heard" Nature complaining against death.[24] These few *vers figuratz*, as they are called in reference to their use of allegorical figures, have little that is either religious or lyric about them. But they do follow the usual pattern of reducing the *chanson d'aventure* opening to the merest gesture, so that the narrator is putative spectator and audience, but not participant. Examples are no more plentiful in German or Italian; around the end of the thirteenth century, Regenbogen (?) writes of how he went into the greenwood and dreamed of two allegorical pictures of religious significance (here we are dealing with the German genre of the *bîspel*, for Regenbogen dares his poetic rivals, especially Frauenlob, to unriddle the paintings), and a sixteenth-century text with a folklike opening turns the *pastourelle* situation into an encounter between the huntsman Gabriel and the maiden Mary out on the heath.[25] Neither is at all typical of vernacular use of the *chanson d'aventure* or the vision in religious lyric elsewhere. The few Italian examples are all marginal. In the Pisa *laudario*, a *planctus Mariae* opens with the minimal frame, "In front of a column/I saw a woman stand"; of three poems with *chanson d'aventure* openings in late fifteenth-century printed collections of *laude*, one begins "Lifting my eyes I saw fair Mary/With book in hand and the angel speaking to her" and concludes with a call to the audience to come see the *annunziata*; another opens similarly, describes the Nativity rather than the Annunciation, and ends with the poet's declaration of love for Mary and resolve to live a better life. Finally, a converted Jew, christened Giovan Battista, suddenly introduces a narrator into stanza four of a short non-*ballata lauda* on the Nativity: "I turned toward the East, I saw three crowned kings coming." This touch is so unusual in late medieval religious lyric that one suspects possible influence from Hebrew poetic tradition; at the very least, its position within rather than at the start of the poem shows it does not derive from the *chanson d'aventure*.[26]

By far the most examples of *chanson d'aventure* and vision openings appear in Old French and in Middle English. The extremely early "Quant li solleiz" combines a *chanson d'aventure* frame with the Song of Songs to create an account of "her" history by the personified Church; Gautier de Coincy writes a religious pastoral, "Hui matin a l'ajournee," in which he encounters the "fresche rose" Mary, but which consists mainly of an elaborate rejection of secular *pastourelle*.[27] In Middle English, the two frames serve as elsewhere for lyrics on the Nativity and Passion scenes, and extra-lyrically for body and soul debates (cf. the Latin tradition and its vernacular derivatives). Most of the numerous cases involving these frames allow them only a cursory role as introduction to a narrative; "I passed þoru a garden grene," however, has the narrator describe a series of three encounters and his movements from one to the next, much in the manner of a Chaucerian dream vision, and it closes with a call to worship and pray to Mary.[28] The relative frequency of these frames in Middle English may have been due to an enthusiasm for French poetic fashions in the fourteenth century, when French was still the language and culture of greater prestige, and thereafter a perpetuation of the acquired practice within the English poetic tradition. Whatever the case, these frames accomplish two important purposes: they establish a speaking human link between the audience and the sacred, and they deautomatize responses by their almost invariable fiction that the narrator does not recognize the sight he sees (Mary weeping or Mary with the Christ child, usually), in effect lending us fresh eyes with which to perceive overly familiar scenes. No doubt the increasing late medieval desire to divinize Mary (in reaction against extreme Franciscan humanization) had something to do with the failure of vernacular poets to make wider use of these frames. To the end, they remained an occasional, easily detachable feature of a few poetic traditions.

One could say that *rhetorical questions* and *exclamations*, like apostrophe or the *chanson d'aventure*, move the speaker toward the subject, rather than (like prosopopoeia or dialogue) the subject toward the speaker. They express a degree of excitement that the audience is to emulate and that is associated in normal speech with confrontations or urgent accounts of what one has just witnessed or experienced. In sum, the effect of these figures is to make the subject to which they are a response become much more immediate to us.

Rhetorical questions seem to be rather rare in Latin religious lyric, particularly in the hymn; poets use them, when they do, for moral poems or complaints. They are much more frequent in the Greek tradition, which is generally more receptive to dramatization of religious material. By contrast, exclamations are common in Latin as well as Greek liturgical and non-liturgical poetry.

Of the vernaculars, the *laude*, which like Greek religious poetry have a strongly dramatic bent, show the heaviest use of these figures. Jacopone da Todi, Guittone d'Arezzo, Bianco da Siena, Feo Belcari, Leonardo Giustinian all treat them as a natural part of their poetic repertory, and they seem especially characteristic of the fifteenth-century literary *lauda*. The ordinary *laudari* of the confraternities show little disposition to use either, however. This pattern has a close analogy in Middle English, where no poem in the first two volumes of Brown's anthologies begins with an exclamatory "O!," whereas the index of the third volume (fifteenth-century material) contains no fewer than nineteen such incipits. Meanwhile, literary religious poetry— for instance, Chaucer's "ABC" or the proem to the Second Nun's Tale—had been using both figures freely since the later fourteenth century. This evidence supports the inference that rhetorical questions and exclamations were perceived as features of high literary style, to be used only by consciously literary poets or only when literary tradition had infiltrated anonymous lyric, as it did in England in the fifteenth century. The fact that Christmas carols are full of instances of these figures is indicative of their clerical authorship and the qualifications one must introduce when describing the carols as "popular."

One finds a similar pattern in most of the other vernacular traditions. Both figures are rare in Old Norse, appearing occasionally in the post-1350 *rímur*, especially for Marian subjects, and almost never in earlier work. They are still rarer in Provençal religious lyric, which prefers a more natural and intimate tone between human speaker and divine subject. Spanish examples are scattered, mainly literary, and in most cases Marian. In Portuguese, Alfonso's *Cantigas* use the two figures sparingly, and Gil Vicente, in a lyric from an *auto* or play, has St. Augustine exclaim over God's goodness— as anyone who has read the *Confessions* would naturally have the saint do.[29] In Catalan, Llull (who is influenced by Latin tradition) and Pero Martines (whose plight would have even justified hysteria) will exclaim or interrogate, as do several poems for the *joyas* and a few semilearned Christmas songs and *planctus*. Except in the works of Gautier de Coincy, the most exuberant of early French writers of religious lyric, neither figure is common in Old French till the late fourteenth and the fifteenth century (cf. Italian, English, and late Latin religious lyric). In the *chansons* collected by Jaernstroem and Långfors from the thirteenth century, there are no examples in the first volume, very few in the second and later volumes. The Old French tradition shows a strong association between these figures and mystic, meditative, and penitential Marian lyric. Most German examples involve Mary in some way, though a few express a response to points of doctrine such as God's incomprehensibility or the notion of the *felix culpa* (fortunate fall). Several are prompted by the image of the Passion. The *Rheinisches Marienlob* and the "Monk of Salzburg" account for half of the occurrences I was able to collect. One can therefore state that, even though from the twelfth century onward these figures were freely available to Middle High German poets, anonymous as well as well-known, they were not often used. Here as elsewhere, vernacular receptivity to "rhetoric" is generally far lower than Latin or Greek receptivity. Vernacular lyrics that rely heavily on exclamation and rhetorical question thereby reveal their authors' literary ambitions.

Since this section deals with figures that enter into the handling of time and space in medieval religious lyric, it might be worthwhile to consider what part *direct references to time*, especially to markers of its passage, play in this poetry. The most important fact about these references is their rarity; another important fact is their conventionality when they do occur. The usual form such reference takes is the word for "today" in liturgical poems associated with particular dates in the church-year. Concerning Greek, the eminent liturgiologist Anton Baumstark stated that the "today" antiphon was "a type of almost infinitely wide distribution in liturgical poetry,"[30] and the same may be said of Latin, whether one is speaking of early hymnody, of the sequence, or of any other form or period. Given the liturgical function of references to "today," it is natural that they seldom figure in vernacular lyric traditions, except when a poem served for quasi-liturgical use. And even the *laude*, despite their frequent association with major feasts, do not often begin with an *oggi*, their equivalent for the liturgical Latin *hodie*. In Middle English, references to "today" belong to the carol, with its (usual) connection to Christmas and its public, collective performance. Catalan examples also belong to Christmas songs. In German, Christmas still dominates, but a few poems on the Passion or the Resurrection will include the reference, and one also finds it in simple prayers ("protect us today"). The few French examples, like most of the German examples, are by named poets: Gautier de Coincy (a translation of the liturgical sequence *Laetabundus* and a piece that also shows a strong local feeling for his monastery) and Guillaume Alexis. Two involve Christmas, the other a penitential prayer.

Spanish examples are equally scarce and concern Good Friday.[31] Old Norse, Portuguese, and Provençal seem to contain no examples at all. One notes that vernacular poems referring to "today" nearly all have to do with the two seasons of the church-year that attracted the greatest popular attention and participation and permitted paraliturgical hymn singing in the vernacular (cf. the German tradition, for example). All in all, the "today" opening is an extremely neutral and colorless way of designating the time of a celebration. It really expresses not the date but the fact of a collective social action at a particular moment all have agreed upon as symbolically meaningful. And that is why this motif or figure nearly always appears together with a declaration of or summons to collective praise and worship.

Though few and far beween, references to the *seasons* play a part in some particularly interesting poems. Unlike "today," they have a real content, even if it identifies one's position in the cycle of the year and not along the time line of history (as phrases like "in olden days" or "long ago" would do, if they ever appeared in medieval religious lyric). In their hunger for transcendence, Greek hymnody and nonliturgical poems spurn any mention of the season during which particular feasts occur. In Latin, however, from Venantius Fortunatus's Easter hymn "Tempore florigero" on, hymns on the Resurrection and processional hymns in particular sometimes open with a reference to or description of spring. The verses on spring in the Song of Songs (1 : 11–13) also provided a precedent for religious lyric to imitate. On occasion, the description can become quite elaborate in Latin,[32] but it is usually only an opening allusion. The frequency of references to spring in the *conductus* of the twelfth and thirteenth centuries, including Christmas (!) *conductus*, probably owes something to the popular motif of the reverdie as well as to the tradition of the Easter poem.

It is certainly the reverdie that underlies references to spring in vernacular religious lyric, sometimes complicated through its extension by analogy to the use of other seasons, a style that Provençal poets exploited with great success. Catalan, Spanish, and Italian contain no religious reverdies, though in the fifteenth century Lucrezia Tornabuoni, mother to Lorenzo de' Medici, and other Italian poets wrote *contrafacturas* of the May song "Ben vengas Mayo!" The Toledo manuscript of Alfonso's *Cantigas de Santa Maria* includes a lyric with the same incipit ("Ben veñas, Maio") and similarly intended to provide a religious substitute for the long popular tradition of secular *kalenda maya* songs;[33] other than in this Marian poem, the reverdie does not figure in medieval Portuguese religious lyric. Provençal examples are few and also Marian; Raimon Cornet, in a love song to the Virgin written for the *jeux floraux* at Toulouse, begins by declaring, "In spring, I'll make a song of fair, prime words, for you illumine the world with your beauty"; a later contestant speaks in his Marian *dansa* of the "new season."[34] The fact that the contest was held in spring and was literary in nature seems to have overcome Provençal reluctance to make seasonal references in their religious lyrics—after all, what object is there in reducing the usefulness of a Marian poem by tying it to some one part of the year, other things being equal? In Old French, thirteenth-century chansons tell how spring incites to longing for heaven or to praise for Mary. But one also encounters poems in which winter's onset prompts the image of Jesus as an orchard where spring never ends, autumn prefaces the expression of penitence, and spring awakens no response, for the world and its beauty is barren for the speaker.[35] The most striking use of the seasonal opening for religious purposes, and the most explicit about its secular antecedents, is perhaps in Gautier's Marian *lai*, "Ne flours ne glais":

> Ne flours ne glais
> Ne chant d'oisel qui s'esnaie
> N'ierent jamais
> En cose que je retraie,
> Ou je sui trais
> Sans ce que ja m'en retraie.
> Chanson voel faire
> Deu plus haut affaire
> Dont nus puist retraire:
> C'est de la tres vraie
> Dont fist sacraire
> Dex et son repaire
> Pour nous tous atraire
> Dex li debonaire,
> Par son sant sanc raire
> De sa douche plaie.[36]

(No flower or iris or song of bird that plumes itself will ever figure in the matter that I tell of, whither I am drawn without ever withdrawing myself. I want to make a song of the highest affair, of which none can tell; it is about the truest woman, of whom God made his sacrarium and repair to attract us all, God the gallant, by the holy precious blood from his sweet wound.)

In German, the fourteenth-century poet Der Huelzing's "Du lentze gut, des jares teurste quarte" modulates from a warm tribute to the beauties of spring into praise of Easter and a series of effective addresses to Christ, Satan, laymen and priests ("sing *Christ ist erstanden!*"), and finally to Spring itself. In this poem, the Latin tradition comes to a fine vernacular fruition. Muscatbluet opens with a reverdie and praises Mary as if she were a maid in the greenwood; elsewhere, he constructs a miniature allegory of redemptive history upon fields, woods, plants, and the coming of spring; a penitential poem begins with the coming of summer, which turns out to be a reminder to the poet that his life too is passing by and turning toward old age. Finally, the gifted Oswald von Wolkenstein writes a fine free paraphrase of Adam of St. Victor's sequence on spring and Eastertide, "Mundi renovatio".[37] Like another French fashion, namely, the *chanson d'aventure*, the reverdie had a special success in Middle English. Examples abound from the thirteenth century on; one of the earliest poems is

> Somer is comen & winter gon,
> þis day biginniþ to longe,
> & þis foules everichon
>   Ioye hem wit songe.
> So stronge kare me bint
> al wit Ioye þat is funde
>   in londe,
> Al for a child
> þat is so milde
>   of honde.[38]

(Summer has come and winter gone; the days begin to lengthen, and every bird you see sings in joy. Such a strong concern holds me, full of the joy found in the land, all for a child that is so mild of hand.)

Besides the reverdie, the stanza form (note the short lines) marks the French derivation of this poem. The child is of course Christ, and the poem's subject the Redemption, but the poet is deliberately veiling these facts behind as close an adherence as possible to his secular models. Interestingly, the association between Christ child, Easter, and spring is the same as one finds in the *conductus* of the same period (thirteenth century).

Yet again, we see how religious lyric can borrow from secular poetry and infuse the borrowed figures and motifs with a new meaning. And we also see how far the distribution of rhetorical features reflects tastes in secular poetry in the various traditions.

References to time take on one further form in medieval religious lyric: the count of years between Creation and the Redemption. Even though the four weeks of Advent were thought, in the late medieval period, to stand for the four millennia before the harrowing of hell,[39] the figure that poems use is usually 5000 years, and occasionally 5200 (in an evident attempt to give a symbolic meaning to the 52 weeks of the church-year). The figure 4000, 5000, or 5200 turns up in connection with mankind's exile almost a dozen times in Middle High German religious lyrics and several times each in French, Italian, and Middle English. Almost always, it reinforces a generally "popular" tone, such as one finds in a particularly irresistible form in the well-known "Adam lay i-bounden, bounden in a bond":

> Adam lay ibounden,
> Bounden in a bond:
> Foure thousand winter

> Thought he not too long.
> And all was for an apple,
> An apple that he tok,
> As clerkes finden
> Written in here book.[40]

(Adam lay in bondage, bound in a bond; four thousand winters he did not think too long. And it was all for an apple, an apple that he took, as lettered men find written in their book.)

The significance of this arithmetic is that the age before Christ was terribly long as well as dark and that it is over and done with. It is no accident that, despite widespread use of anno Domini chronology by the later Middle Ages, poets do not perform the simple calculation that would let them count the years from the Creation, or the Redemption, to the present. As I have said before, the relationship between God's actions and one's own spiritual present was not historical—it was immediate. To tot up the years would be to profane this relationship, even to erode the hope of eternal life by a reminder that centuries have passed and the world has changed and Christ has not yet come again.

The devices discussed in this section vary widely in importance. Some see universal use; some see regular use only in certain traditions; some are rarely used anywhere or have only a minor significance in themselves. In total, however, they constitute a powerful set of instruments with which medieval poets could impose the Christian view of spiritual reality upon their religious lyrics. Perhaps the most effective instrument of all was none of these figures and motifs, but simply the consistent absence of any acknowledgment of a normal human sense of the lapse of physical time and the weary fact of physical distance. Other "transcendental" sorts of medieval poetry express a similar view of "what matters" (cf. the *chanson d'amour*), but there is this-worldly poetry aplenty, particularly in the vernaculars of the later Middle Ages, to show that poets ignored time and space not out of a cultural blindness to them but out of deliberate choice.

ii

The next subject for discussion is the rhetoric of speaker-audience relations in medieval religious lyric. (I here assume the actual audience to be earthly and human, even when it is ostensibly heavenly, in accord with the view advanced in the Introduction.) In his relationship with his audience, the speaker has three major options: he may join it (often as a sort of hieratic cheerleader); he may mediate between it and heaven; or he may face and exhort it directly. These three options correspond to the roles of fellow worshipper, celebrant, and homilist, respectively and are themselves the roles the clergy fill at various points in divine service. Indeed, one may imagine the poet's place in the commerce of heaven and earth as that of a priest standing in the cross of a Christian church at the altar, facing it or the worshippers in turn, representative of an office not of himself, and channeling action and reaction beween heaven and the congregation; in turn, the congregation extends beyond the church door to include the penitents outside, the town, the kingdom, humanity, ultimately the cosmos to its remotest nook. Particularly for the vernaculars, one must add to this model the roles of storyteller, spiritual advisor, mystic, penitent, and man of letters, though all of these can be reduced to variants of the three primary functions of religious discourse (praise, prayer, instruction) and the three options for the speaker outlined above. Finally, the speaker may simply efface himself, vanishing into the traditional structures of his text, a model that is very common, particularly in hymnic poetry.

Here, however, we will be concerned with means available to poets who wish to establish a more active relationship with users of their poems. Several of the most important figures have already received attention in other connections, notably anaphora, argument, and rhetorical questions and exclamations. The first and third cast the speaker in the role of excited guide or insistent preacher, forcing a matter of particular importance upon the hearer's attention. The second may serve indirectly, when addressed for instance to Mary, to persuade the users of the efficacy of their supplication, and it may also serve directly as a device of homiletic persuasion. Since the latter moves us over into the domain of doctrine and morality, it will not be pursued; the former function was discussed in the closing pages of chapter 2. In addition, dialogue between the speaker and a fictive audience or audience member occurs often enough (especially in Byzantine epigram) that it too should be mentioned, but its function is unambiguously didactic rather than lyric.

Certain features of medieval religious lyric affecting speaker-audience relations have escaped much direct discussion, however. Perhaps the most prominent of these, for anyone acquainted with hymnic poems, is the *call to the audience* to praise, pray, mourn, sing, celebrate, or pay heed. Since such a call is aimed at involving all present in a collective action, it naturally occurs most often as part of the opening of liturgical poems, in which the fiction of congregational participation continued despite its actual cessation. Thus, one finds it particularly in Latin and Greek hymnody, in Catalan Christmas songs and Middle English carols, and in the Italian *laude*, which due to the penitential emphasis of many *laudari* are especially rich in calls to lamentation and to repentance. In German, one is called upon to take part in Christmas joy, to contemplate the Passion sorrowfully, or to praise the

Virgin—the meditative poem readily adopted a device originally meant to elicit public response, converting it to a call to private feelings. In Old Norse and Provençal, calls to attention are in a plurality; both traditions lack much in the way of meditative lyric or (during the medieval period) Christmas songs. Calls of any sort are infrequent in Old French, outside of Gautier de Coincy's Marian lyrics from his *Miracles* of the Virgin; by contrast, the lyrics from Alfonso's analogous miracle-collection are much more liturgical, issuing frequent summons to praise. Spanish examples show no particular pattern, except perhaps for a larger emphasis on song than is usual in other traditions. Outside of carols and moral poems, Middle English religious lyric rarely seeks this sort of relationship between speaker and audience.

Third-person descriptions of praise, sorrow, celebration, or the like, or impersonal assertions concerning the appropriateness of a collective activity or attitude often function as the equivalent of a direct exhortation.[41] As far as suasive force is concerned, there is little difference between saying *Deum cuncti concelebremus* (let us all worship God together) or *omne genus Deum celebrat* (every kind worships God). Such alternations play a large role in hymnody and can of course be used for subtle artistic effect; but often they are simply elegant variation.

Much more oblique, but quite normal in the late medieval meditative and in the penitential lyric, is the possibility of letting the *speaker* act *as paradigm*. In such a case, the emotional response to the thought of the Crucifixion or to the thought of one's sinfulness is demonstrated to the audience by the poem itself, with the expectation that we will benefit by the example set. From this viewpoint, even the most desperate penitential poem, with a speaker who doubts his ability ever to stop backsliding or even to take the first step toward reform, is exemplary—it shows us how seriously we should take our own spiritual situation, which may well be even worse precisely because we are complacent about it. Of course, penitential poems that take the form of a general confession were specifically intended to be used as a framework for individual penitence, but I am speaking of a more fundamental rhetorical function common to all penitential lyrics, even when they are unsuitable for universal application.

Less complex, and more common, is the contemplative or meditative poem in which the intense response of the speaker acts as a model for our own response. The normal emptiness of the poem's "I" allows any believer to make the poem and its sentiments his own; as one scholar, imitating Rimbaud, has put it, "Je est un rôle" (I is a role), and this role is open to all comers.[42] Greek examples of paradigmatic emotional response by the speaker are more numerous much earlier than in Latin, which prefers a more impersonal or collective mode up until the twelfth century. In a funeral hymn,

Theodore the Studite speaks of his personal shock at the sudden loss of the dead man; Symeon the New Theologian explicitly presents his response to the presence of God as a model for us; John Mauropus introduces his personal reaction into his poems on the icons for the great feasts (cf. no. 7, on the Crucifixion, where he says, "I must die with You"); and Theodore Prodromos lends an intensely personal turn to an epigram on the conversation between Christ and Nicodemus:

> Τῆς ἡμέρας τὸ δόγμα νυκτὶ μανθάνει
> Ὁ Νικόδημος καὶ φυγὼν νύκτα πλάνης
> Τὸν ὄρθρον εἶδε τῆς νοητῆς ἡμέρας.
> Ὡς εἴθε Νικόδημος ἤμην, Χριστέ μου.[43]

(By night Nicodemus learns the doctrine of day, and fleeing the night of error he sees the dawn of intellectual daylight. Would that I were Nicodemus, Christ mine!)

Shaped by the spirituality of St. Francis, Latin poetic examples of the paradigmatic speaker are quite different in character from these Greek poems. An outstanding passage from John of Howden's long and remarkable *Philomena* should make this difference clear:

> Ut sub sole tristi nascentia
> Pressa gelu pallent rosaria
> Regis languent ora vernantia
> Et exsanguis frons livet regia.
>
> Sed, Rex pie, cur non compatior,
> Cum te dolat manus immitior?
> Adamante nonne sum durior,
> Qui cruore mersus fit mollior?
>
> Mors et dolor, simul irruite
> Et cor mihi, rogo, confodite!
> Mentis petram rigentem scindite,
> Condolentem dolenti facite![44]

(As rosebushes opening under a sad sun turn pale, laden with frost, the blossoming face of the king droops and the royal bloodless brow grows white. But, merciful King, why do I not suffer with you, when a crueller hand batters you? Am I not harder than adamant, which softens when dipped in blood? Death and pain, attack together and pierce my heart, I beg you! Cleave the frozen rock of my mind, make me suffer with the sufferer!)

Turn the apostrophe to Christ in the second stanza into an apostrophe to the hearers, with the first-person verbs changed to the second-person, and you will have the unspoken message of this poem: why do *you* feel so little at the thought of Christ's agonies? Our success would be to attain the

speaker's stricken sense of his own emotional *aporia* before the infinite demands the Passion makes on the limited human ability to respond. One
might even say that our imperfections give us the opportunity of taking the
contemplation of the Passion as our never-to-be-completed lifework, on a
scale suggested by the four thousand lines of John of Howden's poem.

Naturally, most meditative poems do not equal the *Philomena* in vehemence. But the same sense of the human duty to respond and the impossibility of adequate response is pervasive in them. Nativity poems by their
nature take a happier view, yet even here the speaker feels overwhelmed by
the incommensurancy in human terms of what he sets before his mind's eye.
One of the best of the *laude*, perhaps by Neri Pagliaresi, expresses this ag-
ony of tenderness with great beauty, projecting it onto the Virgin:

> Quando chiamar tu ti sentivi mamma,
> come non ti morivi di dolcezza?
> Come d'amor non t'ardeva una fiamma,
> che t'avesse scoppiata d'allegrezza?
> Di ver che grande fu la tua fortezza,
> poiche la vita allor non ti finio![45]

(When you heard yourself called mamma, how did you not die of the sweetness? How did a flame of love not burn you, so that it consumed you with joy?
Truly how great was your strength, since your life did not thereupon end!)

Also in Italian, one encounters Jacopone da Todi blazing the mystic path
or setting an example of contempt for self, the flesh and the world; Bianco
da Siena babbling of the delights of the love of God; Leonardo Giustinian
praying Mary to keep him from melting away at the thought of the Christ
child suffering in the cold of the night of the Nativity.[46] Poets anonymous
and named deluge the users of the *laude* with their responses to sacred subjects, and all might join with the *sacerdos* (priest) in a *lauda* from Pesaro on
the Eucharist when he says, "Pigliate exempio omai del caso mio" (Always
take my case as an example).[47] Even a damned soul may serve for our edification, calling us to repent, though it cannot:

> Pero che el tempo si ma ingannato,
> Como voy vedeti in questo exempio,
> Questo exempio ve basta bene,
> Che sempre staro in queste pene.[48]

(Since time has tricked me so, as you see in this example, let this example suffice you, for I will remain forever in these pains.)

In this example (to echo the unfortunate soul), the didactic intent latent in
penitential and meditative lyric becomes explicit. The lyrical quality of these
poems depends on keeping it from emerging so starkly, as they generally
succeed in doing, but one should not forget that it is nonetheless present.

The other vernacular traditions offer examples aplenty and of much the same sorts. German poets provide us models of contempt for the world, desire for heaven, hunger for penance, mystic longing, anguished *compassio*, love for Mary (or Christ), and pious concern for one's fellow man. Catalan demonstrates the virtue of hope, joy at Christmas, sorrow at the Passion.[49] There is little difference from one tradition to another, except that where meditative poetry is scarce, paradigmatic use of the speaker will be too.

In a sense, all religious lyric is exemplary, and its speakers with it. He who praises or prays shows us how to act, that is, to speak, and at the same time supplies us with the words to do it in. Folquet de Marseille (fl. 1175– 1200) gets this point across quite clearly in a religious alba:

> Qui no sap Dieu pregar obs es que o aprenda
> et auja qu'ieu dirai et escout et entenda:
> Dieus, que commensamemens es de fota [tota?] fazenda
> laus vos ren e merce.[50]

(Whoever doesn't know how to pray to God needs must learn it—let him listen to what I say and hear it and heed it: "God, You Who are the source of all speech, I pay you praise and thanks.")

If what Folquet says in this poem is generally applicable to religious lyric, one sees why the fundamental functions of this poetry are ultimately inseparable: to pray is to praise; to praise is to pray; and to do either is to instruct. Thus, religious poetry as a whole (and not only meditative and penitential lyric) is inherently didactic; the question is merely to what degree it will stress this aspect of itself. No wonder then that it awakens such antagonism in the average modern reader.

Paradigmatic use of the speaker also lies behind the common practice of *self-apostrophe*. Here, the speaker's soul acts as a surrogate for the audience, allowing us to overhear an uninhibited harangue instead of becoming its browbeaten objects. In addition, the speaker's performance shows us what attitude to take toward our selves.

Self-apostrophe belongs particularly to the penitential lyric, with the soul-and-body debate as its objectified, dramatized analogue. A brief, nonliturgical poem in iambic trimeters by Theodore the Studite makes dignified use of this form of address:

> Ψυχὴ ταπεινή, δεῦρό μοι, δέξαι λόγον.
> Ὁ καιρὸς ὀξὺς ὡς δρομεὺς διατρέχων,
> ἐγγὺς τὸ τέρμα, καὶ παρελθεῖν οὐκ ἔνι.
> Μὴ δὴ κάνοιμεν ταῖς ματαίαις φροντίσιν,
> ἀντλοῦντες ὄντως εἰς πίθον τετρημένον,
> ξαίνοντες εἰς πῦρ, ὡς γελοιωδῶς ἔχει·
> ἀλλ' εἴ τι θεῖον εἴ τι σωστικὸν πέλει,

ταῦτα σκοποῦντες καὶ διώκοντες πόθῳ,
ὡς ἂν παρασταίημεν ἐν παρρησίᾳ
τῷ τῶν ἀπάντων καὶ Κριτῇ καὶ Δεσπότῃ,
τὸ πῦρ φυγόντες τῆς Γεέννης, ὡς γράφει,
καὶ προστρέχοντες τῷ παναρρήτῳ φάει.[51]

(Miserable soul, look here, listen to my words! The crisis is as quick as a run-
ner racing, the end near, and none can evade it. Let us not then be caught up in
vain thoughts, drawing water indeed in a sieve, carding into the fire, which is
laughable; but if there is anything divine, anything that can save, [let us] gaze
upon that and pursue it with ardor, so we may dwell in freedom with the
Judge and Ruler of all things, escaping the fire of Gehenna, as it is written, and
hastening forward in unutterable light.)

The Greek liturgical tradition, since it permits the first person singular, also
permits occasional self-apostrophe in penitential hymns; in Latin, self-
apostrophe is confined to nonliturgical poetry. Several of the vernacular traditions do not seem to use it, indicating that like many other figures, it was
felt to be too rhetorical, too much a part of "literature," that is, of Latin.
The only examples of significance I have discovered in Old French occur in
the Lorraine group of lyrics, where they concern the speaker's response to
the Crucifixion.[52] Several Spanish examples arise in the same connection,
while others exhort to Marian praise or issue reproaches for insensitivity to
Christ's love. In German, Heinrich von Laufenberg (fifteenth century) bids
his soul (or perhaps simply "the" soul—it is often hard to know which) to
rise and seek heaven or the Christ child in various poems. With his usual
vigor, Oswald von Wolkenstein apostrophizes himself, "Wach, menschlich
tier" (Wake up, you animal!), going on to argue for belief in God and to
describe his long-lived, obsessive love for his enemy's daughter that led him
to "break his shins" on God's commandments.[53] The literary *lauda* (cf. Jacopone da Todi, the Urbino *laudario*, Bianco da Siena, Feo Belcari, Francesco
d'Albizo, Leonardo Giustinian, Lorenzo de' Medici, and Savonarola) shows
by far the heaviest use of self-apostrophe of any vernacular tradition, which
is consistent with its other dramatic (even historionic) tendencies. Italian
poets call on their heart or their soul, or perhaps their tongue, to take spiritual or poetic actions of all sorts. Perhaps the most famous of these cases is
Jacopone's autobiographical *lauda*, "Que farai, fra Iacopone?" in which the
use of self-apostrophe powerfully communicates the estrangement from and
skepticism toward the self that Jacopone feels we all should cultivate.[54] In
fact, one may say that self-apostrophe is the perfect poetic expression of
that penitential self-discipline and self-examination which the fraternal orders sought to inculcate during the later Middle Ages. The connections between that religious enterprise and the increased awareness of the self and
its faculties that manifests itself in late thirteenth-century Italian secular
lyric would be interesting to investigate.

Often, the speaker maintains no more than a minimal presence in the poem. For objective praise or instruction, a greater prominence would be desirable. In such contexts the speaker may appear in the first person only to vouch for the truth or the importance of what he is saying, in a rhetorical figure sometimes known as *epiphrasis*.[55] In tone, it can be assertive, ironic, professorial, or merely informative.

> If man him biðocte,
> inderlike & ofte
> warde is te fore
> fro bedde te flore,
> wu reuful is te flitte
> fro flore te pitte,
> fro pitte te pine
> wat neure sal fine,
> i wene non sinne
> sulde his herte winnen.

(If a man bethought himself earnestly and often how hard the journey is from bed to floor, how sorrowful the trip from floor to pit, from pit to punishment that will never end, I daresay no sin would win his heart.)

> Ἐγώ, Διονύσιε, τολμῶ καὶ λέγειν,
> ὡς οὐκ ἐπιλάσθης ἐν γυναικὸς κοιλίᾳ.

(O Dionysios, I dare even to say it, that you did not forget in woman's womb.)

> Ut didici pro re triplici lux haec celebratur.

(As I have learned, this day is a day of celebration for three reasons.)

> Illius inquam Sabbati,
> Quod est ignarum termini.

(Of that Sabbath, I say, which is without end.)[56]

Generally, when the speaker's presence is larger than this, it is still no more than an expansion of the impersonal role epiphrasis represents. A troubadour best expressed the genuine feeling that sometimes animates the figure and reminds us of its origins in passionate living speech:

> Ma fes e m·entencios
> me valh·el vejaire
> que·m fan enan traire
> los fagz de dieu els sermos
> qu·ieu conocs ben qu·aondos
> no m·en puesc, tan volentos
> suy de dir sa gran honransa;

> e s·iey fatz outracujansa
> valha mi lo sieus perdos.[57]

(May my faith and my intent and my judgment avail me that make me set forth the deeds of God in speech; I am well aware that I cannot abstain from it, I want so much to tell his great honor—and if I overstep, may he forgive me.)

Even where epiphrasis lacks the impulse this poet describes, it still denotes the presence of a human spirit and a human voice concerned to persuade the audience to share its viewpoint. To some degree, then, it perpetuates the values of oral and aural poetry in the written form. For the Middle Ages, it must have summoned up not only the sermon situation but the jongleur or storyteller who breaks through the objective surface of his narrative to vouch for its human meaning in just the same epiphrastic way.

iii

Frequently in religious lyric, the primary ostensible relationship is between the speaker and an addressee in heaven rather than the speaker and the earthly users of his poem. As with the speaker-audience relationship dealt with in the immediately preceding section, most of the major rhetorical means medieval poets use in speaking to God and the saints have already been discussed. Logical argument and the special cases of *do ut des* and *ut potes* came up in the closing pages of chapter 2, and the dialogue with God, Mary, or the saints in the first section of this chapter. The tones poets use in addressing heaven cover the entire range of religious feeling: exuberant gratitude, hymnic awe, anguished remorse, passionate sympathy, mystic longing, and so forth. However, a few rhetorical figures that enter into these tonalities have so far eluded attention.

One of these is *indirect prayer*, which Aquinas describes in his commentary on the *Sentences* of Peter Lombard as *insinuatio*.[58] Rather than pray directly, the speaker describes intercessory prayer, assumes its results have already been achieved, or simply alludes to the practice of intercessory prayer by Mary or one of the saints. In this way, the citizen of heaven concerned is in effect given to understand what the users of the poem hope to obtain from him or her. Examples of *insinuatio* are not uncommon in Latin and Greek religious lyric; these lines from a sequence on St. Maximian by Hildegard of Bingen show how it is used:

> Tu es fortis et suavis
> in ceremoniis,
> et in coruscatione altaris ascendens
> ut fumus aromatum ad columnam laudis.
> Ubi intercedis pro populo

qui tendit ad speculum lucis
cui laus est in altis.[59]

(You are strong and gentle in ceremonies, and in the glittering of the altar you
rise up like the smoke of incense in a column of praise. There you intercede for
the people who reach out for the mirror of light to whom praise is on high.)

The movement of the smoke traces out the heavenward ascent of prayer, and
we are told that Maximian is there to intervene for his devotees, assuring
that their prayer will avail once it reaches heaven. By contrast to Latin and
Greek, vernacular examples are quite scarce. Pedro Bell, a Catalan poet,
ends a Marian poem for the Valencia *joyas* with indirect prayer; Guiraut Riquier closes a prayer to Jesus Christ with a reference to Mary's power to help
us with her prayers; Guillaume Alexis opens a *balade* to the Virgin by addressing her as "refuge for sinners who ask that it please you to help us in
peril by sea."[60] But by and large, vernacular poets avoid such an oblique
approach in favor of unambiguous supplication. Perhaps they felt less close
to heaven and less confident of its aid than poets who had the use of Latin or
Greek.

   Little has been said about style as such, and indeed stylistics lie outside
the scope of this book. One can usually detect an opposition between popular and learned that cuts across generic lines within a tradition, but for the
most part style is fairly uniform within medieval religious lyrics of a given
type within a single language or school of poets (cf. the Notre-Dame *conductus*, for instance). One striking late medieval stylistic development, not to
say aberration, deserves comment here because of its relevance to speaker—
heavenly addressee relations. Fifteenth-century Middle English writers refer
to it as the use of "aureate" terms or diction. It normally occurs in Marian
poems, where it seems designed to increase Mary's importance and therefore power to act, and perhaps also to prove that the speaker is sufficiently
cultivated to move in the highest circles of the society of the blest. One often
feels that "aureate" poems are guilty of conspicuous consumption, but of
words rather than commodities. The German equivalent is called *gebluemte
Rede* (cf. Frauenlob, Lesch, and other Middle High German poets from
ca. 1300 on). However, German writers usually handle elaborate diction so
that it seems more than merely decorative. In most other traditions, only an
occasional lyric, usually fifteenth century, will show aureate tendencies.
Consequently, one must view Middle English "aureation" as something of a
special case. It is produced by taking Latin words over wholesale and introducing them into one's verses as often as is linguistically possible. What was
natural in Latin becomes extremely artificial in English. Of course, this poetic movement is only one aspect of the assimilation of Latin by English in

the late Middle Ages and Renaissance, but it does seem to reveal a sort of cultural *arrivisme* that vitiates a good deal of late Middle English literature and may have been due to the late start English had as a literary language.

"Aureation" also owed something to the fashion for imitating the French, through whose language many of the Latinate words had in fact passed before being attached by English. The French began to absorb Latin diction and stylistic effects much earlier than most other Romance countries; Gautier de Coincy is a signal example at the beginning of the thirteenth century. As a result, the Latinate quality of French fifteenth-century Marian *balades* and *chants royaux* seems much more natural than it does in their English imitators. Nonetheless, not only do many of these poems resemble Middle English examples in their texture, they awakened conscious resistance in some poets. Pierre Fabri, for instance, bids writers not to practice such "vocabularizing" in "perpulchritudinous terms." [61]

In the right hands, "aureation" could produce splendid results. The so-called Scottish Chaucerians were gifted enough to use it poetically most of the time, and Dunbar in particular shows its possibilities in a famous, or notorious, Marian eulogy:

> Haile! sterne superne, Haile! in eterne,
> In Godis sicht to shine.
> Lucerne in derne for to discerne
> Be glory and grace divine.
> Hodiern, modern, sempitern,
> Angelicall regine,
> Our tern inferne for to dispern,
> Helpe! rialest rosine.
> Ave! Maria, gracia plena,
> Haile! freshe floure feminine,
> Yerne us, guberne, virgin matern,
> Of reuth baith rute and rine. [62]

(Hail! star on high, hail! in eternity, in God's sight to shine. Lamp to see by in the dark with divine glory and grace. Now, new, everlasting, angelic queen, help to dispel our plight below, royalest rose. *Ave Maria gratia plena*, hail!, fresh womanly flower, yearn for us, rule us, Virgin Mother, root and sheath of pity.)

The impulse behind aureation had long been manifesting itself, all over Europe, in macaronic combinations of Latin and a vernacular. As the vernaculars sought to make themselves as much a *grammatica* as Latin, it was natural that they should move from juxtaposing Latin with themselves to an effort to annex it. All speakers of European languages today enjoy the excellent results of this effort, even if it sometimes unbalanced writers of the centuries when it was at its most intense. And after all, what, next to Latin, could be closer to the speech of heaven's court and heaven's liturgy than a Latinized French or English? What better way was there for the aspiring courtier to address his Virgin Queen?

iv

As an adjunct to a discussion of speaker-audience relations in medieval religious lyric, something needs to be said about the startling ways in which pronouns are sometimes handled in religious language and hence poetry. On the one hand, the nearness of the speaker in a religious poem to the un-differentiated gestalt of the audience can lead to a vacillation among the first and second person singular and plural that a modern reader will find very unsettling. On the other, the unusual combination of actual absence and theoretical (or purely semiotic) presence on the part of the sacred persons who figure in religious poetry can lead to an analogous vacillation between second- and third-person pronouns that is at least as unsettling; in the speech of everyday life, we treat animals, prisoners, spouses, and children in this way, now speaking to them as persons, now speaking past them as if they were objects, but one would not expect God and the saints to receive the same treatment.

In many medieval religious poems, singular and plural first-person pro-nominal forms seem to be virtually interchangeable.[63] A few representative stanzas from a twelfth-century Latin *Mariale* (perhaps by Bernard of Cluny) will bear this out:

> Te requiro, ut a diro
>   Hoste me custodias
> Et coronam sempiternam
>   Mihi dari facias . . .
>
> Curam gere, ut videre
>   Mereamur filium,
> Quaere pacem, ne minacem
>   Vibret in nos gladium.
>
> Meam vitam fac munitam
>   Fide et operibus,
> Ut ad cenam intrem plenam
>   Bonis immortalibus.
>
> Dei verbum, qui superbum
>   Cruce vincens zabulum

Expiasti protoplasti
    Noxa tuum populum,

A malignis pro indignis
    Patiens crudelia,
Ut terrenos et egenos
    Sublimares gloria.

Rex caelestis, sic modestis
    Me perorna moribus,
Ut bonorum aeternorum
    Dignus sim muneribus . . .

Innocenter et prudenter
    Fac nos cuncta gerere,
Ne phantasma tuum plasma
    Possit ullum fallere.

Fac me cautum atque promptum
    In hoc vitae stadio,
Ut per fletus fruar laetus
    Summae pacis bravio.[64]

(I ask of you that you guard *me* from the dreadful enemy and have an eternal crown given to me. . . . Take care that *we* deserve to see the Son; seek peace, lest *he* brandish his menacing sword at us. Furnish *my* life with faith and works, that I may enter upon the banquet full of immortal good things. Word of God, who vanquished the arrogant devil on the cross and expiated the sins of the first-made man for *your* people, suffering cruel things from the wicked for the unworthy, that you might lift the earthly and needy up in glory. Heavenly king, adorn *me* so with decorous behavior that I be worthy of the gifts of eternal good things. . . . Make *us* conduct all things harmlessly and prudently, lest delusion be able to deceive anyone of your fashioning. Make *me* wary and quick in this racecourse of life, that through tears I may happily enjoy the prize of ultimate peace.)

When the vacillation is as rapid and continuous as here, the speaker seems to flicker in and out of existence, synecdoche for the whole community of believers.

The situation in Greek is somewhat different. The common practice of including the poet's name in acrostics (see especially the *kontakion*) in liturgical poetry is only one symptom of a firmer sense of and higher regard for the poet's individuality, corroborated by the significant amount of personal petition and personal reference. The speaker as poet ultimately refuses to merge with the mass in Byzantine hymns, and in this respect they stand in clear contrast to Western hymnography. These stanzas from a hymn by Theodore the Studite illustrate the degree of the difference:

Τὸν θείῳ μύρῳ χρισθέντα,
τῶν Μύρων ἀρχιερέα,
ὁ τὰ μύρα σου τερπνῶς
ὀσφραινόμενος τῶν θαυμάτων,
πῶς σε ὑμνήσω
ἁμαρτίαις δυσωδῶν,
ἅγιε Νικόλαε;
Ἀλλὰ νάρδῳ προσευχῶν
μύρισόν μου τοὺς τρόπους,
ἥδυνόν μου τοὺς φθόγγους
εἰς ὀσμὴν εὐωδίας νοητῆς,
πρὸς τὸ ὑμνεῖν σε ἀξίως,
τῶν ἑορταζόντων
προστάτα θερμότατε.

Ὑπὲρ τὰ ἄνθη κυπρίζει
ἡ λάρναξ τῶν σῶν λειψάνων,
νοητῶς μυροδοτεῖς,
προστατεύων ταῖς εὐωδίαις·
τίς γὰρ ἐν πίστει
προφοιτήσας οὐκ εὐθὺς
εὕρατο ὃ ἤτησεν;
Ἀλλὰ δίδου καὶ ἡμῖν
ὀσφραίνεσθαι εὐψύχως πόρρωθεν
οὖσι ταύτης,
τῶν χαρίτων εἰς ῥῶσιν νοητῶς,
πρὸς τὸ ὑμνεῖν σε ἀξίως,
τῶν ἑορταζόντων
προστάτα θερμότατε.

ὁ δι᾽ ἡμῶν σὺ πρεσβεύων,
ἐκ βαθέων ἀνακράζω,
ἀντιλῆπτορ ἀγαθέ,
κινδυνεύοντα πρόφθασόν με,
χεῖρα ὀρέξας
βοηθείας κραταιᾶς,
ἅγιε Νικόλαε,
καὶ ἐξάρας τῶν ἀνθρώπων,
ἵνα πάντες ὑμνῶσι διὰ σοῦ
νῦν τὴν ἐμὴν σωτηρίαν,
τῶν ἑορταζόντων
προστάτα θερμότατε.

Ὑπερκοσμίως ὑπάρχων,
καὶ χαίρων σὺν τοῖς ἀγγέλοις,
μνήσθητί μου πρὸς Θεόν,
ἀναξίου τοῦ ὑμνῳδοῦ σου·

δίδου τὴν χάριν
ὁμοῦ πᾶσι τοῖς τὸ σὸν
τελοῦσι μνημόσυνον,
τῆς εἰρήνης βραβευτά,
ἔκδικε τῶν ἐν λύπαις,
πρεσβευτὰ τῶν ἐν κόσμῳ,
ἱερέων ἐγκαλλώπισμα σεπτὸν,
βασιλέων συμμαχία,
τῶν ἑορταζόντων
προστάτα θερμότατε.[65]

(You annointed with divine myrrh, highpriest of the Myroi, making your per-
fumes smell pleasantly of miracles, how shall I hymn you, Saint Nicholas, I
who stink of sin? But perfume my actions with the nard of prayers, sweeten
my words to an odor of noetic fragrance, so I may hymn you properly, most
ardent advocate of [your] celebrants. Above the flowers blossoms the coffin of
your remains, noetically perfuming, preeminent in fragrances—who that goes
forward with faith has not immediately obtained what he sought? But grant
that we too may be scented with it from afar to our heart's good and the noetic
strengthening of grace, so we may hymn you properly, most ardent advocate
of [your] celebrants. You who intercede for us, from the depths I cry, good
defender, hasten to me in my peril and stretch out your hands of powerful assistance, Saint Nicholas, raising me up from among men so that all may hymn
my rescue by you, most ardent advocate of your celebrants. Dwelling above
the cosmos and rejoicing with the angels, remember me to God, me your unworthy hymnodist; grant your grace to all those together who hold fast to
your memory, granter of peace, avenger of those in trouble, intercessor for
those in good order, august ornament of priests, comrade of kings, most ardent advocate of your celebrants.)

The poet's closing prayer for himself is entirely typical not to say conventional. One notes that he is certainly a part of the congregation; he praises
with it and at times prays with it. But he is no less certainly primus inter
pares, always careful to preserve the distinction between the first person singular, denoting himself in his poetic function, and the first person plural,
denoting himself and the congregation in their common role as Christians.
Whether one finds this egotistical or not, it must be recognized that it is traditional in the East, a matter of custom rather than individual conceit.

In the vernaculars, vacillation of this kind is normally a marker of "artless" or "popular" poetry, except when it is occasionally used for deliberate
effect. Like the Byzantine hymnographers, Western writers of vernacular religious art-lyric have a fairly strong sense of their poetic role and do not confuse themselves in most cases with the rest of humanity, except insofar as
they too are Christians. In particular, the Old French tradition keeps its *je*

and *nos* forms in good order, perhaps because of the central importance of the *chanson d'amour*, with its lyric plot of lover ("I"), beloved ("thou"), and the mostly hostile remainder of the world ("they"). Final prayers often bring a shift from "I" to "we," but this is no more than appropriate, from a Christian viewpoint. Such shifts are also rare or unknown in the generally quite literary linguistic traditions of Spanish, Provençal, Portuguese, Old Norse, and Catalan (even in the "popular" Christmas songs, perhaps because they were written by the clergy in a fairly self-conscious frame of mind). They are also rare in German, despite the considerable amount of unpretentious anonymous verse; the existence of a strong native poetic tradition may have affected nonliterary poetry. Nonetheless, one does find cases like this end of a *Spruch*, by the early poet Reinmar der Zweter: "hilf mir, des ich dich biten wil, / das riuwe unt biht uns von den suenden reine" (help *me*—I want to pray to You for this—that contrition and confession may cleanse *us* from sin).[66] Anonymous Italian *laude* also sometimes show shifts between plural and singular. But the tradition that most often treats different persons and numbers as equivalent is undoubtedly Middle English.

Often, in alternative versions of a Middle English religious poem, one will find substitutions of singular for plural first-person forms or vice versa made apparently at random; or the alternative versions will show the complete insignificance of whether singular or plural is used:

> A. Þru tidigge us cumet iche dei—
>   ful wel leue me his may:
>   On, We sulle honne;
>   Þath oþer, we nite wanne;
>   Þe þridde his of muchel kare—
>   we nite fwider we sulle fare.
>
> B. Vyche day me cumeþ tydinges þreo,
>   For wel swiþe sore beþ heo:
>   þe on is þat ich schul heonne,
>   þat oþer þat ich noth hwenne;
>   þe þridde is my meste kare,
>   þat ich not hwider ich scal fare.[67]

(A. Three tidings come to us daily—one may be quite sure of it: one, we must go hence; the second, we don't know when; the third is of great concern—we don't know whither we will have to go.
B. Three tidings daily come to me, and they are very grievous: the first is that I must go hence, the second, that I don't know when; the third is my greatest concern, that I don't know whither I will have to go.)

One could not ask for a clearer example of the basic equivalency of "I" and "we" in medieval religious poetry, nor a clearer warning against assuming that the choice of "I" or "we" has the automatic meaningfulness that attaches to it in modern poetry. Other texts show the same equivalency within a single version of a poem, much as we saw it at work in the Latin *Mariale* above.[68] A few lines from "Iesus, þat wald efter mid-night" (an "hours of the Cross") will illustrate this:

> Receive, lauerd, me and ma
> Into þi suet armes tua,
> þat er bright and scene.
> Lauerd, þou hele wondes mine
> With þi suet medicine.
> Grant þat it sua bene!
>
> Mak vr bodijs fair and chast . . .[69]

(Lord, receive *me and mine* into your sweet arms, which are bright and beautiful. Heal *my* wounds, Lord, with your sweet medicine. Let it be so! Make *our* bodies fair and chaste . . .)

Cases of fluctuation between first and second person plural are also frequent. They may even be found in St. Paul (cf. Ephesians 1:3–12 or 2:1–10) and in such passages as 1 Peter 1:3–5.[70] Paul, however, is using the second person with deliberate effect, since he is writing to gentiles who once were lost but now are saved and wishes to emphasize that fact in his letter; his addressees are at once received into the Christian community ("we," "us") and considered in their distinct identity as a single group (distant from the writer) of saved beings ("you"). This is not true of the verses in 1 Peter, addressed to Jewish Christians in Asia Minor. Here verse 3 represents a formulaic creedal statement possibly used in worship, whereas in verse 4 the writer turns back to his audience without adjusting the discrepancy—perhaps quotation marks should be put round the preceding verse. Other examples of this phenomenon are plentiful in the New Testament.[71] A medieval Latin poem by Ratpert of St. Gall begins in the third-person subjunctive (equivalent to a call to praise),

> Iam fidelis turba fratrum   voce dulci consonet,

(Now let the faithful band of brothers sing together in a sweet voice)

shifts into the first person at verse 13,

> Nos istorum semper clara   consecuti munia
> Sanctitati tante cantu   personemus bombico

(Since we have always obtained their illustrious gifts, let us sing to such holiness with resounding song) and concludes in perplexity that the editor rightly refuses to remedy by emendation (vv. 21–24):

> Nunc redemptor et creator, auctor veri gaudii
> Largiatur aptam vobis   virtutis fiduciam
> Ut sibi volendo digna   captemus perennia.[72]

(Now may the redeemer and creator, the author of true joy, lavish a fittingly reliable virtue upon *you*, so that *we* may obtain perpetual rewards with his assent.)

This is an extreme case, but the interchange of first and second person, outside the liturgy (which in the West bars "I"-forms and the instructional or homiletic mode), is in itself quite frequent.

In Byzantine poetry, one again finds a much sharper distinction between pronouns. Shifts between the first and second persons are deliberate and expressive. For instance, a fine Christmas poem by John Mauropus begins with the speaker as part of the audience, continues with the speaker assuming the role of guide, and ends with the speaker returning to the collective embrace of the newly enlightened audience, while the pronominal forms reflect the steps in this itinerary faultlessly.[73] This lack of vagueness in its use of first- and second-person forms seems to be still another sign of that Byzantine poetic self-consciousness (even in liturgical poetry) that is much rarer in the West.

As with the shift in number, examples of this shift in person are rare in most vernacular traditions. However, Middle English lyrics mingle first- and second-person-plural pronominal forms no less readily than singulars and plurals:

> All we lufe sum thyng,
> þat knawyng hase of skyll,
> And haves þerin likyng, when it mai come us tyll.
> Forþi do Crystes biddyng,
> and lufe hym, as he wyll,
> And with lufe þat hase na endyng
> þi hert he wil fulfyll.
>
> Þai þat lufes fleschly er lickend
> til þe swyne.
> In fylth þai lat þaim ly,
> þaire fairehed wil þai tyne.
> Þair luf partes porely,
> and putted es to pyne.
> Swetter es luf gastly,
> þat nevermare wil dwyne.

If þou luf, whils þat þou may,
    þe keyng of majeste,
Þi wa wendes away,
    þi hele heyes to þe,
Þe nyght turnes intil day,
    þi joy sall ever be.
When þou ert as I þe say, I pray þe þynk on me.

Owre hedes sal we sett togydyr,
    in heven to dwell;
For þare þe gode ar mett,
    þat Cryste haldes fra hell.
When we owre synnes have grett,
    þen tythans may we tell
Þat we fra fer haves fett
    þe lufe þat nane may fell. . . .

His luf es trayst and trew,
    whasa hym luf and ware.
Sen fyrst þat it I knew,
    hit keped me fra kare.
I fand it ever new
    to lere me Goddes lare;
And now þar me not rew
    þat I have sufferd sare.

In lufe þi hert þou hye,
    and fane to fell þe fende.[74]

(All of us who have knowledge and experience love something and take pleasure in it when it comes to us. Therefore, do Christ's bidding, and love him as
he wishes, and he will fill your heart full of love that has no end.

Those that love carnally are like pigs. They let themselves lie in filth; they destroy their beauty. Their love ends badly and is put to punishment. Spiritual
love is sweeter—it will never fail. If you love a king of majesty while you can,
your sorrow departs, your happiness hastens to you, the night turns to day,
your joy will last forever. When you are as I am telling you, I pray you to think
of me.

We shall put our heads together, to dwell in heaven, for there the good are
gathered that Christ took from hell. When we have wept for our sins, then we
may tell tidings that we have fetched from far away the love that no one can
destroy . . .

His love is trusty and true for whoever is loving toward him. Since first I knew
it, it has kept me from anxiety. I found it was always new in teaching me the
lore of God; and now I need not regret that I have suffered sorely. Keep your
heart in love and ready to destroy the devil.)

The incoherence of thought in this poem, which one often finds in the "mystic" verses of Rolle or his followers, reveals itself in an additional incoherence of address and pronouns—but such fluidity in pronominal forms is quite common in hortatory poems.[75] Doubtless it is an effect of the strong sense of identification the poet felt with his audience in the sins attacked and conduct recommended.

The other major vacillation between pronouns in medieval religious lyric involves a shift between second- and third-person forms in dealing with sacred persons. As usual, the Byzantine tradition avoids such shifts in mode of address. But they are a regular part of Latin hymnody and nonliturgical poetry. For instance, Maximilian Scherner, in his study *Die sprachlichen Rollen im lateinischen Weihnachtslied des Mittelalters*, states that alternation of second- and third-person forms is common in Christmas hymns, ending his discussion of this phenomenon with the well-founded generalization that "shift of roles belongs to the essence of religious speech in all periods."[76] However, I believe that his analysis of the implications of the *tu/ille* shift is incorrect. In fact, it implies a sense of both the absence and the presence of the sacred, or perhaps one should say, of the fact that the sacred is present in objects (words, vestments, incense, architecture, and so forth) and so can readily be objectified into the third person. And I certainly do not agree that one must presume that the third-person forms are also directed at God as hearer. Rather, they acknowledge the fact that the true destination of the hymn, as opposed to the ostensible, is the worshipping congregation, whose sense of distance from God the second-person mode of apostrophe is intended to diminish (see the first section of this chapter).

Similar cases of movement from direct address of sacred persons to a third-person mode addressed to the earthly audience are of course innumerable in the vernaculars. Rather than illustrate this rather banal phenomenon, I will present a few passages in which the shift in mode is especially abrupt and therefore disconcerting to a modern ear unaccustomed to medieval religious lyric.

In Old French, Jean Molinet ends his imaginative Marian love-poem, "Tout a par moy, affin qu'on ne me voye," with this farewell:

> Adieu, madame, adieu vous dy,
> Adieu, belle plus de cent fois;
> Adieu, qui joie nous rendit,
> Quand son fils sur la croix pendit . . .[77]

(Adieu, my lady, adieu I say, adieu, fair a hundred times, adieu, one who gave us joy when *her* son hung on the cross . . .)

In an Old Norse *drápa* by Abbot Arngrímr Brandsson, we find the following:

> Engi skal, þótt illa gangi,
> ǫrvilnan sik láta skilja,
> dauða stig, þviat dæller at vægja,
> dýrligr frá þér himna stýrir . . .[78]

(Even though it go badly for him on death's path, no one should let despair separate him from *You*, glorious helmsman of heaven, for *He* is quick to spare . . .)

The first stanza of an Italian *lauda* attributed to Ugo Panziera di Prato is less abrupt and therefore somewhat more representative; still, it would certainly raise eyebrows today:

> Languisco amando e faime consumare:
> quando di te pigliare gioi' mi rimembro,
> un'allegrezza in me sento creare
> che fa dolzor gustare ad ogni membro;
> sento il mio core in alto levare
> sovr'ogni ciel; pensare a cui rimembro
> cioe Cristo cui tegno nelle braccia
> per contemplare, m'avaccia a danzare.[79]

(I languish with love and *you* make me pine away; when I remember the joy of laying hold of *you*, I feel a happiness grow in me that makes my every limb taste sweetness; I feel my heart lifted on high above every heaven; the thought to which I turn, that is, *Christ whom I hold* in my arms to contemplate, stirs me to dancing.)

The poem then continues to speak of Christ in the third person till its end, even though the *ripresa* or refrain that follows each stanza is a direct address to Christ.

One even finds passages in which a sacred person, speaking in prosopopoeia, will suddenly slip into the viewpoint of the earthly audience. In a Spanish fifteenth-century *contrafactura* of a secular poem, "Dezidme, reyna del cielo," by Juan Alvarez Gato, the Virgin says the following in the course of an antiphonal dialogue with the speaker:

> Yo soy aquel santo templo
> quel quiso santificar,
> en que pudiese morar
> aquel Dios, en quien contenplo,
> y nos dexo por exenplo,
>   siendo Dios,
> querer ser onbre por vos.[80]

(I am that holy temple he wished to sanctify, in which that God could dwell whom I contemplate and which he gave *us* as an example, being God, to seek to be man for *your* sake.")

Of course, despite these lines, Mary was not given to herself as an example; but the aside is just the sort of thing the speaker might say in a Marian poem, and here it is put, illogically, into Mary's mouth. Similarly, the thirteenth-century Old Norse "Líknarbraut" has Christ speak of himself in the third person in the midst of a prosopopoeia:

> Ér megud undir stórar
> yðars graeðis sjá blaeða,
> þaer eru sýnt, þo sárer,
> saklausum mér vakðar,
> min þvi at mildi raunar
> mest ok yðrir lestir
> veldr þvi, at verða skyldi,
> vist, lýðs fyrir píslum.[81]

(You will be able to see the great and bitter wounds of your savior bleed which were opened in innocent me; for verily my grace and certainly your sins caused it, that *he* should be subject to men's tortures.)

As in the Spanish poem, the narrator has temporarily forgotten the dramatic situation and slipped back into his own voice, which he legitimately resumes in the second stanza following this one.

Certainly these passages are at the extreme edge of what was possible to religious poetry. Nonetheless, they do nothing more than reveal in an exaggerated fashion a fundamental fact about religous lyric and religous language, namely, the fictivity and irreality of the sacred, which makes the effort of second-person address or first-person prosopopoeia vulnerable to a collapse back into third-person actuality, with only human beings present. These passages also reflect the unrealism with which sacred persons are handled in poems where they appear as characters rather than simply addressees. There is rarely any attempt at psychological consistency or verisimilitude, even if in most cases the pronouns do stay in order. For example, in a poem from the Urbino *laudario* in which Mary is represented as interceding with Christ on behalf of a sinner, she twice steps out of character to appeal to written records when in her position she would have far superior, direct knowledge of what she is saying:

> Fillo, la Madalena,
> come fo peccatrice a smesurança
> lo representa la sancta Scriptura . . .
> La egeçiaca Maria
> e·t Täysìs, kedd-eran peccatrice

> et offesero molto a·tte, Signor,
> tornando a·bbona via,
> secundo la legenna loro dice,
> le recepisti cun verace amore.[82]

(Son, the Magdalene, Holy Scripture describes how great a sinner she was . . .
Mary of Egypt and Thais, who were sinners and greatly offended you, Lord,
when they returned to a virtuous life, as their legend tells, you received them
with true love.)

In a Christmas *villancico* by Juan del Encina, the shepherds end a discussion
of what presents to take to the Mother and Child by speaking on a subject
about which the audience is well informed, although they could not be at
this point in the story:

> En cantares nuevos
> Gocen sus orejas:
> Miel e muchos huevos
> Para hacer torrejas,
> Aunque sin dolor
> Parió el Redemptor.[83]

(Let her ears rejoice in new songs; honey and many eggs to make fritters with,
even though she bore the Redeemer without pain.)

Frey Ambrosio de Montesino has the Magi gloss their own gifts like good
exegetes (gold is for purity, incense for divinity, myrrh for the crucifixion!)
and call themselves "good Christians."[84] And so forth. Such passages remind us that dialogue, story telling, and characters appear in religious lyrics
not in order to create a convincing, illusionistic fiction but to remind the
audience of sacred history and of its meaning, with the latter very much par-
amount. The plausibility of the fiction will be sacrificed without flinching if
incorporating a significant traditional interpretive motif requires it—even
by a poet like Montesinos, who is capable (in the same poem mentioned just
now) of imagining Mary turning pale at the sound of the camels, frightened
it might be Herod and his henchmen come looking for her child.[85]

Not only do the pronouns and the details of apparently dramatic speech
in religious lyric reflect a radical instability of viewpoint, but sometimes the
verb tenses do as well. Most of the underlying causes of this phenomenon
were discussed in the first section of this chapter. But the causes for other
sorts of category shifting that have been laid out in this section also play
their part. Generally, the tense structure of a medieval religious lyric is quite
simple. Many poems will be entirely in the present tense, with perhaps an
occasional foray into the future. If the past tense occurs, it is used to refer to
past actions by God or Mary that lend credence to the speaker's hopes or

prayers. But in some cases, the tense structure grows more complex and the exact temporal location of the action of the poem becomes obscure. For instance, in an outstanding *planctus Mariae*, "Viva ab gran gauig la Verge Maria," Ramon Llull has Mary vacillating beween the dramatic viewpoint (the Crucifixion as a present, ongoing event) and the viewpoint of the audience (the Crucifixion as a past event); the fact that the narrative passages are in the historical present only adds to the uncertainty.[86] Of course, in a poet like Llull, one is inclined to argue that such tense shifting is an artistically valid way of destroying the meaning of "present" and "past" when we are concerned with the Passion and the compassion we owe Mary and Christ. In a much more directly theological way, Frauenlob represents the paradoxical simultaneity of Mary's virginity, motherhood, and heavenly reign in the opening stanzas of his brilliant *Marienleich*:

> Ei ich sach in dem trône
> ein vrouwen, diu was swanger.
> diu truoc ein wunderkrône
> vor mîner ougen anger.
> Sie wolde wesen enbunden,
> sus gie diu allerbeste,
> zwelf steine ich an den stunden
> kôs in der krône veste.
>
> Nu merket wie sie trüege,
> diu gevüege,
> der natûren zuo genüege:
> mit dem sie was gebürdet
> den sach sie vor ir sitzen
> mit witzen
> in siben liuhtaeren
> und sach in doch gesundert
> in eines lambes wîse
> ûf Siôn dem berge gehiuren,
> Und het ouch daz sie solde,
> jâ diu holde
> truoc den bluomen sam ein tolde.
> vrouwe, ob ir muoter würdet
> des lambes und der tûben?
> die trûben
> ir liezet iuch swaeren.
> dâ von mich niht enwundert,
> ob iuch diu selbe spîse
> kan wol zuo der vrühte gestiuren.

(Ai! I saw a woman on the throne who was with child; she wore a wonderful crown in the field of my eyes. She was about to give birth, thus it stood with the best woman of them all; twelve stones I caught sight of then, fast in the crown. Now mark how far she brought forth, the virtuous woman, in accord with nature: the one she was carrying, him she saw sitting before her cunningly in seven candlesticks and yet saw him separately in the guise of a lamb on Zion the mighty mountain, and also had that which she ought to have, yes, the beloved bore the flower like a branch. Lady, would you be the mother of the lamb and of the dove? With the cluster of grapes [a type of Christ, Numbers 13:24] you let yourself be laden. Therefore I do not feel any wonder that the same food can bring you to fruition.)[87]

The last lines of the second stanza work effectively to undermine one's secure sense of the pastness of the reported vision. In fact, it is the seeing not the seen that belongs to time; Mary's multiple roles are a single eternal fact, always ready for the human eyes that will open to behold her.

Used less artistically, but ultimately for similar reasons, tense shifts may occur at any time in religious lyrics that present the sacred directly. They complement, in their effect, the other rhetorical features—if one can call practices that are usually quite spontaneous "rhetorical"—to which this section is devoted.

Before we leave behind the issue of modes of address and the nature of point of view in medieval religious lyric, however, I want the reader to have the opportunity to examine the complete text of a poem that makes particularly subtle and meaningful use of pronominal and verbal forms. At the same time, the poem shows how a didactic intent can produce highly poetic results when the poet is sufficiently skilled. The poet is Thomas Aquinas, and the poem is *Lauda Sion*, written in the third quarter of the thirteenth century for the Office of the new eucharistic feast of Corpus Christi.

1. Lauda, Sion, salvatorem,
   lauda ducem et pastorem
      in hymnis et canticis;
   quantum potes, tantum aude,
   quia maior omni laude,
      nec laudare sufficis.

2. Laudis thema specialis
   panis vivus et vitalis
      hodie proponitur,
   quem in sacrae mensa cenae
   turbae fratrum duodenae
      datum non ambigitur.

3. Sit laus plena, sit sonora,
   sit iucunda, sit decora,
      mentis iubilatio;

dies enim sollemnis agitur,
in qua mensae prima recolitur
   huius institutio.

4. In hac mensa novi regis
   novum pascha novae legis
      phase vetus terminat;
   vetustatem novitas,
   umbram fugat veritas,
      noctem lux eliminat.

5. Quod in cena Christus gessit,
   faciendum hoc expressit
      in sui memoriam;
   docti sacris institutis
   panem, vinum in salutis
      consecramus hostiam.

6. Dogma datur Christianis
   quod in carnem transit panis
      et vinum in sanguinem:
   quod non capis, quod non vides
   animosa firmat fides
      praeter rerum ordinem.

7. Sub diversis speciebus,
   signis tantum et non rebus,
      latent res eximiae;
   caro cibus, sanguis potus,
   manet tamen Christus totus
      sub utraque specie.

8. A sumente non concisus,
   non confractus, non divisus,
      integer accipitur;
   sumit unus, sumunt mille,
   quantum isti, tantum ille,
      nec sumptus consumitur.

9. Sumunt boni, sumunt mali,
   sorte tamen inequali
      vitae vel interitus;
   mors est malis, vita bonis;
   vide, paris sumptionis
      quam sit dispar exitus.

10. Fracto demum sacramento
    ne vacilles, sed memento

tantum esse sub fragmento
quantum toto tegitur;
nulla rei fit scissura,
signi tantum fit fractura,
qua nec status nec statura
signati minuitur.

11. Ecce panis angelorum
factus cibus viatorum,
vere panis filiorum,
non mittendus canibus;
in figuris praesignatur,
cum Isaac immolatur,
agnus paschae deputatur,
datur manna patribus.

12. Bone pastor, panis vere,
Iesu, nostri miserere,
tu nos pasce, nos tuere,
tu nos bona fac videre
in terra viventium;
tu qui cuncta scis et vales,
qui nos pascis hic mortales,
tu nos ibi commensales,
coheredes et sodales
fac sanctorum civium.[88]

(Zion, praise the Savior, praise the Guide and Shepherd in hymns and canticles; whatever you can do, dare to do it, for He is greater than all praise, nor are you adequate to praise Him. 2. As a theme of special praise, living and vital bread is set before us today which at the Last Supper, there is no doubt, was given to the band of twelve brothers. 3. Let praise be full and sonorous, let there be a pleasant and seemly inner rejoicing, for a solemn day is celebrated today on which the first institution of this meal is renewed. 4. At this meal of the new king a new paschal offering under the new law ends the old Passover; newness routs oldness, truth, the shadow [of typology], light drives night out of doors. 5. Christ laid down that what He did at the Last Supper should be done in His Memory; taught by His sacred ordinances, we consecrate bread and wine as a sacrifice unto salvation. 6. The doctrine is given to Christians that bread is changed into flesh and wine into blood; that which you neither grasp nor see, faith in its courage affirms despite the [natural] order of things. 7. Under different appearances, signs only and not things, extraordinary things are hidden; flesh is food, blood is drink, yet Christ is wholly present in either kind. 8. Unsevered by the partaker, unbroken, undivided, He is received in His entirety; partake one, partake a thousand, He is as numerous as they and, partaken of, remains unconsumed. 9. Partake the good, partake the evil, they do it still with an unequal result, life or destruction; it is death to the evil, life to the good; see, how different the result of an equal partaking is. 10. When the sacrament is broken then, do not waver, but remember that just as much resides in the fragment as is encompassed in the whole; the thing itself is not cut, only the sign is broken, a breach in which neither state nor size of the signified thing is diminished. 11. Behold the bread of angels made the food of wayfarers, truly the bread of the sons, not to be given to dogs; in types it is prefigured, when Isaac is offered as a sacrifice, when the lamb is assigned to Passover, when manna is given to the patriarchs. 12. Good shepherd, true bread, Jesus, take pity on us, feed us, guard us, make us see the good things in the land of the living; You who know and can do all things, who feed us mortals here, make us table companions, coheirs, and comrades there of [Your] holy citizens.)

The content of this regular sequence is the eucharistic theology celebrated by the feast of Corpus Christi, and in particular the doctrine of the Real Presence, which had been subject to heated rationalist objections by scholastic philosophers of the period. Aquinas therefore chooses a persuasively rational approach, keeping emotion firmly in check until intellectual doubts have been allayed. Of the available forms of the conventional opening call to praise, he chooses not the first-person-plural hortatory subjunctive (*laudemus*, "let us praise!") but an imperative directed at the personified Church. And consistent with the pattern the whole poem follows of making the conventional fully explicit and thus revitalizing it, Aquinas virtually paraphrases the standard definition of a hymn in the first three lines (cf. Augustine's *laus Dei cum cantico* [praise of God in song]). In effect, we are to perform an action familiar to us from past occasions (the Eucharist and the act of worship), but this time we will understand each part of it as it occurs.

The second half of the first stanza uses the convention of *aporia* (see the next section of this chapter) but unconventionally casts it as part of the apostrophe to Zion rather than as an authorial gesture of inadequacy. Thus, it both serves as a compelling reason for us to praise and brings to the surface the universal *aporia* that all believers experience at the thought of God and that underlies any authorial *aporia* in religious verse.

Imitating the structure of a sermon, the poet next states his theme but relates it through the conventional "today" motif (see the first section of this chapter) to the liturgical occasion his "sermon" celebrates. In keeping with the detached presentation and the deliberately low emotional temperature an impersonal form (*ambigitur*), itself part of an understated negative phrase, ends the second stanza.

This choice of the third-person indirect mode continues in force during the third stanza (*Sit laus plena*); one feels that *decora* is the key word and here means "decorous" as well as simply "fitting." The themes of the first stanza (praise) and of the second (reasons for praise, i.e., the celebration of the Eucharistic Institution) are restated in order in this stanza, so that the audience has time to contemplate its fortunate duty and the causes behind it before the text proceeds to direct analysis.

The fourth stanza begins this analysis, executing a bold but totally unforced polyptoton on *novus*, which as the key concept (i.e., "new") of the poem fully deserves the stress placed on it at the start of the exposition (cf. the types in stanza 11, the "old" symbols yielding to the "new" reality, and also the "newness" of the feast that occasioned Aquinas's poem).

Stanza 5 contains yet another impersonal of absolute yet unemotional obligation (*faciendum*), but it ends with the only first-person form up to this point, *consecramus* (we consecrate). Note, however, that the word does not exhort, it simply describes the eucharistic action that speaker and audience perform together as communicant members of Christ's body. In describing, it also, discreetly, informs us of the frame of mind that should accompany the action (*docti sacris institutis* [taught by his sacred ordinances]), a frame the poem is intended to establish in its hearers-performers.

The sixth stanza similarly begins with an impersonal (*datur*): note the repetition of "bread" and "wine" from the previous stanza, now chiastically enclosed by their reality (in orthodox theology), "flesh" and "blood." But in its second part, the stanza turns to the professorial mode of address one often finds in religious lyric of the scholastic age from Abelard on, though it states that the audience (concentrated into a single "thou") is doing certain things, rather than ordering the audience to perform them (contrast the usual *nota* or *considera*).[89] Even *firmat* is a confident indicative, not a hortatory subjunctive. The poet leaves it in no doubt that he seeks neither to convince us of the truth nor to impart new knowledge, but instead to clarify knowledge we already possess and conduct in which we already engage.

The theme of the intangible and unseen provides the link to the next stanza (*latent*, "are hidden"), in which the poet carefully defines the nature of the Real Presence; the subtle variation of *vinum* and *panis* (bread and wine) by *cibus* and *potus* (food and drink) is admirable, for it stresses the value of both as (spiritual) nourishment to answer human needs.[90]

This emphasis is taken up in the eighth stanza where polyptoton announces the introduction of a new major theme (*sumente*, *sumit*, etc., all variant forms of the verb "to receive"). The implicit sequence of thought may be described thus: the Real Presence has been fully explained, and the congregation presumably accepts it with both mind and body; but if Christ is literally present in the wine and the bread, if they are he, should one not fear the breaking of Christ's body as it is taken into one's own? The poet properly refuses to acknowledge this undercurrent of anxiety openly (it was very real and very strong in the later Middle Ages) and simply answers the questions it raises with a calm series of assertions. All the while, he keeps consistently to the third person.

The continuing polyptoton on *sumere* introduces the ninth stanza and fixes its place in the order; within it, we have a professorial imperative *vide* (see) to call our attention to the paradox of the two opposing effects of the Eucharist. This form prepares the congregation for the muted imperative *ne vacilles* (do not waver) in the eleventh stanza, where the faithful's doubts are at last permitted to declare themselves. *Memento* (remember) exactly expresses their relationship to the poem's teaching and imposes on them the role of catechumens not free inquirers. They have only to recall what they know, and all will be clear. Meanwhile, forgetting nothing of his craft, the poet has begun to devise an effective ending by adding two verses to the stanza.[91]

Aquinas enters on his peroration now, at last free to celebrate the wonder of what he has expounded, even permitting himself a dramatic *ecce* (behold). But in the midst of conventional typological praise redeemed by its concision and its place in the structure of the poem as a release of pent-up feelings, the poet does not lose his equilibrium; instead, note how he places in the heart of the stanza the vivid understatement *non mittendus canibus* (not to be thrown to dogs). And because he has exercised such restraint on himself, his text, and therefore his audience, denying himself not only any supplication but any direct exhortation or strongly emotional expression until the very end, the convention of closing with a prayer that the last stanza uses regains all its force. The speaker apostrophized Zion at the start, and now he apostrophizes its Head. *Pastor* (shepherd) recalls *pastorem* of line 2, the themes of "bread" and "feeding" are resumed, and the audience at last fully understands the sense in which Christ is the shepherd and on exactly what "pastures" he lets believers feed *in terra viventium* (in the land of the living). "Feed us," the speaker says, and shows a few lines later that it was unnecessary to ask: *tu . . . qui nos pascis hic mortales* (you who feed us mortals here). The poem closes on a note of magnificent certainty, praying not out of doubt but knowledge, knowledge that what is done at the altar is done in eternity and may win eternity for every partaker.[92]

Lauda Sion shows to near-perfection what effects can be drawn from the medieval habit of gliding from pronoun to pronoun, in this case, from apostrophe to impersonal to first person plural to second person singular and back and forth between them. One will not often find such a sure hand at work, however, and one should not demand it. To enter into the world of medieval religious lyric that lies in the shadows behind such noted texts as this one, it is necessary, among other things, to learn to appreciate for its own sake the opalescence of address and point-of-view that shimmers in this poetry like the colors in shot silk.

V

In this penultimate section, we will investigate the rhetoric of self-referentiality in medieval religious lyric, all those devices or motifs that reveal the poet's awareness of what he is doing as a literary act and that simultaneously solicit an esthetic or literary response from the audience. A number of polemic or programmatic statements figured in the third section of chapter 2; they illustrated how far medieval poets sometimes went in making their literary conscience explicit in their work. Here, we will be concerned with less arresting and far more frequent features that work to the same end.

Aporia, or the rhetorical gesture that praises by stating that no praise can do justice to its object, is endemic to medieval religious lyric. It derives from the religious situation, from religious language, and from the poetic tradition. In consequence, particular examples vary in character; sometimes they are scriptural, sometimes they reflect antecedents in pagan epic or panegyric. Whatever its particular character, one finds it is abundant in each linguistic tradition, above all in Marian literature and in art-poetry.

In Catalan, for instance, it is quite rare in the Christmas songs but common in nonpopular material. In Italian, its usage is very unequally distributed; surprisingly, examples are scarce in Jacopone, though he uses it well when he uses it at all:

> O Madonna, quelli atti,
> avivi en quelli fatti,
>
> quelli 'nfocati tratti
> la lengua m'ò mozzata.[93]

(O Madonna, those acts, enjoyed in those deeds, those gestures afire with love have put a check upon my tongue. [Jacopone has just been asking Mary how she could nurse Christ or hear him call her "mother" without dying of the sheer joy of it.])

Aporia is infrequent in a number of other Italian poets as well (cf. Leonardo Giustinian), in the earliest (thirteenth century) *laude*, including those in Cortona 91, in some later *laudari*, and generally in the fifteenth- and early sixteenth-century collections of *laude* reprinted by Galletti. The "Pisa," "Gubbio," and Aquila *laudari* make somewhat more use of the figure, but it is really common only in Ugo Panziera, Feo Belcari, Lorenzo de' Medici, Savonarola, and especially Bianco da Siena—and in Guittone d'Arezzo, if one goes by the number of occurrences relative to the number of poems. Of this pattern, one can say that there is a close correlation between *aporia* and certain "name" authors, whereas the composers of anonymous *laudari* meant for confraternal use and fifteenth-century poets who were trying to imitate the popular manner of the *laudari* avoided using *aporia*.

The figure is a normal part of encomiastic passages in Greek and Latin religious lyric. Here is a conventional example, taken from Peter the Venerable's hymn "Hugo, pius pater, clarus prosapia," in which he sings the praises of St. Hugo of Cluny, like Peter himself an abbot of that monastery:

> Quae addam amplius eius operibus
> Cum haec plus niteant cunctis sideribus?
> Nam eius opera sunt velut sidera,
> Quae propter numerum manet innumera.[94]

(What more should I add concerning his deeds, when these outshine all the stars? For his deeds are like the stars, so numerous they are innumerable.)

Greek examples are of much the same kind (Mauropus speaks in a hymn to the Theotokos of how παραδόξως συμβαίνει / τὸ ἀπορεῖν / ἐκ τῆς εὐπορίας [insufficiency comes paradoxically from abundance], which neatly sums up the rationale for the figure).[95]

Aporia is also very common in German; one of the last wandering poets of the Middle Ages, Michel Beheim (d. 1475) has a Marian panegyric whose eighty-seven verses consist of nothing else,[96] and briefer forms of the figure are prevalent from the twelfth century through the sixteenth. In Old French, the preferred variety is third-person and general (like the example from Peter the Venerable); Gautier de Coincy uses *aporia* several times, and in fact almost all cases occur in poems by known authors. Significantly, the Lorraine group of religious poems and anonymous pieces in general seldom use the figure. In Old Norse, examples are late, mostly Marian or hagiographical, and not very plentiful. Provençal, Portuguese, and Spanish all show the usual concentration in the work of named authors and on Marian subjects; poets in the *Cancionero general* (1514 and later editions) have a great fondness for it. The genuinely literary, authorial *aporia* does not establish itself in Middle English until the fifteenth century, with examples beginning to appear in the last half of the fourteenth (e.g., in Chaucer's ABC). By contrast, a passage of *aporia* borrowed from St. Paul turns up at the very dawn of the thirteenth century:

> ne mei non heorte þenchen ne nowiht arechen,
> neo no muð imelen ne no tunge tegen
> hu muchel god ðu ȝeirkest wið-inne paradise
> ham þet swinke dei & niht i ðine servise.[97]

(Nor may any heart conceive or in any way judge, nor may any mouth speak or tongue tell how much good you work in paradise for them that labor day and night in your service.)

And one will encounter an occasional unpretentious expression of *aporia* such as the lines, "For little have I cunning / to tell of his fairhead," from a poem under the influence of Richard Rolle (mid-fourteenth century);[98] in such cases, one may perhaps detect a faint taste of the literary, but little is left after the Latin tradition has percolated through the stiff clay of native English.

In fact, that last anonymous example of *aporia* might equally well have served as an illustration of the closely related *inadequacy* topos. A variant of *aporia*, it lays the stress upon the deficiencies of the poet rather than the magnitude of his subject. The effect, however, and the distribution among poems in the various traditions is very much the same, except that it usually seems marginally more literary. German authors of major Marian texts— for example, Bruder Hans von Cleve, *Marienlieder*; Konrad von Wuerzburg, *Diu guldîn smide*; the anonymous writer of the *Rheinisches Marienlob*—all repeatedly express their sense of inadequacy. Hans von Cleve is as colorful as always:

> Nym nut miin sprechen, vrou, vuer erch.
> Went zwaer ich prueb daz wol und merch,
> E ennich minsch, ley oder clerch,
> Diin lop volspreech, man solt den berch
> Goddert e mit halm durchboren.
> Zu trotz dem duvel und zu terch
> Tred ich zem creys doch in daz perch,
> Recht sam eyn cleynes cranc gedwerch,
> Daz jegen eynem ruese sterch
> Den camp nut geben wil verloren.
> Went alz calander unde lerch
> Lustliichen zingen an den swerch,
> So is der gouch siinz sangz nut kerch.
> Sus wil ich enden ouch diz werch,
> Al hetz der dubel bi siin oren
> *Beid* gesworen.[99]

(Lady, don't take my words amiss. For well I know and certainly mark that before any man, lay or clerk, expresses your praise completely, one might first bore through Mt. Gothard with a straw. Despite the devil, I step into the ring just like a weak little dwarf who will not give his battle with a mighty giant up for lost. When calender and lark gaily sing upon the spray, the cuckoo too does not begrudge his song. So will I too end this work, even if the devil has sworn by his ears, "Stop!")

Throughout the vernaculars, the inadequacy topos is consistently much less common than simple *aporia*. In Catalan, several *joyas* entries contain it.[100] In Italian, Guittone d'Arezzo and Bianco da Siena use it, as does Savonarola, but it is rare elsewhere.[101] In Spanish, Perez de Guzman accounts for most of the examples in lyrics—he is so insistent about it that one begins to believe he is actually sincere (he needn't have been so diffident). Only late Old Norse poetry uses the inadequacy topos almost as often as *aporia* proper, perhaps in reaction to the sinful pride of the old skalds, just as there was a rejection of skaldic word order and skaldic kennings.

Rather than exalt his subject by asserting its indescribability or denigrating himself, a poet can indirectly claim special importance for his poem and therefore its subject by including an *invocation*. This can be as simple as the liturgical phrase from a Marian antiphon, "Dignare me laudare te, Virgo sacrata" (Make me worthy to praise you, sacred Virgin).[102] As a request for aid in expression, instead of personal worthiness or spiritual illumination, it belongs to literary, even classicizing poetry and to Old Norse, which had its own "classic" native tradition.[103] In fact, so deep and indelible was the mark of skaldic self-awareness, that the invocation is virtually de rigueur in Old Norse religious poetry, particularly in the panegyric narrative form of the *drápa*. Among the fifty-odd occurrences (in perhaps no more than twice as many poems), there is the request for help in finding a new refrain line with which Eysteinn Ásgrímsson marks the midpoint of his *Lilja*:

> Yfirmeistarinn allra lista,
> Jésús góðr, er lífgar þjóðir,
> kenn þú mér at stilla ok stýra,
> steflig orð megi tungan efla.
> (*stef*) Aevinliga með lyktum lófum
> lof raeðandi á kné sín bæði
> skepnan oll er skyld at falla,
> skapari minn, fyr ásján þinni.[104]

(Master in all virtues, Lord Jesus, you who give life to men, teach me to direct and govern so that my tongue can produce words for the *stef*: "All creation must fall on both its knees before your face, my creator, speaking praise forever and ever with joined hands.")

Poets in the tradition show that they agreed fully with Einarr Skulason, one of the earliest Christian poets of significance to write in Norse, who begins his famous *drápa* "Geisli" with the lines, "The one God's Trinity can teach me poem and prayers—very wise is he who can get them from skilful, all-counseling God!"[105]

Invocations both literary and scriptural figure in many Greek and Latin poems, within and without the liturgy in Greek, primarily outside it in Latin, where the liturgical mode permits at most a collective request for aid in praising. In a canon to St. John Chrysostomos, John Mauropus (not

Damascene, among whose works this piece mistakenly appears in the *Patrologia*) makes the following invocation:

Στόματι πηλίνῳ
καὶ γλώσσῃ γεώδει
σὲ τὸν Χρυσόστομον
ὑμνεῖν ορμῶντί μοι,
χρυσοφαὲς
οὐρανόθεν
θείας γνώσεως ἀμάρυγμα
ἐξαστράψας,
φώτισον
τὸν νοῦν καὶ τὴν καρδίαν μου.[106]

(As I strive with mouth of clay and earthy tongue to hymn you the Golden-Mouth, shine the golden splendor of divine knowledge down from heaven and enlighten my mind and my heart.)

The ethereal glitter of these lines is typical of the Greek tradition. Among Latin examples, the opening of John of Howden's *Philomena* is especially elaborate, which is no more than appropriate for a poem over four thousand lines long:

Ave, Verbum, ens in principio,
Caro factum pudoris gremio,
Fac, quod fragret praesens laudatio
Et placeris parvo praeconio.

Et tu, stella maris eximia,
Mater patris et nati filia,
Laude, precor, reple praecordia,
Cum sis laudis mira materia.

Virgo, David orta progenie,
Dola linguam hanc imperitiae
In sonantis lyram placentiae,
Et iam psallas manu munditiae.

(Hail, Word, Being in the beginning, made flesh in the bosom of modesty, make this present praise smell sweet and may you be pleased with slight proclamation. And you, excellent star of the sea, father's mother and son's daughter, fill, I pray, my heart with praise, for you are wonderful material of praise. [Note the pun on *mater* and *materia*.] Virgin, born of the line of David, beat this tongue of inexperience into a lyre of pleasant sound, and then may you pluck it with the hand of cleanness.)

Finally, a hymn by Ratpert illustrates the much earlier, classicizing vein in fashion during the Carolingian period:

Christus ad nostras veniat camenas,
Christus et vocem tribuat salubrem
Christus ad vitam vehat et perennem
Se modulantes.[107]

(May Christ come to our muses, may Christ also confer a saving word, and may Christ bring to life everlasting those who sing of him.)

Even the Sapphic stanza seeks to remind us of Horace's invocations, in distant days and to far other gods!

In the vernaculars other than Old Norse, invocations are relatively infrequent. This is especially true of Portuguese, Provençal, Catalan (except the *joyas*), and Middle English, where examples appear only in the high literary line extending from Chaucer to Lydgate and other fifteenth-century Chaucerians. Of a scattering of instances in Italian, Bianco is responsible for nearly half; a few occur in anonymous *laude*. Spanish invocations are mostly Marian and rather literary (cf. Montesino). Old French examples appear in the anonymous chansons (thirteenth century) collected by Jaernstroem and otherwise in named authors. Jean Molinet begins his "O Trinité parfaite et interine" with several stanzas of invocation on an even grander scale than John of Howden's proem to the *Philomena*.[108] Only German remotely approaches the Old Norse taste for the invocation; with several dozen examples out of ten times as many poems, the frequency is an order of magnitude lower, however. Still, it is yet another indication of the fairly high status of vernacular religious poetry in the German-speaking countries. Like the inadequacy topos, invocations occur mostly in poems by known poets and in the major Marian poems. Early in his series of seventy-two stanzas in praise of Mary (to correspond to the supposed number of "all the tongues of the earth"), Heinrich von Muegeln aims a particularly well-decorated invocation at the object of his encomium:

Mins tichtes stam besnit,
    den rifen grober sprueche wit
von im, der mir gewaldig lit
    in herzen anger, waren mei.

saf und der witze tror
    guess, maget, in mins sinnes ror
und sluess mir uf der kuenste tor,
    das ich dir, kuensteloser lei,

Maria, lob uss bluender zungen webe
    und girdig in dins dienstes silen strebe.
uf tichtes mar ich swebe,
    das mir indren der gnaden tuft.[109]

(Prune my poem's stem, remove the ripening of coarse *Sprueche* from it, which troubles me sorely in the field of my heart, true Virgin. Maid, pour into the reed of my mind the juice and drops of wit and open me the door of the arts, so that I, an artless layman, may weave you, Mary, the praise of blossoming tongues and eagerly strive in your service's harness. On song's horse I sway— may the odor of grace perfume me.)

Even less rococo invocations still imply that the poem is something written by a poet, that it is important enough to justify a request for heavenly aid, and that if successful it will contribute to the fame of its subject. Whatever the terms in which it is couched, this form of self-referentiality is in essence anything but modest. Still, as a Spanish poet puts it, Christian poets could claim that divine inspiration was a necessity of their calling: "el metro ha de ser del cielo / y el poeta el Trino y Uno" (the meter must be from heaven / and the poet the Three and One).[110]

Another way that poets have to draw attention to the status of their poetry as art is to speak within it of *new song* or occasionally *new dance*.[111] It is true that such phrases have a primarily spiritual meaning, suggesting the freshness of the new dispensation since the Redemption and of the soul that has put off the old Adam, and that they echo the *canticum novum* (new song) that Psalm 98 enjoins us to sing to the Lord. Nonetheless, they also refer to the continuous renewal of praise achieved in the religious lyric by individual writers.

The motif is characteristic of the vernaculars, rather than Latin or certainly Greek, at least so far as the emphasis may be felt to fall on "song" and not simply "new" (the sequence, as a new form, is an exception to this rule). One suspects that writing religious lyric in the vernacular, particularly in the early decades of each tradition, did bring with it a heightened sense of the novelty of the act and of the language and forms one was using. From the thirteenth century in France, we hear Gautier say, "Talens m'est pris orendroit / Qu'a mout haut ton / De la plus haute qui soit / Vous die un nouvel son" (The desire has just come to me to say you a new "sound" [= "song"] in a very high "tone" of the highest of women).[112] (Elsewhere, he actually opposes singing of the Virgin to the search for novelty inherent in secular poetry: "Whoever makes a new *rotruenge, pastourelle*, song, songlet, or chanson, I will sing of the holy virgin.")[113] The concept of the "new" had a certain complexity. An anonymous *contrafactura* of a *pastourelle* (and therefore "new" in neither form nor melody!) begins with a secular reverdie, saying "Quant voi la flor novele, / Florir en la praele, / Lors chant chancon novele / De la virge pucele" (When I see the new flower flowering in the meadow, then I sing a new song of the virgin maid), associating the renewal of the year with the renewal of poetry.[114] In the same collection, another *contrafactura* adapts the motif to more loverlike tones: "Fine amour et bone esperance / Me fait un noviau chant chanter / De cele qui touz ceaus avance / Qui de cuer la vuellent amer; / Si vueil la mere Dieu loer / en la chancon que je comence" (*Fin' amours* and good hope make me sing a new song of her who helps all those who will love her from the heart; thus I wish to praise God's mother in the song I am beginning).[115] Exceptionally, still another *contrafactura* ends its envoi with the motif, working it into an oblique quid pro quo: "Can g'en ai mout grant mestier / Et m'envoit tele estancele, / Por ceste chancon novele, / Qui me garde de pechier" (For I have great need [of her remembering me], and may she send such a spark [of spiritual ardor] for this new song that it will keep me from sinning).[116]

In these French poems, which are all to some degree "courtly" chansons, the use of the motif is directly modeled upon its use in secular love-song, that liturgy of the (usually) etherealized earthly beloved that was indeed a new song (or a new constellation of dissociated older ideas) in twelfth-century Europe. Italian examples of the motif seem to owe more to Scripture and less to contemporary lyric. For instance, one of the thirteenth-century *laude* in Cortona 91 has as its *ripresa* or refrain these lines: "Ogn'om canti novel canto / a san Iovanni, aulente fiore" (Everyone sing a new song of St. John, fragrant flower), which is a close paraphrase of the opening verse of Psalm 98.[117] The motif has the same look in texts from a fourteenth-century Florence *laudario*; concerning St. Augustine, one says, "Tutti di si gran Santo, / Novello or faccian canto" (Let all make a new song of so great a saint); another, to St. Zanobio, bids, "Novel canto tutta gente / Canti con divoto core" (Let all people sing a new song with devout heart).[118] However, a Marian *lauda* from Venice (1300/1350), which was much under the influence of French literature at that time, shows the motif in its courtly form again: "A l'onor d'una nobel polcella, / Mare del Re celestial Segnor, / Cantar me plas d'una cancon novella / A tuti quigi k'entendo en lo so amor" (In honor of a noble maiden, mother of the King, the heavenly Lord, I wish to sing a new song for all those who are set upon her love).[119] And later in the century, Bianco da Siena begins a *capitolo ternario* in a style that owes little to Scripture and much to literature: "O primo amor dal Padre procedente / E dal Figliuol, vero Spirito Santo, / O vero Iddio solo onnipotente, / Per lo tuo dono ho fatto nuovo canto" (O first Love proceeding from the Father and from the Son, true Holy Spirit, O true God alone almighty, through your gift I have made a new song).[120]

German and Old Norse uses of the motif sometimes have a more technical sense. For example, Meister Rumezlant (Rûmelant von Sachsen) several times dedicates the "first praise" in a new form or *wîse* to God, which honors both the Lord and the stanza.[121] But the anonymous poet's reference in "Bjoða vil ek" to his "nyium od," (new ode or poem), the reference in "Ain anevanc in ewikeit" to his "niwen gesanc" in the course of an inadequacy topos, and another passage in Muscatbluet that promises a "new song" to Mary without any connection with the stanza form—all of these are of the familiar psalmic type.[122]

As with other motifs and figures, the derivation of the motif of the "new song" is complex, and its use reflects this complexity. In its customary position at the beginning of a poem, however, it acts as a variant on the call to praise or song, heightening the already considerable self-referentiality involved in such a call. It almost always appears in encomiastic lyric, directed at God, the saints, and particularly the Virgin. Since many of the vernacular texts that contain it are in fact *contrafacturas*, one can conclude that it refers not to the superficial but to the essential "newness," literal and spiritual, of each new poetic tribute to the patrons of a sinful humanity. After all, for the medieval religious poet, Christ was "ein sanc / des niemer stunde verdriuzet" (a song of which one never tires).[123] Der alte Missenaere tells us best of all what song, especially "new song," was for the medieval poet and audience:

> Das sank das hoeste si in himele unde uf erden,
> des ziuh' ich an die engel, die mit sange lobent
>   Got in himele dort.
> Mit worten mak von brote Gotes lichnam werden;
> des ist sank unde wort daz hoeste, sit daz ie unde
>   ie was Gotes wort.
> Sank leret tugende pflegen, vlien valschen rat,
>   sank vroeuwet, sank ringet vil der swaere;
> sank ist gotelich, sank der ist lonebaere:
> gedoene ane wort, daz ist ein toter galm, so ist
>   vor Gote sank gehort.[124]

(Song is the highest thing in heaven and on earth; I affirm this because of the angels, who praise God with song up there in heaven. Through words bread can become God's body; so song and word are the highest thing, since ever and ever God's Word was. Song teaches to cultivate virtues, to flee false counsel, song gives joy, song takes away the greater part of heaviness; song is divine, song is worthy of reward; music without words, that is dead noise, but song is heard by God.)

Could one find a higher tribute to the power and value of lyric poetry?

Sometimes, medieval religious lyric may involve self-reference by the poet to himself, and not simply to his "song," either in the form of outright *self-naming* or more discursively through the inclusion of *autobiographical details*.

As a guarantee of orthodoxy and a means of obtaining prayers for oneself it had been an accepted practice to sign hymns from the earliest period on.[125] However, except through acrostics (as in Byzantine hymnography), such signatures were external to the text, and in practice, most hymns were either never signed or shed their signatures in the process of transmission, lapsing back into anonymity.[126] In classical literature, authorial names might appear in a *sphragis* within the text, in a *titulus* or *sillubos* attached to the roll on which it was written, or as part of an initial dedication. The first falls into desuetude, by and large, in the West, especially in religious lyric; the other two practices continue in various forms but of course do not affect the text itself. The one Latin genre that makes special room for signatures is the penitential poem, where, since one is confessing how reprehensible one's conduct has been, one may name oneself as part of the ritual of public self-abnegation at the poem's start or ending.[127]

The practice is rare in vernacular religous lyric. Llull signs his *planctus Mariae*; "Garzo" includes his name in four of the *laude* that Cortona 91 contains; Lambert Ferri imitates the secular custom of incorporating one's name in the envoi of a Marian sirventese, and Gautier de Coincy ends "Puis que voi la fleur novele" with "Ci fenist la chanconete / LE PRIOR" (Here THE PRIOR ends his little song), which in its omission of Gautier's actual name perhaps indicates a higher opinion of himself and his fame than including the name would have.[128] In Old Norse, skaldic pride in one's craft lies behind the riddling close to a *drápa* on St. Catherine, where the poet first slips his name, "Kalfr," into the poem and then Latinizes it a few lines later to *Vitulus vates* (!) (Kalf the bard).[129] German *Spruchdichter*, such as Regenbogen and Muscatbluet, are the most inclined to name themselves; Heinrich der Teichner actually signs all but one of his 729 poems. Konrad von Wuerzburg and Hans von Cleve include their names in their great Marian poems; the author of the *Rheinisches Marienlob* deliberately omits his name as an act of humility, leaving one to infer the expectation that he would normally have stated it within the text.[130]

Autobiographical details appear in a few highly artistic, self-conscious poets' work. Dante provides us a guide to the interpretation of their use when he states (*Convivio* 1.2.12) that one may speak of oneself when it serves a doctrinal point, with Augustine's *Confessions* as his major precedent.[131] Alfonso speaks of his illnesses and how the Virgin brought him recovery, Guittone and Iacopone draw on their own experiences; the penitential section 4 of "The Testament of Dan Lydgate" has at least the appearance of autobiography; a late German poet like Oswald von Wolkenstein, who has an unusually strong authorial personality, or Hugo von Montfort will write about themselves.[132]

In Latin, the ninth-century poets Gottschalk and Notker both refer to personal traits or fortunes, though not in liturgical poetry, and the tenth-century poet, Froumond of Tegernsee, writes a religious poem concerning his refusal of the priesthood—similar examples are scattered through earlier and later Latin religious poetry. In Greek, one finds John the Geometer speaking frequently, much like King David, of persecution by his enemies; John Mauropus refers on several occasions, in his liturgical as well as his paraliturgical *kanons*, to the poor state of his health (a subject his letters are also full of); even Theodore Prodromos's saints' calendar, a rather objective sort of context one would suppose, includes autobiographical references, which have their analogue in this case in twelfth-century Latin begging poems to prelates or magnates, rather than to saints.[133] Mauropus, it would seem, is not alone in his hypochondria; mentions of illness enjoy a privileged status, and one finds them in such disparate poets as Notker Balbulus, Walter of Châtillon, and (in Middle English) Friar John Audelay.[134]

Instead of referring directly to oneself or one's name, medieval poets will far more often lay stress upon their role as poet, upon the formal or generic status of their poem, or upon the occasion or situation for which the poem is meant to serve.

The latter case is characteristic of Latin liturgical poetry; for instance, like other poets, Hildegard refers directly to antiphonal singing in her sequence on St. Disibod: "Membra mirificae laudis aedificasti / in duabus partibus . . ." (You have raised up the members of wonderful praise in two parts). The processional hymn in epanaleptic elegiacs, "Sancta Maria, quid est?" includes a vivid description of the behavior of the multitude during a tenth-century religious festival at Rome.[135] Normally, references are brief and conventional, but even so, they interject some presence of the poem or its performance between the audience and the poem's religious meaning.

Byzantine poets avoid references to mode of performance and instead focus on their role as poets (references the Byzantine liturgy accommodated without resistance) or the poetic status of what they had written. For instance, Theodore the Studite speaks of himself as "your poor hymnodist," in a phrase one finds in various forms either in the text or as an acrostic in many Byzantine hymns.[136] There is also a sizable repertory of terms for referring to the text itself (ἆσμα, ὕμνος, ψαλμός, ᾠδή, μέλος) in regular use. In sum, self-referentiality is quite strong in the Byzantine tradition, and common, though less striking, in Latin as well.

The vernaculars differ a good deal in their use of the various forms of self-reference. None appears often in Spanish: Berceo speaks of himself as Mary's "troubadour"; Ayala apologizes for his old-fashioned style; Alonso de Proaza mentions the number of stanzas in a text, with numerological overtones.[137] In Portuguese, Alfonso (or his assistants) cast themselves, like Berceo, in the role of Mary's troubadours.[138] In Provençal, Cerveri de Girona speaks of the need to write a "good" poem before he dies; Peire de Corbiac mentions that he is singing of Mary "in romance tongue"; Guiraut Riquier complains of the bad reception (religious) verse gets at court; Daude de Pradas deprecates the singing of other sorts of song and invokes a blessing on whoever sings his own; Lanfranc Cigala says he will sing despite his depression and whatever the results as poetry; in a competition poem, Raimon de Cornet describes how he hunts for "rare and subtle rhymes," and other competition entries refer directly to their formal genre (*dansa, tenso,* and so forth).[139] This degree and variety of self-reference is typical of Provençal secular poetry, the source for its presence in religious poetry. In Catalan, only *joyas* entries show much self-reference ("your troubadours," a mention of pen and paper, the act of rhyming, the role of the judges, and so on).[140]

In the thirteenth-century French religious chanson, there is a good deal of talk about the compulsion or desire to sing of the Virgin, particularly at the beginning of the poem; in some cases, the song tends to become the subject, as it does in the *chanson d'amour.* For instance, Moniot d'Arras begins one poem,

> De haut liu muet la cançon que je cant
> Car ele muet de la vierge pucele
> Dont Dieus naqui; si voeil q'a mon vivant
> Ait cascun an de moi cancon novele.
> Ains mais ne fis, pour voir le vous creant,
> Cançon de li, or me vient a creant
> Que de li cant, s'ert ma chanson plus bele.[141]

(From high place comes the song I sing, for it comes from [deals with] the virgin maiden of whom God was born; and I want her to have a new song from me every year of my life. [This was Gautier's practice, as he several times tells us.] I do assure you, I never made a song about her before, and now I feel a desire to sing of her, and so my song will be more beautiful.)

This emphasis on the poet's motives for writing is not confined to Old French poetry, of course, but it seems particularly frequent there.

In German, references to the poem's form (see above, concerning new *wîsen*) are a standard feature of *Spruchdichtung,* where poems are grouped in the manuscripts according to stanza type. Poets also speak of their work or the praises they are singing, sometimes making a formal offering of the poem to the addressee. One hears too about *tône* (tunes/stanzas) wasted on worldly subjects, the strictures of rhyme, or a poem's structural division into sections.[142] Old Norse shows a similar interest in poetic organization and technique. It was traditional in the *drápas*, where the format was well defined and explicit (introduction, sections unified by a refrain-line or *stef*, then the conclusion or *slaem*). Another notable feature is the regular incorporation of a title for the poem into the text—something one rarely finds in other traditions, despite exceptions like Rutebeuf's "Chantepleure." Some sort of minimal reference to "this poem" is extremely common. The absence of even such references is typical of Middle English religious lyric, which surpasses any other tradition (except in the literary strand of its development, which appears in the later fourteenth century and becomes important in the fifteenth) in unpretentiousness and lack of poetic self-awareness.

Most readers will have found the range and degree of self-reference in medieval religious lyric rather surprising. In most traditions and genres, poets feel free to discuss what they are doing, or at least to make some note of it. But one should not allow the evidence presented in this section to obscure the basic facts about this poetry in its normal form. Compared to what we are accustomed to, the author's presence is vestigial; the poetic act as such is secondary or ignored; the particular situation that engendered the poem is thrust aside and usually irrecoverable. Precisely for these reasons, one is irresistibly drawn to the exceptional passages where the mask slips, or the poet takes it off for a moment. But they remain exceptions nonetheless, and one must not demand their presence or resent their absence in medieval religious lyric as a whole.

vi

The last section of the main body of the text of this book concerns rhetorical means for reducing the distance between the subject matter of religious lyric and the life of its users. These include metaphor, details from average human experience, colloquial phrases, and the like. By equation or association, all such means move heaven and earth closer together, and in this respect are analogous to the rhetorical figures that serve to reduce or eliminate historical distance and are discussed in the first section of this chapter. Since these means generally occur in close association—that is, a tradition, a poetic type within a tradition, or an individual poet will use them all or none of them—it is possible to study them together, as variant expressions of the same impulse. However, as metaphor is the most powerful means of bringing the remote into proximity, and as it sees the widest and most interesting use and development in medieval religious poetry, it will receive pride of place in the ensuing pages.

Most of the metaphors in medieval religious lyric are rigorously traditional; their content matters less than their metonymic association with a particular subject matter. In connection with sacred persons, typological symbols act as the core of the repertory, with certain symbols enjoying special favor in poetic usage in all linguistic traditions; thus, in Marian poetry, Jesse's rod, Aaron's staff, Moses' burning bush, Ezechiel's closed door, and Gideon's fleece are the types of preference, each with its nimbus of prescribed metaphors, and poets will not usually venture much outside this list, unless the length of their encomium demands more material. In connection with sacred events, the repertory is no less well defined. For most subject matters (e.g., dawn, the Crucifixion, the Resurrection), an early hymn that won wide acceptance will have established the basic metaphorical matrix (cf. Ambrose for dawn and Fortunatus for the Crucifixion and Resurrection), which can be modified by later poetic successes or shifts in piety but generally shows great staying power. It is the tone and the emphases that change, in the main, not the motifs themselves. Even the paradoxes to which (for example) Nativity hymns give such prominence are thoroughly traditional; certainly they held no surprises for the medieval audience.

As for everyday details or conversational effects, the Latin and Greek traditions largely exclude both from religious poetry, at least up to the thirteenth century. After 1200, Latin religious lyric becomes more hospitable to such elements; except in poets like Symeon the New Theologian or Theodore Prodromos, who incorporate demotic influences into their work, the Byzantine religious lyric will countenance neither. In particular, Byzantine hymnography, whose authors adhered closely to patterns established in the early centuries, makes no attempt to accommodate creaturely feelings by humanizing heaven. It may dramatize sacred history to make it more actual, but it insists on the altitude of heaven and on the human possibility of divinization. The fundamental difference may have been that where the West saw an abyss between heaven and earth, the East saw only a great but unbroken and continuous distance that connected as much as it separated.[143]

There were excellent reasons for the resistance of Greek and Latin, especially in the liturgy, to a free expansion of metaphor or free association of time and eternity through naturalistic detail or language. (Incidentally, those who doubt the ability of medieval Latin or Byzantine Greek to achieve the colloquial should examine the work of the Archpoet or Hugh Primas, on the one hand, or Symeon or Prodromos, on the other. Both were languages of education, to be sure, but they were also spoken languages.) As was discussed in the Introduction, the purpose of medieval religious lyric was not exploratory. Rather, it was commemorative, celebratory, community affirming. It looked inward to the beliefs, knowledge, and experiences the orthodox faithful shared, not out to the dubious fringes of speculative theology. With this circumscription of subject matter came a necessary limitation on contact between the sacred and the worldly. Indeed, when creaturely life intrudes in religious poetry beyond a certain point, attention may shift to its fresh vitality and away from the fixities it is supposed to illustrate and support. One can see from the apocryphal gospels of antiquity that from the start popular piety exerted considerable pressure in favor of a further humanization of the relative austerity of scriptural accounts. Against this pressure, the Church led the long and ultimately unsuccessful resistance in the West, succumbing in the twelfth and thirteenth centuries to a combination of change from within (new monastic forms of piety) and from below (popular movements, co-opted through Church acceptance of the fraternal orders). The age that was born then we still inhabit.

The Church did of course tolerate the free play of analogy and speculative thought, to a large extent, but in the privileged zone of learned exegesis, not in the public sphere of liturgical or even nonliturgical poetry. Gregory the Great, in a famous passage from the *Moralia in Job*, celebrates the amorphous fluidity of scriptural interpretation, rising and expanding like water flooding a hilly terrain, taking its shape at each moment from the lay of the land but presumably tending toward a plenum in which everything participates in a universal ocean of analogy.[144] Where metaphor might distract or confuse, it was cabined and confined; where only a limited and trustworthy audience would be affected, it could and did run riot. Joachim of Fiore's comparison of Scripture to "liquid wax" echoes Gregory's conceit; in the same period, one may also find Alanus de Insulis joking about medieval uses of authority (which were licentiously metaphorical in many cases) as treating texts like a "wax nose," to be squeezed into and out of shape, as one desired.[145] Curiously, the same period that saw the beginnings of a humanization of the sacred, conducted in large part through metaphors with naturalistic vehicles, also saw a reaction against the unbridled use of metaphor previously dominant in exegesis; one can detect a good deal of unease in Joachim's and Alanus's phrases, and it is symptomatic of the change in attitude that Rupert of Deutz compares the task of interpreting Scripture to well-digging.[146] Instead of spreading edifying, spiritually vivifying waters over the thirsty ground, the exegete has become a toilsome laborer casting aside that ground to win with difficulty some narrow access to the hidden waters of life below.

Medieval ideas about metaphor are too extensive and complex to receive full treatment here. Instead, I will concentrate on the theological rationale for metaphor, since it casts a unique and revealing light on the use of metaphor, either explicit or implicit, in later medieval religious lyric in the West. In a valuable article published some fifteen years ago, Hennig Brinkmann summarized medieval views about "naming God," drawing especially on Alanus de Insulis's summa "Quoniam homines" and his *Theologicae regulae*, both early scholastic texts of considerable influence.[147] God transcends all creation and therefore language, which is in effect condemned to the status of metaphor in anything it says about God. It can describe only God's effects on mankind, not God himself. There are four methods of description open to it: (1) God may be named as the cause of the various virtues; (2) things like God because of their positive qualities may be compared to God; (3) the human motives consistent with God's actions as revealed through Scripture may be ascribed to God (e.g., God can be said to have been "angry" when he is known to have punished the people of Israel); and the most interesting for our purposes, (4) since God is in the end *unlike* anything we can experience, the most accurate method of description is through negation. This last alternative bears a close kinship to the theory of metaphor contained in the "negative theology" of the late antique mystical writer, Dionysios the pseudo-Areopagite, which had a diffuse effect on medieval Western thought thanks to Erigena's translation in the ninth century and renewed scholarly activity concerning the Dionysian canon beginning in the twelfth century.[148] With the radicalism of a mystic, Dionysios takes the notion of description through negation (i.e., the fundamental indescribability of God, who is the unnameable) to its logical conclusion: the more grotesque and inappropriate the symbol, the fitter it is to signify the divine mystery. By outraging good taste and reason, it liberates the aspiring soul from the bonds of human socialization and human intellect; only then can it attain the "noetic light" that lies beyond the cloud of unknowing, that inky mass of language negated and symbols burnt to ashes.

Of course, no one would contend that the writers of late medieval religious lyric were all practicing mystics or negative theologians, though some of them (including Jacopone da Todi or Bianco da Siena in Italy, the Englishman Rolle, and German writers like Mechthild of Magdeburg) certainly were. But it is only such ideas about the function of metaphor that can explain the more bizarre aspects of its use in religious lyric, as we shall see below. In addition, these ideas find good support outside the speculations of mysticism in literary theory and in the mechanics of human perception. For example, one can look at literary discourse as an array of procedures for persuading the reader to make comparisons between words and their elements that would normally never arise in nonartistic language. Poetry in particular arranges language to create complex equations between words grouped into lines or stanzas and brought into association by their position within formal units and by the recurrence of sounds (cf. rhyme words, initial words in a series of lines, final lines in a series of stanzas, words in a line or stanza sharing consonant or vowel sounds, and so forth). But the effect of such equations is not simply to make us see likenesses where we had seen none before. Rather, they also, as a necessary consequence, awaken us to the differences between words, which may in turn enter into the creation of meaning (the most obvious illustration is perhaps an antithetical couplet in the manner of Pope, where an extreme degree of similarity between the structure and rhythm, and usually the sounds, of two lines of the same length serves to isolate and highlight what is different between them). In talking about God, Dionysios and Alanus hit upon a basic feature of artistic and, particularly, poetic language: the power to make us see likeness in unlikeness and unlikeness in likeness, in fact, to grasp something like the reality of objects and persons through the unreality of ultimately false comparisons. Similarly, it is becoming clear that perception is based upon the measurement of difference. Visual perception, for instance, exploits the eye's ability to register and the brain's ability to interpret differences of brightness along edges dividing areas under different illumination from one another.[149] Even in infants, the auditory perception of language appears to involve the ability to categorize sounds by systematic differences that the brain discriminates and applies to incoming speech sounds long before there is any comprehension of their symbolic meaning.[150] Language acquisition at a later stage proceeds by the same process of perception of difference and abstract categorization. For example, a young child at a certain stage will use "tall" and "short" as synonyms, not because the child is incapable of an adequate degree of abstract thinking, but because he or she must first grasp the abstract category of "words designating the vertical dimension of a human being" and only then can distinguish between words belonging to that category. In fact, the child who "confuses" short and tall has correctly perceived that these two words share an important *likeness* that makes them different from other groups or classes of words. Through the same procedure, the child can continue to make ever finer judgments about difference within likeness, about likeness within difference. Indeed, the child will play with the latter concept from early on, bringing together words that contain similar sounds (especially rhyming syllables) to test out whether they belong together in some other way as well.[151]

I believe that a solid cognitive basis exists for the apparent absurdity of the notion of description through negation. I would even claim that the deepest medieval thinking about language and poetry was done in theology, as part of the reflection on what Kenneth Burke calls, in an excellent book, "the rhetoric of religion."[152] God is not only the Word, God is also a word, and a word that challenges one to consider how words work. Alanus and Dionysios are worth heeding on both scores.

Whatever the causes, the second half of the Middle Ages in the West saw a general opening of literature to life, manifested not least in the rise to literary status of the birth tongues of Christian Europe. In literature that dealt with the sacred, this opening proceeds primarily through the oblique channels of metaphor, either as explicit verbal equation of one thing to another or as implicit equation of sacred persons and events to merely human persons and events through describing the former in the same terms and with the same imaginative details as one would the latter. At the very least, theological warrants for religious use of metaphor such as we have just been examining did nothing to impede this process, and in many cases, where poets had acquired a degree of theological sophistication as part of their education, may have given it important support. However, one must look to Provençal poetry for the origins of an extensive use of fresh, nontraditional metaphor, which spreads thence to the other vernacular traditions.[153] As chapter 2 should have demonstrated, secular influence on later medieval religious lyric was very considerable, and the use of metaphor in secular vernacular poetry made its impact along with features of form and motif. The fact that Latin religious lyric, especially the Latin hymn, was a tissue of inherited, frozen metaphors made it all the more impressionable—one could continue to work in the traditional mode but also revitalize it by substituting here and there new metaphors in the old niches.

Of course, most of the old metaphors, and the old ways, stayed securely in place, and most poets made no attempt to dislodge them. Still, one may say that the future was with those who did. It seems appropriate that in his treatise on how to write poetry, Matthew of Vendome treats metaphor as the prince of tropes, a claim no one today would think it necessary to assert or dare to challenge.[154] It seems appropriate, too, that one of the Latin terms for metaphor was *conversio*, which happens also to have been the word for religious conversion (something the crusaders and missionary friars were much exercized about) and a near relation of *conversatio*, the word for lifestyle frequently used of monks and their self-devotion to the Lord. One might say that the poets of religious lyric tried to "convert" the carnal world to sanctified ends by applying the *conversio* or conversion of metaphor.[155] It makes sense then that so much of the material they used came from the lower levels of life, the fleshiest and earthiest and most unethereal, because those were the levels that most needed to be converted. Like Christ, whose historical incarnation and sacrifice and especially its daily renewal in the Eucharist were at the center of late medieval piety, their language descended from its heights, seeking to redeem the depths by incorporating them into its substance, *sermo humilis* finding a new way of exaltation in a new self-abnegation. For us, metaphor works to rejoin the innumerable fragments of reality, scattered across the levels of history and the life of the senses; it offers us the role, too, of an overmastering consciousness that has the power to forge a new universe, for the space of a text at least. For the Middle Ages, metaphor healed the split between heaven and earth, promising that in the mind of God "all manner of things" might be well and whole again, for the space of eternity. As the body of each believer was to be glorified at the Last Day, so in the poetry of the sacred the body of human experience might put off corruption too.

The actual result was very different. Heaven did not raise up earth and consecrate it—earth pulled down heaven and absorbed it. As the centuries pass, the best work of the best poets puts more and more energy into elaborating the body of its metaphors, and the spirit turns ghostly. Better, it becomes a transparent pretext for the inclusion of as much human reality as possible. In allegories, the literal sense gets the upper hand, and the reader must remind himself to translate the fascinating letter into the faded, no longer controlling meaning.[156] Typological symbols lapse into simple metaphors; Gideon's fleece, type of the Virgin, becomes the picturesque "white fleece of thy womb virginall" in Hoccleve, and the fructifying dew of the Holy Spirit is the gentle unmeaning rain of Leonardo Giustinian's "come piogia in lana / che descendendo in terra piana / non opera macchia ne diffecto" (like rain in wool which falling on level ground causes neither harm nor damage).[157] As Achilles, Judas Maccabaeus, and Helen infiltrate Marian encomium, the glory of the Virgin turns to pomp, the Virgin to a Queen.[158] In short, the sacred is secularized. When heaven sups with earth, it had better use a long spoon.

As Chenu demonstrates, the typological equation of New and Old Testament proved to contain similar dangers. Innocent III said that sometimes they christianized the Old Testament, sometimes they judaicized the New; Christ's sacrifice threatened to become "a special case of the ritual laws of Leviticus."[159] In effect, the "shadow" eclipsed the "light" of its typological fulfillment, just as the letter eclipsed the allegorical significance and the vehicle of metaphor the tenor in the final centuries of the Middle Ages. It is likely that thinkers and writers had no choice in any of these matters, and that they were simply carried along in currents far vaster and deeper than theology or poetry. Certainly the use of metaphor, in the broad sense meant here, by the authors of medieval religious lyric reflected rather than produced large-scale change. Still, opening this lyric to the reality of daily life was part of the process of conferring dignity and meaning upon the latter by giving it an increasing place in artistic and religious expression. Insofar as we are late heirs to the results of the protracted sanctification of the commonplace and the lowly that began with the New Testament, the details of a crucial stage when the pace of change accelerated and the direction became definite ought to be of interest to us. It is to the details that I now turn.

By way of illustration of the general evolution toward a *sermo humilior* in later medieval religious lyric, I have chosen a thoroughly traditional motif, here christened the "container contained." After its vicissitudes have been traced, the chapter will close with an account, with numerous illustrations, of the more interesting varieties of metaphor in each linguistic tradition.

In religious lyric, the motif of the "container contained" appears almost exclusively in the form of a paradox concerning the fact that God, who encompasses all, was himself encompassed as the incarnate Christ in the Virgin's womb. The idea of enclosure that this motif involves has great and primordial symbolic significance of a highly ambiguous kind that the happy accident of the rhyming pair of English words *womb* and *tomb* perfectly conveys. On the one hand, enclosure can mean protection within the realm of the known, safe, and warm. On the other hand, it can mean imprisonment within the unknown, perilous, dark, and cold realm of death.[160] Logically, then, Christmas *conductus* show a frequent association between the image of Christ in Mary's womb and the image of Christ in the Passover tomb. The fact that Christ turns both that tomb and the tomb of hell into a womb out of which he and the imprisoned people of the Old Testament are reborn further justifies the association. In consequence, in at least one case, the "container" paradox is actually used directly of Christ in the grave, which like Mary miraculously contains him who contains the universe.[161]

Since this discussion of metaphor focuses on the second half of the Middle Ages, my first examples of the "container" motif in action will come from twelfth-century Latin poetry, whose antecedents can be disregarded here.[162] To Walter of Châtillon goes the honor of achieving what is undoubtedly the finest poetic statement of the motif; in a Marian hymn, he describes the Virgin as "claudens in utero / claudentem sidera" (enclosing in her womb / him who encloses the stars).[163] To the notion of "infinity in a little room" that tradition gave him, Walter adds an imaginative perception of the analogy between the darkness of the womb and the darkness of the nighttime universe contained within God and scattered with the stars that for a medieval mind betokened the order (and the close proximity just beyond) of heaven. Much more typical of Latin examples of the motif is this quatrain from Bernard of Morlaix's(?) *Mariale*, a text I have drawn on before:

> O felicem genetricem,
>   Cuius sacra viscera
> Meruere continere
>   Continentem aethera![164]

(O fortunate mother, whose holy vitals earned the right to contain him who contains the heavens!)

The abstract poetic plural *aethera* entirely lacks the poetic impact of the no less poetic but much more concrete and suggestive *sidera*.

In most early instances, vernacular use of the motif is much like its use in Latin. Around the end of the twelfth century, Reinmar der Zweter exclaims

den des himels wîte   nie umbevie, diu ende nie gewan
  Noch mit der hoehe in umbevie
noch mit der wîten tiefen   grundelosen helle nie,
den umbevie ir cleiner lip: da merket alle wunder an![165]

(Him whom the width of heaven never encompassed which has never found
ending—neither with its heights has it ever encompassed him nor the broad
deeps of bottomless hell—him your little body encompassed: all take note of
the wonder therein!)

In the mid-thirteenth century, the *Rheinische Marienlob* tells how the angels
praise and marvel at Mary:

Si wundert ser, wi got belive
genzlich in dim engem live,
des götlich gewalt ervült aleine
himel ind erde algemeine,
Dat du in dregs, de alle dinc dreget,
de alle creaturn beweget,
si wundert, dat du dem gefs spise,
de in himelrich is der engel spise.[166]

(They are greatly astonished that God dwells wholly in your slender body,
God whose divine power fills by itself heaven and earth entire, that you bear
him who bears all things, who sets all creatures in motion, they are amazed
that you give him his food who in the kingdom of heaven is the angels' food.)

Even in this passage, however, one can see the impulse to soften the sublimity of the "container" paradox by including, rather periphrastically,
Mary's suckling of Christ in the same extended sentence. The same impulse
takes a humoristic turn in a slightly later poem by Konrad von Wuerzburg:

Wilder schepher wunderhaft,
jâ gebar dich dîn geschaft
und diu crêâtiuer dîn . . .
durch sîn tougenlich geberc
slouf ein rise in ein getwerc,
dô dîn bilde almehteclich
hal in kindes forme sich.[167]

(Wild and wonderful creator, truly your creation and your creature bore
you . . . through his secret embrace, a giant slept in a dwarf, when your all-
powerful shape clad itself in a child's form.)

The same "popular" quality appears in a thirteenth-century Old French religious chanson, whose author retains this structure but varies the motif by
stressing God's power rather than his infinity:

Virge concut au tesmoing d'Ysaye
Et enfanta sanz dolour endurer
Celui par cui en deus fu departie
La Rouge Mer pour son peuple sauver,
Puis la rejoinst et la fist reverser
Seur Pharaon et sa grant compaignie.
Bien doit estre loee et graciie
Cele qui cainst neuf mois de sa couroie
Celui qui fist si merveilleuse voie.[168]

(As Isaiah testifies, a virgin conceived and brought forth without pain him through whom the Red Sea was divided in twain to save his people, and then he reunited it and let it fall back upon Pharaoh and his great host. Well should she be praised and thanked who for nine months girt with her belt him who made so marvellous a route.)

Even the shift from the concept of something so vast it holds all one can see—a concept that is very hard to grasp—to the far more accessible story of God dividing the Red Sea shows an accommodation to a less sophisticated audience. But it is that *couroie* or "belt" that really brings the miracle of the Incarnation down to the human level. It is interesting that earlier in the century Gautier de Coincy, like the earlier German writer Reinmar, still preserves the mystery and sublimity of the motif, even though the scriptural antecedents of the phrase of potter and pot do not entirely exclude a response to it as a detail from everyday life: "Quant cil forme prist humaine / Qui en son poing tot enclot, / Mers entra en la fontaine / Et li potiers en son pot" (When he assumed the human shape who holds all enclosed in his fist, the sea entered into the fountainhead and the potter into his pot).[169]

In later medieval lyric, as the process of humanization proceeds, the motif temporarily becomes vestigial or falls into disuse. Even in mitigated form, it was apparently too metaphysical, too paradoxical, too sublime in its appeal to the imagination to enter into the domestic arrangements of most Marian lyric between 1250 and 1400. In German, Frauenlob's *Marienleich* is sufficiently high style to include the motif, though it has been merged with a rather baroque development of the conceit of God as tailor cutting out the cloth of his incarnation.[170] But the motif shows few signs of coming back into fashion until the early sixteenth century (i.e., 200 years later) in the period just before the Reformation when there was a great deal of hymn translation, vernacular competition with Latin hymnody, and an attendant incorporation of the hymnic mode into German religious lyric.[171] As a result, one finds Johannes von Rinkenberc returning to something like the original form of the "container" motif:

Unt den du tougen sunderbar
hatost umbevangen in dir reinecliche,

> der alliu ding umbevangen gar
> hat, wazzer luft viur erde unt himelriche:
> des waere du ein klose hie.[172]

(And in a mysterious and wonderful way you encompassed him purely in
yourself who embraced all things whatsoever, water air fire earth and heaven:
of him you were a cloister here.)

Besides reviving the old typological notion that makes Mary the *hortus con-
clusus*, the "cloistered garden" of the Song of Songs, and that underlies the
"container" motif throughout the tradition, this (very) late medieval poet
has returned to the sublime mode of Walter of Châtillon and Reinmar and
Gautier de Coincy—the four elements may not have the visual power of
Walter's *sidera*, but they are at least as grand and primal (and liturgical to
boot).

In other traditions in the late Middle Ages (fifteenth and early sixteenth
centuries), one finds the same pattern. The "container" motif appears here
and there, but in its hymnic, traditional form, befitting the dignity of the
Marian poetry of the period.[173] Certainly Leonardo Giustinian's uses of the
motif are of this kind; one of his *laude* makes no more of it than this:

> O vaso piccolino, in cui riposa
> Colui, che il ciel non piglia.[174]

(O little vessel, in which he rests whom heaven does not contain.)

Even late medieval Italian Marian poetry will rarely forego the tender touch
of a diminutive ("piccolino"), but there is little else in this text to challenge
the regal station she enjoys on her "si sublime ed eccellente seggio" (so sublime and excellent throne—l. 18).

Not only the handling of the "container" motif, but the handling of naturalistic detail, naturalistic speech, and naturalistic comparisons follows the
same pattern: movement away from the "high" mode and metaphors traditional in Latin hymnody toward a greater and greater lifelikeness, sometimes taking grotesque forms, and offset to a degree at the end of the Middle
Ages by a resurgence of the hymnic style that affects Latin religious lyric as
well as the vernaculars. Narrative poetry (and the drama) seems to lag somewhat behind, reaching a climax of naturalism in the fifteenth century when
lyric had already begun to retreat from the naturalistic extremes reached in
the thirteenth and fourteenth centuries. The sequence seems to have been
first a metaphorical use of ordinary life and then direct translation of sacred
history into the mode of the profane.

Greek poetry, whether liturgical or nonliturgical, deals almost entirely in
the high and the sublime, including what it takes from Scripture. This eleva-

tion does not exclude warmth of feeling, but it does exclude naturalism.[175] The additional factor of an ongoing humanist tradition among the educated in the East abetted the theological tradition of Greek thought, with its high speculative and transcendental bent, in excluding the "low" from poetry (Symeon and Theodore are the major exceptions). In consequence, Byzantine metaphor and language have few surprises for the reader. Like Walter's phrase "claudens in utero/claudentem sidera," its victories come from a purification and intensification of highly selective, inherited means.

Latin religious lyric up to 1200 contains many isolated cases of brilliantly successful metaphor, but it is largely abstract in nature, and those images it admits are, as stated, usually prescribed by tradition. Outside paradigmatic texts by figures like Ambrose or Venantius Fortunatus, one sees relatively little use of novel metaphor. Among examples from the Carolingian period through the twelfth century, there is Ekkehard IV's comparison in an Ascension poem of Christ and the apostles to a swarm of bees and their leader, a comparison that was more decorous then than it seems now (for the Middle Ages, the bee was a kind of bird, the source of their sweetening, and the object of much admiration).[176] Taking a leaf from a famous passage in Orosius, Walter of Châtillon describes the approach of the end of the world as an evening in mountainous country, where darkness rises up from the valleys.[177] Adam of St. Victor compares the faith of the martyrs to mustard seed, which grows by attrition; another martyr resounds like a plucked chord with Christ's praises when he is struck, and fire to him is like the fire of a kiln to a pot, or the fire that releases the full odor of mustard (again) or incense; despite their scriptural origins, these metaphors are used in a novel enough way that they regain their freshness.[178] The line between "high" and "low" that Adam approaches without transgressing is tested further in the next century in Franciscan Latin poems like John Pecham's *Philomena*, where the vehemence of the poet's response to the Crucifixion expresses itself in sometimes shocking imagery:

> Hoc reclinatorium
>   quotiens monstratur
> piae menti, totiens
>   ei glutinatur,
> Et sicut accipiter
>   totus inescatur
> Super carnem rubeam,
>   per quam revocatur.[179]

(Every time this bed [i.e., Christ on the cross] is shown to the pious mind, it cleaves to it, and like the hawk it swallows down completely the bait of the red meat by which it is called back.)

The image of the bed is common in devotional literature of the period; the hawk taking the bait is not. However, though it is startling, it remains within the "high" matter of falconry. And yet, the grotesque quality that Dionysios's views on metaphor and the naming of God commend is very near.

This quality emerges completely in the vernaculars. Sometimes a grotesque metaphor is borrowed from religious prose; sometimes, it seems to be original to the poem where it appears. In any case, the ingenuities of late medieval sermons work hand in hand with the ingenuities of late medieval religious lyric, which was used in sermons and which had similar aims for its clerical writers. Reinmar offers not Christ but Mary as the believer's bed, a chaste bed to be sure, with Mary's beneficence as its mattress and coverlet; here one suspects the *al fresco* bed of Middle High German *pastourelle*, spread with leaves and rose blossoms, has been deliberately translated into something more homely and less erotically stimulating.[180] The bed and bedding metaphor enjoys a flourishing career in religious lyric on into the *Meistersang* tradition. In Italian, Guittone d'Arezzo, whose grotesqueries were rejected by the young Dante of the "New Style" but reappeared transfigured in the Comedy, asks Christ to make our hearts as full of lamentation for the Crucifixion as a sponge, speaks of honor growing like a fish in the great sea, and describes us as oarsmen rowing hard toward evil.[181] (Of course, strictly speaking, all these "diminishing" metaphors are directed toward men, not heaven.) Jacopone makes Christ into a university teacher with himself as the textbook and compares his decision to redeem mankind to becoming an ant to save an anthill, and an unworthy one at that.[182] An anonymous penitential *lauda* of the fourteenth century compares its speaker to a kidney wrapped up in fat; again, the object of the metaphor is human and earthly, but it still acts to physicalize the spiritual (the effects of irony being always complex).[183] In Catalan, a late poem on the joys of Mary uses the by-then traditional metaphor of Christ as the bread in the oven of Mary's womb or of the cross and further literalizes it by describing Christ as the "pure dough" of "celestial bread."[184] Most hair-raising of all, in his *Guldîn smide*, Konrad von Wuerzburg (d. 1287) adopts the bestiary mode and compares Christ at length to a crab: the crab moves sideways, against nature, and Christ's birth was against nature; the crab seizes anything you push at it, and Christ accepted all the torments thrust upon him; the crab has a much finer color once it has been boiled, and Christ's form was far brighter in heaven than it had been on earth.[185]

Most of these grotesque metaphors do not involve a break with existing metaphors but rather take them a step or two further, at which point the reader has to look head-on at what might otherwise have been accepted as a passing fancy. In addition, some of them diminish man's stature rather than bridge the gap between us and heaven; nonetheless, as I noted, to speak of spiritual matters in such a way tends to naturalize, even profane them. Certainly it appealed to the same tastes as grotesque metaphor directly involving Christ or Mary. Finally, the reader must not think that metaphor of this sort ever became dominant. Even in the vernaculars, traditional metaphors persist, with the centuries gradually bleaching all color out of them, and a majority of those metaphors that are either new features of late medieval religious literature or freshly invented by an individual poet come from "high" rather than "low" zones of human experience. In either case, though, it is still the orbit of human experience into which the sacred is being drawn. Zones with a "noble" connotation for a medieval audience include the following: falconry, nightingales, and certain other "attractive" birds; flowers and most trees; orchards and gardens; warfare (duels, knights, armor, weapons); precious substances (especially gold); seafaring (especially ship metaphors); most forms of music; most forms of dancing; courts and court ceremonies.

With these provisos in mind, it is possible for us to embark at last upon the brief survey of naturalistic metaphor and details of language in the various vernacular traditions with which this chapter will end. Chronological order will be observed within each tradition so far as possible.

In Catalan, Llull says that people read his works like a cat crossing hot coals. Ausias March confesses to God how he has bent his straight commandments into a curved sickle. The Christmas songs fill the Nativity scene with little boys and girls and their toys and favorite dainties; in one of them, Mary tells Joseph not to worry—she is more closed than an egg. Like Frauenlob and many others before him, Roiç de Corella uses the cloth metaphor for the Incarnation, praising Mary for spinning out of her blood the cloak God put on, broidered round with green lilies; later in the same poem, he describes how she rose to heaven, her hand on Christ's shoulder. Pero Martines assures Christ he is still a branch in his orchard and praises the Dominicans (*domini canes*, as the Latin folk etymology went, the "Lord's hounds") for calling back the straying with their barking. In one poem, he actually equates himself with Christ, claiming that the mob of this world cries, "Let him die!" In the *joyas* poems of 1474, humanist simile appears, but also a conversion of Dante's *selva oscura* of spiritual bewilderment (out of Augustine) into the "dark wood" in which eulogists of Mary become entangled.[186]

German received a disporportionate share of the attention earlier in this discussion, but it deserved it, and there is much more to tell. Of all the vernacular traditions, German is perhaps the most inventive and uninhibited in its naturalism. Even in the twelfth century, one can see precursors of its graphic concreteness; Der junge Spervogel describes a house in heaven whose pillars are of marble the Lord adorns with jewels and whose door is reached via a golden road, and Der von Kolmar's heaven is free of stinking huts, leaky roofs, and old age—the morning is over, evening is here, and we pilgrims had better choose the right road now. Evening is falling in a poem by Bruder Wernher, too, and the soul that was pure as a glass when baptism washed it is spotted now, like the black feet on a white swan; death comes like a snuffer to the soul's brightness. Reinmar sees in the glassmaker's ability to make a mirror out of sad ashes God's ability to make our lump of earth into a glorified and everlasting body.[187] A Mary-Psalter of the middle of the thirteenth century tells Mary that compared to him she carried in her arms, heaven and earth weigh less than a grain of wheat on his finger; Mary herself is like a silkworm. In the *Rheinisches Marienlob*, Mary is a richly decorated altar and God's house where God as bishop sings mass; her body is pure as beaten gold, worked upon by winter and summer and fatigue and sorrow. For the anonymous author of a *contrafactura* of a secular *leich*, Mary's chastity is like the gold of Araby given the Kaiser. In reply to Friedrich von Sonnenburg's eloquent stanzas in praise of the world, a poet blames it most for its ingratitude to God, who made clothes out of it to his hurt, and compares it to a foul bog around a fresh spring, without refreshment or purity.[188] Konrad von Wuerzburg outdoes even these other thirteenth-century poets in the boldness of his conceits; not only is Christ very like a crab, he was once grey, but got back his blondness at the Incarnation; in another poem, God is both a dark-haired youth and an old grey-headed lord who feeds us daily. Der alte Missenaere advises the sinner to strip off his skin of sins like a snake moulting by passing through the crack in a rock. (Moral lyric, or moralizing religious lyric, was especially hospitable to such pungent comparisons, and not only in German.) Meister Rumezlant tells how God was the T-square that drew a line for us to follow straight across the circle of this universe.[189] The pseudo-Gottfried *Marienlob* (thirteenth century) states that only those with a huntsman's steadfast heart can catch the prey of God's love; those without God's love are like a shadow on the wall, senseless to life; the poet's sins are more numerous than the waves in the Bodensee; the praise of Mary rises like leaf, grass, blossom, and clover through a green meadow from the goodness of fruitful rain; Mary blooms in the pure heart as a fruitful tree blooms in the bright meadow, laughing, opening its blossoms to the morning dew; Mary is deeper than the wild sea's depths, reaching from the stars down into bottomlessness.[190]

To do the rest of German religious lyric justice (i.e., texts dating from the end of the thirteenth century on) would require too much space. Certain authors stand out: Frauenlob, in the *Marienleich* especially (the sexual imagery of st. 9 leaves one amazed, or aghast), but in the *Kreuzleich* and his

Sprueche too; the Monk of Salzburg (who may or may not have been in reality two different poets), whose finest moment is perhaps a description of dawn with which he begins a *horae passionis*; Hans von Cleve, whose *Marienlieder* overflow with ideas (Mary is like solder or a brimming vessel full of grace; her grace roars like a sluice gate; men are like puppies chasing everything they see; the devil lies in ambush like dogs waiting for deer; the human self lives like owls in filth and in darkness; and so forth); Heinrich von Muegeln, who makes skillful use of simple, familiar metaphors; and the anonymous poets who adapted folk-song situations to the story of Christ and Mary or Christ and the soul.[191] In general, outside of a brilliant exception like Oswald von Wolkenstein or Hans von Cleve, the later fourteenth and fifteenth centuries do not produce much new naturalistic metaphor or detail. The categories have been set, for low as well as high, and the reader recognizes most of what he encounters as long-familiar to poets and audiences by that time. The really creative period is from 1175 to about 1325, in this respect, and in most others.

Italian religious lyric is neither so rich nor so audacious as German religious lyric in its naturalism. It tends toward effects of sweetness and tenderness; rather than trying to shock the reader into thought, it tries to touch his heart. Jacopone da Todi shows by far the greatest range. He tells how the wine of the love of God is too strong for any hoop he has to hold it; one should be discreet if one's love for God is great, he says elsewhere, just as a man who has a candle shelters it from the wind and stops every hole in the house; he reminds a man who is reluctant to give up his pleasures and follow God that in prison, even royalty has gotten so hungry it eats its shoes, mud and all—why be so fastidious? He is particularly adept at applying the values of middle-class, urban, mercantile, and legal Italian life: the lover of God is like a quiet house where duties have been rationally assigned; Love treats him like a rich man who lets his wife go begging or a merchant who tempts the customer with his merchandise and then withholds it. And he can turn an image from romance to new purpose, crying to his soul, "Run to drink of the fountain of Christ's love till you are drunk, don't leave it, let yourself die in it!" Even the power of mystical experience does not elude his grasp: the soul in its ascent says, "Of the light I made my shield / and of the dark my spear; / I concentrated on my balance and began to ride," striking down the deadly sins in the manner of Parzival, the Holy Fool, or the later Tom O'Bedlam; in the state of self-annihilation, time is arrested, the seasons are still, they cannot turn, the heavens are stopped, in their silence they make him cry, "O abyssal sea, your depth has swallowed me up and I drown." Even a disciple finds the right touch, describing how the perfect soul puts its head out above the treetops through the power of love.[192]

The Urbino *laudario* continues his manner, though not his high quality. An excuse is like a featherless bird trying to fly; the lover of God licks teeth and lips as he goes, for love has honeyed them; love treats the soul as one teases silly children, showing them what they want and then snatching it away;[193] a penitent confesses how he fled Christ's gaze like a bad falcon; death rides on a palfrey night and day that neither water nor land ever delays; repent, another poem says, and cross the river before the flood comes down (wise advice in a country of torrential streams or *fiumari*); yet another describes a man emerging from the world as muddied water that gradually clears. Later poets are more timid, though Bianco proves to be not entirely unworthy of Jacopone's influence in passages where he describes his soul as "limping like an old cat" or literalizes the spiritual wrestling a Christian must go through. Dancing and seafaring continue to be productive, and classical material infiltrates into the *laude* as Renaissance humanism spreads out from Latin into vernacular poetry (particularly the *ternario*). But Italian religious lyric at the close of the Middle Ages is mostly rather thin stuff, sometimes successful through its delicacy and its exclusions, rarely attempting new things.[194]

At its very beginnings, Provençal religious lyric attains its apogee, I believe, in Cerveri de Girona's verse sermon on *Surgens Iesus mane*. Certainly the description of heaven is incomparably the finest attempt at that intractable subject in medieval literature, excepting only the thirty-three cantos of Dante's *Paradiso*. It is unfamilar enough to deserve translation in full here:

> Let's rise early, do our day's work, for all pleasures here are weariness to heaven's. This world is nothing to paradise, for it is the womb where the little child lies—one could not believe how great the pleasure is, or how powerful, or how precious, any more than a child in its mother's womb—if it were possible to speak to a man before his birth—would believe it, if one told him, "Think of leaving here, and you will see sun and moon and stars shine, and heaven, earth, and sea, castles, towns, cities, ladies and knights, gardens and orchards and meadows, rivers and fountains and trees and birds; and by my faith, the world, were it good, the world is very fair in May, when one sees green fields and trees in flower—yet for all their fairness, my words do not lie." I believe the child would leave the womb eagerly and seize the chance to see this world, knowing it was such. So, since our Lord has given us sense and knowledge and sight and hearing and all that is good to serve us, we ought to desire eagerly to win Christ and His love and save the soul.[195]

Certainly one could not ask for a better or more complete example of "converting" the world into heaven! In general, Provençal poets get their effects, in religious lyric at least, as much from pungent colloquialism as from naturalistic comparisons. For instance, Peire d'Alvernha says he wouldn't give

two cents for a mountain of money after death and that people who worry
too much about property lease a narrow field; the same poet also creates the
vivid picture of Christ staying no longer here after the Resurrection than it
takes to leap from a hill in Jehoshaphat, from atop a stone to heaven and
beyond, which has the same colloquial force. Or one has Cadenet (early
thirteenth century) beginning a poem with the mock-ingenuous wish that all
the good he has done might become evil and vice versa, for then the good
would be so great that he would be equal to a saint. Again, it is the informal
relationship the poem establishes with the reader that is its main attraction.[196]

Fourteenth-century Provençal religious lyric relies less on the charm of
authorial personality and more on straightforward popular metaphor. A
treatise on the Names of God describes God as writing on Mary's skin and
wanting to wear her wool; the speaker asks for light, since we are at sea and
can't see to go without it, and the enemy wants to put out the candle;
nothing evil or cruel mounts the ladder to heaven because Mary clips its
wings; Mary is valuable flat ground in which one ought to sow one's wheat,
for it will yield good and saving food; similarly, Mary is the sure, level, and
straight way to the city of God.[197] Competition poems show a liking for
miniature allegories, as labored as the Middle English example quoted at
the end of chapter 2 or worse. However, Raimon de Cornet's entries are several cuts above the rest, and he shows a characteristically Provençal knack
for pungent phrasing and comparisons in his "El mes d'abril," part of which
has been cited above: Adam did not languish as much for the forbidden fruit
or the mariner for lack of oars (?) as Raimon does for the Virgin; if he loses
her, he will be more joyless than Cain and pine away worse than a stricken
dove; Mary is the branch that puts out flower and leaf together against the
winter, up high where the fruit will surely mature; his heart burns with a
smokeless fire in its love. But what Raimon really cares about, as a child of
his times, is his rhymes, to which his tornada draws our attention, in case we
might have failed to observe their virtuosity.[198]

In Old French, as in Provençal, the most striking use of metaphor comes
early in the tradition of religious lyric. Gautier chides Eve for causing Christ
to lack a bed for his friends and tells Mary that we have put our bets on her,
asking her to teach her pawns to play and to pull up such a netful of us that
we can all move to the great king; he speaks of how our beds are already
made in heaven; he who loves Mary is whiter than milk and will sit at a rich
table; due to the loss of St. Leucadia's relics, her church is uglier than an old
barn; Mary is like a great blossoming rose (surely he is thinking of contemporary rose windows); we should give *fole amor* ("mad love" of a worldly
kind) a raspberry; one candle of Mary's love is worth more than all the gold
of Frisia (Phrygia?); Mary's servant has taken a great fish and reaped a great

harvest; whoever serves Mary from the heart sings higher than his highest note.[199] Another early figure, Thibaut de Champagne, also excels in the freshness of his phrasing and his metaphors: offered the chance to taste the fruit of loving Mary, he is like the child who goes round and round the tree, hanging from the branches, and never climbing up it; in our sinfulness, we have pushed God behind our backs. And he can sustain metaphor without becoming tedious, as in the beast fable of "Diex est ainsi comme li pelicans."[200] Other religious chansons of the thirteenth century also have their moments: Mary was as oblivious to the act of conception as a sleeping man is when one is looking at him; the incarnation and birth left no more trace in her than a fish's path in the sea or a falcon's in the air; a devotee of the Virgin says he wants to do her will more than be king of Tyre; still another passage on the incarnation tells how rain does not fall so gently onto wool (note a further case of Gideon's fleece reduced to metaphor!) as he who saved Jonah in the whale descended into Mary's holy body (since Jonah was a type of Christ and the Resurrection, this passage illustrates how complex the ramifications of the "container" motif and its underlying theme of enclosure were). In other chansons in the same collection, Mary is the miner who gave us the gold with which the true engineer redeemed us; without Christ, we would all be lost like the Albigensians; Christ paid on a Friday for all Adam wasted; God loved tomb, cross, and selpulchre, but he must have loved Mary's womb best, since he spent nine months there; life is a gust of wind. Guillaume li Viniers imagines Mary and Christ in heaven, Christ taking his pretty golden-haired mother by the chin and consenting to do as she asks, because she carried him gently in her sides; he speaks of Mary watering the world and bringing spring weather, worries about being hit in the tournament of life in this world without bridle or saddle, pictures death waiting and holding the handle of the frying pan, prays to St. Michael to sing his "new song" to God till God commands him to accept Guillaume's soul when Death cuts its coat.[201] Rutebeuf says that if Mary isn't present at the Last Judgment, he'll have gotten a bad bargain from the palmer and swears he knows a woman doctor who is better than any surgeon at Lyons or Viane—she even cured Mary the Egyptian. An anonymous macaronic prayer to Christ, in Anglo-Norman and Middle English, calls the love of Christ "sweeter than honey when it is hot."[202]

From the early fourteenth century, a Beguine devotional poem marshals a series of similes concerning the devout life and God's use of adversity: rubbing a rusty sword till it shines, knotting a cord to help one's memory, plunging wool into dye, adding a little weight making the difference on a scale, and going to school in the glorious book of Christ's side. In the same group of poems, prayer is like an arbalest on a tower, wounding whatever it touches, the quarrels being tears, the cords cries of prayer, the stirrups humility, the bolt the devout soul that goes straight to heaven.[203]

The mid-fourteenth century group of nine religous songs from Lorraine, edited by Richard Otto in 1890, is especially rich in metaphor; there seems to have been a flowering of religious poetry in Metz in the late Middle Ages, and these particular poems reflect the mystical bent so noticeable in the prose treatises that appear in the same manuscript.[204] The second poem apostrophizes Christ as the "joyous meat which the fire of love roasted!"; the heart should not be like a scurvy old dog that loses the scent of noble venison through laziness but like a bold harrier that runs full tilt at the smell of blood; Christ is also a nightingale who made his nest in the branches of the cross; his wounds are flowers with which he is adorned, his lily is changed to violet, and there are roses aplenty. In the third poem in the group, the temple curtain has torn itself in two to make dressings for Christ, who is the pool (of Bethesda) with five red healing rivulets; Mary is the spicer of love, the altar where God's fire burns constantly, the spark that kindled living faith; further, Christ is a candle formed from the honey and wax his wounds shed, the stag the prophets and patriarchs sounded their horn after and who had long lain embosqued in his covert; Mary, the sweet turtledove, could well lose her feathers from her long sorrow. In the fourth poem, Jesus is the great sea to which one should make God's part of oneself return daily; in the fifth, the doves gaze into the abyssal rivulet of Christ's wound, shedding their flesh by bathing in it. In the eighth poem, the speaker praises the lamb for the poultice of life it has steeped in its blood, promises to make an orchard in his or her heart with the cross planted in its midst laden with the fruit of the tree of life, and calls Christ's wounds five taverns he has made for us in his flesh.[205]

The Lorraine poems demonstrate the fructifying effect of mystical literature and a mystical spirit on religious poetry. Elsewhere in the fourteenth and fifteenth centuries, metaphor tends to become allegorical as it elaborates itself. In addition, as in European poetry in general, one begins to see the inclusion of classical lore in comparisons. Jean Brisebarre for instance begins a balade with the declaration to Mary that Helen never loved as her son loved humanity when he consented to fulfill the prophecy of Isaiah. Abstract, "metaphysical" metaphors also come into fashion, some two or three centuries after their arrival on the poetic scene in Latin (cf. Alanus de Insulis); for instance, an Ave Maria gloss uses grammatical terms like *optative*, *superlative*, and *conjunction* in rhyme position as a way of implying that Mary is as fundamental a reality as the structure of language. Machaut's "Lai de la fonteinne" expounds a sustained allegory for the Trinity (the conventional late-medieval comparison of the three Persons to spring, rivulet, and channel), enlivening it with a colloquial passage in the seventh stanza: "Better at Rome or overseas in exile or cast in the Somme, the Jordan, or the Nile than to believe anything a good man cannot believe without peril—for is he worth an apple without God? I say no!" Similarly, Deschamps builds a Marian prayer, which is followed by Mary's reply in another ballade, around a sustained ship allegory that the poem itself glosses. In a long poem cataloguing Marian patristic passages, doctor by doctor, Christine de Pisan, in a flash of associative imagination, addresses Mary as the dove whom Christ carried to heaven at the Assumption "like a branch" in his arms—real doves on everyday branches, the dove that brought the olive branch to Noah, the herald on a mission of peace, perhaps even Aeneas meet in these lines.[206]

The simplicity of this moment in Christine's work, however, is scarcely representative of the religious lyric of the end of the Middle Ages in France. Rather, one finds a poem like Georges Chastellain's Mary-Psalter of fifty stanzas, wherein he tells how "veins, heart, and all my entrails open to you and offer trellises for the admirable root from which your ears may gather living flowers" (one might almost think one were reading Lorca), and less surrealistically, how Christ preserves pure deity and humanity contained together as in an apple (a symbolic fruit for certain!), how Mary has "borne the grain and straw of him whose humble sowing you were before," and how (in stanzas that recall Bernart de Ventadorn's "Quan vei la lauzeta mover") his heart seeks to fly high and he is like the lark that has to descend back down to where it knows its food and its leaf, because of the heat up aloft on its plumage, and then recovers, returning to its homage with throat, heart, and every vein bent on song (stt. 32 and 34). Yet in the midst of this lyrical flight, the poet talks about how the phoenix lays its egg in Mary and how there is nothing to hold onto or shave on an egg! The curious mix of the grand and the grotesque reflects beautifully the opposing impulses toward homely naturalism and ceremonious sublimity that racked the fifteenth century.[207]

Toward the end of the century, Jean Molinet sums up its tendencies. In a *chant royal*, he carefully develops a miniature Marian allegory based on the structure of a seven-stringed harp. In an *Ave Maria* gloss, he praises Mary's name for its power to lull to sleep the mad dogs of black Pluto, in effect putting pilasters on the medieval hell mouth. And in yet another Marian poem, he mingles the poetic and the grotesque, the homely and the exotic, as Chastellain had done: "As a father teaches his child, as the clever master teaches a heavy elephant, your clear clear soul guided your body." The taste for little allegories, the often incongruous erudition, the unbalanced fancy—all are here.[208]

There is little to tell about naturalistic metaphor or details from life in Portuguese religious lyric, principally because what we have consists of some forty lyrics dispersed through Alfonso's *Cantigas* from the thirteenth century, and virtually no strictly religious lyric otherwise from the early period, and a rather undistinguished group of plainspoken, simple texts from the fifteenth century. In general, Alfonso's (or his collaborators') language is fresh and vigorous,[209] but the metaphors are largely conventional, and details from life appear mainly in the narratives of Marian miracles that form the bulk of the collection. One gleans little in these fields. A lyric account of how the Virgin cured Alfonso of a fever says that the fear of Death and encircling evils make his heart "greener than cambric"; the refrain of an account of how a pious woman opened the church doors at St. Mary of the Martyrs describes Mary as "she who opens up heaven's doors to save us," turning the story into a metaphor; one of the lyrics, taking *alba* as its motto-word, achieves a sustained and powerful development of a comparison between Mary and the dawn (e.g., "You are the dawn through whom was seen the Sun . . . God for your sake sought from on high to be born of you, His created, and made dawn of you"; each stanza explores a different aspect of the comparison). And much later, upon the borders of the Middle Ages and the Renaissance, the gifted Gil Vicente writes a romance, "Remando vão remadores" (The oarsmen are rowing), as the opening of his *auto* on the "ship of Purgatory," an *auto* that gracefully develops the immemorial ship metaphor, with the son of God the steersman and angels at the oars. But the material is too scanty and too unevenly distributed for one to draw any conclusions about trends.[210]

Spanish has much more to offer the investigator. Like the *Cantigas*, their approximate contemporary Gonzalo de Berceo shows a turn for effective popular language, which relieves the extended *locus amoenus* allegory of the prologue of his *Milagros de nuestra señora* with allusions to "Sancho or Domingo, Sancha or Domenga" and how "we are striving in vain, the well is without bottom." As with Portuguese, there follows a considerable chronological gap (approximately 125 years in this case), after which Spanish became, in the form of Castilian, a medium suitable for art-poetry in contemporary eyes. In the first half of the fifteenth century, the Marquis of Santillana (d. 1458) asks God to help his miserable soul, for "carts are hard to move," and Pero Veles de Guevara ingenuously avers that he believes "more than a thousand times" in the son Mary carried for nine months. Such use of naturalistic language becomes rarer later on. Unfortunately, the great collection that covers the earlier fifteenth century, the *Cancionero de Baena* (datable poems from 1406 to 1449), includes relatively little religious poetry, and one therefore has little to compare to texts of the second half of the century and the beginning of the sixteenth.[211]

In a Nativity *villancico*, Nicolas Nuñez has Mary answer the congregation's questions in a very natural and human way, contrasting agreeably with Marian poetry of the same period elsewhere in Europe. Spanish religious lyric in fact shows a general gift for humanizing, but not sentimentalizing, the sacred and for achieving grandeur without pretension or pompousness. With a fine austerity, Frey Gauberte's "Como en salir del rosal" develops a metaphor of bush, flower, and light as the emblem of our relation to God: "As a flower withers rising from the rosebush, so life quickly dies in rising from eternal good." The intellectualism of this six-stanza poem, particularly in the conceit that the light of God is like a parent plant and that the physical beauty of blossoming is a separation and deterioration from one's origin, is typical of its tradition and quite different from its more mechanical, less genuinely thoughtful equivalents in late medieval German or Middle French religous lyric. Juan Alvarez Gato (1433–1496) makes good use of the metaphor of battle in a dialogue with Mary after the Resurrection, "Di nobis, Maria, / que viste en la vya?" having Mary reply for instance that "I saw our good captain who won the victory that those in his (military) company enjoy"; the hortatory *contrafactura* "Pues tienes libre poder" tells those who seek the spiritual life how they "must go alone and as pilgrims in the steps of the Triune God," lyrically elaborating the metaphor of pilgrimage.[212]

A glossed *Ave* (possibly by Friar Hernando de Talavera) that is far superior to any Latin examples I have seen launches a veritable barrage of metaphors in midcourse: because of Mary, gloomy Cerberus does not bark at us (cf. Molinet!); Mary is the promised land of Israel, running with white milk and sweet honey; hers is the storage-chest where God folded his garments, and the liquor of her vial fills the heavens; God made her his nest, a short cloak to cover him whom a thousand worlds would not cover (a variant on the "container" motif); Jesus disdained all flesh till Mary laid hold of his jesses, and at the first "hucho! hu!" he then dropped down with a good will, for the bait of Mary's purity filled him with longing; Mary (again) is not only the rich cloak God put on, but the sea where God sailed as a merchant and across which all those sail who are heaven-bound.[213] Frey Iñigo de Mendoza, Franciscan author of an incomplete *Vita Christi*, asks the Christ child in a *villancico*, "Since charity burns in you at birth, what will you do when you grow up?," basing the whole poem on the traditional metaphor of the "fire of charity." The Marquis of Santillana calls Mary a "copious library, text of admirable gloss, history of the prophets," all of which she indeed proved to be by the end of the Middle Ages. Lucas Fernandez, in a dialogue between Dionysios and Matthew about the Passion, has one speaker say of

Christ, "Among the hawks dies the red-tailed eagle, with legions of angels looking on." Juan Tallante, who wrote only religious poetry and practiced a deliberately difficult manner, intellectualist and compressed, expounds the harmony within the Trinity through an elaborate musical metaphor in a poem on the Cross and closes another poem with an effective parallel between himself and Simon of Cyrene, who helped carry Christ's cross.[214]

It is characteristic of religious lyric in Spanish toward the end of the fifteenth century that its comparisons and its language become more studied and more extended, except in imitations of popular poetry such as the religious *villancico*. Like Tallante, Friar Ambrosio Montesino (d. 1513) turns to music for a metaphor, saying of Mary's visit to St. Elizabeth that as keys touched by a musician cause harmonies on an organ, so John moved his mother (Elizabeth) not to stop singing the melody he could not sing (being in his mother's womb still). But simple direct metaphor in the older manner does not disappear; Alonso de Proaza, in a panegyric to St. Catalina (Catherine), writes of Christ, "the hawk eats only hearts—so the divine falcon took yours."[215]

The *Cancionero general* of 1511 (and later editions) and the *Cancionero musical* of 1530 contain a representative selection of religious lyric from the final period of the Middle Ages (1470–1530), the one representing the tastes of the court *literati*, the other the tastes of courtly musicians (composers' names appear, but not the names of the poets). One notices a regular and rather heavy use of conventional metaphor in the *Cancionero musical*, particularly involving cloth, clothing, and embroidery. In the *Cancionero general*, poets play with metaphors of sailing, jousting, archery, alchemy, and the orchard. Beyond this, one finds Andrés Quebedo experimenting with the shadow-light duality of typology; starting with the traditional type of the rock Moses struck as Christ's side wounded with the spear, Quebedo embroiders on it by making Peter the keybearer to its opening and then by extending the notion of *sombra* (shade; Latin *umbra*, the standard metaphor for the Old Testament member of typological pairs): seeing the sun from shadow is like seeing God, the sun of justice, in the shadow of humanity, whence comes Christ's ability to raise with his shadow those it touched. The intellectualism of this poem, like that of many others around the end of the fifteenth century, looks forward to the "conceptualism" of poets like Góngora. In the same vein, Lazaro Bejarano compares Paul's soul to a vessel full of liquid, reflecting heavenward. An anonymous poet makes the ill-assorted combination of a classicizing comparison of Paul to Antaeus and the traditional medieval metaphor of Christ as bread, which in this case was only kneaded when Peter, James, and John partook of it but was given to Paul fully baked. Another poet, Ruy García Alleman, also compares Paul to Antaeus and, even more incongruously though ingeniously, to a bouncing ball. Finally, Bartolomeo de Torres Naharro, in a poem on the Veronica, turns *pintar* (to paint) into a unifying metaphor by consistent use of various . forms of the word's root and of its synonyms.[216]

There are important analogies between the development of Spanish religious lyric and its use of naturalistic metaphor or details and the development of European religious lyric in general, particularly in Old French and German. Colloquial language becomes rarer; metaphor expands toward allegory; panegyric becomes more abstract and intellectualizing in its figures. The telescoping of its development into one and one-half centuries (1375– 1525), however, means both that tendencies natural to the early period are underrepresented, on the one hand, and, on the other, that these tendencies survive more easily until the end of the Middle Ages and help balance contrary tendencies (which enjoyed a freer hand in French and German), simply because there was less time for one ethos to yield gradually to the next. This persistence of the medieval into the Renaissance in Spain may be one reason why its sixteenth century was indeed a *siglo de oro*.

The same might be said of Middle English, which also did not begin significant development as a secular literary language until the mid-fourteenth century. But neither it, nor the other remaining tradition, Old Norse, proved especially creative, so far as metaphor is concerned, in its religious lyric. Middle English moralizing lyric does achieve a frequently fine use of realistic details, proverbial comparisons, colloquial speech (cf. the Vernon manuscript),[217] and narrative retellings of the life of Christ sometimes equal the Spanish in dignity, immediacy, and force. One finds rather the same situation in Old Norse, where a moralizing poem on the Last Things like *Solarljóð* easily eclipses all of the strictly religious poems but *Lilja* in any respect one would care to name. However, Middle English religious lyric, up to the fifteenth century, cannot be denied an appealing directness. For instance, "Unkynde man, gif kepe til me" has Christ tell man-soul, "Tow & thyrty yhere & mare / I was for þe in trauel sare / with hungry, thirst, hete, & calde" (Two-and-thirty years and more I was in sore travail for you with hunger, thirst, heat, and cold). Passages like this have a strikingly balladlike quality (cf. a stanza from "The Black Bull of Norroway": "Seven long years I served for thee, / The glassy hill I clamb for thee, / The bluidy shirt I wrang for thee, / And wilt thou not wauken and turn to me?"). The same may be said of the brilliantly imaginative exceptions to the generally unimaginative level of the Middle English religious lyric, "I syng of a myden þat is makeless," and the early-sixteenth-century Corpus Christi carol, "Lully, lulley, lully, lulley, / The fawcon hath born my mak away." As Davies says, in his excellent anthology of medieval English poetry, such poems are "peculiarly English, and peculiarly good." They are also very few.[218] Otherwise, the carol provides somewhat coarse but hearty popular (or popularizing) fare, making up in rhythmic enthusiasm and general high spirits what it lacks in originality. Of fifteenth-century literary religious lyric, one may say that it develops along the same lines as contemporary Continental literary religious lyric, even to exaggeration, as in the case of "aureate diction." It is ironic, in fact, that Middle English religious lyric has been so well served by editors and scholar-critics when it is on the whole one of the less interesting or significant traditions of religious lyric in medieval Europe.

The kennings of early Old Norse religious poetry are either drawn directly from the traditional skaldic stock or modeled closely upon traditional kennings, in a kind of "calquing." Poems of the post-*Lilja* period generally use the equally traditional stock of metaphors that had developed in Latin religious lyric, after 1350 the major model for Old Norse work. Very occasionally, they include a metaphor or phrase that testifies to their northern origins or to an independent poetic talent. For instance, the poem "Rosa" ("Fader og son àà haestum haedum," in *dróttkvaett*) has the poet pray John the Baptist to make his tongue bear fruit and ask for a "sweat-bath" of penitential tears—the sauna has a long history! With refreshing simplicity, a Norwegian Marian poem calls the Virgin "bright as a polished stone." And there is a fine dance-song, with suspended phrases rather like those of "Maiden in the mor lay," beginning "Maria meiann skiaera" and appearing in a multitude of manuscripts. This song compares Mary to "blood-red gold on brass" and a "sapphire on black loam" and shows an eye for sensuous detail that late medieval Marian poetry, in its sumptuous but insubstantial fabrics, badly needed.[219] For something in the later period that shows real control as well as inspiration, one must go to the fountainhead, Eysteinn Ásgrímsson himself; his *Lilja* excels by perfection of statement and powers of dramatization (the use of Satan and the mastery of dialogue recall the Byzantine hymns of Romanos) rather than through its imagery, but near its end, the poet produces a finely original metaphor for the labors of the Marian eulogist. Since this book has had so much to do with the results of just those labors, it seems appropriate to end this survey of medieval religious lyric and its metaphors with Eysteinn's words:

> Tungu-saetr et einnhverr ýta
> orðum hygz i kvaeði at skorða
> mjukan dikt at makligleikum,
> min drotning, af heiðri þinum,
> þvi er likast, sem rasi eða reiki
> raðlauss seggr at ýmsum veggjum
> faeldr ok byrgdr, of feti þó hvergi
> fúss i brott úr vǫlundarhúsi.[220]

(When a sweet-tongued man thinks about laying out eloquent words in a poem that will do justice to your glory, my queen, he is most like him who staggers and stumbles, a man who has lost his head, from path to path, frightened and trapped, and cannot find a way for his feet out of Volund's house [i.e., the labyrinth].)

He is not the only one to entertain such thoughts of desperation when confronted with the intricate, indeterminate ways of religious lyric. But unlike Eysteinn, we may feel free to strike the labyrinth and call it a day. And that, save for a final retrospect over the trampled field where the great throngs moved, now empty and silent, is precisely what I shall do.

POSTSCRIPT

Upon the common religious, poetic, and rhetorical stock of antiquity, each medieval linguistic tradition sets its individual stamp. Aesthetic principles and poetic genres, even subgenres, unite the traditions; differences in emphasis, in tone, in form, in structure, in fictive author, in fictive audience, in degree of self-reference, in choice of rhetorical figures divide them and divide period from period. Within most of the traditions, there is a clear awareness of the difference between "artistic" and "popular" religious lyric; both are impersonal, only the latter genuinely anonymous. In this and in other respects, within and among the traditions, antinomies play a crucial role. Religious lyric sets itself against secular, trying to compete with the world on its own ground. Similarly, the vernacular traditions at once reject and emulate the diction, tone, and rhetoric of the Latin religious lyric, achieving their own identities but increasingly prey to the desire to acquire the prestige of Latin by adopting its habits. And yet the figures and *topoi* of ancient rhetoric and poetry penetrate surprisingly little into the vernacular religious lyric; in turn, Latin and Greek religious lyric are characterized at least as much by their opposition in form, content, and manner to the literature of antiquity as by their common features. One may justly speak of a pan-European continuity in the development of religious lyric, but only in the complex sense that sees negation and conscious divergence as a natural and necessary part of any cultural continuum.

Further, though religious lyric turns its back on life, its feet rest upon the shared ground of humanity. Larger cultural changes affect it powerfully, even though these changes are themselves mediated for the most part by religious practice and prose literature before they begin to act upon the lyric. One must never forget that the minds of its authors bound together languages and values that their culture defined as separate and distinct. Time has disintegrated what men and women once integrated; as men and women studying the past, we must seek a new integration of the remains of the Middle Ages.

Since the sixteenth century, the religious lyric has pursued various paths. One of the most important has brought its assimilation to the traits of secular lyric: privatized, particularized, historicized, the expression of a religious person rather than a religion. Another has led to a rapprochement between the late medieval devotional poem, with its first-person-singular speaker, its emotivity, its solicitation of response, and the church hymn. All paths lead back to the Middle Ages and arise out of tendencies already present in their closing centuries. Yet it would be impossible to mistake a nineteenth-century hymn or a lyric by Herbert for a medieval product.

Faced with a choice of asserting either our continuity or our discontinuity with the Middle Ages, I would deny the validity of such an antithesis. Truly, the Middle Ages have their "alterity," the Middle Ages are "other," but this Other has a human face. Like our fellow man, it is both very much like oneself, and infinitesimally, infinitely different, in an uncountable number of ways. If irrefutable historical knowledge of our antecedents in the past is ultimately a delusion, are we any less deluded when we claim irrefutable knowledge of the inner, hidden reality of our friends and family—or of ourselves? Our condition is otherness; we approximate to the truth with fictions; we are cut off and isolated, and yet we are in touch. The mysteries we reach for—whether the soul of one's lover or the spirit of the past—elude our grasp. And yet one reaches out, and sometimes less than everything slips through one's fingers.

What these hands hold of the religious song of the Middle Ages, they offer to you. May it prove useful.

ORIENTATIONS

CATALAN

For geographical and political reasons, Provence exercised a heavy influence on Catalonia. From the mid-twelfth to the late thirteenth century, most Catalan poets wrote as "troubadours" and in Provençal (cf. Cerveri de Girona). Ramon Llull created Catalan art-prose in the second half of the thirteenth century and also wrote some sixteen poems in Catalan, but his verse is still laced with frequent Provençalisms. The manuscript Ripoll 129 includes a fragmentary collection of Catalan items amid its Latin and allows a glimpse of Catalan poetry early in the next century; a school of Majorcan poets shows a special penchant for the Provençal form of the *dansa*, which much later becomes a major form for Provençal Marian competition poems.

At the beginning of the fifteenth century, Ausias March initiates the use of pure Catalan in lyric poetry. The influence of French poetry, as well as (to a lesser degree) Italian, overtakes that of Provençal poetry, though Provençal treatises on poetry remain in the ascendant. Their hold is largely due to Catalan involvement in poetic contests at centers such as Toulouse (1323–1484), Llerida (1388), and Barcelona (1393), which were subject to the rules laid down in the treatises. As the century proceeds, the cultural center of gravity shifts south from Barcelona to Valencia, where the *Trobes en lahors de la Verge Maria* composed for a *jocs florals* in 1474 became the first book to be printed in Spain. Catalonia falls subject to Castile in 1468, and Castilian replaces Catalan as the language of nonanonymous poetry by the early sixteenth century; one finds a considerable amount of Castilian verse in the *Cancionero general* (1511 and later editions) that was written by aristocratic poets from Valencia. Not till the romantic period and the nineteenth century does Catalan again become a language of art-poetry; those seeking to treat Spain as the single unified nation it is not (most recently Franco) have always been hostile to those writing in Catalan.

Popular religious poetry is very scarce between 1200 and 1400. Thereafter, it becomes plentiful, and many late medieval texts remain current down to recent times among the folk (popular piety being one of the major refuges of a beleaguered ethnic culture). Artistically, it largely outclasses the artifi-

cial, academic products of the competitors at Barcelona, Valencia, and elsewhere. Its authorship seems to have been clerical, as is also the case for
"popular" religious lyric in England and Italy.

Select Bibliography

For a general history of Catalan literature, consult Arthur Terry, *Catalan Literature* (1972) or Martín de Riquer, *Història de la literatura catalana, part antiga*, 3
vols. (Barcelona, 1964–66); the latter's *Literatura catalana medieval* (Barcelona,
1972) conveniently summarizes his full-scale treatment of the subject: see especially
chap. 4 "La poesia del 1300 al 1500," (pp. 75–98), and the "Guia bibliogràfica"
(pp. 121–36). The *Anthology of Catalan Lyric Poetry*, ed. Joan Triadù and Joan
Gili (Berkeley, 1953) includes a 79-page introduction in English (trans. Pring-Mill)
on the Catalan lyric from its beginnings to the twentieth century.

The most convenient text of Llull's vernacular poems is Ramon Llull, *Poesies*, ed.
Ramon d'Alòs-Moner, 2d ed. (Barcelona, 1928); more complete is *Obras rimadas
de Ramon Llull . . .* , ed. Jeroni Rossello (Palma, 1859); see also *Obres essencials*, ed.
R. Riera Sala and Valls Taberner, 2 vols. (Barcelona, 1957–60). The Catalan poems
in Ripoll 129 appear in Jordi Rubio, "Del manuscrit 129 de Ripoll (Arxiu de la Corona de Aragó), del sigle xivᵉ," *Revista de bibliografia catalana* 5 (1905): 285–378
(nos. 10 and 12 are religious lyrics). On the borders between Catalan and Provençal
lie *Les "Coblas" ou les poésies lyriques provençocatalanes de Jacme, Pere et Arnau
March*, ed. A. Pagès (Toulouse, 1949) (see i, v, and vi). For a complete edition of
Ausias March's poetry, see Ausias March, *Poesies*, ed. P. Bohigas, 5 vols. (Barcelona,
1952–59) (bibliography in vol. 1); the Edinburgh Bilingual Library includes *Ausias
March: Selected Poems* (no. 12), ed. and trans. Arthur Terry (Edinburgh, 1976) (see
pp. 142f. for a brief bibliography). The "Cant espiritual" appears as poem cv on
pp. 114–27 with facing English prose translation. For later fifteenth-century religious lyric, see the *Cançoner dels Masdovelles (Manuscrit n.° 11 de la Biblioteca de
Catalunya)*, ed. R. Aramón i Serra (Barcelona, 1938) (cf. nos. 45, 95, 129, 130, 148,
149, 172, 173, 174–78, 183–84); Grajales; and the *Cançoner de les obretes en
nostra lengua materna mes divulgades durant los segles xiv, xv e xvi*, ed. Mariano
Aguiló y Fuster (Barcelona, 1900). This last book, a bibliophile's edition in black
letter, is of particular interest because it includes reproductions of the ornamental
borders and woodcuts of early printed editions of anonymous Catalan religious poetry. A generous collection of late fifteenth-century Christmas songs appears in *Cançons nadalenques* (see list of abbreviations). For Roiç de Corella, see his *Obras*, ed.
Ramón Miguel y Planas (Barcelona, 1913); for Pero Martines, see Pero Martines
(list of abbreviations).

GERMAN

There is very little in Old High German that could be called religious lyric;
none of it has much poetic interest. The earliest Middle High German reli-

gious poetry consists of long didactic texts and scriptural paraphrase. Marian lyric begins to be written in the second quarter of the twelfth century, and with the rise of vernacular poetry in the latter decades of the same century, religious lyric gains a prominent place in German literature. Its authors include Minnesingers like Walther von der Vogelweide (whose Marian *leich* is an exception to the Minnesingers' avoidance of Marian subject matter) and *Spruchdichter* like the two Spervogels (the term *Spruchdichter* is a nineteenth-century coinage); of course, a poet could write both *Minnesang* and *Sprueche*, and both religious and secular verse. The religious *Spruch* reflects briefly on a doctrinal or moral fact, exhorting, praising, sometimes praying. It forms the bulk of Middle High German religious lyric between 1200 and 1350, and the Meistersinger (whose guilds begin to appear in the second half of the fifteenth century) consciously continue the tradition of *Spruchdichtung* in their voluminous production, intensifying its formalism and intellectualism.

Alongside the religious *Spruch* and *Leich*, the thirteenth and fourteenth centuries produced important large-scale Marian poetry; the *Niederrheinisches Marienlob* (1200s; over 5,000 lines), Konrad von Wuerzburg's *Diu guldîn smide* (ca. 1280, 2,000 lines), the "Lobgesang auf Maria und Christus" falsely ascribed to Gottfried von Strassburg (over 1,300 lines), a *Rosenkranz* from ca. 1250 (over 1,100 lines), and Bruder Hans von Cleve's *Marienlieder* (1391/1400, 5,280 lines). In addition, popular religious song begins to be recorded in fourteenth-century towns, and religious art-song in the following century. Translation of Latin hymns, which starts in the thirteenth century, becomes common by the late fourteenth century (cf. the works of the "Monk of Salzburg"); some translations are isosyllabic, in order to make it possible to use the original music without alteration, others are mere cribs, and still others genuinely artistic in nature. The first decades of the sixteenth century see the culmination of over a hundred years' intensive activity in printed collections of translated hymns like the *Ortulus animae* of 1501 and the Sigmundsluft *Hymnary* of 1524.

Besides hymn translations, songbooks including religious lyric (cf. the Lochaimer, Rostock, and Klara Haetzlerin collections, for instance), and the Meistersang, the fifteenth century also brought systematic *contrafactura* of secular music and texts (cf. the works of Heinrich von Laufenberg) and the first true German church songs (i.e., texts sung in church during the service by the congregation and tolerated by the clergy). The *Ruf* (cry) or *Leise* (perhaps a popular corruption of the response "Kyrieleison") goes back at least to the tenth century, consisting often of a single supplicatory line such as one finds the people using in late medieval religious movements (recorded examples appear only from 1400 on, though); a few songs such as "Crist ist erstanden" had been in extraliturgical use for several hundred years; but it is only in the last two decades of the fifteenth century that vernacular song wins a toehold within the liturgy proper. By the Reformation, nonetheless, the ground for the German *Kirchenlied* had been thoroughly prepared.

Finally, two ancillary factors affecting Middle High German religious lyric need to be mentioned. First, the influence of the mystical movement centering on figures like Eckhart, Mechthild of Magdeburg, Suso, and Tauler and propagating itself through groups like Rulman Merswin's fourteenth-century *Gottesfreunde* begins to be felt in poetry around 1250 and becomes an important general influence on poetic sentiment, language, and motifs in the next two centuries. Second, the true *Volkslied* (Herder's term) surfaces in the fifteenth century alongside the urban *Gesellschaftslied* (Hoffmann von Fallersleben's term) and provides new secular material for religious lyric to use; however, it is the *Gesellschaftslied* of the towns (which by our standards were still very countrified, of course) that most fifteenth-century poets (from Heinrich von Laufenberg on) use but that we think of as an adaptation of the "folk song."

Select Bibliography

Paul Salmon, *Literature in Medieval Germany* (New York, 1967), includes an extensive and very useful bibliography, pp. 167–267 (with index). Most German religious lyrics (and a good deal else) appear in the double-columned pages of Wack.; however, as a fire-breathing nineteenth-century German anti-Papist, he is prone to omit Marian lyrics without warning, and in addition, many *Sprueche* are capriciously excluded, whereas others like them are admitted, and major Marian poetry appears only in excerpt or not at all (cf. the *Niederrheinisches Marienlob* or *Diu guldîn smide*). Strictly speaking, *Kirchenlied* is at best an anachronism, at worst a misnomer for the texts Wackernagel presents; the German church song is almost entirely a post-Reformation phenomenon. Hoffman von Fallersleben, *Geschichte des deutschen Kirchenlieds bis auf Luthers Zeit* (Hannover, 1861, 3d ed.; reprint, Hildesheim, 1965), makes an honest attempt to trace the antecedents of the church song in the German Middle Ages and remains a valuable book, if only as an antidote to Wackernagel; the connective material between the carefully selected poems in von Fallersleben is still very readable and useful. The best way to track down texts that Wackernagel and Fallersleben leave out is to consult the latest editions of the different volumes of the multivolume *Geschichte der deutschen Literatur von den Anfaengen bis zur Gegenwart*, gen. ed. Helmut de Boor (Munich). Volume 3 : 1 (1962) includes references to editions of the various *Spruchdichter* who wrote between 1250 and 1350 on pp. 475–81 in the alphabetical order of their names; volume 4 : 1 (1970), by Hans Rupprich, contains a chapter on lyric poetry and *Spruchdichtung* that covers poets, songbooks, and *Kirchenlied*, and the early history of *Meistersang* in the period from 1370 to 1520 (see pp. 165–235), with bibliography on pp. 747–56. References in de Boor will lead one to the following principal collections: Friedrich Heinrich von der Hagen, *Minnesinger*, 4 vols. (Leipzig, 1838) (still indispensable for many *Spruchdichter*); Carl von Kraus, *Deutsche Liederdichter des 13. Jahrhunderts*, 2 vols. (Tuebingen, 1952–58); Karl Bartsch, *Deutsche Liederdichter des 12.–14. Jahrhunderts*, rev. Wolfgang Golther, 8th ed. (Berlin, 1928); Karl Bartsch, *Die Erloesung, mit einer Auswahl geistlicher Dichtungen* (Quelinburg/Leipzig, 1858). Old High German and early Middle High German shorter poems appear in W. Braune and Karl Helm, *Althochdeutsches Lesebuch*, rev. Ernst Ebbinghaus, 14th ed. (Tuebingen, 1962); Erich Henschel and Ulrich Pretzel, *Die kleinen Denkmaeler der Vorauer Handschrift* (Tuebingen, 1962); Albert Waag, *Kleinere Gedichte des 11. und 12. Jahrhunderts*, rev. Werner Schroeder (Tuebingen, 1972); Karl V. Muellenhoff and Wilhelm Scherer, *Denkmaeler deutscher Poesie und Prosa aus dem 8. bis 12. Jahrhundert*, rev. E. von Steinmeyer, 3d ed. (Berlin, 1892); Emil von Steinmeyer, *Die kleinen althochdeutschen Sprachdenkmaeler* (Berlin, 1916). Twelfth-century Marian lyrics may be found in Waag.

The best single connected account of medieval German religious lyric is by Richard Kienast in the article "Die deutschsprachige Lyrik des Mittelalters," in *Deutsche Philologie im Aufriss*, ed. Wolfgang Stammler, 2d ed., vol. 2 (Berlin, 1960), sec. 7, "Die geistliche Lyrik des 13. bis 16. Jahrhundert (bis zu Luther)," col. 120–32. Most articles and monographs on medieval German poetry focus on the long, non-lyric texts of the eleventh and twelfth century. The best recent study of Marian poetry from the "Vorauer Marienlob" to Frauenlob's *Marienleich* is Gerhard M. Schaefer, *Untersuchungen zur deutschsprachigen Marienlyrik des 12. und 13. Jahrhunderts*, Goeppinger Arbeiten zur Germanistik, no. 48 (Goeppingen, 1971). For a careful exposition of the actual uses to which German religious lyric was put in the Middle Ages, see Johannes Janota, *Studien zu Funktion und Typus des deutschen Geistlichen Liedes im Mittelalter*, Muenchener Texte und Untersuchungen zur deutschen Literatur des Mittelalters, vol. 23 (Munich, 1968). For a wide-ranging, comparative treatment of *Spruchdichtung*, see Hugo Moser, "Die hochmittelalterliche deutsche 'Spruchdichtung' als uebernationale und nationale Erscheinung," *Zeitschrift fuer deutsche Philologie* 76, no. 3 (1957): 241–68. On the *Meistersang*, see Bert Nagel, *Meistersang*, Sammlung Metzler, no. 12 (Stuttgart, 1962) (full references to the literature). On stanza forms, see Anthonius Touber, *Deutsche Strophenformen des Mittelalters* (Stuttgart, 1975).

GREEK

The history of Byzantine Greek liturgical poetry begins with *troparia*, passages of poetic prose introduced between Psalm verses that developed into verse strophes by the fifth century. What little of these early texts survives exhibits a very close dependence on the Bible and the liturgy (cf. the later Western "trope," ninth century on). Associated with the names of Anastasios, Kyriakos, and Romanos, the *kontakion* appears in the early sixth century (see "Forms" in chapter 2 for details; the term dates from the eighth century). In turn, it is superseded by the much more elaborate form of the *kanon* in the late seventh century. In the meantime, *troparia* of various kinds continue to be written; among them are some of the finest Byzantine hymns. In the ninth century, monks at the Studios monastery (Constantinople) revive the *kontakion*, following the lead of Romanos but without approaching his mastery of the form. The *kanon*, which started its career as a penitential text for Lent, spreads to the weeks between Easter and Pentecost and thence to feast days throughout the year. Production of liturgical poems largely ceases in the eleventh century, due to a lack of room for new material in the liturgy, but an Italo-Greek school in Calabria and the monastery of Grottaferrata (established in the tenth century by St. Nilus) continue to be active till about 1150.

Select Bibliography

Students of Byzantine religious lyric are fortunate to have Egon Wellesz, *A History of Byzantine Music and Hymnography*, 2d rev. ed. (Oxford, 1961), which should be their constant companion. Chapters 8 and 9 (pp. 171–245) give a short history of Byzantine hymnography, and on pp. 442–43 there is a list of hymnographers with dates (as far as they can be ascertained). Pages 133–45 describe the full range of Byzantine liturgical books; pp. 239–45, the shorter hymn forms. A valuable bibliography appears on pp. 428–41. On the *heirmoi*, see Miloš Velimirovič, "The Byzantine Heirmos and Heirmologion," *Gattungen*, pp. 192–244; on the *kontakion* and *kanon*, see José Grosdidier de Matons, "Le Kontakion," *Gattungen*, pp. 245–68. See also Hans-Georg Beck, *Kirche und theologische Literatur im byzantinischen Reich*, Handbuch der Altertumswissenschaft 12:2:1 (Munich, 1959), pp. 262–66, 425–30, 472f., 515–19, 601–9, 662f., 701–7, and 796–98; Josef Szoevérffy has recently published *A Guide to Byzantine Hymnography: A Classified Bibliography of Texts and Studies*, vol. 1 (Brookline, Mass./Leyden, 1978). I have not seen it.

For information concerning nonhymnic poetry, one should consult Karl Krumbacher, *Geschichte der byzantinischen Literatur*, 2d ed., Handbuch der klassischen Altertumswissenschaft 9:1 (Munich, 1897); Franz Doelger, "Die byzantinische Dichtung in der Reinsprache," 2d ed., in *Eucharisterion, F. Doelger zum 70. Geburtstag* (Thessalonica, 1961), pp. 1–64; and the copious notes in the second volume of Raffaele Cantarella, *Poeti bizantini*, 2 vols., Edizioni dell'Università cattolica del sacro cuore, series "Corsi Universitari" 21 and 22 (Milan, 1948).

Cantarella's book is still the best single anthology of Byzantine poetry. Some Byzantine texts appear in Constantine Trypanis, *Medieval and Modern Greek Poetry: An Anthology* (Oxford, 1968), but with only light annotation and without an English counterpart to Cantarella's helpful Italian prose translation of the selections he includes. As an introduction to Byzantine hymns, John M. Neale, *Hymns of the Eastern Church*, 2d ed. (London, 1863), is very outmoded but still useful. To find most hymns, one must turn to Orthodox liturgical books, the best editions of which are listed on pp. 429–32 of Wellesz, *A History of Byzantine Music* (note the edition of the *Heirmologion* by Sophronios Eustratiades, which appeared in 1931 as the ninth volume in the *Hagioreitike Bibliotheke*). Important texts probably antedating the *kontakion* appear in Paul Maas, Giuseppe Mercati, and Sofronio Gassisi, "Gleichzeilige Hymnen in der byzantinischen Liturgie," *Byzantinische Zeitschrift* 18 (1909): 309–56. Much more convenient, but selective, are Jean Baptiste Pitra, *Analecta sacra spicilegio solesmensi parata*, vol. 1 (Paris, 1876; reprint, Farnsborough, Hants., England, 1966) and Wilhelm von Christ and Matthaios Paranikas, *Anthologia graeca carminum christianorum* (Leipzig, 1871). For examples of the early *kontakion* not by Romanos, see Constantine A. Trypanis, *Fourteen Early Byzantine Cantica*, Wiener Byzantinistische Studien, vol. 5 (Vienna, 1968). Italo-Grecic work is appearing in the *Analecta hymnica graeca e codicibus eruta Italiae inferioris*, ed. Joseph Schirò; see for instance vol. 1, *Canones Septembris*, ed. Ada Gonzato (Rome, 1966) and vol. 8, *Canones Aprilis*, ed. Constantine Nikas (Rome, 1970). Enrica Follieri has edited a group of canons by John Mauropus in the *Archivo italiano per la storia della pietà* 5 (1968): 1–200, *Giovanni Mauropede, Metropolita d'Eucaita—otto canoni paracletici a N.S. Gesu Cristo* (with facing Italian prose translations). She has also produced an invaluable index to Greek hymnography, the *Initia hymnorum Ecclesiae Graecae*, 5 vols., Studi e testi 211–215 bis (Rome, 1960–66).

Editions of nonhymnic religious (and secular) poetry by Byzantine poets are too widely scattered to be listed in detail here; Cantarella's notes on each author in *Poeti bizantini* should be consulted for books and articles prior to 1948 and later than 1897 (the date of Krumbacher's *Geschichte*). For the Greek Anthology see *Anthologia graeca*, ed. Hermann Beckby, 4 vols. (Munich, 1965). For Christophoros's saints' calendar, see Enrica Follieri, *Analecta bollandiana* 77 (1959): 245–304; for Romanos, see the editions by Paul Maas and Constantine Trypanis, *Romani Melodi Cantica genuina* (Oxford, 1963) (bare text), and by José Grosdidier de Matons, *Hymnes*, 4 vols., Sources chrétiennes 99, 110, 114, and 128 (Paris, 1964–67) (with facing French prose translation); there is also a rather pedestrian translation of part of the oeuvre by Marjorie Carpenter, *Kontakia of Romanos, Byzantine Melodist* (Columbia, Mo., 1970); for Symeon the New Theologian, see *Hymnes*, ed. Johannes Koder and Joseph Paramelle, 3 vols., Sources chrétiennes 156, 174, and 196 (Paris, 1969–73); see also *Hymnen*, ed. Athanaios Kambylis, *Supplementa byzantina* 3 (New York/Berlin, 1976); for Theodore Prodromos's tetrastichs on the fixed feasts and the saints, see Ciro Gianelli, *Analecta bollandiana* 75 (1957): 299–336; for Theodore the Studite's trimeter poems, see the oustanding edition (with full commentary and German translation) by Paul Speck, *Iamben*, Supplementa byzantina 1 (Berlin, 1968).

ITALIAN

Apart from a relatively small number of sonnets, *canzoni*, and *capitoli ternari* (discussed in chapter 2, "Forms"), the history of the Italian religious lyric is identical with the history of the *lauda*. Before the flagellant movement of 1260, extant precursors of the *lauda* take the form of monorhymed quatrains (a form borrowed from Latin); after the movement, the secular dance-song, the *ballata*, becomes the well-nigh universal form for the *laude*, and confraternities proliferate, beginning in Tuscany and Umbria and spreading thence throughout central and northern Italy. As the custom of daily singing of *laude* also spreads (apparently originating in Siena), *laudari* for confraternal use are composed, or compiled, with a free interchange of texts and much scribal reworking (an early oral phase of transmission seems to have yielded to written transmission before the end of the thirteenth century). Today, more than two hundred *laudari* are still in existence, many as yet unpublished.

The friars sponsored the confraternities, created the *laudari*, and instilled their spirituality into the laity involved. (This is in sharp contrast to the non-lyric religious poetry of the late thirteenth and early fourteenth centuries in its Lombard and Umbrian centers, which was the work of aristocrats of characteristically "heretical" leanings.) A similar desire to reach the people shows itself in mid-thirteenth century Italo-Latin paraliturgical pieces on secular models. In its later development, the *lauda* takes several directions. One leads through a distribution of the "parts" in dialogue-*laude* among various speakers to full-blown religious theater (1330–40, Perugia and Orvieto, then Umbria, then Siena and Florence, then Rome, and so on). Another continues the original impulse behind the conventual *laudari*, but with less and less force as the energies of 1260 dissipate. A third develops the private, literary *lauda* such as one finds at the very beginnings of the form in Guittone d'Arezzo and Jacopone da Todi. In consequence, non-*ballata laude* become more common, since for the literary *lauda* there is no congregation that needs a *ripresa* (refrain) to sing. At the same time, the musical settings become more complex, moving from chantlike monody to three-part polyphony (cf. the *conductus*) to the complex polyphony of the Ars Nova period; *lauda* singing ceases to be a confraternal act of worship and turns into something the lay members pay professionals to do on their behalf. Attendance declines, the confraternities grow more and more secular (in a Florence confraternity, the Virgin is being invoked in Ovidian verses by the fifteenth century!), or they are converted into exclusive clubs for the local aristocracy or for craft guilds. Even the impact of a mass movement like that of the Bianchi in 1399 has only a transitory effect on the decay of the confraternities. By the fifteenth century, the *lauda* is almost entirely a literary form, relying on the use of anonymous secular tunes (including popular French songs and carnival numbers) to give itself an interest the insipid words usually lack. The Italian religious lyric has entered an age of mediocrity from which it is not to emerge until the nineteenth century.

Select Bibliography

For a general account, see Giorgio Petrocchi, "La letteratura religiosa," in *Storia della letteratura italiana*, vol. 1: *Le origini e il Duecento* (Milan, 1965), pp. 627–88, with bibliography (especially sec. 6 and 7, on the *lauda* and on Jacopone). For detailed bibliography and a century-by-century history, see the *Storia letteraria d'Italia*: Giulio Bertoni, *Il Duecento*, 3d ed. (1939; reprint, with bibliographical updating, Milan, 1960); Natalino Sapegno, *Il Trecento*, 3d ed. (Milan, 1955); Vittorio Rossi, *Il Quattrocento*, rev. ed. (Milan, 1938; reprint, 1956). Important articles include the following: Benedetto Croce, "Letteratura di devozione," in *Poesia popolare e poesia d'arte: Studi sulla poesia italiana dal tre al cinquecento* (Bari, 1933), pp. 163–87 (fundamental for the question of evaluation), and idem, "Il secolo senza poesia," *Poesia populare*, pp. 209–37 (fundamental article on the century from 1375 to 1475); Ignazio Baldelli, "La lauda e i Disciplinati," *La Rassegna della letteratura italiana* 64, no. 3 (1960): 396–418 (seminal work on filiation of *laudari* and sociopoetic differences in the *laude* of different regions, in this case, east of the Tiber versus west of the Tiber); Giovanni Getto, "La letteratura religiosa," in *Letteratura e critica nel tempo* (Milan, 1968), pp. 117–91 (ends with an excellent bibliography on mysticism, style, the religious orders, general histories and reference works, and periodicals, pp. 184–91); Gerard G. Meersseman, "Etudes sur les anciennes confréries dominicaines," a series of three monographs in *Archivum fratrum praedicatorum* 20 (1950): 5–113; 21 (1951): 51–196; and 22 (1952): 5–176 (largely supersedes the earlier work by Gennaro M. Monti, *Le Confraternite medievali dell'Alta e Media Italia* [Venice, 1927]).

Aside from the bibliographies already noted above, one may consult Gennaro M. Monti, "Bibliografia della laude," *La Bibliofilia* 21 (1921): 241–57; 22(1922): 289–99; 23 (1923): 260–67; 24 (1924): 29–40, and 25 (1925): 71–75 and 256–65 (hereafter cited as Monti). For an index by incipit to the *laude*, see Annibale Tenneroni, *Inizii di antiche poesie italiane religiose e morali* (Florence, 1909), and Ludovico Frati, "Giunte agli inizii di antiche poesie italiane religiose e morali a cura di Annibale Tenneroni," *Archivum romanicum* 1 (1917): 441–80; 2 (1918): 185–207 and 325–43; and 3 (1919): 62–94.

Anthologies of the *laude* by period include Giorgio Varanini, *Laude dugentesche*, Vulgares eloquentes, vol. 8 (Padua, 1972) (a valuable introduction, a map on p. xlvif. placing significant events and manuscripts, a list of manuscripts on pp. 206–9, and well-edited thirteenth-century texts); Gianfranco Contini, *Poeti del Duecento*, vol. 2:2, pt. 6, *La Letteratura italiana, storia e testi*, vol. 2:2, (Milan/Naples, 1960), pp. 7–166 (basic bibliography); and Natalino Sapegno, *Poeti minori del Trecento*, sec. 7, *La letteratura italiana, storia e testi*, vol. 10, (Milan/Naples, 1952), pp. 1011–1134 (basic bibliography for fourteenth-century religious poetry). For early *laude* and precursors, one may also consult Ernesto Monaci, *Crestomazia italiana dei primi secoli*, rev. Felice Arese, 2d ed. (Rome/Naples/Città di Castello, 1955), nos. 36, 141, 159. For the fifteenth-century *lauda*, the best source remains [Gustavo Galletti], *Laude spirituali di Feo Belcari, di Lorenzo de' Medici, di Francesco d'Albizzo, di Castellano Castellani, Lucrezia Tornabuoni, Bianco da Siena, Girolamo Savonarola, Giovanni Dominici, Ugo Panziera, Jacopone da Todi e di altri, comprese nelle prime quattro edizioni* (Florence, 1863). In addition to the poets listed in the title, it includes pieces by Antonio Bettini da Siena, Antonio di Guido, Michele Chelli, Gherardo d'Astore, Bernardo Giambullari, and Suora Hieronyma de' Malatesti. Most of the major authors appear elsewhere, in better editions; Galleti simply reproduced the "four editions" of *laude* printed in 1480 (*Laudi di Feo Belcari*, Florence?;

Monti, no. 4), 1485 (*Laude facte e composte da più persone spirituali*, Florence; Monti, no. 7), 1489 (same title, Florence; Monti, no. 8; paid for by Lorenzo the Magnificent and including his own *laude*), and 1510 (*Libro di laude composte da più persone spirituali*, Florence, Monti, no. 22; Piero Pacini da Pescia was the petitioner). However, most of Belcari's *laude* and the work of Castellano Castellani (fl. 1448–1518, Florentine) and Francesco d'Albizzo are still available only in Galletti. For individual poets and *laudari*, see the following editions:

1. Guittone d'Arezzo, *Le Rime*, ed. Francesco Egidi (Bari, 1940).
2. Jacopone da Todi, *Laude*, ed. Franco Mancini (Rome/Bari, 1974).
3. Cortona 91, "Laudi cortonese del secolo xiii," ed. Guido Mazzoni, *Propugnatore* 22, n.s. 2 (1889): 205–70 and 23, n.s. 3 (1890): 5–48.
4. Ugo Panziera, *I Cantici spirituali del b. Ugo Panziera di Prato*, ed. Cesare Guasti (Prato, 1861) (see also Alfredo Mori, *Giullari di Dio* [Milan, 1920]).
5. Aquila *laudario*, "Laudi e devozioni della città di Aquila," Erasmo Percopo, *Giornale storico della litteratura italiana* 7 (1886): 153–69 and 345–65; 8 (1886): 180–219; 9 (1887): 381–403; 12 (1888): 368–88; 15 (1890): 152–79; 18 (1891): 186–215; and 20 (1892): 379–94.
6. Florence (S. Eustachio?) *laudario* [Eugenio Cecconi], *Laudi di una compagnia fiorentina del secolo xiv fin qui inedite* (Florence, 1870).
7. Pisa *laudario* (= Arsenal MS 8521), Erik Staff, *Le Laudario de Pise*, vol. 1, Humanistiska Vetenskaps-Samfundet i Uppsala, Skrifter 27:1 (Uppsala/Leipzig, 1931); thanks to "missionary" activity emanating from the Roman confraternity of the Gonfalone, this *laudario* and the next two items are closely related.
8. Genoa *laudario*, "Laudi genovese del secolo xiv," Vincenzo Crescini and Gian Domenico Belletti, *Giornale linguistico di archeologia, storia e letteratura* 10 (1883): 321–50.
9. Turin *laudario*, Ferdinando Gabotto and Delfino Orsi, *Le laudi del Piemonte*, Scelta di curiosità letterarie, vol. 238 (Bologna, 1891) (includes a few *laude* from Bra); on the relations of items 7 through 9, see Ferdinando Neri, "Di alcuni laudari settentrionali," Accademia delle scienze di Torino, *Atti* 44 (1908–9): 1009–33.
10. Modena *laudario*, Giulio Bertoni, "Il laudario dei Battuti di Modena," *Beihefte zur Zeitschrift fuer romanische Philologie* 20 (1909).
11. Urbino *laudario*, Rosanna Bettarini, *Jacopone e il laudario urbinate* (Florence, 1969).
12. Bianco da Siena: *Laudi spirituali del Bianco da Siena povero gesuato del secolo xiv* (Lucca, 1851; 92 items); *Il Bianco da Siena: notizie e testi inediti*, ed. Franca Ageno, Biblioteca della "Rassegna," vol. 24 (Genoa/Rome/Naples, 1939; 19 additional items); Gennaro M. Monti reprints 28 items from Bini's edition (nos. 8, 9, 10, 11, 15, 18, 19, 20, 22, 33, 35, 38, 41, 44, 45, 50, 51, 52, 53, 54, 57, 58, 63, 64, end of 69, 83, 84, 85) in *Laude mistiche del Bianco da Siena* (Lanciano, 1925) in far more readable type.
13. Neri Pagliaresi, *Rime sacre di certa o probabile attribuzione*, ed. Giorgio Varani (Florence, 1970).
14. Ferrara *laudario* (includes Latin texts), Giuseppe Ferraro, *Poesie popolari religiose del secolo xiv*, Scelta di curiosità letterarie, vol. 152 (Bologna, 1877).

15. Leonardo Giustinian: in the absence of modern editions, one must turn to early printed collections (cf. Monti, no. 1, 1474 ed., Venice; no. 2, 1475 ed., Vincenza; no. 6, 1483 ed., Venice; no. 10, 1490 ed., Venice; no. 19, 1506 ed., Venice—the last is held by the New York Public Library, which should now have a microfilm copy on file to be reproduced on request).

16. Feo Belcari: see pp. 1–53, 68ff., 72, 75, 86f., 96ff., 100f., 105f., 283 and 285–87 of Galletti's 1863 reprint of the 1480 edition of Belcari's *Laude* (cited above); Luisa Delucchi, *Alcune laudi inedite di Feo Belcari* (Genoa, 1930); Feo Belcari, *Sacre rappresentazioni e laude*, ed. Onorato Allocco-Castellino (Turin, 1926), reprints of 28 *laude* from Galletti.

17. Lucrezia Tornabuoni de' Medici, *Le laudi* ed. Guglielmo Volpi (Pistoia, 1900).

18. Lorenzo de' Medici, *Opere*, ed. Attilio Simioni 2d ed., 2 vols. (Bari, 1939).

19. Girolamo Savonarola, *Poesie*, ed. Mario Martelli (Rome, 1968).

Finally, the reader without Italian will find a useful discussion of the *laude* in English in David L. Jeffrey, *The Early English Lyric and Franciscan Spirituality* (Lincoln, Neb., 1975), pp. 118–54 (chap. 4, "The Earliest Lyrics in Italy"). And for the music of the *laude*, see Fernando Liuzzi's splendid *La Lauda e i primordi della melodia italiana* (Rome, 1935).

LATIN

The beginnings of Christian religious lyric in Latin, liturgical and non-liturgical, lie in the fourth century A.D. In mid-century, Hilary of Poitiers composed his *Liber hymnorum* in various meters; in the 380s, Ambrose created the hymn in iambic dimeter quatrains that became known as the *ambrosianus* and dominated the first centuries of the Middle Ages. At the end of the century, Prudentius achieved a reasonably successful synthesis of classical literary traditions and Christian material in his large and various output; centos from the *Cathemerinon* and the *Peristephanon* were assimilated by the liturgy, though Prudentius's intentions were purely literary and his audience the same educated elite to whom Augustine addressed his *De civitate Dei*. Shortly thereafter, Paulinus of Nola, pupil to the then-famous Ausonius, also made an important contribution to the new-born Christian literary religious lyric.

In the next two centuries, various Ambrosian hymns whose authors are now unknown entered liturgical use, but there was no notable writer of religious lyric until Venantius Fortunatus, toward the end of the sixth century. His hymns enjoyed a huge and well-deserved influence throughout the Middle Ages. In the period between the close of antiquity and the Carolingian dynasty, certain "national" traditions make contributions of varying degrees of importance: the Visigothic, in Spain, known after the Arab conquest in the eighth century as the "Mozarabic" tradition (suppressed everywhere except Toledo by the Roman church at the end of the eleventh century); the Celtic, in Ireland and in Continental monasteries founded by Irish monks such as St. Columban; the Anglo-Saxon (rather undistinguished, and poor in lyrics); the Frankish, or Gallican, in which the *versus* or processional hymn (in accentual verse, often with refrain) is the most interesting early development (it continues in fashion till the end of the ninth century and beyond at St. Gall). Each of these traditions has its own distinctive traits: for example, the classicizing tendencies, including a liking for classical lyric stanzas such as the Sapphic, of Visigothic and Mozarabic hymns, or the baroque "Hisperic" diction of Celtic-Latin work.

The court of Charlemagne produced a great deal of "learned" poetry, some of it religious and some of that lyric, but generally not very successful; exceptions include the hymn "Ut queant laxis," Paulinus of Aquileia's *rhythmi* (rather than his quantitative, "classical" verse), and the poems of the gifted Spaniard Theodulf, bishop of Orleans (notably his "Gloria laus et honor," which became the Palm Sunday processional hymn). On the borders of religious lyric, Alcuin (originally of York) did some excellent work, successfully fusing the classical and the medieval Christian in a way that usually eluded both himself and his contemporaries. Poetically, the accentual, nonlearned Latin verse of the Age of Charlemagne is by and large more interesting than the court poetry.

The major contribution of the ninth century came after the breakup of the Carolingian empire, in the creation of the "prose" (later, "sequence") and the trope (see "Forms" in chapter 2). The trope went out of favor in the twelfth and thirteenth centuries but was an important liturgical genre for several hundred years. The sequence begins as art-prose raised to the power of poetry but takes on the regular metric and stanzaic form of the hymn in the late eleventh century; at the same time, along with other sorts of Latin lyric, it gains the additional feature of rhyme, which can be traced back in its monosyllabic guise to at least the fifth century (cf. "A solis ortus cardine") but which becomes disyllabic ca. 1100 and transforms the face of Latin poetry—it may even have been the desire to obtain two-syllable rhyme that motivated the shift from the iambic norm of early medieval hymnody to the trochaic norm of the regular sequence, because a trochaic line has a two-syllable, feminine, rather than a one-syllable, masculine, cadence. The archaic, proselike sequence went into eclipse, to return to frequent use in the fourteenth and fifteenth centuries.

The twelfth and thirteenth centuries also see the rise of the *conductus* (see "Forms" in chapter 2) and various sorts of *cantio* (paraliturgical lyric), all bearing the evident marks of a desire to incorporate popular elements into religious song. This is also the period in which medieval polyphony enters upon a rich and rapid development, one which often reduced Latin texts to a secondary or purely decorative role. Outstanding writers of religious lyric include Abelard, Hildegard of Bingen, Adam of St. Victor (regular sequence), Philip the Chancellor, John Pecham, John of Howden, Bonaventura, Aquinas, and Arnulf of Louvain. Franciscan poetry dominates thirteenth-century Latin religious lyric (cf. the Dies irae and the Stabat mater), as it does the vernacular in England and Italy, but there is a wide range of liturgical, devotional, and literary work being done by authors of all clerical descriptions.

The output of hymns, sequences, and *cantiones* increases to unheard of dimensions in the fourteenth and fifteenth centuries, continuing on into the middle of the sixteenth century, when liturgical reform put an end to medieval religious poetry (in the Roman missal of 1570, the tropes have vanished, and only four sequences—the "Veni sancte spiritus," the "Victimae paschali," the Lauda Sion, and the Dies irae—remain in place, to be joined in the eighteenth century by the long-beloved Stabat mater, in time to be set by some of the greatest Baroque composers). This period remains ill-studied (as it is for most of the vernaculars as well), but the general consensus is that few authors do more than live off the capital of the past, repeating its achievements. One suspects, however, that a revaluation is possible, and needed.

Select Bibliography

Josef Szoevérffy, "L'hymnologie médiévale: recherches et méthodes," *Cahiers de civilisation médiévale* 4 (1961): 389–422, is a good brief survey of the hymn and a prelude to his *Annalen* (see below). The standard reference work in English remains Frederic J. E. Raby, *A History of Christian-Latin Poetry From the Beginnings to the Close of the Middle Ages*, 2d ed. (Oxford, 1953); for editions, monographs, and articles prior to the 1950s, one should consult its bibliography (pp. 461–94) and the bibliography at the end of its companion, Frederic J. E. Raby, *A History of Secular Latin Poetry . . .*, 2d ed., 2 vols. (Oxford, 1957), as well as the footnotes at the start of the discussion of each poet or work (see indexes). (Editions and secondary material covered by Raby will not, in principle, be mentioned below.) Much more complete, but in German only, is Josef Szoevérffy, *Die Annalen der lateinischen Hymnendichtung*, 2 vols. (Berlin, 1964–65), with lavish, somewhat indiscriminate references to all the relevant literature (for strictures on this work, see Peter Dronke's review in the *Journal of Theological Studies*, 2d ser. 17 [1966]: 496–502). Antiquated, but compendious and very convenient, is John Julian, *A Dictionary of Hymnology*, 2d ed. (London, 1907). For general literary-historical information, see Max Manitius, *Geschichte der lateinischen Literatur des Mittelalters*, 3 vols. (Munich, 1911–31); a good guide to medieval Latin is Karl Strecker, *An Introduction to Medieval Literature*, rev. and trans. Robert Palmer (Dublin/Zurich, 1957).

By far the most important collection of medieval religious poetry, the 55 volumes of the AH must still be relied on for most poets and most poems. The long-standing lack of an index under which hymnological studies have labored has at last been remedied by a comprehensive index in two volumes to *all* the incipits of medieval Latin poems: *Initia carminum latinorum saeculo undecimo antiquiorum*, ed. Dieter Schaller and Ewald Koensgen, with John Tagliabue (Goettingen, 1977), and *Carmina medii aevi posterioris latina*, vol. 1 : 1 *Initia carminum ac versuum medii aevi posterioris latinorum*, ed. Hans Walther, 2d ed. (Goettingen, 1969) (for lists of incipits omitted by Walther, see *Mittellateinisches Jahrbuch* 7 [1972]: 293–314; 8 [1973]: 288–304; 9 [1974]: 320–44; and 12 [1977]: 297–315). These two volumes between them cover close to forty thousand items. For religious poetry, Ugo Chevalier, *Repertorium hymnologicum*, 6 vols. (Louvain, 1892–1920), though cumbersome to use and superseded, technically at least, by the two volumes just listed, can still prove useful, in part because it concentrates on hymnography, and in part because of volume 6, whose indexes cover (1) feasts, saints, and so forth, (2) authors and editors, (3) liturgical books, and (4) sources and which provides a great deal of information about manuscripts and the literature up to the turn of the century. (With it, use Clemens Blume, *Repertorium repertorii* [Leipzig, 1901].)

On the development of the liturgy, Dom Gregory Dix's *The Shape of the Liturgy* (London, 1943) is easily the most readable and thorough account. For more technical studies, see Josef A. Jungmann and Aimé-Georges Martimort, et al., eds., *Handbuch der Liturgiewissenschaft*, 2 vols. (Freiburg, 1965); the French version is *L'église en prière* (Paris/Tournai/Rome/New York, 1961). For a brief recent bibliography, see Jonsson, *Tropes*, pp. 44 and 51. On medieval Latin prosody, see Dag Norberg, *Introduction à l'étude de la versification latine médiévale*, Studia latina stockholmiensia 5 (Uppsala, 1958) (with references to earlier literature). On the hymn, see Szoevérffy's article in the *New Catholic Encyclopedia*, vol. 7 (New York, 1967), pp. 287–96 and the list of articles in his *Annalen* 1 : 35; major studies and editions appear on pp. 35–38. On the archaic sequence, see Richard Crocker, *The Early Medieval Sequence* (Berkeley, 1977) (bibliography on pp. 449–52); Crocker's chapter, "The Sequence," in *Gattungen*, pp. 269–322, is an excellent short study of its subject, far easier going than the later book. On the trope, see *Annalen* 1 : 275–81 (full references), and Richard Crocker, "The Troping Hypothesis," *Musical Quarterly* 52 (1966): 183–203. On the *conductus*, see *Annalen* 2: 48–51 (footnotes); Jacques Handschin's article in the *New Oxford History of Music*, vol. 2 (Oxford, 1954), chap. 5, "Trope, Sequence, and Conductus," is helpful concerning all three forms.

In the last century, there have been a number of valuable monographs on particular genres of hymns, or national traditions. For Sweden, see Carl Allen Moberg, *Die liturgischen Hymnen in Schweden*, vol. 1 (Copenhagen, 1947) (valuable general discussion of the liturgy); for Poland and Silesia, see two works edited by Henryk Kowalewicz, his *Cantica Medii Aevi Polono-Latina*, vol. 1: *Sequentiae*, Bibliotheca Latina Medii et Recentioris Aevi 14 (Warsaw, 1964) (a collection of 140 sequences) and his *Zasób, Zasięg Terytorialny i Chronologia Polsko-Łacińskiej Liryki Średniowiecznej* (Extent, Distribution, and Chronology of the Polish-Latin Lyric of the Middle Ages), Seria Filologia Polska, no. 13, Adam Mickiewicz-University (Posen, 1967) (Szoevérffy discusses both books in detail in "Ostmittel-europaeische Streifzuege I: Mittellateinische Lyrik aus Polen und Schlesien nach neuer polnischer Forschung," *Mittellateinisches Jahrbuch* 12 [1977]: 97–122); for Iberia, see Szoevérffy,

Iberian Hymnody: Survey and Problems (Wetteren, Belgium, 1971). On Christmas hymns, see Maximilian Scherner, *Die sprachlichen Rollen im lateinischen Weih- nachtslied des Mittelalters*, Mittellateinisches Jahrbuch no. 4, suppl. (Wuppertal, 1970); on Mary Magdalene hymns, see Wiltrud aus der Fuenten, *Maria Magdalena in der Lyrik des Mittelalters* (Duesseldorf, 1966); on St. James hymns, see J. O'Mal- ley, "An Introduction to the Study of the hymns of St. James," *Traditio* 26 (1970): 255–91; on St. Martin hymns, see Marie M. Keane, "Martin Hymns of the Middle Ages" (Ph.D. diss., Catholic University, 1969); on Cross hymns, see Szoevérffy, "Crux fidelis . . . Prolegomena to a History of the Holy Cross Hymns," *Traditio* 22 (1966): 1–41; on St. Peter hymns, see Szoevérffy, *A Mirror of Medieval Culture: Saint Peter Hymns of the Middle Ages*, Transactions of the Connecticut Academy of Arts and Sciences 42, no. 3 (New Haven/Copenhagen, 1965); on eucharistic hymns, see Wilhelm Breuer, *Die lateinische Eucharistiedichtung des Mittelalters von ihren Anfaengen bis zum Ausgang des 13. Jahrhunderts*, suppl. to Mittellateinisches Jahr- buch 2 (Wuppertal/Kastellaun/Duesseldorf, 1970).

The best general anthologies of medieval Latin religious lyric are Guido Dreves and Clemens Blume, *Ein Jahrtausend lateinischer Hymnendichtung*, 2 vols. (Leipzig, 1909); Franz Joseph Mone, *Hymni Latini Medii Aevi*, 3 vols. (Freiburg im Breisgau, 1853–55) (still valuable for its commentary and the vernacular materials it in- cludes); and, underannotated but easily accessible, Frederic J. E. Raby, *The Oxford Book of Medieval Latin Verse*, rev. ed. (Oxford, 1959). For the early centuries of hymnody, see Walther Bulst, *Hymni antiquissimi LXXV—Psalmi III* (Heidelberg, 1956) (Hilary to Venantius Fortunatus), and Arthur Walpole, *Early Latin Hymns* (Cambridge, 1922) (same span for named authors, to eighth century for anonymous texts—127 items in all; copious and extremely helpful notes) (see also AH 51; pp. 1–256, fifth to eleventh centuries). For Visigothic and Mozarabic hymns, see AH 27 and the important textual improvements suggested by Birgitta Thorsberg, *Etudes sur l'hymnologie mozarabe*, Studia latina stockholmiensia 8 (Uppsala/Stockholm, 1962). For Celtic hymnody, see AH 51, pp. 257–365, and the editions listed in Raby, *A History of Christian-Latin Poetry*, p. 134f. For Scandinavian hymns, see Moberg, *Die liturgischen Hymnen in Schweden* and the rare nineteenth-century col- lection by Gustaf E. Klemming, *Latinska Sånger fordam använda i Svenska Kyrkor, Kloster och Skolor*, 2 vols. (Stockholm, 1885–87) (further literature in *Annalen* 2:291–97 and 347–54; references to volumes of AH for individual texts, esp. vols. 42–43). For Polish hymns, see the collection of sequences edited by Kowalewicz, *Cantica Medii Aevi Polono-Latina*, vol. 1: *Sequentiae*, and the listing of incipits with printed sources in Szoevérffy's review article, "Ostmittel-europaeische Streifzuege I." For sequences, see especially AH 53–55 (historically ordered collection from origins to end of Middle Ages) and 7 (sequences from St. Martial's of Limoges prosers); for Notker Balbulus and the early sequence, see the outstanding work of Wolfram von den Steinen, *Notker der Dichter*, 2 vols. (Bern, 1948). For tropes, see AH 47 and 49, and the ongoing collective edition under the general editorship of Ritva Jonsson, the *Corpus troporum*, of which two volumes have appeared: Jonsson, *Tropes* and *Pro- sules de la Messe, Tropes de l'allelulia*, ed. Olof Marcusson, Studia latina stock- holmiensia 22 (Stockholm, 1976). For the *conductus* and *cantiones* of all sorts, see especially AH 20–21, and also AH 1 (Bohemian *cantiones*), 2, and 45b. For the motet, see Friedrich Gennrich, *Bibliographie der aeltesten franzoesischen und lateinischen Motetten* (Darmstadt, 1957). For verse offices (*historiae rhythmicae*) see AH 5, 13, 17 (Spanish), 24–26, 28, 45a. For devotional poems (*pia dictamina*), see AH 15, 29–33, and 46.

As stated, references to editions of individual poets or manuscripts can be found in Raby and Szoevérffy by consulting the index and the bibliographical references to which it will guide one. However, a number of important editions have appeared in the last twenty-five years that require mention here, since those relying on Szoevérffy or (a fortiori) Raby alone can easily miss them. Ten poems published earlier without ascription have been restored to Gottschalk of Orbais and appear in PLAC 6.1:97–106 (including the long penitential lyric "O mi custos"). The poems of Peter Damiani have been edited by Margareta Lokranz, *L'opera poetica di S. Pier Damiani*, Studia latina stockholmiensia 12 (Stockholm, 1964). The shorter poems of Hildebert of Lavardin have been given a critical edition by A. Brian Scott, *Carmina minora* (Leipzig, 1969). Szoevérffy has issued a two-volume study and text of Abelard's *Hymnarius paraclitensis*, Medieval Classics: Texts and Studies 2–3 (Albany, N.Y./Brookline, Mass., 1975) (but see Peter Dronke's review in *Mittellateinisches Jahrbuch* 13 [1978]: 307–11; it is still advisable to consult Dreves's edition in AH 48, pp. 141–223 [items 111–243]; for the *planctus*, use Wilhelm Meyer's edition in his *Gesammelte Abhandlungen zur mittellateinischen Rhythmik*, vol. 1 (1905), pp. 340–74, and Dronke's text of the lament of Samson, "Abissus vere multa" in his chapter, "Peter Abelard · *Planctus* and Satire," in *Poetic Individuality in the Middle Ages* (Oxford, 1970), pp. 121–23. The most convenient edition of Adam of St. Victor's sequences (though no great advance on earlier scholarship) is that edited by Franz Wellner (see list of abbreviations). For Hildegard of Bingen's poems, see *Lieder*, ed. Pudentiana Barth, Immaculata Ritscher, and Joseph Schmidt-Goerg (Salzburg, 1969).

A great deal remains to be done. Medieval Latin poetry suffers from an embarrassment of riches and a dearth of scholars. One hopes for an improvement in this situation in the future, but the reverse is more likely. Still, it is possible that one day Latin and contemporary vernacular literature will be properly correlated in the as-yet-unwritten literary history of the Middle Ages in their full diversity and unity.

MIDDLE ENGLISH

For some three centuries after the conquest in 1066, English stood last of a group of three languages, with Latin at the top and Anglo-Norman French in the middle. By contrast, during the Old English period, it had vied with Latin as a language of culture and literature. Nonetheless, Anglo-Saxon proved to be remarkably unproductive in the area of religious lyric, perhaps because the long alliterative line is far more suitable for discursive and narrative verse than for lyric poetry, and the lyric forms of the Celtic and Latin traditions were not adopted to provide an alternative to it. There are a few outstanding poems, such as "The Dream of the Rood" and so-called elegies like "The Seafarer" or "The Wanderer," which resolve (or dissolve) a first-person description of anguish and near-impasse with the general truths of the Christian faith. And there are paraphrases of liturgical texts and some Psalms. The first group is too anomalous, the second too uninteresting to have been included in the discussion in this book. In any case, the reader will find that the major Old English poems have all received excellent individual editions and a degree of critical discussion few works in other traditions have been blessed with.

About twenty years after the advent of the friars in England (Dominicans, 1221; Franciscans, 1224), vernacular lyrics begin to appear in significant numbers in English manuscripts. The authorship of Old English religious poetry had been monastic, in keeping with the monastic dominance of early medieval culture; now the religious lyric becomes the work of the friars, and more particularly, of the Franciscans (from 65 to 90 percent of work up to 1350). Most lyrics appear in a number of manuscripts assembled by friars for homiletic or devotional use; these include Digby 86 (ca. 1275; Dominican or perhaps Franciscan); Trinity (Cambridge) 323 (1255–60, a compilation of English, French, and Latin texts; Dominican?); Jesus (Oxford) 29 (1250–75; Franciscan); Digby 2 (1282; Franciscan?); Cotton MS Caligula A ix (second half of the thirteenth century); and Harley 2253 (1330s?; half of the lyrics also appear in Franciscan miscellanies). Befitting the popular audience to which they were directed, these lyrics succeed, when they do, through the directness and simplicity of their language and the uncomplicated strength of their devotional feeling.

An eminent scholar of Middle English has estimated that about 10 percent of Middle English lyric consists of translations. In Philipps 8336 (British Museum MS Additional 46919), there is an interesting set of 17 hymn translations by the Franciscan friar William Herebert (d. 1333); later translations include work by Lydgate, Ryman, and others (e.g., cf. the late fifteenth-century "Hymnal from MS Additional 34,193 British Museum," ed. Frank A. Patterson, in *Medieval Studies in Memory of Gertrude Schoepperle Loomis* [Paris/New York, 1927], pp. 443–88). One may compare Germany and France for a similar increase in hymn translation in the fourteenth and especially the late fifteenth centuries. For England, the subject has been exhaustively treated by Helmut Gneuss, *Hymnar und Hymnen im Englischen Mittelalter* (Tuebingen, 1968) (pp. 257–413 contain the text of a late Old English "Expositio Hymnorum").

After the Black Death of 1349, Franciscan authorship falls off to about 25 percent, reflecting the friars' increasing cultivation of the wealthy rather than the common folk and perhaps the increasing use of English as a literary language suitable for art-lyric. Nonetheless, Franciscans remain important

in the history of the Middle English religious lyric. One of the more extensive fourteenth-century collections was the work of Friar John Grimestone
(Advocates MS 18.7.21, dated securely to 1372), and Friar James Ryman
was responsible for a quarter of all carols written up to 1550.

In general, fourteenth-century religious lyric in English is more subject to
courtly and literary influences, particularly in the "high" tradition that appears in the last quarter of the century. Music ceases to be a normal part of
the experience of the poem. At the same time, the number of Christmas
poems increases dramatically, the lullaby is adapted to religious uses, and
the *chanson d'aventure* becomes a popular model for the opening of a lyric.

The great poets of the close of the century, such as Chaucer, Gower,
Langland, the "Gawain-poet," seem to have avoided the religious lyric. In
this respect, they are like the major Italian poets (the *stilnovisti*, Dante, Petrarch, Boccaccio) and the major fourteenth-century French poets (Machaut
and Deschamps, to a degree). Still, Chaucer's Marian ABC acted as a model,
mediated by Lydgate, for fifteenth-century Marian lyric in the high style,
and his Prioress and Second Nun speak nobly if briefly in the hymnic mode.

The fifteenth century took Lydgate as a sufficient approximation to Chaucer for its purposes (and a far more imitable writer). In particular, his aureate Marian poems found wide imitation in lyrics whose forms come from
France and whose manner, it would appear, from late Latin religious poetry.
The fifteenth century also produced some moving, original anonymous
poems, but pomp and circumstance dominates the religious art-lyric.

More enjoyable to read, but artistically no better in most cases, the carol
appears in the late fourteenth century. It shares motivation and authorship
with the clerical "popular" *contrafacturas* that proliferate in German and
Italian religious lyric in the fifteenth century. The monophonic settings of
the first decades yield to polyphony ca. 1400, so that only the "burden"
could thenceforth be sung by the audience. The name suggests an origin in
the round dance; the refrain form, an origin in the *conductus* or something
like the Italian *lauda*. Whatever the ultimate resolution of the long-standing
scholarly controversy on its origins, the carol is clearly one of many late medieval examples of the marriage of high and low, learned and popular—
even the language of the carols, that is, their frequent macaronic blending of
Latin and English, with passages or lines from hymns appearing in the burden, bears witness to this.

At the very end of the Middle Ages, Dunbar, one of the most brilliant of
the so-called Scottish Chaucerians, closes out the medieval religious lyric in
English with a long-disused panache; his "Done is a battell on the dragon
blak" (Resurrection) and "Hale, sterne superne! Hale, in eterne" (Marian)
suddenly reveal to the reader how drab and clumsy, or meretricious and
clumsy, most fifteenth-century English religious lyric is.

Select Bibliography

There is an excellent short bibliography on pp. xiii–xvi of Douglas Gray, *A Selection of Religious Lyrics* (Oxford, 1975) that includes a number of hitherto unpublished texts and can be recommended as the best anthology specializing in Middle English religious lyric. For fuller information on the literature, one should turn to John E. Wells, *A Manual of the Writings in Middle English* (1916; 9 suppl., 1919–52), chap. 13 (revision now in progress edited by Jonathan Severs and Albert Hartung, 3 vols. issued, 1967–); the alphabetical inventory of fifteenth-century authors and texts in Henry S. Bennett, *Chaucer and the Fifteenth Century*, Oxford History of English Literature 2 : 1 (Oxford, 1947); and the *New Cambridge Bibliography of English Literature*, vol. 1 (1974) (complete but bewildering to use). Manuscripts and incipits of poems are covered in Carleton Brown and Rossel Robbins, *The Index of Middle English Verse* (New York, 1943), and in Rossel Robbins and John Cutler, *Supplement to the Index of Middle English Verse* (Lexington, Ky., 1965). For the devotional context of fifteenth-century lyric, Peter Revell, *Fifteenth Century English Prayers and Meditations: A Descriptive List of Manuscripts in the British Library* (New York/London, 1975) is a recent and valuable aid to research.

Part 2 of George Kane, *Middle English Literature: A Critical Study of the Romances, the Religious Lyrics, Piers Plowman* (London, 1951), is the best short introduction to the Middle English religious lyric, though I would disagree with Kane's view that "the religious *subject* [my italics] as a whole had a restrictive effect upon its poets" (p. 179). Pages 25–56 (Anglo-Saxon religious poetry), 94ff. (friars' miscellanies), 120ff. (fourteenth century), and 243ff. (fifteenth century) of Derek Pearsall's *Old English and Middle English Poetry*, Routledge History of English Poetry, vol. 1 (London, 1977) represent an admirable synthesis of the best in current scholarship and criticism on these matters. Among earlier, more specialized books and studies, I would recommend Theodor Wolpers, "Geschichte der englischen Marienlyrik im Mittelalter," *Anglia* 69 (1950): 3–88; Rosemary Woolf, *The English Religious "Lyric" in the Middle Ages* (Oxford, 1968); and Douglas Gray, *Themes and Images in the Medieval English Religious Lyric* (London, 1972). David Jeffrey, *The Early English Lyric and Franciscan Spirituality* (Lincoln, Neb., 1975), is a major historical study which demonstrates that Franciscan "influence" on the Middle English religious lyric before 1350 was more like control; for all its virtues, though, the book is less illuminating critically than one might have hoped, and Latin material is often badly mishandled. A good deal may be gleaned from Raymond Oliver, *Poems Without Names: The English Lyric 1200–1500* (Berkeley, 1970) and Stephen Manning, *Wisdom and Number* (Lincoln, Neb., 1962). Least successful of the surprising number of books on the Middle English lyric that include religious lyric in their discussion are Edmund Reiss, *The Art of the Middle English Lyric* (Athens, Ga., 1972), which suffers from a lack of proportion in its critical method (a licentious New Criticism), and Sarah Weber, *Theology and Poetry in the Middle English Lyric* (Columbus, Ohio, 1969), which fails to make its case for a significant close relationship between the "proportions" of Middle English lyric and the liturgy. Among important specialized studies, one should be aware of William Wehrle, "The Macaronic Hymn Tradition in Medieval English Literature" (Ph.D. diss., Catholic University,

1933) (a mediocre first attempt that needs to be replaced but the best available on the subject), and Helen Sandison, *The "Chanson d'Aventure" in Middle English*, Bryn Mawr College Monographs, no. 12 (Bryn Mawr, Pa., 1913) (altogether a better job; see pp. 135–39 for a list of the twenty-seven religious examples).

Among anthologies, Gray's *A Selection of Religious Lyrics* has already been cited; other useful examples include Reginald Davies's excellent *Medieval English Lyrics* (London, 1963; Evanston, Ill., 1964), Theodore Silverstein's *Medieval English Lyrics* (London, 1971), and Celia and Kenneth Sisam, *The Oxford Book of Medieval English Verse* (Oxford, 1970). More limited in coverage, but deserving of mention, are Edmund Chambers and Frank Sidgwick, *Early English Lyrics* (London, 1921), Frank A. Patterson, *The Middle English Penitential Lyric* (New York, 1911), and Henry Person, *Cambridge Middle English Lyrics* (Seattle, 1953). The standard collection remains Carleton Brown's *English Lyrics of the XIIIth Century* (Oxford, 1932) (essentially complete for both secular and religious lyric); *Religious Lyrics of the XIVth Century*, rev. G. V. Smithers (Oxford, 1952) (selective); and *Religious Lyrics of the XVth Century* (Oxford, 1939) (very selective; ca. 10 percent of available material).

Richard Greene, *Early English Carols* (Oxford, 1935; rev. ed., 1977), is the major source for that genre (see also his *A Selection of English Carols* [Oxford, 1962]). For carol settings, see John Stevens, *Medieval Carols*, Musica Britannica 4 (London, 1952). For MS Trinity College (Cambridge) 323, A.D. 1255–60, see Karl Reichl, *Religioese Dichtung im englischen Hochmittelalter* (Munich, 1973). For Digby 86, ca. 1275 (a selection of texts in Anglo-Norman and Middle English and a full discussion of contents), see Edmund Stengel, *Codicem manu scriptum Digby 86 in Bibliotheca Bodleiana asservatum* (Halle, 1871). For MS Harley 913, early fourteenth century, see Wilhelm Heuser, *Die Kildare-Gedichte*, Bonner Beitraege zur Anglistik 14 (1904). For Harley 2253, 1330s, see Brown XIII, nos. 72–91 and XIV, nos. 6–11; George L. Brook, *The Harley Lyrics*, 2d ed. (Manchester, 1956); and Neil Ker, *Facsimile of B.M. MS. Harley 2253*, EETS, no. 255 (London, 1965). For Richard Rolle, see Carl Horstmann, *Yorkshire Writers: Richard Rolle of Hampole, an English Father of the Church and his Followers*, 2 vols. (London, 1895–96); Hope E. Allen, *Writings Ascribed to Richard Rolle* (London, 1927) and *Richard Rolle, English Writings* (Oxford, 1931); and Frances M. Comper, *The Life and Lyrics of Richard Rolle* (London/Toronto, 1928). For the contents of Grimestone's collection, A.D. 1372, see Edward Wilson, *A Descriptive Index of the English Lyrics in John of Grimestone's Preaching Book*, Medium Aevum Monographs, n.s. 2 (Oxford, 1973) (= MS Advocates 18.7.21). For the lyrics in the Vernon manuscript (= Bodleian English poetry a.1; late fourteenth century), see Carl Horstmann, *The Minor Poems of the Vernon Manuscript*, vol. 1, EETS, orig. ser. 98 (London, 1892), and Frederick Furnivall, *The Minor Poems of the Vernon Manuscript*, vol. 2, EETS, orig. ser. 117 (London, 1901) (most of the English poems in *A Worchestershire Miscellany, Compiled by John Northwood c. 1400*, ed. Nita Baugh [Philadelphia, 1956] also occur in the Vernon manuscript). For Hoccleve, see Frederick Furnivall and Israel Gollancz, eds., *The Minor Poems*, rev. Jerome Mitchell and Anthony Doyle, EETS, 2d ser. 61 (London, 1892), and Frederick Furnivall, ed., *The Regement of Princes and Fourteen of Hoccleve's Minor Poems from the Egerton MS 615*, EETS, 2d ser. 72 (London, 1897).

(Both were reprinted in one volume in 1970.) For Lydgate, see Henry McCracken, ed., *The Minor Poems of John Lydgate*, pt. 1, EETS, 2d ser. 107 (London, 1911), and Otto Glaning, ed., *Lydgate's Minor Poems: The Two Nightingale Poems* [only the second is by Lydgate; the first is a worthy translation of John Pecham's *Philomena*], EETS, extra ser. 80 (London, 1900). For John Audelay, see EETS, no. 184 (London, 1931), ed. Ella Whiting. For MS Sloane 2593, ca. 1450, see Thomas Wright, *Songs and Carols*, Warton Club 4 (London, 1856). For MS Trinity College (Cambridge), 1450, see A. G. Rigg, *A Glastonbury Miscellany of the XVth Century* (Oxford, 1968). For Ryman, see Greene's *Early English Carols*. For Dunbar, see James Kinsley, ed., *The Poems of William Dunbar* (Oxford, 1979). For MS Arundel 285, early sixteenth century, see Jack A. W. Bennett, Devotional Pieces in Verse and Prose, Scottish Text Society, 3d ser. 23 (1949). For MS Balliol 354, also early sixteenth century, see Roman Dyboski, *Songs, Carols, and Other Miscellaneous Poems*, EETS, extra ser. 10 (London, 1907). Other editions of medieval manuscripts may be found in the many-score volumes of the Early English Text Society in its various series, including the *Lay Folk's Mass Book*, EETS, no. 71 (London, 1879), *The Prymer for Marian horae*, EETS, nos. 105 and 109 (London, 1895–97), the Wheatley manuscript, EETS, orig. ser. 15 (London, 1866); EETS, orig. ser. 46 (London, 1871); and EETS, no. 124 (London, 1904).

Despite the considerable literature on the Middle English religious lyric, the book that would integrate its history with that of contemporary Anglo-Norman and Latin religious lyric has yet to be written—even the foundations have yet to be fully laid.

OLD FRENCH

There is a good deal of religious verse in Old French written before the late twelfth century, including hagiographical narrative, verse sermons, farced epistles, drama, and various didactic poems, but none of it is religious lyric. The first important author of Old French religious lyric is Gautier de Coincy (b. 1177/78), who interpolated his lyrics by groups into his *Miracles de Notre Dame*. They were used in church and found a wide audience, both monastic and lay. Popular in tone, technically brilliant, fresh in inspiration, they closely resemble the best of contemporary Latin *conductus*, and in fact, Gautier was the first to compose *conductus* with an Old French text. No later writer of medieval French religious lyric really was able to equal Gautier's consistent excellence. A trouvère of the next generation, Thibaut de Champagne, perhaps comes closest.

In Old French, secular and religious lyrics typically use the same forms, and in both *contrafactura* of earlier stanzas and melodies is common. Authorship of religious chansons and other forms seems to be mainly lay, for professional performance. The virtuosic bent that Old French shares with Provençal is much in evidence, and intensifies in the following centuries (contrast Iberian and Italian lyric, where complex sound play and demanding rhyme schemes are very exceptional). The *balade* appears ca. 1250, and the *virelai* and *rondeau* begin their careers. Marian lyric in particular proliferates, as it does throughout Europe at this time, and dominates the religious chanson, which is closely modeled in language and motifs on the secular song of *fin' amour*.

In the second half of the thirteenth century, Arras is the major urban center for literature (cf. Adam de la Halle, Guillaume li Vinier, and others). Anglo-Norman lyric is remarkably scarce; linguistic drift has sufficiently separated the dialect of the Norman nobility in England from continental dialects by 1250 that dictionaries of "correct" French begin to appear (cf. Gautier de Biblesworth).

There is a good deal of translation of sequences and hymns and glossing of Latin texts, including the Psalter. In part, this activity may have been encouraged by official projects such as Bible translation (Paris, 1221 on) and the revision of the Vulgate. Franciscan and Latin influence is strong (contrast the south of France), and one may see their effects in the large number of prayers to Mary, Christ, or (much less often) the saints, and in Marian laments. Beginning about 1240, secular and religious lyrics are written down in *chansonniers* or song books (ca. thirty in northern France, 1250–1400); another major source, of a humbler sort of religious poetry, is the great mass of the *livres d'heures* for which the upper class and the bourgeoisie provided a busy market in the fourteenth and fifteenth centuries (major *ateliers* at Paris, in the Low Countries, and elsewhere).

In the fourteenth and fifteenth centuries, the output of religious lyric by well-known poets is relatively slight. There is much anonymous material, but it is generally mediocre or worse. After Machaut, lyrics cease to be songs—at least, music no longer accompanies their texts in the manuscripts. Literary religious lyric is confined to certain forms, notably the *chant royal*, which is the Marian form used at the *puys* competitions (first example of the form dates to A.D. 1316), and the *lai*. Treatises lay down strict rules about which forms are to be used for what subject matter (cf. the *Arts de seconde rhétorique*), much as they do in the same period (fifteenth century) in Provence and Iberian areas under Provençal influence. Toward the end of the century, there is a revival of courtly dance-song and *Gesellschaftslied*, with the music written by professional composers, in still another example of late medieval archaizing nostalgia—but this has little effect on the religious lyric. The professional court writers who go under the collective name of *grands rhétoriqueurs* produce the most interesting work, religious and secular, of the late fifteenth century, their verbal ingenuities surpassing but still recalling the high-spirited flourishes of Gautier de Coincy three hundred years before. On the whole, however, there is little to praise in Old and Middle French religious lyric after the thirteenth century.

Select Bibliography

For an outstanding general introduction to Old French literature, see Zumthor, *Histoire*. Standard accounts available in English include Urban T. Holmes, *A History of Old French Literature from the origins to 1300*, rev. ed. (New York, 1962) and Carl Voretzsch, *Introduction to the Study of Old French Literature*, trans. Francis M. DuMont (New York, 1931). For concentrated data, see the *Grundriss der romanischen Philologie*, ed. Gustav Groeber, vol. 2:1, pt. 3, sec. B.1, "Franzoesische Literatur" (Strassburg, 1902), pp. 440–44, 477f., 685–87, 971–77, 1190f., and references for individual authors in the index, and Gustav Groeber, *Geschichte der Mittelfranzoesischen Literatur*, rev. Stefan Hofer, 2d ed., 2 vols. (Berlin/Leipzig, 1933), 1:14–71, and 2:14–73, 86–89, 89–100, 112–23, 183–93, 193–214; here one will find essential details on nineteenth (and in part, early twentieth) century editions of texts and secondary literature and on manuscripts and authors. The new *Grundriss*, under the editorship of Jean Frappier, Hans Gumbrecht, Hans Robert Jauss, and Erich Koehler, has just issued two fascicles of the volume on the lyric (ed. Koehler), vol. 2:1; its fasc. 5.B.iii, sec. n covers the "religioeses Lied" (1979), presumably superseding the old *Grundriss* in this area (I have not seen these fascicles). The standard bibliographical source is Robert Bossuat, *Manuel bibliographique de la littérature française du Moyen Age* (Melun, 1951) and its *Suppléments* (Paris, 1955 and 1961). The basic catalogue of Old French lyric is Hans Spanke, *G. Raynauds Bibliographie des altfranzoesischen Liedes*, vol. 1 (Leiden, 1955) and, since Spanke never completed his revision, Gaston Raynaud, *Bibliographie des chansonniers français des XIIIe et XIVe siècles, comprenant la description de tous les manuscrits, la table des chansons classées par ordre alphabétique de rimes et la liste des trouvères*, 2 vols. (Paris, 1884). For prayers, see Jean Sonet, *Répertoire d'Incipit de prières en ancien français* (Geneva, 1956). For motets, see Friedrich Gennrich, *Bibliographie der aeltesten franzoesischen und lateinischen Motetten* (Darmstadt, 1957). For *rondeaux* and refrains, see Nico van den Boogaard, *Rondeaux et refrains du xiie siècle au début du xive*, Bibliothèque française et romane (Strasbourg), ser. D, no. 3 (Paris, 1969). On verse forms, see Roger Dragonetti, *La technique poétique des trouvères dans la chanson courtoise*, (Bruges, 1960), chaps. 5 and 6, and Fritz Noack, "Der Strophenausgang in seinem Verhaeltnis zum Refrain und Strophengrundstock in der refrainhaltigen altfranzoesischen Lyrik" (Ph.D. diss., Greifswald University, 1898). (Pages 651–98 of Dragonetti constitute a valuable alphabetical "biobibliographical" guide to the trouvères from 1170 to 1300.) On the *livres d'heures*, see Victor Leroquais, *Les Livres d'heures manuscrits de la B.N.*, 2 vols. (Paris, 1927). Alfred Jeanroy, *Les origines de la poésie lyrique en France au moyen âge*, 3d ed. (Paris, 1925), is also valuable on matters of poetic form, and much else besides.

Unfortunately, a great deal of Old and Middle French religious lyric is scattered through well over a century of learned journals and must be ferreted out by assiduous use of the references listed above. The most important single collection of religious lyric is still the *Recueil de chansons pieuses du 13e siècle*, ed. Edward Jaernstroem and Edward Jaernstroem/Artur Långfors, respectively, 2 vols., Suomalaisen Tiedeakatemian Toimituksia, Helsinki, Annales Academiae Scientiarum Fennicae,

B.III.1. and B.V.20 (1910–27). One may also consult Gaston Raynaud's *Recueil de Motets français*, 2 vols. (Paris, 1881–83), and Friedrich Gennrich, *Rondeaux Virelais und Balladen*, 2 vols. (Dresden, 1921–27), and *Cantilenae piae*, Musikwissenschaftliche Studien-Bibliothek 24 (Langen bei Frankfurt, 1960). Richard Otto, "Altlothringische geistliche Lieder," *Romanische Forschungen* 5 (1890): 583–618, contains the texts of a group of outstanding religious poems mentioned several times in the course of this book. The Jaernstroem/Långfors *Recueil* includes work by the following poets not covered below: Aubertin des Arenos, Lambers Ferris (third quarter of the thirteenth century), "Gilles de la croix," Guillaume li Vinier (d. 1245; Arras), Richart de Fournival (d. ca. 1260, canon at Amiens), Moniot d'Arras (fl. 1213–1239), Jacques li Vinier (fl. 1250– 1275), "Pierot de Niele," Adam de La Halle (d. ca. 1288; Arras), Guillaume de Béthune, "li quens de Bretagne" (*quens* = *comte*), and Ernaut Caupain. Editions of the works of individual authors are as follows:

Baudouin and Jean de Conde, *Dits et contes* . . . , ed. Auguste Scheler, 3 vols. (Brussels, 1866–67) (cf. nos. 14f and 44).

Georges Chastellain, *Oeuvres*, ed. Kervyn de Lettenhove, vol. 8 (Brussels, 1866), pp. 269–92.

Christine de Pisan, *Oeuvres poétiques* . . . , ed. Maurice Roy, vol. 3, SATF 41:3 (Paris, 1896), pp. 1–26.

Eustace Deschamps, *Oeuvres complètes*, ed. Le Marquis de Queux de Saint-Hilaire and Gaston Raynaud, 3 vols., SATF 16 (Paris, 1878–91), nos. 14, 134f., 186, 197f, 223, 261, 274, 276, 289, 1353, 1356, and 1358.

Gautier de Coincy, *Les Miracles de Nostre Dame*, ed. Vernon F. Koenig, 4 vols. (Geneva/Lille/Paris, 1955–70), 1:20–49, 3:249–61 and 265–302, and 4:542–92. Artur Långfors, "Mélanges de poésie lyrique française: Gautier de Coinci," *Romania* 53 (1927): 474–538, remains useful for its apparatus.

Gilles le Muisit (1271–1350), *Poésies*, ed. Kervyn de Lettenhove, vol. 1 (Louvain, 1882), pp. 38–42 and 68–78.

Guillaume Alexis, *Oeuvres poétiques*, ed. Arthur Piaget and Emile Picot, 3 vols., SATF 4 (Paris, 1896–98), 2:58–70, 3:37 and 3:181–200.

Guillaume de Machaut, *Poésies lyriques*, ed. Vladimir Chichmaref, vol. 2 (Paris, 1909) (see the *lais* "de Nostre Dame" and "de la fonteinne").

Huon le Roy de Cambrai, *Oeuvres*, ed. Artur Långfors, vol. 1, Classiques français du moyen âge (Paris, 1913), "Li Ave Maria en roumans."

Jacques de Cambrai, see *Recueil* 2, nos. 30–36.

Jean Brisebarre, "Trois poèmes . . . ," ed. Amédée Salmon, in *Mélanges de philologie romane dédiés à Carl Wahlund à l'occasion du cinquantième anniversaire de sa naissance* (Macon, 1896), pp. 213–24.

Jean Molinet, *Les faictz et dictz* . . . , ed. Noël Dupire, vol. 2, SATF 81:2 (Paris, 1937), pp. 425–566.

Philipe de Rémi de Beaumanoir, *Oeuvres poétiques*, ed. Henri Suchier, vol. 2, SATF 38:2 (Paris, 1855), pp. 299–301.

Jean Regnier, *Les fortunes et adversitez* . . . , ed. Eugénie Droz, SATF 69 (Paris, 1923), pp. 15ff., 50–52, 120f., 123f., and 145f.

Rutebeuf, *Oeuvres complètes*, ed. Edmond Faral and Julia Bastin, 2 vols. (Paris, 1959–60), vol. 1, no. 40 and vol. 2, nos. 46–49.

Thibaut de Champagne, *Les chansons* . . . , ed. Alex Wallenskjoeld, SATF 70 (Paris, 1925) (see *Recueil* 2, nos. 66–70 for the religious chansons alone).

Watriquet de Couvin, *Dits* . . . , ed. Auguste Scheler (Brussels, 1868), nos. 9 and 21.

OLD NORSE

In A.D. 1000, it was decided at the Althing that Iceland should become (nominally) Christian. Nonetheless, there are relatively few extant Christian poems in Old Norse till the thirteenth century, and the native pagan poetic tradition remains dominant until 1350 or so.

Preconversion texts (of which there are a few) and texts from the eleventh and the first half of the twelfth century survive, so far as they do, only by grace of citation in historical works or sagas or as examples in Snorri Sturluson's textbook for skalds (ca. 1200). Since the conversion was effected by missionaries from German-speaking countries where a vernacular vocabulary for Christian matters had already developed, Icelanders found it relatively easy to absorb religious words into their poetic lexicon; assimilation of Latin or Romance terms would have been far more difficult. Early fragments show that in some cases conversion was scarcely even skin-deep. Until the mid-twelfth century, authors were skalds and laymen, not members of the clergy (churches began to be built only toward the end of the eleventh century); they include Thrand the Faroese (a bizarre Credo), Thorbjoern Disarskald (on a baptism), Eilif Godrunarson (on Christ), Thorvald Kodransson (on heathen resistance to Christian preaching), Skapti Thoroddsson (on God's power as creator), Arnór Jarlaskald (on St. Michael and the Last Judgment), Thorarin Loftunga (on the just-deceased saint-to-be, King Olaf, written 1031/32), and (in the twelfth century) Runolf Ketilsson (on the dedication of a church). Doctrinally, Icelandic Christianity was very old-fashioned, closer to the Carolingian age than to the contemporary St. Anselm; Christian material tends to remain *en marge* up to 1150, at the start or end of poems, leaving their heart untouched.

About the middle of the twelfth century, the growing population of settled clergy, especially in the new monasteries, took up the writing of religious poetry, but still in the traditional skaldic style. This led to the recording of poems for their own sake, rather than as illustrations; the very first poem, skaldic or eddic, to be written down in Iceland seems to have been the anonymous "Placitusdrápa" (recorded ca. 1200). From 1200 to 1350, the panegyrical *drápa* continues as the favorite form (introduction, section or sections with *stef*/refrain, and *slaem*), its usual subject being a saint, often royal; Marian poetry also begins to appear, though in small quantities as yet. The favorite stanza forms are *drottkvaett* (eight lines of six syllables and three stresses with alliteration, rhyme, and internal rhyme at fixed places) and *hrynhent* (*drottkvaett* with one extra stress and therefore two extra syllables per line). The former had always been the favorite stanza form in skaldic verse; the latter, which appeared in the Hebrides ca. 1050 and spread thence into general skaldic use, gave more room to the poet and permitted a simpler, more easily understood manner, suitable to the humbler aesthetic of Christianity—hence its great popularity among clerical poets.

In the mid-fourteenth century, poets like Arngrím Brandsson and Eysteinn Ásgrímsson openly declared their opposition to the formidable word order and dark kennings of the traditional skaldic style. The success of Eysteinn's 100-stanza poem on redemptive history in honor of Mary, *Lilja*, showed the way to a new Christian style of poetry, stressing meaning over form and opening the doors to direct influence from contemporary Latin and Continental poetry. In honor of the poem, the 300-year-old *hrynhent* stanza that Eysteinn used was rechristened "liljulag." Both it and the *drottkvaett* stanza continued in use in the succeeding centuries, but after 1400, rhymed stanzas borrowed from Continental tradition (known as *rímur*) became the norm; the first example is the fourteenth-century "Olavsrima." They reflected Old Norse native practice in their use of systematic alliteration as well as rhyme and spread to secular as well as religious material, finding use as songs and even lyrics to dance to, and incorporating such features as refrain-lines, motto-words, and macaronics. The *drápa* becomes rare in this period, and Marian and hagiographical lyric dominates. Nonetheless, Old Norse religious poetry is far from surrendering outright to foreign models. There is virtually no use of allegory; scriptural paraphrase is notably lacking since the first translation of the Bible into Old Norse dates to 1540, which is extraordinarily late; mysticism has no effect, though a mystic and saint like Brigitta of Sweden was widely adored, and there is little of the highly charged poetry on the Passion characteristic of the rest of Europe from the thirteenth through the fifteenth centuries. One reason for the absence of Passion poetry is no doubt the failure of the friars to play an important part in late medieval Iceland; authorship of religious literature remains monastic, for the most part. Anglo-Saxon and Celtic native verse traditions showed similar staying power, and Iceland had the additional advantage (or disadvantage, as one prefers) of relative isolation. Still, the persistence of at least a skaldic flavor, and sometimes much more, in Iceland through the end of the Middle Ages is an impressive fact. And indeed, the writing of skaldic verse is still an avocation for Icelanders today.

Select Bibliography

Skaldic poetry up to 1400, including all Christian work, is collected together in *Skjaldedigtning*. The "B" volumes contain a normalized text and a Danish prose translation at the foot of the page; the "A" volumes contain the unnormalized text and critical apparatus. For late medieval religious poetry (1400–1500), consult Helgason; over 100 poems are included, most of them *rímur*. For notes on a few of the poems in Jónsson and Helgason, see the earlier collection by Bernhard Kahle, *Islaendische geistliche Dichtungen des ausgehenden Mittelalters* (Heidelberg, 1898) (on "Máríuvísur" nos. 1, 2, and 3, "Vitnisvísur," "Katrínardrápa," and "Petrsdrápa," see introduction, pp. 1–7 and 12–19, and notes, pp. 98–103 and 105–13; on "Máríugrátur," see introduction, pp. 8–11, and notes, p. 104f.). On Jón Arason (1484–1550), see Finnur Jónsson, *Jón Arasons religiose Digte*, Kongelig Danske Videnskabernes Selskab, historisk-filologlisk Meddellelser 2:2 (1918), pp. 1–24; Helgason's edition supersedes Jónsson's textually speaking. (Cf. 1.2:189–206, 111–39, 212–38, and 247–60; item 3 in Jónsson, a paraphrase of Psalm 51, does not appear in Helgason.) Wolfgang Lange, *Christliche Skaldendichtung* (Goettingen, 1958), consists of German prose and verse translations, with headnotes, of the early (eleventh and twelfth century) Christian fragments and of several important religious poems (Skulason's "Geisli," "Gamli's" confessional "Harmsól," the anonymous "Leiðarvisan," the sapiential "Sólarljóð" with its stunning portrait of death and the last things, and the *Lilja*).

Lange is also the author of the single recent book-length work on Old Norse religious poetry, *Studien zur christlichen Dichtung der Nordgermanen; 1000–1200* (Goettingen, 1958); unfortunately, as the title indicates, he does not deal with the later Middle Ages. For further information, one may turn to Frederik Paasche, *Kristendom og Kvad* (Kristiania, 1914), and to a standard literary history like Jón Helgason, *Norges og Islands Digtning*, Nordisk Kultur 8 B (Copenhagen/Oslo/Stockholm, 1953). For relations between medieval Scandinavian and Latin literature, the apposite monograph is Paul Lehmann's *Skandinaviens Anteil an der lateinischen Literatur und Wissenschaft des Mittelalters*, Akademie der Wissenschaft, Munich, philosophisch-historische Abteilung, Sitzungsberichte, no. 2 (1936) and no. 7 (1937), 76 pp. and 136 pp., respectively.

As one can see, there is more than a little room for work on Old Norse religious poetry, particularly after 1200—indeed, skaldic poetry in general has not received anything like definitive treatment.

Iceland was not the only part of Scandinavia to produce literature in the Middle Ages, even though I am ignoring other countries of the North in this book. For an example of late medieval Danish religious poetry, see Ernst Frandsen, *Mariaviserne* (Copenhagen, 1926); for Scandinavian-Latin literature, see references cited in the Select Bibliography for Latin above (AH 42 and 43, especially, and also Moberg, *Die liturgischen Hymnen in Schweden*, and Klemming, *Latinska Sånger fordam använda i Svenska Kyrkor, Kloster och Skolar*); Georg Reiss, *Musiken ved den middelalderlige Olavsdyrkelse in norden*, Videnskapsselskapet i Kristiania, historisk-filosofisk

Klasse, Skrifter 2, no. 5 (Oslo, 1911), prints the texts and music of Latin lyrics concerning St. Olaf from the Scandinavian Middle Ages.

PORTUGUESE

In medieval Portuguese poetry, there are two distinct periods separated by roughly a century in which Castilian replaced Portuguese (or, more strictly speaking, Galician-Portuguese) as the language of art-lyric; the first period, lasting from about 1185 to about 1325, produced a splendid body of secular poetry (extant today in three *cancioneiros*, "Ajuda," "Vaticano," and "Biblioteca Nacional") and Alfonso X's *Cantigas de Santa Maria*; the second, beginning about 1440, is represented in Garcia de Resende's *Cancioneiro Geral* (1516), which collects poems by over three hundred poets, mostly from the decades between 1480 and its date of publication.

Well into the fourteenth century, while Catalan poets were writing in Provençal, the rest of Iberia used Galician-Portuguese for its lyrics. It was for that reason that the King of Castile and Leon, Lord of Galicia, Alfonso X el Sabio, "the Wise," chose Galician-Portuguese for the *Cantigas* produced at his court, while the prose works he produced or commissioned were written in Castilian. Among the 429 items in the *Cantigas*, some 40 are lyrics, and these poems constitute virtually the entire corpus of Portuguese religious lyric extant today from the early period (it is reported that his grandson, King Dinis of Portugal, composed a religious *cancioneiro*, but if it ever existed, it has left no traces). Three-fourths of the texts in the *Cantigas* are in the *zejel* or *virelai* form; there are few pure *rondeaux*, *balades*, or *canciós* (close, more or less contemporary analogues exist in the *ballata* of Italy and the Latin *conductus*). Alfonso and his copoets make fluent use of their stanza forms (which are a virtual repertory of thirteenth-century Romance lyric stanzas), enjambing freely, even across the refrain. One notices that "joys" and "sorrows" *cantigas* omit the refrain and emulate the high style of the chanson (cf. the fifteenth-century Castilian *gozos*). The narratives themselves that make up the bulk of the collection take on a lyrical character because of their form, and one is not surprised that they too were sung. Four thirteenth-century manuscripts survive, dating from 1257 to 1279 and showing that the collection went through three versions, growing from a mere 100 to over 400 items in the end. The narratives of the miracles are organized according to their provenance (a variety of Marian churches). Literarily, musically, and pietistically, the *Cantigas de Santa Maria* is one of the fundamental texts of the high Middle Ages.

Lyric poems in Galician-Portuguese continue to be produced as late as the fifteenth century (cf. Gomez Manrique, a Spaniard), but by the end of the fourteenth century, the former situation has reversed itself: instead of Spanish poets writing in Portuguese, Portuguese poets write in Spanish. Motives for this choice were literary and cultural, not political (after all, Portugal *won* the crucial battle of Aljubarrota in 1385). About 1440, court poetry in Portuguese begins to revive; at least, Portuguese poets become literarily bilingual, working in both Castilian and their own language. Unfortunately for the history of religious literature, the one great collection of fifteenth century poetry from Portugal that saw print, the *Cancioneiro Geral*, includes religious lyrics only by accident, as it were: there are no more than seven or eight among the hundreds of secular lyrics. Because the material Garcia de Resende did not anthologize remained unprinted, much of it has since been lost. In addition, as of 1959, twenty-eight of the thirty-five extant fifteenth-century *cancioneiros* were still languishing in manuscript, unedited. As a result, printed fifteenth- and sixteenth-century Portuguese religious lyric amounts to no more than a modest handful, indistinguishable in manner from contemporary Castilian work. Of all the linguistic traditions dealt with in this book, it is Portuguese that has perhaps left too little record of its religious lyric (though who knows what may be gathering dust in the libraries of Portugal?) for meaningful statements to be made about its general characteristics.

Select Bibliography

No general literary history has much to say about Portuguese religious poetry, understandably enough, outside of Alfonso's *Cantigas*. For background, and for the excellent bibliography by Bernardo Vidigal on pp. 358–78 of the latest printing (current through 1970), we are lucky to have Aubrey Bell's *Portuguese Literature* (1922; reprint with new bibliography, Oxford, 1970). For a more detailed but fifty-year-old bibliography of Portuguese poetry of the earliest period, see Silvio Pellegrini, *Repertorio bibliografico della prima lirica portoghese* (Modena, 1939); see also Maria A. Valle Cintra, "Bibliografia de textos medevais portugueses publicados," *Boletim de Filologia* 12 (1951): 60–100. Alvaro J. de Costa Pimpão, *História da literatura portuguese*, vol. 1 (twelfth–fifteenth centuries) (Coimbra, 1947), discusses the *Cantigas* on pp. 167–74 and the religious lyrics in the *Cancioneiro Geral* on p. 371f. Manuel Rodrigues Lapa is silent on religious poetry in his *Liçoes de literatura portuguese*, 7th ed., rev. (Lisbon, 1970), but chap. 2 (pp. 29–102) is a thorough discussion of the thorny problem of the origins of the Romance lyric (see also Pierre Le Gentil, *Le Virelai et le villancico: Le problème des origines arabes* [Paris, 1954]). Pierre Le Gentil, *La Poésie lyrique espagnole et portugaise à la fin du moyen âge*, 2 vols. (Rennes, 1949), is essential for the later period; chap. 6 of vol. 1 (pp. 295–336) covers religious poetry in Spanish and Portuguese and its connections to French, Catalan, and Provençal work, and vol. 2 analyzes in exhaustive detail Iberian verse and stanza forms. Finally, the old edition of the *Grundriss der romanischen Philologie*, vol. 2.2, pt. 3 (Strassburg, 1893 for 1897), includes a still-useful monograph by Carolina Michaelis de Vasconcellos and Teofilo Braga, "Geschichte der portugiesischen Literatur" (pp. 129–382); see especially p. 273, a paragraph on fifteenth-century religious lyric, and Michaelis's chapter on the *Cancioneiro Geral*, pp. 264–80, in which this paragraph appears.

Among anthologies, Guilherme de Faria, *Antologia de poesias religiosas desde o século xv . . .* (Lisbon, 1947), assembles most of the exiguous remains of fifteenth-century religious lyric in one place; pp. 17–49 include King Duarte's translation of "Juste Judex," João Claro's version of the Te Deum, an anonymous Ave Maris Stella gloss, Queen Philippa's prayer, Joam Manuel's meditation on Christ in Gethsemane, Diogo Brandam's *vilancete*, Luis Anriques's paraphrase of the Pater noster, the Nativity song "Branca estais e colorada" and other passages from plays by Gil Vicente, and an anonymous prayer to Christ that makes effective use of *leixa-pren*, that is, repetition of the last line of one stanza as the first of the next. Two of the religious poems in the *Cancioneiro Geral* and a gloss on the Pater noster by Vicente appear in Jose J. Nunes, *Crestomatia arcaica*, 6th ed. (Lisbon, 1967), pp. 506–13; on pp. 529–46, there is a useful lexicon of medieval Portuguese authors with citation of early remarks on them.

For the *Cantigas de Santa Maria*, see the recent edition by Walter Mettmann in four volumes (Coimbra, 1959–72; vol. 4 is an invaluable glossary); see also Higini Anglès, *La música de las Cantigas de Santa Maria*, 3 vols. in 4 (Barcelona, 1943–64), and, on the forms of the *Cantigas* and for general information, Higini Anglès's article on pp. 346–64 of *Gattungen*. For João Claro's poems, see Fr. Fortunato de S. Boaventura, *Collecção de ineditos portuguezes dos seculos xiv e xv*, vol. 1 (Coimbra, 1829), pp. 173–208 (the gloss poem on the Ave Maris Stella reproduced by Faria appears on pp. 5–13, and the *Opusculos do Doutor Fr. João Claro* (Coimbra, 1829). As yet, there is no critical edition of Garcia de Resende's *Cancioneiro Geral*; one may use either Gonçalvez Guimaraes's edition, 5 vols. (Coimbra, 1910–17) or Eduard H. von Kausler's, 3 vols., Bibliothek des literarischen Vereins, vols. 15, 17, and 26 (Stuttgart, 1846, 1848, 1852) (note the facsimile by Archer M. Huntington, 1904). In von Kausler's edition, see 1 : 219 (Diogo Brandão), 1 : 230ff. (Alvaro de Brito Pestana), 1 : 330 (Anrique de Sá), 1 : 383–86 (João Manuel), and 2 : 252–61 (Luís Anriques). For the *Cancioneiro de Évora*, see the edition by Arthur Askins, University of California Publications in Modern Philology, vol. 74 (Berkeley, 1965).

PROVENÇAL

Provençal art-lyric begins ca. 1100 with the poems of Guillaume IX; the religious lyric scarcely exists except for a penitential song on the eve of pilgrimage by Guillaume until the "late classical" troubadour period, toward the end of the twelfth century (but see Karl Bartsch, *Chrestomathie provençale*, 6th ed. [Marburg, 1904], pp. 18–22). Its first authors seem to have been Peire d'Alvernha and Folquet de Marseille, but in fact very little religious lyric is extant that can be dated to earlier than ca. 1230. (In the mean-

time, the tradition of prayers in verse and *contemptus* poems, which got under way in the early twelfth century, continued, of course.) The first Marian
lyric was the work of Peire de Corbiac at the start of the thirteenth century;
Marian panegyric and love-poems become frequent after 1230, and in the
last half of the century, poets deliberately create the maximum ambiguity in
some of their Marian poems, leaving modern scholars (and probably contemporaries) uncertain whether the subject is an earthly lady or the Lady of
heaven (cf. Guiraut Riquier and Folquet de Lunel). Around the middle of
the century, the religious lyric comes to be defined as belonging to the
"high" genre of *canso* rather than the lower genre of *sirventes*, which indicates the increasingly important role it played in late Provençal poetry.
Nonetheless, religious lyric remains a highly literary product, without the
religiosity of contemporary work in most other parts of Europe. There was
notably little response to the Franciscans and their spirituality in the south
of France, and mysticism of any kind fails to affect Provençal religious lyric.
One may see an impact from (primarily) the Dominican order in the rise of
Marian poetry in the thirteenth century, in certain penitential poems, and
perhaps even in the relatively cool and reserved intellectuality with which
theological matters are handled (when they are). But in the main, the characteristics of the native secular tradition persist, rather as they do in Old
Norse.

The fourteenth century opens with the appearance of the Marian *planctus* in Provençal (some half-dozen surviving examples) and the increased
popularity of "joys" and "sorrows" poems (the prevailing number of joys or
sorrows was seven, rather than five). In addition, Provençal poems begin to
be recorded in *chansonniers* (some thirty antedate A.D. 1400). Institutionally, the major event is the establishment of the Toulouse *Consistori* and
its poetic competitions that involve amateur poets from a wide variety of
urban occupations and that support the production of a large amount of
carefully orthodox Marian poetasting. Only seven entries from the fourteenth century survive today, and about sixty from the fifteenth, including a
total of thirty-nine Marian items. Alongside this "academic" poetry was a
sizable amount of anonymous, less pretentious, sometimes subliterary religious verse that has been printed in a number of collections listed below.

The Provençal tradition is unusual in several important respects. The
troubadours who wrote Provençal religious lyric (and who included many
Catalan and Italian poets in the twelfth and thirteenth centuries) were laymen, though some of them may have entered monasteries late in life. The
spirit of their work is fundamentally secular, or at least "this"-worldly.
Their poetry is exceptionally personal and "local," thanks in part to the existence of functioning literary circles and a well-trained and appreciative literary audience in Provençal towns and courts. Even in their religious lyrics,

they often address their words to specific people, named more or less openly, in dedications, apostrophes, and closing *endreças* or *tornadas*. The traditional stress on novelty of form also meant that originality and individuality were favored, as well as a high degree of self-consciousness about the creation of the text. These poets want to talk, to you, to each other, to anyone who will listen, even (on occasion) to God or Mary—to include the whole world of talkers and listeners in their circle. This quality of intimacy, of direct, addressed speech is what distinguishes their Marian lyric and gives the reader so strong a sense of the human space that surrounded the writing and the saying or singing of their work. In all these respects, they look foward to the modern age and therefore have won strong friends in our own century. And yet, their strengths are also strong constraints. One will not find the more impersonal beauties or the deep feeling of late medieval devotional literature in Provençal poetry, nor much of the excitement of the truly "other" that the discourse of the past can sometimes give.

Select Bibliography

The basic reference source remains Alfred Pillet, *Bibliographie der Troubadours*, rev. Henry Carstens (Halle, 1933). Istvan Frank, *Répertoire métrique de la poésie des troubadours*, 2 vols., Bibliothèque des hautes études, sciences historiques et philosophiques, vols. 302 and 308 (Paris, 1953–57) includes a bibliography of troubadours and anonymous lyrics through the mid-1950s (2:83–214; see the indexes to various formal features as well, 2:59–67); it is also the major study of Provençal stanza forms. Alfred Jeanroy, *La poésie lyrique des troubadours*, 2 vols. (Toulouse/Paris, 1934), contains a "Liste bio-bibliographique des troubadours" (1:326–436); chap. 8 (2:305–14) briefly treats religious poetry in Provençal. There is also a brief discussion (with references to the nineteenth-century literature) in the *Grundriss der romanischen Philologie*, ed. Gustav Groeber, vol. 2, pt. 2, sec. 3, "Provenzalische Literatur" (Strassburg, 1902), pp. 34–36.

The major studies, however, are two monographs in the journals. The first is Victor Lowinsky, "Zum geistlichen Kunstliede in der altprovenzalischer Literatur bis zur Gruendung des Consistori del Gai Saber," *Zeitschrift fuer neufranzoesische Sprache und Literatur* 20, no. 1 (1898): 163–271, and a series of three articles by Dimitri Scheludko, "Die Marienlieder in der altprovenzalischen Lyrik," its continuation, and "Ueber die religioese Lyrik der Troubadours," *NM* 36 (1935): 29–48; 37 (1936): 15–42; 38 (1937): 224–50. The first section of Lowinsky's study takes up the religious lyrics in Provençal and their authors, one by one, in chronological order. On the poetry of the *Consistori*, see Alfred Jeanroy, *La poésie lyrique*, 2: 347–64, and Jeanroy, *Joies*. For a complete repertory of the melodies of troubadour lyric, see Friedrich Gennrich, *Der musikalische Nachlass der Troubadours*, 3 vols., Summa musicae Medii Aevi, vols. 3, 4, and 15 (Darmstadt, 1958–65). Somewhat specialized, but very thoroughgoing, is Diego Zorzi's *Valori religiosi nella letteratura provenzale: la spiritualità trinitaria*, Pubblicazioni dell'Università cattolica del S.

Cuore, n.s., vol. 44 (Milan, 1954). A long and valuable bibliography appears on pp. 347–62.

Major collections that include Provençal religious lyric are the following:

Anglade, Joseph, ed., *Poésies religieuses du xive siècle en dialecte toulousain tirées des Leys d'Amour* (Toulouse, 1917), cf. pp. 4–26 and 30–48.

Appel, Carl, ed., *Provenzalische Chrestomathie*, 3d ed. (Leipzig, 1907), cf. nos. 58, 102–4, and 106.

Azaïs, Gabriel, ed., *Les Troubadours de Béziers*, 3d ed. (Béziers, 1869; reprint, Geneva, 1973), cf. pp. 12–14, 16–18, 52–54, and 109–15.

Bartsch, Karl, ed., *Chrestomathie provençale*, 4th ed. (Elberfeld, 1880), cf. coll. 277–81.

Bertoni, Giulio, ed., *I Trovatori d'Italia, Biografie, Testi, Traduzioni, Note* (Modena, 1915; reprint, Rome, 1967), cf. Lanfranc Cigala, nos. 37–39 and 46, and Peire Guilhem de Luserna, no. 25.

Jeanroy, *Joies.*

Meyer, Paul, ed., *Anciennes poésies religieuses en langue d'oc publiées d'après les manuscrits* (Paris, 1860).

————, *Daurel et Beton*, SATF 14 (Paris, 1880), cf. poems nos. 1–7, from the mid-fourteenth-century MS Didot.

————, *Les Derniers troubadours de la Provence* . . . (Paris, 1871), see esp. pp. 43–45.

————, *Recueil d'anciens textes bas-latins, provençaux et français* (Paris, 1874), see pp. 206, 354f., 374ff.

Noulet/Chabaneau, nos. 15, 17, 19, 25, 27, 28, 33, 37, and B.3 and 5.

Suchier, cf. pp. 85–97, 214–40, 272–83, 285–89, and 290–96.

A number of poems are still available only in classic but antiquated collections of the earlier nineteenth century, namely,

Raynouard, François, ed., *Choix des poésies originales des troubadours*, vol. 4 (Paris, 1819).

Mahn, *Werke.*

Mahn, Carl, ed., *Die Gedichte der Troubadours*, 4 vols. (Berlin, 1856–73).

The work of some authors has received a separate edition; others appear only in the collections just cited:

Aimeric de Belenoi: Mahn, *Gedichte*, vol. 2, no. 570.

Bernart d'Auriac: Azaïs, *Les Troubadours*, pp. 102–4.

Bernart de Venzac: Raynouard, *Choix des poésies*, pp. 432–33.

Cerveri de Girona: Martín de Riquer, ed., *Obras completas* . . . (Barcelona, 1947)

Daude de Pradas: Mahn, *Gedichte*, vol. 3, no. 1040f.

Folquet de Lunel: Franz Eichelkraut, ed., *Der Troubadour Folquet de Lunel* (Berlin, 1872) (see Lowinsky, "Zum geistlichen Kunstliede," pp. 196–98, footnotes, for emendations).

Folquet de Marseille: Stanislaw Strónski, ed., *Le Troubadour Folquet de Marseille* (Cracow, 1910), see no. 28f.

Guilhem d'Autpol: Appel, *Provenzalische Chrestomathie*, no. 58, and Meyer, *Les derniers troubadours*, pp. 43ff.

Guilhem d'Ieras: Mahn, *Gedichte*, vol. 1, no. 7.

Guiraut Riquier: Mahn, *Werke* 4:1–100; see nos. 21, 24, 26, 37–39, 42, 44, 46–49, 51, 53, 67f. and Ulrich Moelk, ed., *Las cansos*, Studia romanica 2 (Heidelberg, 1962).

Guy Folquet: Suchier, pp. 272–83.

Jaime II: Cesare de Lollis, ed., "Ballata alla Vergine de Giacomo II d'Aragon," *Revue des langues romanes* 31 (1887): 289–95.

Joan Esteve: Camille Chabaneau, "Deux retroensas inédites," *Revue des langues romanes* 32 (1888): 98–101 (German translation of one lyric by Lowinsky, "Zum geistlichen Kunstliede," pp. 269–71).

Lanfranc Cigala: Francesco Branciforti, ed., *Il Canzoniere* . . . (Florence, 1954), cf. nos. 27–30.

March, Jacme et al.: Amédée Pagès, ed., *Les "coblas" ou les poésies lyriques provenço-catalanes de Jacme, Pere et Arnau March* (Toulouse, 1949), see Arnau March, nos. 1, 5, and 6.

Peire d'Alvernha: Alberto del Monte, ed., *Liriche* (Turin, 1955), see nos. 10 and 16–19.

Peire Cadenet: *Der Trobador Cadenet*, ed. Carl Appel (Halle, 1920).

Peire Cardenal: René Lavaud, ed., *Poésies complètes* . . . (Toulouse, 1957), cf. nos. 30, 36, 38, and 40.

Peire de Corbiac: Raynouard, *Choix des poésies*, p. 465.

Peire Espanhol: Edmund Stengel, ed., "Peire Espagnol's Alba," *Zeitschrift fuer romanische Philologie* 10 (1886): 160–62.

Peire Guilhem de Luserna: Bertoni, *I Trovatori d'Italia*, no. 25.

Perdigo: Henry Chaytor, ed., *Les Chansons de Perdigon* (Paris, 1926), cf. no. 6.

Raimon de Cornet: Noulet/Chabaneau, nos. 15, 17, 19, 25, 27, 28.

Raimon Gaucelm: Azaïs, *Les Troubadours*, pp. 12–14 and 16–18.

Wolfenbuettel MS extravagans 268: Emil Levy, ed., "Poésies religieuses françaises et provençales, du ms . . ." *Revue des langues romanes* 31 (1887): 173–288 and 420–35.

Zorzi, Bartolome: Emil Levy, ed., *Der troubador Bèrtholome Zorzi* (Halle, 1883), nos. 1 and 5.

SPANISH

In the thirteenth century, when Galician-Portuguese was the language of nonnarrative poetry everywhere among the people in Iberia (save for Catalonia), Gonzalo de Berceo was alone in writing religious lyric in Spanish. His *Milagros de Santa Maria* (cf. Gautier de Coincy and later Alfonso X) and his shorter poems were meant for pilgrims who had come to San Millan, and knowledge of his work remained confined to the monasteries and churches of the Rioja district. Two hundred years later, the Marquis of Santillana, chief literary figure of the mid-fifteenth century, did not even know of its existence. Berceo's form was the so-called *mester de clerecía*, the monorhymed "long-line" quatrain that went out of fashion at the end of the fourteenth century and that owes an obvious debt to the Goliardic quatrain of medieval Latin.

From ca. 1300 on, the Iberian political and military center of gravity moved away from the northwest as the conquest progressed southward. Similarly, the lyric moved away from Galician-Portuguese toward Castilian, with many poets still bilingual in the second half of the fourteenth century but Castilian winning sole place by the fifteenth. At the same time, new forms, or simplified versions of the old, come into fashion; the tripartite stanza yields to the bipartite (octaves resolving into two quatrains), the number of rhymes per stanza rises from three to four, the custom (derived from Provençal practice) of writing an entire poem on the same rhymes lapses by 1450 in favor of new rhymes in each stanza or perhaps only one of the rhymes carried through the poem. Music loses its old importance (as it was doing all over Europe, though not necessarily to the same degree or without revivals), and the appeal and themes of lyric poetry become much more intellectual and reflective. In the course of the fifteenth century, fixed forms such as the *villancico* and *canción* gain regular use by writers of art-lyric (cf. the *rondeau* and its cogeners in the French fifteenth century). Refrain forms (i.e., structures analogous to the *virelai* or *ballata*) in general flourish. The fifteenth century takes particular delight in exchanges of poems, entered into by the first poet (*preguntas* and *respuestas*) or initiated unilaterally by the second (through a *glosa* or a one-stanza *canción*, for instance). All of these "genres" figure in religious lyric, and it is notable that hymn forms were not borrowed from Latin; instead, poets kept within the vernacular tradition, content with its possibilities and immune to the formalisms of Provence, Burgundy, and France.

Except for narrative *romances* (axbxcxdx . . .), religious poetry in the fifteenth century is strophic and mostly in short fixed forms. Various members of the clergy (cf. Juan de Padilla or Iñigo de Mendoza) also produced large-scale poems into which they often introduced lyric responses to the religious history they were retelling. In addition, as the "highest" genre, there were more discursive, open-ended doctrinal lyrics that directly reflected the spirit of the great church councils of the first decades of the century. Poets favored dance forms (such as the *villancico*) particularly for Marian lyric; but in their *gozos* and *dolores* (joys and sorrows) they rejected the popular note of the refrain and aimed at the solemn ceremoniousness typical of European Marian lyric of the period. Their most frequent subjects were the Immaculate Conception (a highly topical issue), the Nativity, and the Passion; one also finds panegyrics to saints (mostly from the Gospels) and paraphrases of prayers and hymns (again, with evident parallels elsewhere).

Poetry from the fifteenth century is contained in several dozen *can-*

cioneros, most of which have been published in part or whole. The major collections are the *Cancionero de Baena* (1449/54), the *Cancionero general de Hernando del Castillo* (1511 for the first edition), and the *Cancionero musical* (1530). The first is invaluable for its representation of the early fifteenth century, though little of its content has much poetic interest; the second provides the most comprehensive picture of the second half of the century, though with major gaps or underrepresentation of particular poets, and it includes much genuinely excellent work; the last was compiled by musicians for musicians and therefore shows the role poetry was playing in polyphonic (three or four part) song between 1470 and 1530. For further details, see below.

Select Bibliography

For the classic literary history of Spanish medieval poetry, see Menéndez y Pelayo; some volumes consist entirely of the editor's prose. Volume 1 opens with an excellent essay on Spanish anthologies; Berceo is discussed in vol. 2, *Baena* in vol. 4, the *Cancionero general* in vol. 6 (sec. 10) (all the "introductions" to the volumes of the *Antología* have been published separately, without the exemplary selection of texts with which the editor originally accompanied them). For a general account in English see A. D. Deyermond, *A Literary History of Spain: The Middle Ages* (London/New York, 1971). On the later Middle Ages, Pierre Le Gentil (see list of abbreviations) is essential; the second volume covers late Spanish versification in all the detail one could wish. However, Henry R. Lang's article, "Las formas estróficas y términos métricos del Cancionero de Baena," in *Estudios eruditos in memoriam de Adolfo Bonilla y San Martín (1875–1926)*, vol. 1 (Madrid, 1927), pp. 485–523, is a more convenient reference source, since it provides brief definitions of terms in alphabetical order; one may also consult Rudolf Baehr, *Spanische Verslehre auf historischer Grundlage* (Tuebingen, 1962), and Tomás Navarro, *Métrica española* (Syracuse, N.Y., 1956). On the *villancico*, there is a recent study by Antonio Sanchez Romeralo, *El Villancico. Estudios sobre la lírica popular en los siglos XV y XVI* (Madrid, 1969).

For further information concerning the literature, there is a variety of bibliographical sources. These include José Simón Díaz, *Bibliografía de la literatura hispánica*, vol. 3 : 1 (Madrid, 1963); Homero Serís, *Manual de Bibliografía de la literatura española*, pt. 1 (Syracuse, N.Y., 1948); Gerhard Rohlfs, *Manual de Filología hispánica*, trans. Carlos Rosselli (Bogota, 1957) (for help with linguistic issues involving Portuguese and Catalan as well as Spanish); and Anthony Cardenas, John Nitti, Jean Gilkison, eds., *Bibliography of Old Spanish Texts*, Literary Texts, Edition 1 (Madison, Wis., 1975) (covers all manuscripts of a given work, with references to Simón Díaz's bibliography and other data). For a complete listing of the incipits of medieval Spanish lyrics, see the recent, computer-generated *Bibliografía de los cancioneros castellanos del siglo xv y repertorio de sus géneros poéticos*, ed. Jacqueline Steunou and Lothar Knapp, 3 vols. Documents, études et répertoires publiés par l'Institut de recherche et d'histoire des textes (Paris, 1975–); vol. 1 inventories the contents, in order of appearance, of ninety manuscripts and early printed editions (listed and described on pp. 106–23); vol. 2 contains the alphabetical list of incipits and a classification of all texts by author; in vol. 3, when it appears, the texts will be grouped according to the nature of their content, form, and number of syllables per line and combinations of lines within the stanza. The introduction (1:13–32) briefly surveys the poetry of the *cancioneros*, fifteenth-century poetic style and theory of the arts, and poetic forms of the period. This monumental project is a priceless aid to research.

The principal anthologies of Spanish religious poetry are Roque E. Scarpa, *Poésia religiosa española*, 2d ed. (Santiago de Chile, 1941), pp. 15–109, and José M. Peman and Miguel Herrero, eds., *Suma poética*, 2d ed. (Madrid, 1950) (texts of all periods are mingled together). Both are intended to serve Catholic piety rather than literary scholarship, and neither is very good. But they are convenient as an introduction to the texts. The major collections are as follows:

Menéndez y Pelayo.

Cancionero de Juan Alfonso de Baena, ed. José M. Azáceta, 3 vols. (Madrid, 1966). CC.

CG, see esp. vol. 2, pp. 287–381.

Cancionero general . . . (1511) ed. Antonio Rodriguez-Moñino, 2 vols. (Madrid, 1958–59) (vol. 1 is a facsimile of the 1511 edition, with an extensive introduction on the bibliography of the CG; vol. 2 prints the texts added in the later editions from 1514 to 1547).

CM; for the music, see *La música en la Corte de los Reyes' Católicos*, vol. 3, pt. 2: *Polifonía profana: Cancionero musical de Palacio*, ed. Higini Anglès (Barcelona, 1951).

Romancero y cancionero sagrados, ed. Justo de Sancha, Biblioteca de autores españoles, vol. 35 (Madrid, 1855).

The bulk of fifteenth-century religious poetry is in the *Cancionero castellano*. Most poets and their works can be found in it, in the *Cancionero general*, or in the *Cancionero de Baena* (in fact, there is relatively little religious lyric in the 1511 edition of the CG or in Baena). For the works of Gonzalo de Berceo, see *Obras completas*, ed. Brian Dutton, vol. 2, Collección Támesis, ser. A. 15 (Madrid/London, 1971) (*Los milagros* . . .) and *Obras completas*, ed. Rufino Briones (Logroño, 1971) (*Loores* and other shorter poems). For Juan Alvarez Gato, see *Obras*, ed. Jenaro A. Rodríquez, Los clásicos olvidados 4 (Madrid, 1928). Ambrosio Montesino's *cancionero* is reprinted in Justo de Sancha's *Romancero y cancionero sagrados*, pp. 402–66. Finally, for Bartolomeo de Torres Naharro, see *Propalladia, and Other Works*, ed. Joseph Gillet, 3 vols. (Bryn Mawr, Pa., 1943). The shorter poems are in vol. 1, pp. 240ff. and 255ff.

NOTES

NOTES TO THE INTRODUCTION

1. The theoretician in question is the semiotician Juri Lotman; see Lotman, *Structure*, pp. 95, 107, and 112f.

2. It is in terms of this centripetal, normative tendency that Zumthor accounts for the medieval preference for anticlimactic series, moving from extremes to center or general to particular, thereby frustrating our own precisely opposite expectations (cf. Zumthor, *Essai*, p. 44; on p. 93 Zumthor discusses the closely related tendency of medieval texts to "close upon" what is most typical in themselves).

3. Lotman, *Structure*, p. 125f., sets the use of inflectional or grammatical rhyme in medieval poetry into relation with the "aesthetic of identity," viewing the former as an affirmation *in parvo* of the world view generally expressed by the latter.

4. Chenu, p. 170 n. 2.

5. Of course, "glossing" was not always and everywhere viewed with favor; for examples of distrust of glossing in the later Middle Ages, cf. Morton Bloomfield, "Symbolism in Medieval Literature," *Modern Philology* 56, no. 2 (1958): 80f., and Chenu, p. 258 n. 2 (concerning St. Francis's devotion to the letter of Scripture and dislike of the gloss, which he expressed in his will as well as in his life). Nonetheless, in the midst of the fifteenth century, one will still find the Marquis of Santillana calling Mary "texto de admirable glosa" (CC, vol. 1, no. 218, p. 531, st. 5).

6. Cf. Frauenlob (i.e., Heinrich von Meissen), *Marienleich*, ed. Ludwig Pfannmueller, *Quellen und Forschungen*, no. 120 (Strassburg, 1913).

7. Zumthor, *Langue*, p. 16.

8. Zumthor, *Essai*, pp. 441–43.

9. See Joseph Sauer, *Symbolik des Kirchengebaeudes und seiner Ausstattung in der Auffassung des Mittelalters*, 2d ed. (Freiburg im Breisgau, 1924; reprint, Muenster, 1964).

10. See Antonio Viscardi, *Saggio sulla letteratura religiosa del medio evo romanzo*, Pubblicazioni della Facoltà di lettere e filosofia, vol. 3 (Padua, 1932), pp. 23ff. On discontinuity in liturgical texts, see also Léon Gautier,

Histoire de la poésie liturgique au moyen âge: les tropes, vol. 1 (Paris, 1886), p. 274f. (concerning *Regnum tuum solidum* tropes).

11. See Zumthor, *Essai*, pp. 43–46; see also pp. 71–74. For some examples of the extent of variation among different versions of the "same" poem, see the following: "Rayna potentissima," in Ernesto Monaci, ed., *Crestomazia italiana dei primi secoli*, rev. Felice Arese, 2d ed. (Rome/Naples/Città di Castello, 1955); Ferdinando Gabotto and Delfino Orsi, eds., *Le Laudi del Piemonte*, Scelta di curiosità letterarie 238 (Bologna, 1891), pt. 1, no. 36, and pt. 2, no. 4, or pt. 1, nos. 25 and 35, and pt. 2, no. 5; Franz Spechtler, ed., *Die geistlichen Lieder des Moenchs von Salzburg*, Quellen und Forschungen zur Sprach- und Kulturgeschichte der germanischen Voelker, n.s. vol. 51 (Berlin/New York, 1972) (= vol. 175), G.24, pp. 232–42.

12. On the "invisibility" of art in a culture centered on the sacred, see Maurice Blanchot, *L'Espace littéraire* (Paris, 1955), p. 277 ("l'hymne—où l'oeuvre, l'art et le monde sont absents" [the hymn—where work, art, and world are absent]), and p. 311f.:

> Quand l'art est le langage des dieux, quand le temple est le séjour où le dieu demeure, l'oeuvre est invisible et l'art, inconnu. Le poème nomme le sacré, c'est le sacré qu'entendent les hommes, non le poème . . . L'oeuvre est donc tout à la fois cachée dans la profonde présence du dieu et présente et visible de par l'absence et l'obscurité du divin.

> (When art is the language of the gods, when the temple is the dwelling place which the god inhabits, the work is invisible and art, unknown. The poem names the sacred, it is the sacred that men hear, not the poem. . . . Thus, the work is at once hidden within the profound presence of the god and present and visible by virtue of the absence and the obscurity of the divine.)

See also Roman Guardini, *Ecclesia orans*, vol. 1: *Vom Geist der Liturgie*, 7th ed. (Freiburg im Breisgau, 1922), especially pp. 11, 52, and 83 ("Nur wenn wir von der Wahrheit der Liturgie ausgehen, werden uns die Augen aufgetan, dass wir schauen, wie schoen sie ist" [Only when we leave behind the truth of the liturgy are our eyes opened and we see how beautiful it is]). By alluding to Genesis 3:7, Guardini treats the moment of aesthetic epiphany as a sort of Fall, which in a sense it is.

13. On variation in medieval literature and architecture, respectively, see Zumthor, *Histoire*, p. 23; and Henri Focillon, *The Art of the West: Romanesque Art*, 2d ed. (New York/London, 1969), p. 5.

14. Twentieth-century music has sometimes sought to incorporate the "aesthetic of opposition" into the internal structure of its "texts," not just into their intertextual relationships, refusing (as in Webern) to allow any

repetition of pattern within a piece, so that its notes have the collective character of a single word rather than a speech or a conversation. Equally notable is that the modern audience for music has stubbornly resisted this radical step and that we are now seeing composers react against the orthodoxy of the middle part of this century and in favor of musical forms involving some or even an extreme degree of repetition. Of course, folk and popular music have gone on repeating themselves, intra- and intertextually, as they always have.

15. Cf. for instance Ritva Jonsson's remark on the lack of specific "sources" for most tropes (Jonsson, *Tropes*, p. 38f.), or the conclusion to Stroppel. Sarah Weber attempts but fails to demonstrate a close relationship between Middle English religious lyric and the liturgy in her *Theology and Poetry in the Middle English Lyric* (Columbus, 1969); for a critique see Jeffrey, "Introduction."

16. Robert M. Jordan, *Chaucer and the Shape of Creation: The Aesthetic Possibilities of Inorganic Structure* (Cambridge, Mass., 1967). A closely related doctrine from the same source is the distinction between the poetry of the "Fancy" and that of the "Imagination." It is consistent with Dronke's unawareness of the possibility of anachronism in critical assumptions that he applies precisely this distinction to twelfth-century Latin poetry: see Peter Dronke, *Poetic Individuality in the Middle Ages: New Departures in Poetry 1000–1150* (Oxford, 1970), p. 179.

17. Jonathan Saville, *The Medieval Erotic Alba: Structure As Meaning* (New York, 1972), p. 10.

18. Paul Zumthor, "Style and Expressive Register in Medieval Poetry," in *Literary Style: A Symposium*, ed. Seymour Chatman (London/New York, 1971), pp. 263–75.

19. Zumthor, *Essai*, p. 272.

20. Cf. Paul Zumthor, "De la circularité du chant," *Poétique* 1 (1970): 129–40.

21. Cf. Zumthor (op. cit., note 18 above), p. 265.

NOTES TO CHAPTER 1

1. See Eduard Norden, *Agnostos Theos* (reprint, Stuttgart, 1956) and *Die antike Kunstprosa*, 2 vols. (reprint, Darmstadt, 1971); Francesco di Capua, "Preghiere liturgiche, poesia, ed eloquenza," *Archivo italiano per la storia della pietà* 1 (1951): 1–24; Hans Rheinfelder, "Zum Stil der lateinischen Orationen," *Jahrbuch fuer Liturgiewissenschaft* 11 (1931): 20–34; and especially Ricarda Liver, *Die Nachwirkung der antiken Sakralsprache im christlichen Gebet des lateinischen und italienischen Mittelalters; Unter-*

*suchungen zu den syntaktischen und stilistischen Formen dichterisch ge-
stalteter Gebete von den Anfaengen der lateinischen Literatur bis zu Dante,*
Romanica Helvetica, vol. 89 (Berlin, 1979).

2. On the influence of the Akathistos hymn, see Meerssemann, *Akathistos.*

3. Cf. Maximilian Scherner, *Die sprachlichen Rollen im lateinischen
Weihnachtslied des Mittelalters,* Suppl. to Mittellateinischen Jahrbuch 2
(Wuppertal/Ratingen/Duesseldorf, 1970), pt. 1, chap. 2, sec. 4.

4. Origen, *De Originibus* 1.12.

5. Augustine, *Enarrationes in Psalmos,* no. 72, in PL, vol. 36, col. 914;
echoed in, for instance, Josef Szoevérffy, ed., *Peter Abelard's Hymnarius Paraclitensis,* vol. 1: *Introduction to Peter Abelard's Hymns,* Classical Folia
Editions, Medieval Classics: Texts and Studies 2 (Albany, N.Y./Brookline,
Mass., 1975), preface. See also Augustine, *Erarrationes in Psalmos,* no. 148,
PL, vol. 37, col. 1947f.; Isidore of Seville, *De ecclesiasticis officiis* 1.6, in PL,
vol. 83, col. 743, and *Origines* 1.39.17 and 6.19.17 (ed. Lindsay, Oxford
Classical Texts); Alcuin, *Epistula* 164 (ad Carolum imperatorem), in PL,
vol. 100, col. 429; Hrabanus Maurus, *De universo* 5.9, in PL, vol. 111, col.
129; and Walafrid Strabo, *De ecclesiasticarum rerum exordiis et incremen-
tis xvv,* in PL, vol. 114, col. 954. (These references are mostly drawn from
Wiltrud aus der Fuenten, *Maria Magdalena in der Lyrik des Mittelalters:
Zum Wesen religioeser Lyrik,* Wirkendes Wort, Schriftenreihe 3 [Duessel-
dorf, 1966], p. 10 n. 7.)

6. Cf. Friedrich Heiler, *Das Gebet,* 3d ed. (Munich, 1921), p. 157: "In
purpose and form, the hymn is a prayer"; see also p. 444f.

7. See Peter von Moos, "Gottschalks Gedicht *O mi custos*—eine confessio," *Fruehmittelalterliche Studien* 5 (1971): 338, 343, 346f. (including
nn. 119–22), and p. 356f (part two of a two-part article that begins in vol.
4 of the same journal, pp. 201–30).

8. See Hennig Brinkmann, "Voraussetzungen und Struktur religioeser
Lyrik im Mittelalter," *Mittellateinisches Jahrbuch* 3 (1966): 37f. His students include aus der Fuenten, Breuer, Georgi, and Scherner.

9. Cf. Gregory Dix, *The Shape of the Liturgy* (London, 1943), chap.
12, opening.

10. One should be aware, however, of the stubborn *resistance* to song
(indeed, to speech) on the part of the monks of the desert in the Near East:
cf. Egon Wellesz, *A History of Byzantine Music and Hymnography,* 2d ed.
(Oxford, 1961), pp. 171–74.

11. Ambrose, "Sermo contra Auxentium," chap. 34, cited in Walther
Bulst, *Hymni latini antiquissimi LXXV Psalmi III* (Heidelberg, 1956),
p. 161.

12. One should also be aware of a strong current of suspicion of the

effects of verse (and music) that sets in toward the end of the twelfth century and leads to the "derhyming" of many texts; this attitude is well expressed in Johannes von Saaz's, *Der Ackermann aus Boehmen*, chap. 2 (ca. 1400): "Dein klag ist on reimen und on done, davon wir prufen, du wellest durch dones und reimens willen deinn sinn nicht entwerken" (Your complaint is without rhyme or music, from which we surmise, you do not wish to distort your meaning for the sake of music and rhyme).

13. Cf. Schroeder, chap. 3, sec. 8; according to sec. 10a, up to 1578, Christmas in fact did double duty as New Year's in Germany.

14. Cf. August H. Hoffmann von Fallersleben, *Geschichte des deutschen Kirchenlieds bis auf Luthers Zeit*, 3d ed. (Hannover, 1861; reprint, Hildesheim, 1965), p. 416f.

15. Cf. Schroeder, chap. 3, sec. 10.

16. Cf. Johannes Janota, *Studien zu Funktion und Typus des deutschen geistlichen Liedes im Mittelalter*, Muenchener Texte und Untersuchungen zur deutschen Literatur des Mittelalters, vol. 23 (Munich, 1968), 3.a.1, pp. 84ff.

17. Ibid., 3.b.1.a., pp. 151ff.

18. Cf. Zumthor, *Historie*, pt. 1, chap. 1, p. 20.

19. Cf. Peter von Moos, "Gottschalks Gedicht *O mi custos*—eine confessio," pt. 2, *Fruehmittelalterliche Studien* 5 (1971): 336 n. 82 (full discussion with references to the literature).

20. Cf. Ignazio Baldelli, "La lauda e i Disciplinati," *La Rassegna della letteratura italiana* 64, no. 3 (1960): 406, and Carl Allen Moberg, *Die Liturgischen Hymnen in Schweden*, vol. 1 (Copenhagen, 1947), p. 23, col. 1.

21. Cf. Carl Horstmann, *The Minor Poems of the Vernon Manuscript*, vol. 1, EETS, orig. ser. 98 (London, 1892), p. 169: "Þis newe feste" refers to Corpus Christi in a poem from the later fourteenth century! Similarly, a fourteenth-century Italian *lauda*, in Giuseppe Galli, *Laudi inediti dei disciplinati umbri* (Bergamo, 1910), p. 184, l. 29, says of Corpus Christi, "Festa novella è tracta" (a new feast is ordained).

22. Cf. *Ars Nova and the Renaissance (1300–1540)*, ed. Anselm Hughes and Gerald Abraham, The New Oxford History of Music, vol. 3 (London, 1960), chap. 10, "European Song (1300–1530)," p. 3.

23. In the seventh century Gallican Sacramentary (from Bobbio), however, Assumption was celebrated on 18 January! See Schroeder, p. 99.

24. Medieval people were not entirely unaware of the competition between Mary and her Son for ecclesiastical position. For instance, there is a funny and irreverent Middle French debate from the fifteenth century between "God" and "His Mother" printed in Ernest Langlois, "Notice du ms Ottobonien 2253," *Mélanges d'archéologie et d'histoire de l'Ecole française de Rome* 5 (1885): 54–61; Christ complains that Mary has the finest part

of Laon and that all he has is a few hospitals where rascals, runaways, and pilgrims lodge who have neither luggage nor money; Mary retorts that "my son left me without a penny to my name, and so did his father," and so forth. The judgment goes against Christ, who has to pay all expenses and manage his mother's people for her while they live, with Mary getting the souls when they die, not He.

25. Cf. Dimitri Scheludko, "Die Marienlieder in der altprovenzalischen Lyrik," pts. 1 and 2, and "Ueber die religioese Lyrik der Troubadours," *NM* 35 (1934): 29—42; 37 (1936): 15—42; 38 (1937): 224—50.

26. Cf. Schroeder, p. 205f. A late medieval Old Norse poem gives an explanation of why Saturday was Mary's day: "Alone I did not doubt Christ the pure would rise on Saturday" (cf. *Skjaldedigtning* B.2, "Máríugrátr," p. 515, st. 36: "Efalaus var ek at upp mundi risa / ein þráttdaginn Kristr enn hreini"). The daily recitation of the little Office of the Virgin dates to the late tenth century (adopted by Cluny after 1050); cf. Victor Leroquais, *Les livres d'heures manuscrit de la B.N.*, vol. 1 (Paris, 1927), introduction, p. xviiif.

27. For instance, an Assumption poem in Middle High German of ca. 1300, "Do got zů im in ewikeite," relates how Mary goes down and harrows Hell, on a smaller scale than Christ, after she has been raised on the third day and taken up bodily into heaven; cf. Wack., no. 438.

28. Cf. Theodor Wolpers, "Geschichte der englischen Marienlyrik," *Anglia* 69 (1950): 3—88, esp. p. 50.

29. Cf. Schroeder, pp. 111—15.

30. Cf. Friedrich Ohly, "Zum Dichtungsschluss *Tu autem, domine, miserere nobis*," *Deutsche Vierteljahrsschrift fuer Literaturwissenschaft und Geistesgeschichte* 47, no. 1 (1973): 56.

31. Cf. Jonsson, *Tropes*, p. 10f.

32. Cf. Stroppel, p. 93 and n. 76; and Meerssemann, *Etudes*, p. 32.

33. Cf. Janota (op. cit., note 16 above), p. 78. The surrounding "Exkurs" (pp. 77—84) is an excellent concise discussion of lay participation (and nonparticipation) in the medieval liturgy, with copious quotations and references.

34. Einar Loefstedt, *Late Latin* (Oslo, 1959), pp. 2 and 4.

35. In response to the incomprehensibility of Latin, one presumes, monks began to insert vernacular pieces into the liturgy as early as ca. 840 in Provence (ever precocious!); the practice is common by the eleventh century, and vernacular influence on religious poetry in Latin in fact begins to show itself toward the end of the eleventh century (cf. Jeffrey, p. 21, which is in turn based upon Claude Fauriel, *History of Provençal Poetry* [New York, 1860], pp. 155 and 158—63).

36. Cf. Janota (op. cit., note 16 above), p. 78, and Stroppel, p. 24 n. 18,

concerning a ninth-century prayer book for laymen in PL, vol. 101, coll. 1383–1416.

37. As is well known, production or use of vernacular versions of sacred texts was viewed as an indication of heretical leanings by the Church; Paris, 1210, for instance, commanded that all such versions and in fact all vernacular religious texts be submitted to one's bishop for clearance (Chenu, p. 321 n. 2).

38. Cf. Chenu, pp. 244–57.

39. Cf. Janota (op. cit., note 16 above), p. 81.

40. Cf. Mariano Aguiló y Fuster, ed., *Cançoner de les obretes en nostra lengua materna mes divulgades durant los segles xiv, xv e xvi* (Barcelona, 1900), "Cobles religioses: Cançoneret y miracles en lahor del Psaltiri o Roser," first two pages (i.e., the fourteenth item in the table of contents under "Cobles religioses"; there are no page numbers in this book).

41. On the matter of confraternities, see Meerssemann, *Etudes*, and Gabriel Le Bras, *Etudes de sociologie religieuse*, vol. 2 (Paris, 1956), "Esquisse d'une histoire des confréries" and "Les confréries chrétiennes," pp. 418–62 (p. 423 n. 2 directs one to the major earlier studies).

42. Cf. *Poeti del Duecento*, ed. Gianfranco Contini, La letteratura italiana, storia e testi, vol. 2:2 (Naples/Milan, 1960), pt. 6, "Laude," preface (p. 4); and Giulio Bertoni, *Il Duecento*, 3d ed., Storia letteraria d'Italia (Milan, 1939), p. 225.

43. No religious *ballata* can be proven to antedate the Disciplinati movement of 1258–60. Guittone d'Arezzo's five religious *ballate* could be earlier than the movement but were probably written later in Guittone's life; cf. Giorgio Varanini, *Laude dugentesche* (Padua, 1972), p. xxxif.

44. Though antiquated, the major study of the 1260 *moto* is still G. Galli (op. cit., note 21 above; to be used more for its account of the *moto* than for its ideas about the connection between the *moto* and the confraternities and their *laude*).

45. See *Studi in onore de A. Schiaffini*, vol. 1 (Rome, 1965), pp. 347–63.

46. Cf. Varanini (op. cit., note 43 above), p. xxif.

47. Cf. Ibid., p. xviii, citing G. Meerssemann, "Nota sull'origine delle compagnie dei Laudesi (Siena 1267)," *Rivista di storia della Chiesa in Italia* 17 (1963): 396.

48. Apparently, confraternities and *puys* failed to "take" in England (cf. Jeffrey, p. 274f.), with the exception of London.

49. Cf. Jeffrey, end of chap. 5, pp. 203–14.

50. Cf. Jeanroy, *Joies*, p. xvi n. 1.

51. Cf. Martín de Riquer, *Literatura catalana medieval* (Barcelona, 1972), chap. 2, sec. 14, p. 36 (the dialogue in question is the "Libre de Sancta Maria").

52. Cf. Zumthor, *Histoire*, pt. 4, chap. 2.

53. Cf. José Grosdidier de Matons, "Le Kontakion," in *Gattungen*, pp. 264–68.

54. Ibid.

55. Cf. Ohly (op. cit., note 30 above), p. 57.

56. According to a source cited by von Fallersleben (op. cit., note 14 above), p. 49 n. 30, in the year 1291 the whole chapter of St. Gall's, once a monastery famous for its learning, was unable to write. Of course, this does not mean the abbot and his monks were truly illiterate, but it represents the degree of monastic decay in the later Middle Ages. (On medieval illiteracy, see Franz Baeuml, "Varieties and Consequences of Medieval Literacy and Illiteracy," *Speculum* 55, no. 2 [Apr. 1980]: 237–65, with full bibliography.)

57. A very large proportion of fifteenth-century *laude* are *contrafacture*, as are many German religious lyrics of the same period. For references to Franciscan religious *contrafacture* in the British Isles at the end of the Middle Ages (notably in *The Red Book of Ossory*, though see Rossel H. Robbins, "Friar Herebert and the Carol," *Anglia* 75 [1957]: 194), see Jeffrey, pp. 259 and 268 nn. 60–62.

58. Cf. Jeffrey, pp. 187ff. (use as *exempla*) and pp. 127–31 (use in sermons in Italy and Germany), and pp. 172–202 (in England). A German lyric, "Jhesus christ, der junckfrowen sun, das liebste kindlin," Wack., no. 853, serves as the heading to a long prose homily.

59. See [Joseph] Victor Le Clerc, *Histoire littéraire de la France*, vol. 23, p. 256, cited in Artur Långfors, "Les traductions et paraphrases du *Pater* en vers français du moyen âge; Essai de bibliographie," *NM* 14 (1912): 35.

60. In one case at least, she intervenes to help a poet find the perfect rhyme for a poem to her; cf. *Cantigas*, no. 202: "Muito a Santa Maria, / Madre de Deus, gran saber, / d'ajudar quen lle cantares / ou prosas faz de loor" (Mary, Mother of God, is very clever at helping those who sing to her or write sequences in her praise). The (Latin) rhyme is "nobile triclinium," a grandiloquent and perfectly traditional Marian epithet.

NOTES TO CHAPTER 2

1. Among the most important discussions of genre and medieval literature are Hans R. Jauss, "Littérature médiévale et théorie des genres," *Poétique* 1 (1970): 79–101, and Zumthor, *Langue*, pp. 108–24.

2. Cf. below pp. 147f. and 155 (Christ as child), pp. 143ff. and 159 (Christ crucified), and p. 180ff.

3. See below, pp. 101, 123, 124f., 127, 138f., 154, 160, 167f., 177, 187, 188ff., 191f., 205, 206ff., 209. Most of the metaphors canvassed at the end of chapter 3 involve Mary.

4. However, the rate of production of Latin hymns to saints is far from uniform; it is quite low, for example, between Prudentius and the Carolingian age (cf. Zumthor, *Histoire*, p. 28).

5. For Greek verse calendars, see Ciro Giannelli, "Tetrastici di Teodoro Prodroma sulle feste fisse e sui santi del calendario bizantino," *Analecta Bollandiana* 75 (1957): 229–336, and Enrica Follieri's edition of a calendar by Christophoros of Mytilene in *Analecta bollandiana* 77 (1959): 245–304. For examples of the German *cisiojanus*, see *Oswald von Wolkenstein: Die Lieder*, ed. Karl Klein, with musical appendix by Walter Salmen (Tuebingen, 1962), nos. 28 or 67.

6. On Mary Magdalene, see aus der Fuenten (op. cit., note 5, chapter 1).

7. See the Select Bibliography for Latin in the "Orientations."

8. Cf. Stephan Beissel, *Die Verehrung der Heiligen und ihrer Reliquien in Deutschland waehrend der zweiten Haelfte des Mittelalters*, Stimmen aus Maria-Laach, Suppl. 54 (Freiburg im Breisgau, 1892), chap. 8, sec. 1, p. 96.

9. *Annalen* 2:283.

10. For a Spanish Christmas poem, see below, p. 178.

11. For Mauropus's Christmas poem, see chapter 3, note 11.

12. For Latin Christmas poems, see especially AH 7–10, 24, 37, 39, 40, 42, and 44.

13. See the Select Bibliography for Old French in the "Orientations."

14. See the Select Bibliography for Portuguese in the "Orientations."

15. Joseph Anglade, *Poésies religieuses du xive siècle en dialecte toulousain* (Toulouse, 1914), pp. 30–48.

16. See below, pp. 000 and 000, and also note 106 below.

17. For examples of the hymnic mode, see below, pp. 101, 164f., and 205 (Latin); 140 (Greek); 163f. (Provençal); 142f., 154ff., and 192f. (Old French); 125f., 166, and 187 (Middle English); and 188, 206ff., and 207f. (Middle High German).

18. On educational use of hymns, see Helmut Gneuss, *Hymnar und Hymnen im englischen Mittelalter* (Tuebingen, 1968), chap. 9, "Die *Expositio hymnorum*," pp. 194–206.

19. Cf. *Iberian Hymnody*, pp. 164 and 166.

20. For examples, see below, pp. 167f., 169f., or 189ff.

21. Cf. Victor Lowinsky, "Zum geistlichen Kunstliede in der altprovenzalischen Literatur bis zur Gruendung des Consistori del Gai Saber," *Zeitschrift fuer neufranzoesische Sprache und Literatur* 20, no. 1 (1898): 163–271, esp. 212.

22. For two examples, see below, pp. 146 and 180ff.

23. For a few examples of the moral mode, see below, pp. 161f., 163, and 171ff.

24. Serlo of Wilton, *Les poèmes de Serlo de Wilton*, ed. Jan Oeberg, Studia latina stockholmiensia 14 (Stockholm, 1965).

25. For examples, see below pp. 146, 159, and 163.

26. On Medieval Latin epigram, see Priscilla Miner, "Eleventh and Twelfth Century Latin Epigram" (Ph.D. diss., University of California at Berkeley, 1970).

27. For a collection of Carolingian *tituli*, see PLAC 1:99–115 and 429–43 (eighth and early ninth centuries), and 5:415–63 (early Ottonian).

28. Cf. p. 146 below.

29. *Skjaldedigtning* B.1, no. 23, p. 185.

30. For examples, see below, p. 159ff., and chapter 3, note 11.

31. Neri Pagliaresi, *Rime sacre di certa o probabile attribuzione*, ed. Giorgio Varanini (Florence, 1970), no. 10, "Di, Maria dolce," and appendix 2, "Amor[e] transformato," pp. 251–53.

32. Here I follow David Jeffrey rather than Rosemary Woolf; cf. Jeffrey, Introduction, p. 5ff; Brown XIII.

33. Cf. Zumthor, *Histoire*, chap. 4.

34. For the purposes of this discussion, I treat penitential lyric as a single mode or genre; however, at the same time I fully agree with von Moos (op. cit., note 19, chapter 1), p. 335 n. 80, in which the author criticizes the habit of treating penitential lyric as if it were homogeneous and suggests a preliminary list of genres into which it ought to be distinguished. For Italian examples of the mode, see below, pp. 143ff. and 160.

35. Cf. Peter Dronke, *The Medieval Lyric* (London, 1968), p. 63, for an anachronistic response to the "I"'s appearance.

36. Frank A. Patterson, *The Middle English Penitential Lyric* (New York, 1911); to be used with caution!

37. Guillaume Alexis, *Oeuvres poetiques*, ed. Arthur Piaget and Emile Picot, 3 vols. SATF 3:1–3 (Paris, 1896–1908), 3:188ff.

38. Suchier, "Des Suenders Reue," pp. 214–40.

39. Guy Folquet, in Suchier, pp. 272–83.

40. On the penitential psalms, see Giuseppe Bernini, *Le preghiere penitenziali del Salterio*, Analecta Gregoriana 62, Series facultatis theologiae, sectio A, no. 9 (Rome, 1953), esp. pp. xvi, 77ff., and 266ff.

41. For examples see below pp. 173f. and 176.

42. Cf. especially numbers 47, 78, 79, 84, 86, and 90 in Mancini's edition. The incipits are as follows: "Povertat'ennamorata" (no. 47), "Un arbore è da Deo plantato" (no. 78), "O Amor, che mme ami" (no. 79), "Fede, spen e caritate" (no. 84), "All'Amor, ch'è venuto" (no. 86), "La Fede e la Speranza" (no. 90).

43. Reinmar, "Ez ist vil manegem minner leit," p. 420.

44. *Hugo von Montfort*, ed. Karl Bartsch, Stuttgart Literarischer Ver-

ein, Bibliothek, no. 143 (Tuebingen, 1879), "Mir kam ein priester vuer im trôn," pp. 175–84.

45. Rosanna Bettarini, *Jacopone e il laudario urbinate* (Florence, 1969), no. 24, "Ihesù Cristo, a Vui m'accuso," p. 593, ll. 69f.

46. Giustinian, item no. 25, "Io scripsi gia d'amor piu volte rime," pp. [fiv]-gi^v.

47. Lydgate, no. 49, "Ballade at the Reverence of our Lady," p. 254, st. 1 ("A thowsand storiis kowde I mo reherse").

48. Gautier de Coincy, ed. Koenig 3:292, "Hui matin a l'ajornee," ll. 20–23. See also *Recueil* 2, no. 118, "Chançon ferai, puis que Diex m'a doné," p. 151f.

49. Cerveri de Girona, *Obras completas*, ed. Martín de Riquer (Barcelona, 1947), "Juglar, prec vos ans que mortz vos aucia," p. 92, st. 5, and Riquier, ed. Pfaff, no. 48, "Kalenda de mes caut ni freg," st. 1.

50. Guilherme de Faria, *Antologia de poesias religiosas desde a século XV* (Lisbon, 1947), pp. 30–32, Joam Manuel, "Poetas ou trovadores," pendant to "Apostolo santeficado."

51. Ramon Llull, *Poesias*, ed. Ramon d'Alòs-Moner, 2d ed. (Barcelona, 1928), "Los cent noms de Deú," preface, p. 36.

52. *Skjaldedigtning* B.2, "Petersdrápa," p. 546ff, st. 7.

53. Wolfgang Lange, *Studien zur christlichen Dichtung der Nordgermanen: 1000–1200* (Goettingen, 1958), pp. 276–82.

54. *Skjaldedigtning* B.2, Arngrímr ábóti Brandsson, "Gudmundar kvaedi byskups," p. 372, st. 2: "Eagle's droppings" are the "poetaster's share" of the mead of poetry, dropped by Odin while fleeing in the guise of an eagle back to Asgard with a cargo of same in his stomach. See *The Prose Edda*, trans. Jean Young (Berkeley, 1966), pp. 101–3.

55. *Skjaldedigtning* B.2, Arni Jonsson ábóti, "Gudmundar drápa," p. 461, st. 78 (the penultimate stanza).

56. Ibid., Eysteinn Ásgrímsson, *Lilja*, pp. 415ff., stt. 97ff.; see also pp. 390ff., stt. 2ff.

57. See Theodor Kochs, *Das deutsche geistliche Tagelied*, Forschungen und Funde, vol. 22 (Muenster, 1928), and Philipp A. Becker, "Vom geistlichen Tagelied" (in Latin), *Volkstum und Kultur der Romanen* 2 (1929): 293–302. Cf. below p. 161.

58. Examples are numerous in Wack.; cf. nos. 106 or 107, for example.

59. Cf. Helen Sandison, *The Chanson d'Aventure in Middle English*, Bryn Mawr College Monographs 12 (Bryn Mawr, Pa., 1913); pp. 135–39 list the twenty-seven religious examples.

60. On Middle English lullabies, see Wolpers (op. cit., note 28, chapter 1), chap. 5, sec. 2c, pp. 40–42, and cf. below pp. 147f.

61. See below, pp. 155 and 192f.

62. See below, pp. 143ff. (laude), 142f. (rondeau), and 125f. (carol).

63. On the "genres" of the *chanson d'amour*, cf. Le Gentil 1:230.

64. Jean Molinet, *Les faictz et dicts* . . . , ed. Noël Dupire, vol. 2, SATF 81:2 (Paris, 1937), no. 23, "Dame sans per, tres precieuse image," pp. 531–35.

65. Jonathan Saville, *The Medieval Erotic Alba: Structure as Meaning* (New York, 1972), pp. 101ff.

66.

> Aeterne rerum conditor,
> noctem diemque qui regis
> et temporum das tempora,
>
> ut alleves fastidium.
> Praeco diei iam sonat,
> noctis profundae pervigil,
> nocturna lux viantibus,
> a nocte noctem segregans.

Raby, *Oxford*, no. 9, p. 8.

67. Cf. Richard Crocker, *The Early Medieval Sequence* (Berkeley/Los Angeles/London, 1977), p. 382.

68. See below, p. 190f., for an example of religious Sapphics.

69.

> Pange, lingua, gloriosi proelium certaminis
> et super crucis tropaeo dic triumphum nobilem,
> qualiter redemptor orbis immolatus vicerit.
>
> De parentis protoplasti fraude factor condolens,
> quando pomi noxialis morte morsu corruit,
> ipse lignum tunc notavit, damna ligni ut solveret.

Raby, *Oxford*, p. 74.

70.

> Tempora florigero rutilant distincta sereno
> et maiore poli lumine porta patet.
> altius ignivomum solem caeli orbita ducit,
> qui vagus Oceanus exit et intrat aquas,
> armatis radiis elementa liquentia lustrans
> adhuc nocte brevi tendit in orbe diem.

Raby, *Oxford*, no. 57, p. 77.

> Primus init Stephanus mercedem sanguinis imbre
> afflictus lapidum Christum tamen ille cruentus
> inter saxa rogat ne sit lapidatio fraudi

hostibus o primae pietas miranda coronae
En vice nos Stephani dominum pulsando canamus
agite
ETENIM SEDERUNT

Jonsson, *Tropes*, p. 160 (dactylic hexameter).

71. Cf. the famous *rhythmus*, cited by Bede in the early eighth century, "Apparebit repentina":

1. Apparebit repentina	dies magna domini,
Fur obscura velut nocte	inprovisos occupans,
In tremendo die iudicii.	
2. Brevis totus tum parebit	prisci luxus saeculi,
Totum simul cum clarebit	praeterisse saeculum,
In tremendo die iudicii.	
3. Clangor tubę per quaternas	terrae plagas concinens
Vivos una mortuosque	Christo ciet obviam
In tremendo die iudicii.	

PLAC 4.2:507.

72. Cf. Bernhard Bischoff, "Ein Brief Julians von Toledo ueber Rhythmen, metrische Dichtung, und Prose," *Hermes* 87 (1959): 247–56.

73. A patriarch of Constantinople, Methodios Homologetes (d. 846) also experimented with hymns in iambic trimeter. To illustrate the form, here are a few lines from John Damascene's canon on the Nativity:

Ἔσωσε λαὸν θαυματουργῶν δεσπότης,
ὑγρὸν θαλάσσης κῦμα χερσώσας πάλαι·
ἑκὼν δὲ τεχθεὶς ἐκ κόρης, τρίβον βατὴν
πόλου τίθησιν ἡμῖν, ὃν κατ' οὐσίαν
ἰσόν τε πατρὶ καὶ βροτοῖς δοξάζομεν.

Constantine Trypanis, ed., *Medieval and Modern Greek Poetry: An Anthology*
(Oxford, 1968), p. 27 (no. 15).

74. Cf. below p. 140.

75. For sources on the *kontakion*, see the Select Bibliography for Greek in the "Orientations."

76. See Paul Maas, G. Mercati, and S. Gassisi, "Gleichzeilige Hymnen in der byzantinischen Liturgie," *Byzantinische Zeitschrift* 18 (1909): 309–56.

77. For an excerpt from a *kontakion*, see below, p. 169f.

78. See Wellesz (op. cit., note 10, chapter 1), p. 204 (concerning the council "In Trullo" of A.D. 691), and *Gattungen* (Miloš Velimirovič, "The Byzantine Heirmos and Heirmologion"), p. 201.

79. See Wellesz (op. cit., note 10, chapter 1), pp. 214–16, and *Gattungen*, p. 196. The nine canticles (in order) were the following: Exod. 15:1–19 (I); Deut. 32:1–45 (II); 1 Sam. 2:1–10 (III); Hab. 3:2–19 (IV);

Isa. 26:9–19 (V); Jon. 2:2–9 (VI); Dan. 3:26–45 (VII); Dan. 3:57–88 (VIII); and Luke 1:46–55 and 68–79 (IX). For examples of the *kanon* (too long for reproduction here), see Trypanis (op. cit., note 73 above), pp. 24–26 (no. 14; odes A and B only), or Raffaele Cantarella, *Poeti bizantini*, 2 vols., Edizioni dell' Università Cattolica del sacro cuore, series "Corsi universitari" 21 and 22 (Milan, 1948), 1:100–20, nos. 50–52.

80. See below pp. 159, 161f., 163, and note 11, chapter 3.

81. See below, p. 146 and compare the following acrostic, cited in Trypanis (op. cit., note 73 above), p. 255, no. 15:

> Εὐεπίης μελέεσιν ἐφύμνια ταῦτα λιγαίνει
> υἷα θεοῦ, μερόπων εἵνεκα τικτόμενον
> ἐν χθονὶ καὶ λύοντα πολύστονα πήματα κόσμου.
> ἀλλ', ἄνα, ῥητῆρας ῥύεο τῶνδε πόνων.

82. Compare Trypanis (op. cit., note 73 above), p. 32 (no. 19), ll. 1–5: (Simeon the New Theologian).

> Εἰ τοίνυν σὺ ἐνδέδυσαι σαρκός σου τὴν αἰσχύνην
> καὶ νοῦν οὐκ ἀπεγύμνωσας, ψυχὴν οὐκ ἀπεδύσω,
> τὸ φῶς ἰδεῖν οὐκ ἴσχυσας σκότει κεκαλυμμένος,
> ἐγώ σοι τί ποιήσαιμι; τὰ φρικτὰ πῶς σοι δείξω;
> πῶς εἰς τὸν οἶκον τοῦ Δαβὶδ εἰσενέγκω σε οἴμοι;

83. See below, p. 164f. or 101.

84. Cf. *Gattungen* (J. Crocker, "The Sequence"), p. 276f. For Dronke's article, see *Beitraege zur Geschichte der deutschen Sprache und Literatur* 87 (1965): 43–73. For a sensible, brief, and recent article on the sequence, see Stephen Ryle, "The Sequence: Reflections on Literature and Liturgy," in *Papers of the Liverpool Latin Seminar 1976: Classical Latin Poetry/Medieval Latin Poetry/Greek Poetry*, ed. Francis Cairns (Liverpool, 1977), pp. 171–82.

85. *Gattungen*, p. 276. Most of my discussion of the sequence is drawn from this article and Crocker's book, op. cit., note 67 above.

86. *Gattungen*, p. 289.

87. Crocker (op. cit., note 67 above), pp. 402–9.

88. Cf. the late medieval revivals of secular forms such as the *chanson de femme* and the *cantiga de amigo* (Le Gentil 1:287–93).

89. Though note the presence of forty-eight tropes in the great Las Huelgas manuscript of the fourteenth century, discussed in *Iberian Hymnody*, pp. 141–49.

90. For examples of the trope, cf. note 70 above and the famous "Quem quaeritis" Easter trope:

> Quem quaeritis in sepulchro,
> o christicolae?

Iesum Nazarenum crucifixum,
o caelicolae.

Non est hic;
surrexit, sicut praedixerat.
ite, nuntiate,
quia surrexit.

Alleluia, resurrexit Dominus,
hodie resurrexit leo fortis,
filius Dei.
Deo gratias: dicite, eia,
resurrexi et adhuc tecum, etc.

Raby, *Oxford*, no. 99, p. 136ff.

91. Cf. Richard Crocker, "The Troping Hypothesis," *Musical Quarterly* 52 (1966): 183—203.

92. On the divergent traits of the two major periods in the development of the trope, see Léon Gautier (op. cit., note 10, introduction), chap. 12, pp. 147—73.

93. See Jonsson, *Tropes*, p. 16.

94. See Gautier (op. cit., note 10, introduction), chap. 9, p. 70. For a discussion of L. Gautier, see Select Bibliography for Latin.

95. Cited in Gautier (op. cit., note 10, introduction), p. 70 n. 1; see *Iohannis Beleth Summa de Ecclesiasticis officiis*, ed. Herbert Douteil, Corpus Christianorum Continuatio Medievalis, vol. 41A (Turnholt, 1976), *capitulum* 59, sec. d, p. 107f.

96. Gautier, (op. cit., note 10, introduction), chap. 11, p. 143.

97. Gautier (op. cit., note 10, introduction), chap. 10, p. 108f.

98. See Gautier, (op. cit., note 10, introduction), p. 5, and chap. 15, p. 227; at Rouen, Sens, and Lyons, tropes were also in use.

99. Cf. *Annalen* 1:250—54; but see also Jónsson, *Historia: Etudes sur la génèse des offices versifiées*, Studia latina stockholmiensia 15 (Stockholm, 1968), esp. pp. 115—17 and 130—40.

100. For an example of the verse office, see Raby, *Oxford*, no. 260 (too long to reproduce here).

101. Cf. *Iberian Hymnody*, chap. 4, p. 78, and *Annalen* 2:215ff.

102. Cf. Paul Lehmann, *Skandinaviens Anteil an der lateinischen Literatur und Wissenschaft des Mittelalters*, Akademie der Wissenschaft, Munich, philosophisch-historische Abteilung, Sitzungsberichte, no. 7 (1937), appendix, item no. 2, pp. 105ff. For a German verse office to Ursula and the eleven thousand Virgins, see Wack., no. 840, "O ir Cristi glentzende rose."

103. For examples of *carmina quadrata*, see PLAC 1:416—23 (Bernowin); 2:421f., (Walafrid Strabo); 3:562—65 (Milo); and 5.2:3, 4f. (Josephus Scottus), and 470f. (Abbot of St. Fleury). For a good recent discussion, see

Zumthor, *Langue*, "Carmina figurata," pp. 25–35 (see acrostic opposite).
Cf. also the following, PLAC 3 : 564f., from Milo's *Life of St. Amandus*.

III.

Salve, rector ovans, aeterno munere fretus.
Aurea vestra decens tenui pangente Talia
Limina pulsare et radians orare tribunal
Viribus exiguis audens haec pagina vorsu
⁵ Exerto properat, o rex, tibi plaudere laude;
Cursio sed voto pavitanti deficit in haec:
Artatur nimium proprio sub calle modesta
Rara videns vestigia, quis artata tenetur
Vilis, et exiguo columen; nec littera ductu
¹⁰ Sufficit ulla sacrum metiri nomen amoris
Aut laus arta valet vivaci cludere lingua.
Mitto tamen ludos et sudat pagina rithmum.
Orbe rubens medio species candore polito
Reddit enim pure metris signata verenter
¹⁵ Aptius has laudes, quas promit rite Camena
Etsi nam multi teneant tua sceptra poetae
Tollentes astris et sertum numinis orent,
Excipe clementer famulum, pietatis amice.
Respicias istic patienti corde libenter
²⁰ Nodo multiplici perlatum, quaeso, ligamen
Ardenterve legas, quo, per tua ludere gesta
Laurea dum vellem, conpegi munera, quae vel
Alta petunt radiis divexo calle repressa
Vel decliva ruunt et plurima digna notatu
²⁵ Depingunt vario: peto, lucri munus ut istud
Excipias placidi terrae iam notus in orbe,
Cernuus excurram parens quo mitius ex hoc,
Optima vel laeto depingam munera plectro.
Rex pie, rex fortis, legis rectissime lator,
³⁰ Vates ornatum tibimet modo fretus in ausu,
Sancte, tuo laetus cecini diadema salutis,
Conisus talem tibi laudem plaudere, donec
Ad maiora queam reverenter abire canenda.
Numen avi portans et laudem culminis exin
³⁵ Salve, rector ovans, aeterno munere fretus.

104. Cf. Carl T. E. Wendel, "Die Technopaegnien Ausgabe des Rhetors Holobolos," *Byzantinische Zeitschrift* 16 (1907): 460–67, and *Anthologia palatina*, bk. 15, nos. 21f. and 24–27.

105. Albert Seay, *Music in the Medieval World* (Englewood Cliffs, N.J., 1965), p. 170.

106. Cf. Davies, no. 152, "See/Me/(kinde)/Be," p. 259, ca. A.D. 1500:

```
SALVERECTOROVANSAETERNOMVNEREFRETVS
AVREAVESTRADECENSTENVIPANGENTETALIA
LIMINAPVLSAREETRADIANSORARETRIBVNAL
VIRIBVSEXIGVISAVDENSHAECPAGINAVORSV
EXERTOPROPERATOREXTIBIPLAVDERELAVDE
CVRSIOSEDVOTOPAVITANTIDEFICITINHAEC
ARTATVRNIMIVMPROPRIOSVBCALLEMODESTA
RARAVIDENSVESTIGIAQVISARTATATENETVR
VILISETEXIGVOCOLVMENNECLITTERADVCTV
SVFFICITVLLASACRVMMETIRINOMENAMORIS
AVTLAVSARTAVALETVIVACICLVDERELINGVA
MITTOTAMENLVDOSETSVDATPAGINARITHMVM
ORBERVBENSMEDIOSPECIESCANDOREPOLITO
REDDITENIMPVREMETRISSIGNATAVERENTER
APTIVSHASLAVDESQVASPROMITRITECAMENA
ETSINAMMVLTITENEANTTVASCEPTRAPOETAE
EXCIPECLEMENTERFAMVLVMPIETATISAMICE
RESPICIASISTICPATIENTICORDELIBENTER
NODOMVLTIPLICIPERLATVMQVAESOLIGAMEN
ARDENTERVELEGASQVOPERTVALVDEREGESTA
LAVREADVMVELLEMCONPEGIMVNERAQVAEVEL
ALTAPETVNTRADIISDIVEXOCALLEREPRESSA
VELDECLIVARVVNTETPLVRIMADIGNANOTATV
DEPINGVNTVARIOPETOLVCRIMVNVSVTISTVD
EXCIPIASPLACIDITERRAEIAMNOTVSINORBE
CERNVVSEXCVRRAMPARENSQVOMITIVSEXHOC
OPTIMAVELLAETODEPINGAMMVNERAPLECTRO
REXPIEREXFORTISLEGISRECTISSIMELATOR
VATESORNATVMTIBIMETMODOFRETVSINAVSV
SANCTETVOLAETVSCEINIDIADEMASALVTIS
CONISVSTALEMTIBILAVDEMPLAVDEREDONEC
ADMAIORAQVEAMREVERENTERABIRECANENDA
NVMENAVIPORTANSETLAVDEMCVLMINISEXIN
SALVERECTOROVANSAETERNOMVNEREFRETVS
```

Acrostic from *Milonis carmina*. Monumenta Germaniae Historica, Poetae Latini Aevi Carolini, vol. III, 2: 565.

STEPHEN HAWES
A pair of Wings

See
Me   (kinde
Be
Againe
My paine   (in minde   5
Retaine
My swete bloode
On the Roode   (my brother
Dide thee good
My face right redde   10
Mine armes spredde   (thinke none other
My woundes bledde
Beholde thou my side
Wounded so right wide   (all for thine owne sake
Bledinge sore that tide   15
Thus for thee I smerted
Why arte thou harde-herted   (and thy sweringe aslake
Be by me converted
Tere me now no more
My woundes are sore   (and come to my grace   20
Leve sweringe therfore
I am redy
To graunte mercy   (for thy trespace
To thee truely
Come now nere   25
My frende dere   (before me
And appere
I so
In wo   (see see
Dide go   30
I
Crye   (thee
Hy

107. Among these students are Richard Crocker and Stephen Ryle.

108. For an outstanding example, see below, pp. 180ff.

109. Cf. Dronke's invidious comparison of Hildegard and Adam of St. Victor in his review of Szoevérffy's *Annalen, Journal of Theological Studies,* 2d ser. 17 (1966): 501, or S. Ryle's association between the regular sequence and the "assembly line" in his article on "The Sequence" (op. cit., note 84 above), p. 178.

110. An example of the *conductus:*

Christo sit
  laus in coelestibus
Consonis
  plaudite cantibus
Ecce ver
  nec eget testibus
    Teste praesenti flore,
Consonis
  plaudite cantibus
    Floris orto splendore.

Caput ver
  de terrae sedibus
Consonis
  plaudite cantibus,
Exserit
  decorum floribus
    Miro splendens nitore
Consonis
  plaudite cantibus
    Floris orto splendore.

Nostris flos
  consonat lusibus
Consonis
  plaudite cantibus
Qui suo
  dat nostris mentibus
    Laetitiam decore,
Consonis
  plaudite cantibus
    Floris orto splendore.

AH 20, no. 100, p. 93.

111. See *Iberian Hymnody*, p. 109.

112. See Anselm Hughes, ed., *Early Medieval Music up to 1300*, New Oxford History of Music, vol. 2 (Oxford, 1954), chap. 10, for a discussion of the *conductus* (on caudae and secular dance tunes, cf. pp. 334 and 337). David Hughes, "Music and Meter in Liturgical Poetry," *Medievalia et humanistica*, 2d. ser. 7 (1976): 29–49, also deals with the *conductus* (cf. pp. 33–42), identifying three major schools: Norman-Sicilian, Aquitanian, and Parisian (Notre-Dame).

113. On organization by musical type, see Hughes, p. 32; on the omission of the second half of stanzas, see Spanke, *Beziehungen*, p. 84.

114. *Iberian Hymnody*, p. 114 (introduction to lessons).

115. See for instance *Recueil* 1, no. 45, "Trois choses font une flor" (Raynaud 1985), p. 116f.

116. Cf. below, p. 125f.

117. For references and an overview of the controversy concerning the derivation of the carol (and other matters), see Rosemary Woolf, *The English Religious Lyric in the Middle Ages* (Oxford, 1968), appendix D, "The Carol."

118. Cf. Hans Spanke, "Zum Thema 'Mittelalterliche Tanzlieder,'" *NM* 33 (1932): 13.

119. On Mary-Psalters, cf. Meerssemann, *Etudes*, p. 44 (esp. n. 12); Stroppel, chap. 5, sec. 1c, pp. 143ff.; and Meersemann, *Akathistos* 2 : 3−28. An example from the end of the fifteenth century follows (only the "first fifty" are reproduced here):

Prima quinquagena

1. Ave, plasma deitatis, ab eterno preconcepta.
   Ave, arca trinitatis, ante tempus preelecta.
   Ave, virgo generosa, ab angelo presagita.
   Ave, mater gratiosa, virtutibus redimita.
5. Ave, germen prophetale, a patriarchis edita.
   Ave, genimen regale, pontificibus genita.
   Ave, in conceptu pura, carens labe primitiva.
   Ave, matrem egressura, mundo decus allativa.
   Ave, vivens in hac vita sine reprehensione.
10. Ave, velut margarita exsul a contagione.
   Ave presentata templo, ibi deo servitura.
   Ave, laudanda exemplo degens sub divina cura.
   Ave, crebro angelorum dulci colloquio freta.
   Ave, per quam mundanorum sunt gaudia spreta.
15. Ave, pie salutata alloquio archangeli.
   Ave, mire gravidata a divo rectore poli.
   Ave, per spiritum sanctum divinitus obumbrata.
   Ave, in partu, post partum et ante intemerata.
   Ave, visitans cognatam Elisabeth servitura.
20. Ave, Christum ad prophetam portans pereruditura.
   Ave, in celici partu subolis fecundissima.
   Ave, in stupendi ortu sideris letissima.
   Ave, iubilatione angelica gloriosa.
   Ave, que accessione pastorum es gaudiosa.
25. Ave, circumcisione alumni fundens sanguinem.
   Ave, que a livione fedum mundasti hominem.
   Ave, percipiens a magis munera quam largiflua.
   Ave, sublevatis plagis inopie melliflua.
   Ave, que purificaris labe carens puerpere.
30. Ave, prolem sacris aris sueto redimens munere.
   Ave, persecutione herodiana fugata.

Ave, premonitione angelica revocata.
Ave, precatura deum Ierosolymam ascendens.
Ave, duodennem natum docentem doctores cernens.
35. Ave, predicatione alumni que donis crescis.
Ave, multiplicatione fidelium hilarescis.
Ave, miraculis Christi mira affecta stupore.
Ave, ubertim fuisti eodem compta decore.
Ave, gladium doloris sacro ferens in pectore.
40. Ave, que fontem amoris ictibus cernis deficere.
Ave, mesta deficiens seculi extinxta luce.
Ave, lacrimis effluens sublato celico duce.
Ave, Christo resurgente suaviter consolata.
Ave, mortem destruente filio speificata.
45. Ave, mundum deserente redemptore gaudiosa.
Ave, celos penetrante alumno hic fastidiosa.
Ave, charisma spiritus sancti abunde hauriens.
Ave, sublimes instinctus in linguis igneis sumens.
Ave, in defunctione dolore mortis orbata.
50. Ave, in assumptione summis civibus stipata.

> Meerssemann, *Akathistos* 2:146ff. (no. 15).

120. Cf. Meerssemann, *Akathistos* 2:79–159.

121. Cf. Lydgate, no. 16, "Hauyng a conseit in my sympill wyt," p. 80, st. 11.

122. CC, vol. 1, no. 302, "Alma mya, / noche e dia, / loa la Virgen Maria," pp. 698–702, by Fernan Perez de Guzman.

123. For the French verse psalter to Christ, see Marius Valkhoff, "Le Ms 76 G 17 de la Haye et l'ancienne hymne Wallonne," *Romania* 62 (1936): 20f.; for the German verse psalter to Christ, see Wack., no. 1094, p. 884f.; for Middle English verse psalters, see Carl Horstmann, *The Minor Poems of the Vernon Manuscript*, vol. 1, EETS, orig. ser. 98 (London, 1892), poems nos. 23 and 24, pp. 49ff. and 106ff.

124. Cf. Wack., no. 1061, p. 853f.

125. An example of the tripartite-stanza structure, which is also macaronic:

> III C'est li roys de majesté
> *Splendor eterni patris*
> Qui covrit sa deïté
> *In nube claritatis;*
> *In utero virginis*
> Vesti nostre humanité
> *Ut esset passibilis.*
>
> IV Cil qui por nous vost morir
> *Caritate nimia*

De ses cieux nous vint servir
Dulcia servicia;
De patris sentencia
Vost son servise acomplir
In obediencia.

Recueil 2, "De chanter m'est pris envie," pp. 70ff., stt. 3-4.

126. Spanke, *Beziehungen*, p. 146.
127. Ibid., p. 149.
128. Le Gentil 2:15f. (bk. 1, chap. 1).
129. For examples of the *Spruch*, see below, pp. 191f., 194ff., 206 or 207f.
130. Cf. below, pp. 169f. (kontakion), and note 71 above.
131. Cf. Hans Spanke, "Das lateinische Rondeau," *Zeitschrift fuer franzoesische Sprache und Literatur* 53 (1930): 113-48. See also Spanke, *Beziehungen*, pp. 104-41, for a general discussion of use of the rondeau form in the later Middle Ages (pp. 140f. touch on the *runteli* written in Latin in Bohemia in the fourteenth and fifteenth centuries). To illustrate Abelard's use of internal and of final refrains here are two stanzas from the *Hymnary*:

Veris grato tempore
RESURREXIT DOMINUS
Mundus reviviscere
Cum iam incipit
Auctorem resurgere
Mundi decuit.

Remissionis numerum
Lux signat quinquagesima,
Quo iubilaeus omnium
Annus relaxat debita.
SUMMA SUMMO REGI
DEO SIT GLORIA,
CUIUS CUNCTA
SUBSISTUNT GRATIA,
EX QUO, PER QUEM,
IN QUO SUNT OMNIA.

The refrain lines are in upper case. From Peter Abelard, *Hymnarius*, ed. Guido M. Dreves (Leipzig, 1905), no. 61; "Veris grato tempore," st. 1, and no. 70, "Remissionis numerum," st. 1; AH 48, nos. 171 and 180, pp. 180 and 185.

132. Systematic use of refrains in Old French can be dated at least as early as 1147/1148, though (cf. Nico van den Boogaard, *Rondeaux et refrains du xiie siècle au début du xive*, Bibliothèque française et romane, Strasbourg, ser. D, no. 3 [Paris, 1969], introduction, p. 9ff.).

133. Cf. p. 142f., however.

134. For a *lauda*, see below, p. 143ff.

135. See also *Cancionero de Juan Alfonso de Baena*, ed. José M. Azáceta, 3 vols. (Madrid, 1966), nos. 317f. and 560, from the earlier part of the fifteenth century, and by Pero Veles de Guevara and Garci Ferrandes de Jerena, respectively (in Azáceta's edition, 2:691–94 and 3:1123). As a sample of the form, here is Gil Vicente's famous "Remando vão remadores":

> Remando vão remadores
> Barca de grande alegria;
> O patrão que a guiava
> Filho de Deus se dizia;
> Anjos eram os remeiros
> Que remavam á porfia;
> Estandarte d'esperança:
> Ó quam bem que parecia!
> O masto da fortaleza
> Como cristal reluzia;
> A vela com fé cosida
> Todo o mundo esclarecia.
> A ribeira mui serena
> Que nenhum vento bolia!

Vicente, no. 5, p. 10.

136. Cf. Jeffrey, p. 133f.; to the references given in Jeffrey's notes to material on medieval dancing, add Hans Spanke, "Tanzlieder in der Kirche des Mittelalters," and "Zum Thema Mittelalterlichen Tanzlieder," *NM* 31 and 33 (1930 and 1932): 143–70 and 1–22, respectively.

137. The scheme of the ballade was three times ababbcbC + bcbC; of the *chant royal*, five times ababccddedE + ddedE. Here is an illustrative ballade by Jean Brisebarre:

> Onques tant n'ama Elainne,
> Vierge royaus, com vos fils
> Ama no nature humainne,
> Quant il se fu assentis
> A paier la prophezie
> Ainsi qu'il l'avoit promis
> Par le prophète Ysaïe.
> Por ce vous et vo lignie
> De qui nasqui telz amis
> Weil servir toute ma vie.
>
> Ainsi com la tresmontainne
> Qui estoile est de haut pris,
> A droit port conduit et mainne

> Ciaulz qui par mer sont marris,
> Ainsi par vous radrecie
> Est ame cui anemis
> A de vo fil eslongie.
> Por ce, etc.
>
> Molt est courtoisie humainne:
> Quant pechieires est bannis
> De la gloire souverainne
> Qui nomée est paradis,
> Se, repentens, merci prie,
> Par vo confort est rescris
> De Dieu ou livre de vie.
> Por ce, etc.

ed. Amédée Salmon, in *Mélanges de philologie romane dédiés à Carl Wahlund . . .*
(Macon, 1896), pp. 222–23.

138. For the Vernon manuscript, see Brown XIV, nos. 95–120, pp. 125–308.

139. Cf. note 163 below.

140. On the *leich/lai*, see *Gattungen* (J. Maillard, "Lai, Leich"), pp. 323–45; for references to further literature, see p. 337 n. 49.

141. *Gattungen*, p. 340.

142. See "Orientations" for German and the entry for *leich* in the glossary.

143. Cf. below, p. 179f.

144. *The Lay of Our Lady*, trans. Adolf E. Kroeger (St. Louis, 1877) (dedicated to H. W. Longfellow).

145. See also Gautier de Coincy, ed. Långfors, no. 32, "Mere de pitié," pp. 532–36, and no. 33, "Ne flours ne glais," pp. 536–38, and Thibaut de Champagne, *Les chansons de Thibaut de Champagne*, ed. Alex Wallenskjoeld, SATF 70 (Paris, 1925), no. 61, "Conmencerai / A fere un lai," pp. 214–17.

146. *Gattungen*, p. 343.

147. Cf. Le Gentil 1 : 321–24. For a full dress *glosa*, cf. the following, by Tapia:

> *Copla esparsa de Tapia al duque de*
> *Medina Celi, porque le mando glosar*
> *esta cancion siguiente.*
>
> Gran Señor, muy mas real
> que los reyes mas reales,
> cuya virtud da señal
> quel loor debe ser tal,
> pues que sus obras son tales:

mando vuestra señoria
que glossase esta cancion
hecha ala Virgen Maria,
a quien ternes cada dia
por amparo y defension
por vuestra gran deuocion.

LA CANCION DIZE:

Oyga tu merced y crea,
ay de quien nunca te vido!
ombre que tu gesto vea
nunca puede ser perdido.

Pues tu vista me saluo,
cesse tu saña tan fuerte;
pues que, Señora, de muerte
tu figura me libro,
bien dira qualquier que sea,
sin temor de ser vencido:
ombre que tu gesto vea
nunca puede ser perdido.

LA GLOSA

Corona delas mejores
de quien el cielo se arrea;
esfuerço de mis temores,
ala boz de mis dolores
oyga tu merced y crea
que dira con amargura
qualquier que fuere nascido,
no viendo tu hermosura,
con dolor, lloro y tristura:
ay de quien nunca te vido!

Pues crea quien te a mirado
y sepa quien lo dessea,
que no sera condennado,
lastimado ni penado,
ombre que tu gesto vea:
por que viendo la presencia
de tu ser tan infinido,
y esperando la clemencia
del rayo de su excellencia,
nunca puede ser perdido.

Pues, alta reyna del cielo,
madre de quien te crio,

de mi tristeza consuelo,
ninguna cosa recelo,
pues tu vista me saluo:
pues para mi, pecador,
que alcançe de poder verte,
piedad te pido, amor,
que al tiempo de mi dolor
cesse tu saña tan fuerte.

Virgen despues de parida,
parida sin corromperte,
madre de Dios escogida,
reparadora de vida,
pues que señora de muerte:
plegate ser piadosa
del triste que no te vio,
pues por mi dicha gozosa,
dela muerte peligrosa
tu figura me libro.

Pues casa santificada
do mi espiritu recrea,
de mano de Dios labrada,
llamandote consagrada,
bien dira qualquier que sea:
y pues eres por quien fue
todo el mundo socorrido,
tu eres a quien dire
reparo de nuestra fe,
sin temor de ser vencido.

CC, vol. 2, no. 831, p. 460.

148. The analogous practice in Middle High German had one poet propose a riddle or "bispel" and challenge another to unriddle it (cf. a *Spruchdichter* like Regenbogen).

149. Cf. p. 193, below, for an example (in excerpt). See Salvator Tosti,
"Due laudi francescane del 300 e un Ternario del 400," *Archivum francis-
canum historicum* 8 (1915): 342–45; Giuseppe Ferraro, ed. *Raccolta di sacre
poesie popolari fatta di Giovanni Pellegrini nel 1446*, Scelta di curiosità, no.
152 (Bologna, 1877), pp. 77–83 (by Pellegrini); Bianco da Siena, *Il Bianco
da Siena; notizie e testi inediti*, Franca Ageno, Biblioteca della "Rassegna"
24 (Genoa/ Rome/ Naples, 1939), nos. 96–98 and 105–8; and Bianco da
Siena, ed. Bini, nos. 65–72 (Penitential Psalms), 59, 62, 64, and 92; Pagliaresi (op. cit., note 31 above), pp. 199–215; Feo Belcari, *Sacre rappresentazioni e laude*, ed. Onorato Allocco-Castellino, Collezione di Classichi Ital-

iani, vol. 13 (Turin, 1926), p. 84; Lorenzo de' Medici, *Scritti scelti*, ed. Emilio Bigi, 2d ed. (Turin, 1965), pp. 89–107; Adolfo Bartoli, ed., *I Manoscritti italiani della Biblioteca nazionale di Firenze*, vol. 1: *Codici Magliabecchiani: Poesie* (Florence, 1879), pp. 15, 17, 21, and 379 (incipits and brief description of *ternari* in various manuscripts); Roberto Tissoni, "Un ternario inedito attribuibile al Bianco de Siena . . . ," *Giornale storico della letteratura italiana* 147 (1970): 367–90 (text on pp. 369–74; probably not by Bianco, in my opinion); Giustinian, item nos. 25, pp. [fiv]-gi[v], and 27f., pp. qiii[v]-hi (the latter two poems lack rhyme linking between tercets); Galletti, nos. 6, 7, 307, and 407 (pp. 4, by Belcari; 148f., anon.; and 287, by Belcari).

150. See Arthur Askins, ed. *The Cancioneiro de Evora*, University of California Publications in Modern Philology 74 (Berkeley, 1965), poem no. 63, pp. 56–64.

151. A typical fifteenth-century religious sonnet, perhaps by Giustinian:

> O sum[m]a sapie[n]tia: che tuto governi
> Cio chel ciel: e la terra i[n] se co[n]clude
> De no[n] guardar[e] ale n[ost]re op[er]e crude
> Ma vogili a nui de gratia li ochi eterni
> Ritien del corso dei cieli superni:
> Che le tue zente e nele gran palude
> De guerra lassi e dogni pace ignude
> Tu solo dio la verita discerni
> Padre merce: per lo tuo caro verbo:
> Che per aprire la beata strada
> In su la croce gusto aceto acerbo
> Manda langelo tuo: manda la spada:
> Che tagli: e vinca ogni valor superbo
> Si che in abysso ogni malicia cada.
>
> Giustinian, pp. ciiii - [cv[R]].

152. Cf. below, pp. 127ff.

153. In Latin, monosyllabic "rhyme" involves either an unstressed syllable or a syllable receiving only secondary stress (with rare exceptions when the last word in a line is also a monosyllable). This is because the primary stress cannot fall on the final syllable in Latin polysyllabic words. To obtain a fully stressed syllable in rhyme position, one must therefore resort to disyllabic rhyme between feminine verse endings. Monosyllabic rhyme:

> Clausae parentis víscerà
> caelestis intrat grátià
>
> (vv. 9f. of "A solis ortus cardine")

Disyllabic rhyme:

> Verbum bonum et suáve
> personemus illud *Áve*

Of course, disyllabic rhyme may also involve masculine endings, but note how much weaker the effect of the masculine rhyme is compared to that of the feminine rhyme in the last stanza of Adam of St. Victor's "Heri mundus exsultavit":

> Martyr, cuius est iucúndum
> nomen in ecclésià,
> languescentem fove múndum
> caelesti fragrántià.

154. On the complex terminological evolution that lies behind the word *rhyme* (and on the history of rhyme and rhythm in late antiquity and the Middle Ages), see Zumthor, *Langue*, "Du rhythme à la rime," pp. 125–41.

155. Northrop Frye, *Anatomy of Criticism* (New York, 1966), p. 294, acutely observes that

> In religious poetry with elaborate stanzaic patterns . . . we realize that the discipline of finding rhymes and arranging words in intricate patterns is appropriate to the sense of chastened wit, a type of *sacrificium intellectus*, that goes with the form. Such intricate verbal patterns go back through the acrostics of Aldhelm at the very beginning of poetry in England to the Hebrew psalms themselves.

156. Cf. Hughes (op. cit., note 112 above), pp. 381ff.

157. Cf. Carl Appel, "Zur Formenlehre des provenzalischen Minnesangs," *Zeitschrift fuer romanische Philologie* 53 (1933): 170.

158. See especially Friedrich Gennrich, "Zu den Melodien Wizlavs von Ruegen," *Zeitschrift fuer deutsches Altertum* 80 (1943): 86–102 (cf. p. 100: "Like the melody the text of many poems also develops from a single cell"), or Christoph Petzsch, "Text-Form-Korrespondenzen im mittelalterlichen Strophenlied," *Deutsche Vierteljahrsschrift fuer Literaturgeschichte* 41 (1967): 27–60.

159. Cf. Juri Lotman, *Analysis of the Poetic Text*, trans. D. Barton Johnson (Ann Arbor, 1976), pp. 37ff. ("Belletristic Repetition") and introduction, pp. xviiff.

160. See Liu Hsieh, *The Literary Mind and the Carving of Dragons*, trans. Vincent Shih (New York, 1959), "Linguistic Parallelism," pp. 190–94. I owe this reference to a remarkable text from ca. A.D. 500 to a graduate student in the Department of Comparative Literature at Berkeley, David Liu.

161. Cited in Eduard Norden, *Agnostos Theos* (reprint, Stuttgart, 1956), p. 174; other terms include *eulogia*, *aretalogia*, and *doxologia* (cf. Liver [op. cit., note 1, chapter 1], p. 205f.; for further discussion of anaphora in medi-

eval lyrics, see pp. 297ff., where Liver claims that the thirteenth-century
finds structural use of anaphora as a marker of regular units at its peak).
   162. See the texts collected in Meerssemann, *Akathistos*, for example.
   163. An example from the Pisa *laudario*:

> D'amor non faccia uista,
> che non poria neente
> chi non-na nella-mente|
> giouanni evangelista.|

Fol. 146ʳ.

1. 5. Come poria sentire
gioia d'amor alcuna| |
cui non fusse ad-gradire
lo-datore che| la don(n)a
che nulla cosa e buona
10. s'a|mor nolla notrica
et amor non (a)e mica|
sensa l'euangelista.|

2. Addunqua chi-diçia
d'amor sentir| dolcessa
15. conuien che in-lui sia
humilita| *et* pianessa

et fede con-fermessa
la-mente necta| *et* pura
del-prossimo auer cura
20. come l'evangelista.|

3. E solo fu dilecto
di-cristo nominato
alla| cena in-sul-pecto
li-fu addormentato
25. allor| chierse il-beato
uidde la trinitade
di-don| di-caritade
fu pien l'euangelista.|

Erik Staff, *Le Laudario de Pise*, vol. 1, Humanistiska Vetenskaps-Samfundet i Uppsala,
   Skrifter 27, no. 1 (Uppsala, 1931), no. 83, pp. 212–13, stt. 1–3.

   164. Cf. Friedrich Gennrich, "Die musikalischen Formen des mittelalterlichen Liedes," *Der Deutschunterricht* 11, no. 2 (1959): 73.
   165. German: Wack, nos. 472, 474, 514, 518, and Monk of Salzburg
(op. cit., note 11, introduction), G. 12 ("Maria, pis gegrusset"). French:
Chrestomathie de l'ancien français, ed. Karl Bartsch, rev. Adolf Horning,
7th ed. (Leipzig, 1891), coll. 393–96; Provençal: Carl Mahn, ed., *Die
Gedichte der Troubadours*, 4 vols. (Berlin, 1856–73), p. 4f. (no. 7); Por-

tuguese: Vicente, no. 3, "Quem he a desposada?" Spanish: CM, nos. 305 and 309. Catalan: Aguiló y Fuster (op. cit., note 40, chapter 1), "Cançoneret" from Lluch de Majorca (item 12 under "Poesies religioses"), poem 100, "Puix en l'altura." Middle English: Brown XIV, no. 101, pp. 143ff., vv. 1 and 179ff. (See also pp. 147f. below.) John of Howden, *Philomena*, ed. Clemens Blume, Hymnologische Beitraege 4 (Leipzig, 1930), stt. 1 and 1131 (p. 3 and p. 87); see also Adam of St. Victor, no. 34, pp. 212ff., and no. 31, pp. 194ff.; and Aquinas, "Lauda Sion" for borderline cases. John Mauropus, *Johannis Euchaitorum Metropolitae quae in codice vaticano graeco 676 supersunt*, ed. Paul de Lagarde, Gesellschaft der Wissenschaft, Goettingen, historisch-philologische Klasse, Abhandlungen 28 (1881), no. 92, vv. 1 and 105ff. repeat the Greek word for storm.

166. *Le Troubadour Folquet de Marseille*, ed. Stanislaw Strónski (Cracow, 1910), p. 35. Cf. also Bertran de Born, "Puois lo gens terminis floritz," vv. 10–12, in *Introduction à l'étude de l'ancien provençal*, ed. Frank Hamlin, Peter Ricketts, and John Hathaway (Geneva, 1967), p. 78.

167. *Also sprach Zarathustra*, Goldmanns gelbe Taschenbuecher 403 (Munich, n.d.), p. 72.

168. Cf. notes 124, 130, and 136 above.

169. See Arthur Walpole, *Early Latin Hymns* (Cambridge, 1922), pp. 316–19 (also AH 2, no. 33, p. 41, or AH 27, no. 19, pp. 74 and 34, where Blume discusses the relatively wide distribution of this hymn).

170. Cf. Alfred Jeanroy and Artur Långfors, eds., *Chansons satiriques et bachiques*, Classiques français du moyen âge 23 (Paris, 1921), p. 84 (cf. p. 132. appendix).

171. Cf. Helgason, 2:195–199, "Haestur heilagu andi."

172. See Le Gentil 2:259ff. (Chap. 3).

173. Hildegard von Bingen, *Lieder*, ed. Pudentiana Barth, Immaculata Ritscher, and Joseph Schmidt-Goerg (Salzburg, 1969), p. 262 (no. 42).

174. Cf. note 119 above.

175. For Audradus Modicus, see PLAC 3:67ff. and 738ff. and also Ludwig Traube, Akademie der Wissenschaft, Bavaria, Abhandlungen 19:374ff., and Augusto Gaudenzi, *Bollettino dell'instituto storico italiano* 7 (1889): 39–45. For Sedulius Scottus, see *Liber de rectoribus christianis*, ed. Siegmund Hellmann, in *Sedulius Scottus*, Quellen und Untersuchungen zur lateinischen Philologie des Mittelalters 1:1 (Munich, 1906), pp. 19–91.

176. See Dag Norberg, *Introduction à l'étude de la versification latine médiévale*, Studia latina stockholmiensia 5 (Stockholm, 1958), p. 63.

177. See *Annalen* 2:212ff., where the following series of hymn *incipits* appears as the final lines of an eight-stanza hymn:

1. Christe, redemptor omnium,
2. Exsultet coelum laudibus,

3. Aeterna Christi munera,
4. Summae Deus clementiae,
5. Vexilla regis prodeunt,
6. Jam lucis orto sidere,
7. Beata nobis gaudia,
8. Ad coenam agni providi.

178. Cf. Raby, *Oxford*, no. 196, "Propter Sion non tacebo," p. 284, vv. 82–84, by Walter of Châtillon, or no. 206, "Prosa asini," p. 307ff., refrain.

179. Cf. AH 21, no. 7, "Christicola, recordare," p. 16ff.

180. The dialects of French and Middle English are, respectively, southern Picard and London with Kentish features; cf. Richard Kienast, "Die deutschsprachige Lyrik des Mittelalters," in *Deutsche Philologie im Aufriss*, ed. Wolfgang Stammler, 2d ed., vol. 2 (Berlin, 1960), col. 125. The first stanza illustrates the pattern:

> Ave alpha du stercher god!
> Je diroy volentiers un mot
> Of *that* swete *ladi deer*,
> Cuius venter te portavit.
> Ich meyn miin vrou dye alrebest,
> Qui dam de toutes dammes est.
> Thye in yr blisset woomb *shy* beer
> Et te dulci lacte pavit
> Et tam ardenter te amavit,
> Daz ir myn dich cund neder zeen.
> Thier thu ars kinc schol se bi queen,
> La noble *fillie* dou roye Davit.

Bruder Hongers Marienlieder, ed. Michael Batts, Altdeutsche Textbibliothek 58
(Tuebingen, 1963), p. 1.

181. Oswald von Wolkenstein, *Die Lieder* . . . , ed. K. Klein, Altdeutsche Textbibliothek 55 (Tuebingen, 1962), no. 69, "Do fraig amors," pp. 189–92; cf. also the *descort* in five languages by Raimbaut de Vaqueiras. Oswald von Wolkenstein surpassed this demonstration a few years later with a secular poem incorporating even more languages.

182. Pero Martines, no. 10, "Clare Thomas, doctor sancte, del orde precador," pp. 131–34.

183. A Spanish example of a Salve Regina gloss by Tapia, where the Latin phrases tend to open the stanzas but also appear within the body of the stanza:

> Salue, regina escogida
> para ser reyna del cielo,
> *ab initio* establescida,
> de Dio padre elegida

> para ser nuestro consuelo.
> Yo que ningun bien espero
> sino por tu intercession,
> te demando que al Cordero
> tu Hijo, Dios verdadero,
> presentes mi peticion.
>
> *Vita, dulcedo,* esperança
> delos tristes aflegidos;
> templo de gran alabança,
> consolacion y holgança
> delos santos escogidos.
> Reyna de tanta virtud,
> yo te suplico, Señora,
> pues peque en juuentud,
> que por ti aya salud
> la mi alma pecadora.
>
> *Ostende, o clemens! o pia!*
> llena de toda virtudes,
> *o dulcis* siempre Maria!
> Por tal carrera nos guia,
> Señora, que nos ayudes
> a uenir al perdurable
> reyno que nunca fallesce.
> O madre muy honorable!
> plegate ser consolable
> a mi alma que peresce.

CC, vol. 2, no. 832, pp. 461—62, stt. 1, 3, and 11.

184. Helgason 2:269f.

185. Cf. Lydgate, no. 58, "O thow ioyfull lyght! eternall ye shyne," pp. 294f.; Helgason 2:261; and *Recueil* 2, no. 81, pp. 69—74.

186. Cf. Wack, no. 480, p. 317, st. 22, and Paul Meyer, "Les manuscrits français de Cambridge," *Romania* 32 (1901): 22f. (the English stanzas paraphrase the French).

187. Cf. Zumthor, *Masque,* p. 166.

188. Cf. Garcia de Resende, *Cancioneiro Geral,* ed. Eduard von Kausler, 3 vols., Bibliothek des literarischen Vereins, vols. 15, 17, and 26 (Stuttgart, 1846—52), 2:252ff. (Luis Anriquez, on Ave Maris Stella); Vicente, no. 21 "A ti, dono de adorar," p. 48 (paraphrase of the Te Deum); and *Cançons nadalenques,* appendix 3, pp. 168—70 (farced Marian sequence), "Verbum caro factum est."

189. Brown XIII, no. 178, p. 26ff. (thirteenth century):

> Of on that is so fair and bright,
> Velud maris stella,

> Brighter than the dayes light,
> Parens et puella:
> Ic crye to thee—thou se to me—
> Levedy, preye thy sone for me,
> Tam pia,
> That ic mote come to thee,
> Maria.

190. Cf. Helgason 2:26–28, 240–42, 251–54, 259–61, 269f., and *Skjaldedigtning* B.2, "Páter ertu ok princeps feiti," p. 496. See also Lehmann (op. cit., note 102 above), pt. 2, pp. 60–64.

191. Cf. *Recueil* 2, no. 81, "De chanter m'est pris envie."

192. Hoffman von Fallersleben's monograph on "Mischpoesie" in his *Geschichte des deutschen Kirchenlieds* is concerned mostly with postmedieval developments. William Wehrle, *The Macaronic Hymn Tradition in Medieval English Literature* (Washington, D.C., 1933) needs to be superseded. The opportunity is there for anyone who will seize it.

193. On the tradition of the Joys of Mary, see Meerssemann, *Akathistos* 2:33–43, and "Von den Freuden Mariens . . . ," in *Lebendiges Mittelalter; Festgabe fuer Wolfgang Stammler* (Freiburg, 1958), pp. 79–100. See also Woolf (op. cit., note 117 above), chaps. 4 and 8, and Sarah Weber, *Theology and Poetry in the Middle English Lyrics: A Study of Sacred History and Aesthetic Form* (Columbus, Ohio, 1969), pt. 2.

194. AH 31, no. 189, p. 198ff.

195. Meerssemann, *Akathistos* 2:190–213; Franz J. Mone, ed., *Lateinische Hymnen des Mittelalters*, 3 vols. (Freiburg im Breisgau, 1853–55), vol. 2, nos. 453–66, pp. 160–80; AH 31, nos. 170–94, pp. 170–203.

196. Cf. AH 31, nos. 165–69, pp. 171–75.

197. Suchier, pp. 272–83, and 295ff.

198. CG, vol. 2, appendix, p. 344ff., by Salazar (1540 ed.); Menéndez y Pelayo 6: ccxxxvi (in Juan de Luzón, *Cancionero*, 1508); Gonzalo de Berceo, *Obras completas*, ed. R. Briones (Logroño, 1971), "De los signos . . . ," pp. 296–98, stt. 48ff.

199. Cf. *Skjaldedigtning* B.2, "Máríugrátr," pp. 516–18, stt. 41–47, and Helgason 2:61f., stt. 8ff.; 2:56, stt. 20–24; 2:65f., stt. 9ff.; 2:68f, stt. 4–12; 2:71f., stt. 4–9; and 2:73ff., stt. 3ff.

200. Cf. *Cantigas*, no. 1.

201. On secular use of enumerative composition, an article by Jean Batany, "Paradigmes lexicaux et structures littéraires au Moyen Age," *Revue d'histoire littéraire de la France* 70, no. 5/6 (1970): 830–35 (sec. 2), is particularly interesting. There is a considerable literature on "enumerative composition," especially in German, where it is known as *Zahlenkomposition*. For bibliography, one may consult Theo Stemmler, "Interpretation des mittelenglischen Gedichtes *God þat al þis myhtes may*," Anglia 82 (1964):

63f. n. 12; Edmund Reiss, "Number Symbolism and Medieval Literature,"
Medievalia et Humanistica 2d ser. 1 (1971): 169–74, and Heinz Rupp, "Zu
Form und Bau mittelalterlicher Dichtung," *Deutschunterricht* 11 (1959):
117–24 (esp. p. 117). Recent books on the subject include [Ian] Christo-
pher Butler, *Number Symbolism* (London, 1970), and Alistair Fowler, ed.
Silent Poetry: Essays in Numerological Analysis (London, 1970). Tony
Hunt, "The Structure of Medieval Narrative," *Journal of European Studies*
3, no. 4 (1973): 295–328, includes a discussion of Eleanor Bulatkin's *Structural Arithmetic Metaphor in the Oxford 'Roland'* (1972), in which the author lays down some useful guidelines for numerical analysis. Friedrich
Ohly, "Der Prolog des St. Trudperter Hohenliedes," *Zeitschrift fuer deutsches Altertum und Wissenschaft*, 84 (1952/1953): 198–232, suggests that
we look for proportions rather than numbers in isolation. Von Moos (op.
cit., note 19, chapter 1), p. 331, cites St. Augustine, *De Trinitate* 4.6.10 (PL,
vol. 42, col. 895): "Different people will arrive at different views on the reasons for these numbers, but no one would be so foolish and absurd as to
argue that they were set down without purpose" (*Et horum quidem nume-
rorum causas . . . potest alius alias indagare, frustra tamen eos esse positos
nemo tam stultus ineptusque contenderit*). One wishes modern scholars
were always as diffident about the exclusive validity of their numerological
conclusions, realizing that (as Augustine's remark shows) medieval interpre-
ters looked to numerology for edification rather than scientific fact. Finally,
the most accessible, and most fundamental, text on the subject remains Excursus xv, "Numerical Composition," in Ernst R. Curtius, *European Literature and the Latin Middle Ages*, trans. Willard Trask (New York, 1963),
pp. 501–9.

202. Six stanzas is the standard length of the poems written for a competition and included in the 1540 edition of the *Cancionero general* (cf. CG,
vol. 2, no. 94, p. 353, by Pedro Navarro, l. 6f.: "En seys coplas no hiziera /
ni en seys mil, obra tan digna . . ." [I would not create so worthy a work *in
six stanzas* or in six thousand], and there are other instances of such special
cases).

203. Sedulius's hymn "A solis ortus cardine" is a well-known, early
(fifth-century) Latin example; see Bulst (op. cit., note 11, chapter 1), pp. 71ff.

204. On Latin acrostics, see Norberg (op. cit., note 176 above), pp. 53–
57; on Greek, see Karl Krumbacher, *Geschichte der byzantinischen Literatur*, 2d ed., Handbuch der klassischen Altertumswissenschaft 9 : 1 (Munich,
1897), pp. 697–700, and Wilhelm Weyh, "Die Akrostichis in der byzantinischen Kanonesdichtung," *Byzantinische Zeitschrift* 17 (1908): pp. 1–
69. On the Hebrew and Syrian background, cf. Anton Baumstark, *Liturgie
comparée* (Paris, 1953), pp. 123–26. On the pagan acrostics in the Anthologia palatina, bk. 9, no. 52ff. (to Dionysios and Apollo, ca. A.D. 500),

pp. 320–24f, see Albrecht Dieterich, "ABC-Denkmaeler," *Rheinisches Museum*, 3d ser. 56 (1901): 77–105.

205. On ABC's, see Walther Lipphardt and Heinrich Schauerte, "Abecedarius," in *Lexikon der Marienkunde*, ed. Konrad K. Algermissen, Ludwig Böer, Carl Feckes, and Julius Tyciak, vol. 1 (Regensburg, 1957), pp. 17–19, and references to "abecedarius" and "akrostichon" in the indexes to *Annalen* 1 and 2.

206. For an especially elaborate acrostic, itself a piece of quantitative verse, cf. note 81 above.

207. Exceptions include AH 52, p. 44; AH 27, pp. 169–71 and 186–88 (both Mozarabic); and AH 46, pp. 169–71—as well as Carolingian *carmina quadrata*, of course.

208. Cf. Zumthor, *Essai*, chap. 3, p. 142.

209. Cf. Le Gentil 1:189 (n. 280 deals with French and Italian acrostics also).

210. Cf. CC, vol. 1, no. 161, p. 448.

211. Cf. Lydgate, no. 63, p. 303, stt. 15–17, or Brown XV, no. 31, p. 55f.

212. Cf. Bianco da Siena, ed. Bini, nos. 46 and 54.

213. Cf. Monk of Salzburg (op. cit., note 11, introduction), G.2 and G.3, pp. 125–32, and Wack., no. 1052, p. 838f.

214. Cf. Spanke, *Beziehungen*, p. 14f.

215. Respectively, AH 21, no. 50, p. 41; AH 20, no. 247, p. 185f.; and Spanke, *Beziehungen*, p. 14f.

216. Cf. Helgason 1.2:58, st. 89f., and also the "moral" poem, *Skjaldedigtning* B.2, p. 182f., st. 12.

217. Cf. Faria, *Antologia de poesias religiosas desde o seculo xv* . . . (Lisbon, 1947), p. 49, "Oh Verbo divino."

218. Cf. *Cançons nadalenques*, no. 29, pp. 135–38; *Cançoner dels Masdovelles* (*Manuscrit n° 11 de la Biblioteca de Catalunya*), ed. R. Aramón i Serra (Barcelona, 1938), no. 174, p. 250ff.; and Grajales "Sou Vos sens par / verge dona polída" [pp. 38–40; unpaginated, diplomatic text].

219. Cf. Theo Stemmler, "Interpretation des mittelenglischen Gedichtes God þat al þis myhtes may," *Anglia* 82 (1964): 61ff.

220. Cf. Brown XIII, nos. 65 and 75, pp. 124ff. and 134–36, or Brown XIV, no. 6, pp. 3–7.

221. Cf. Guiraut Riquier, *Las Cansos*, ed. Ulrich Moelk, Studia romanica 2 (Heidelberg, 1962), nos. 10 and 25, pp. 57–61 and 111–13; Riquier, ed. Pfaff, nos. 24 and 48. See also *Les "Coblas" ou les poésies lyriques provençocatalanes de Jacme, Pere et Arnau March*, ed. Amédée Pagès (Toulouse, 1949), pp. 124–32 (Arnau March, no. 6, "Un novell fruyt"); and Suchier, pp. 214–40 ("Dona Santa Maria, flors de virginitat").

222. Cf. Le Gentil 2:169ff. (bk. 3, chap. 1).

223. Cf. Jacopone, no. 90, "La Fede e la Speranza"; "Laudi cortonese del secolo xiii," ed. Guido Mazzoni, *Propugnatore*, n.s. 2 (1889) (= vol. 22): 205–70, and n.s. 3 (1890) (= vol. 23): 5–48, nos. 1, 24, 28, 34, 36, 42f.; E. Staff (op. cit., note 163 above), nos. 6, 17, 19, 33, 43, 46, 50, 53, 57 (well-used in this poem), 63, 68, 74, 95; Bianco da Siena, ed. Bini, nos. 1, 4–7, 12, 23, 24.4ff., 25.1–5, 26, 28.1–7, and others (and most of the *laude* reprinted by Monti). There are only half a dozen examples in the more than five hundred *laude* collected in Galletti, which by and large date from the fifteenth century.

224. Cf. note 183 above.

225. Cf. Marie Koch, "An Analysis of the Long Prayers in Old French Literature with Special Reference to the 'Biblical-Creed-Narrative' Prayers" (Ph.D. diss., Catholic University, 1940), bibliography of general works, pp. 193–97; see also Grégoire Lozinski [= Grigorii L. Lozinskii], "Recherches sur les sources du *Credo* de Joinville," *NM* 31 (1930): 170–231, and Francesco di Capua, "Preghiere liturgiche, poesia, ed eloquenza," *Archivo italiano per la storia della pietà* 1 (1951): 1–24, esp. p. 10. Like their model, imitations of the *commendatio animae* may ignore the chronological order of the events they commemorate—cf. Stroppel, p. 122; Dimitri Scheludko, "Ueber die religioese Lyrik der Troubadours," *NM* 38 (1937): 230; or Joaquín Gimeno Casalduero, "Sobre la 'oración narrativa' medieval: estructura, origin, supervivencia," *Anales de la Universidad de Murcia: Filosofía y Letras* 16, nos. 1–2 (1957–58): 117ff.

226. Beissel (op. cit., note 8 above), p. 99; cited in Stroppel, p. 157ff. See also Brinkmann (op. cit., note 8, chapter 1), p. 53, where the author cites Caesarius of Heisterbach's comparison of prayer to God and petition to a great man (*salutatio, commendatio, postulatio*), and the medieval *artes dictaminis* (discussed in James J. Murphy, *Rhetoric in the Middle Ages* [Berkeley, 1974], chap. 5, pp. 194–268, esp. 221–23). A rhetoric of prayer by William of Auvergne, the *Rhetorica divina*, is cited and briefly discussed in Harry Caplan, "Classical Rhetoric and Medieval Theory of Preaching," *Journal of Classical Philology* 38, no. 2 (Apr. 1933): 76ff.

227. Here the fundamental book is Barbara H. Smith, *Poetic Closure: A Study of How Poems End* (Chicago, 1968); though the author does not discuss medieval texts, my treatment of closure is much indebted to her work.

228. On the lack of true endings in medieval texts, see Lotman, *Structure*, chap. 8, where there is also a valuable discussion of beginnings; on the "openness" of the medieval text, see Zumthor, *Essai*, pp. 70–74, especially the phrase on p. 73 that precisely states the case "incomplétude virtuelle" (potential incompleteness).

229. *Terminal modification* is a term coined by Barbara H. Smith ([op.

cit., note 227 above], p. 53) for that alteration of pattern at the end of a poem that signals its conclusion and makes it seem "right" to the reader; the most obvious analogies are musical (cf. a slackening of tempo, or a shift from running counterpoint to block chords, at the end of a piece). An example from medieval religious lyric would be the alteration of stanza length that certain writers of regular sequences introduce toward the end of their poems.

230. Cf. Smith (op. cit., note 227 above), pp. 131–39, and Raymond Oliver, *Poems Without Names* (Berkeley, 1970), chap. 6.

231. On *do ut des*, see Heiler (op. cit., note 6, chapter 1), pp. 71–80 and 483; he also discusses argument and prayer on pp. 80–89 and 372–78.

232. AH 50, no. 198, p. 193, stt. 3–6.

233. Brown XIII, no. 41, p. 67, vv. 53–56.

234. Adam of St. Victor, no. 2, pp. 34–36, stt. 4–6.

235. *Early English Carols*, ed. Richard L. Greene (Oxford, 1935), no. 175A, p. 131ff.

236. Auguste Scheler, ed., *Trouvères belges du xiie au xive siècle* (Brussels, 1876), p. 212ff., vv. 214–37 of "uns dis sor les .V. lettres de Marie."

237. Bartsch (op. cit., note 44 above), no. 40, pp. 222–27.

238. On poetic plot, see Lotman (op. cit., note 159 above), pp. 103–6, and idem, *Structure*, chap. 8.

NOTES TO CHAPTER 3

1. See the monographs listed above, chapter 1, notes 1, 3, 5, 6 and 8.

2. See the Select Bibliography for Latin in the "Orientations."

3. Wack., no. 214, "Das erste leit das erste wip," st. 7 speaks of King David's "sprueche und getihte" (i.e., as examples of contemporary genres of Middle High German poetry). This is only a particularly graphic example of how close medieval writers felt themselves to be to the Bible, and thus, of how open they were to its influence.

4. The possible influence of the rhetoric of documents has already been noted; see above, p. 120ff. and note 226, chapter 2.

5. Cf. Annette Georgi, *Das lateinische und deutsche Preisgedicht des Mittelalters in der Nachfolge des genus demonstrativum*, Philologische Studien und Quellen 48 (Berlin, 1969), p. 13ff., discussing the Rhetorica ad Herennium 3.6.11.

6. Zumthor, *Langue*, p. 92.

7. Cf. *The New Catholic Encyclopedia*, vol. 14 (New York, 1967), "The Week's Other Days," p. 842 [by Josef A. Jungmann]. The proliferation of votive masses leads to the dedication of the various days of the week to particular sacred occasions or persons (e.g., Sunday to the Father or to the

Archangel Michael; Monday to the Son or John the Baptist or the dead; Tuesday to the Holy Spirit or to the Angels; Wednesday to the Apostles; Friday to the Passion; Saturday to Mary).

8. A set of hymns by Odilo, abbot of Cluny (d. 1048), printed in AH 50, nos. 232–35, pp. 299–301, on St. Maiolus illustrates how formalistic use of apostrophe can be; the first hymn is in the third person, save for the doxology; the second apostrophizes Christ; the third apostrophizes the saint; the fourth again apostrophizes Christ. Clearly, the nature of the addressee, or even the existence of the addressee, is of only superficial moment in this truly "rhetorical" use of rhetoric.

9. Cf. Brown XIV, no. 59, p. 8off., l. 21ff., or no. 65, p. 83ff., l. 10; and Greene (op. cit., note 235, chapter 2), no. 81A, p. 51ff., st. 9.

10. Jacopone, no. 32, pp. 85–90, esp. vv. 139ff.

11.

Τί τοῦτο; φῶς ἤστραψεν ὡς ἐξ αἰθέρος,
ἀὴρ δὲ μεστὸς μουσικῆς συμφωνίας·
πρόσσχωμεν ὡς μάθωμεν. ὦ μυστηρίου·
παρεμβολή τις ἀγγέλων κράζει μέγα,
,θεῷ 'λέγουσα ,δόξα τῷ σαρκουμένῳ'·
,καὶ πῶς θεὸς σάρξ; ποῦ τὸ θαῦμα, καὶ πόθεν;
τὸ θαῦμα ποῦ; βάδιζε σὺν τοῖς ποιμέσιν·
ἐκεῖ γὰρ αὐτοῖς ὡς ὁρᾷς ἠπειγμένοις
καταφρόνησις γίγνεται τῶν θρεμμάτων·
τούτοις συνελθὼν ἐμφοροῦ μοι τοῦ πόθου.
ἄντρον θεωρεῖς, ἄντρον ἠμελημένον·
ἐν ᾧ φάτνη τις καὶ βρέφος καὶ παρθένος·
οὐκοῦν θεὸς σὸς τοῦτο τὸ βραχὺ βρέφος·
,θεὸς πένης; ἄοικος; ἐν φαύλῳ ῥάκει;
εἰς φῶς προελθὼν ἄρτι; φεῦ, τί μοι λέγεις;΄
ψεῦδος μὲν οὐδὲν ἀλλ᾽ ἀληθῆ μανθάνεις·
καὶ μάρτυς ἀστὴρ ὄν κατ᾽ οὐρὰνὸν βλέπεις,
ἐκεῖθεν ἦκον τὸ βρέφος σοι δεικνύων,
οὗτοί τε, συντρέχοντες ὡς πρὸς δεσπότην,
ὧν καὶ τὸ τερπνὸν ᾆσμα τῆς εὐφημίας,
οἷς συμμελῳδεῖν, οὐκ ἀπιστεῖν σε πρέπον·
εἰς γὰρ χάριν σὴν ταῦτα πάντα συντρέχει—
θεὸς βροτωθείς, ὡς θεώσῃ σὴν φύσιν·
πένης ὑπὲρ σοῦ, πλούσιον σέ δεικνύων·
ἐπικροτοῦντες ἄγγελοι ταῖς ἐλπίσι·
μήτηρ ἄνανδρος· παρθένος βρεφοτρόφος.
μάγων τὰ λαμπρὰ δῶρα· ποιμένων δρόμος·
χαρᾶς τὰ πάντα μεστὰ καὶ θυμηδίας·
τούτοις μὲν οὖν σύγχαιρε καὶ συμπροσκύνει.
ἔα δὲ τόνδε τὸν κατηφῆ πρεσβύτην·

δάκνει γὰρ αὐτὸν ἄλλο τι κρυπτὸν πάθος.
ἕξει δὲ τούτου μικρὸν ὑπνώσας λύσιν,
καὶ συγκροτήσει πᾶσιν ἡμῖν ἡδέως.

(Mauropus [op. cit., note 165, chapter 2], no. 2, p. 2f.)

(What's this? Light flashed as if from high heaven, the air full of harmonious music. Let's go find out. O the mystery! a great stronghold of angels shouts, saying "Glory to God incarnate." "But how is God flesh? where is the wonder, and wherefore? the wonder, where?" "Go with the shepherds, for to them in their haste there, as you see, indifference for their flocks has come; go with them for me, satisfy desire. You see the cave, the neglected cave, and in it a manger and a child and a maiden. Why yes, your God is this little child." "God is poor? homeless? in mean rags? emerging thus into the light? alas, what are you telling me?" "Nothing is false—it is truth you hear, and that star you see in the sky is witness. I came here to show the child to you, and those also who run together as if to their master, whose delight is a song of praise, with whom it is fitting for you to sing, not disbelieve, for all these things concur for your sake: God made mortal in order to divinize your nature; poor for you, revealing you made rich; angels applauding in anticipation; a mother without a husband; a maiden bearing a child; the shining gifts of the magi; the race of the shepherds; all things filled with joy and celebration. So rejoice with them and do obeisance. And let him be, that hangdog old man—for some other hidden passion eats him. In a little while, he'll sleep and find a remedy from it, and he'll join with all of us in applauding sweetly.")

12. Pero Martines, no. 5, pp. 114–18.

13. *Das rheinische Marienlob*, ed. Adolf Bach, Bibliothek des literarischen Vereins in Stuttgart, vol. 281 (Leipzig, 1934), pp. 25–28, vv. 779–896.

14. Jean-Baptiste Pitra, ed., *Analecta sacra spicilegio Solesmensi parata*, vol. 1 (Paris 1876; reprint, Farnborough, Hants., 1966), p. 383, st. 6 of Josephus no. 1. See also Gottschalk of Orbais, "O mi custos," PLAC 6.1: 94, st. 5off.

15. Cf. *Cançons nadalenques*, no. 28, pp. 152–54 (Catalan); "Rheinauer Paulus," in *Die religioesen Dichtungen des 11. und 12. Jahrhunderts*, ed. Friedrich Maurer, vol. 2 (Tuebingen, 1965), pp. 47–56 (German); Manuel, *Anthologia graeca carminum christianorum*, ed. Wilhelm von Christ and Matthaios Paranikas (Leipzig, 1871), p. 105, vv. 5–9 (Greek); Galletti, no. 41, p. 25, by Feo Belcari (Italian); Abelard, "Planctus," *Gesammelte Abhandlungen zur mittellateinischen Rhythmik*, vol. 1 (Berlin, 1905), pp. 340–74 (Latin); *Hoccleve's Works: The Minor Poems*, ed. Frederick Furnivall and Israel Gollancz, rev. Jerome Mitchell and Anthony Doyle, EETS, 2d ser. 61 and 73 (London, 1892–97; reprint in one volume, 1970), "Regement," no. 12, p. 12 (Middle English); Gerhard Moldenhauer, "Nachweis aelterer franzoesischen Handschriften in portugiesischen Bibliotheken," *Ar-

chiv 151 (1926): 75 (Old French); Garcia de Resende (op. cit., note 188, chapter 2), 1:383ff. (Dom Joam Manuel, "Apostolo santeficado"), stt. 1–3 (Portuguese); Cerveri de Girona (op. cit., note 49, chapter 2), no. 118, p. 367 (on *Surgens Iesus mane*), vv. 120–26 (Provençal); and Ambrosio Montesino, "De quin tomais lengua," Menéndez y Pelayo 4:318–23 (Spanish).

16. Jacopone, no. 73, p. 215, *ripresa.*

17. Alexis (op. cit., note 37, chapter 2), 2:60f.

18. Cf. *percontatio,* discussed in Heinrich Lausberg, *Elemente der literarischen Rhetorik,* 3d ed. (Munich, 1967), p. 143.

19. Galletti, no. 241, p. 105f.

20. Cf. Wack., nos. 438, 526, 540, 703, 854, 1293ff., and Frauenlob (op. cit., note 6, introduction), p. 403, "Koufdôn," no. 1 ("Moises der rette ân allen haz").

21. Cf. the Marquis of Santillana, "Remoto a vida mundana," CC, vol. 1, no. 216, pp. 527–29; Gomez Manrique, "O viejo desuenturado," CC, vol. 2, no. 372, pp. 53–56 (playlet); and "Desque Juan le vió llegado," *Suma poetica,* ed. José Peman and Miguel Herrero, 2d ed. (Madrid, 1950), pp. 314–16.

22. Prodromos, PG, vol. 133, col. 1123A.

23. Cf. Édélstand du Meril, ed., *Poésies populaires latines antérieures au douzième siècle* (Paris, 1843), p. 415f., "Dum coepissent crescere damna noctis prima."

24. Jeanroy, *Joies,* nos. 23f. and 33, pp. 103–14 and 151–55.

25. Wack., nos. 424 and 1137.

26. For Italian examples, see Staff (op. cit., note 163, chapter 2), no. 26, "Davanti una colonna"; Galletti, no. 268, "Alzando gli occhi," p. 121f.; no. 210, "Vidi virgo Maria," p. 95; and no. 211, "Eran pastori intorno," p. 95.

27. Paul Meyer, *Recueil d'anciens textes bas-latins, provençaux et français* (Paris, 1874), p. 206; Gautier de Coincy, ed. Koenig 3:292–96.

28. Cf. one of the Italian *laude* described above. Cf. Brown XV, no. 78, pp. 115–17; see also Oliver S. Pickering, "An Unpublished Middle English Resurrection Poem," *NM* 74, no. 2 (1973): 269–82 (start of Ascension section), and Brown XIV, no. 11, p. 13f., and XV, no. 6, pp. 8–13; in the version Brown prints, XV, no. 7, pp. 13–16, is a straightforward Marian lament, but in another version, extant in two manuscripts, it opens with a *chanson d'aventure* frame, which is as detachable here as it is in most Middle English examples (cf. the note on p. 297 of Brown XV).

29. Vicente, no. 6, "Alto Deos maravihloso," pp. 12–17.

30. Cf. Baumstark (op. cit., note 204, chapter 2), p. 111; see also his article, "Die Hodieantiphonen des roemischen Breviers und der Kreis ihrer griechischen Parallelen," *Die Kirchenmusik* 10 (1909/ 1910): 153–60.

31. Cf. Alfred Jeanroy and Artur Långfors, eds., *Chansons satiriques et*

bachiques du xiiie siècle, Classiques français du moyen âge, vol. 23 (Paris, 1921), "Hui enfantez," pp. 83ff., ascribed to Gautier de Coincy (?); Gautier de Coincy, ed. Koenig 3:258–61, "De sainte Leocade"; and Alexis (op. cit., note 37, chapter 2), 3:181, "Roÿne qui fustes mise," st. 1.

Cf. CM, no. 290, "Ya somos del todo libres," and CG, vol. 2, no. 23, "Ans qu'el gran sol," p. 304, st. 5 (in Valencian), by Vincent Ferradis (1527 ed.).

32. Cf. Sedulius Scottus, "Haec est alma dies," a nonliturgical literary piece from the ninth century. See AH 50, no. 172, p. 230, or PLAC 3:218.

33. Cf. *Escolma de poesia galega*, ed. José María Alvarez Blasquez, 2 vols. (1952–59), 1:133ff.

34. Noulet/Chabaneau, no. 15, "El mes d'abril, quan vey per mieg los cams," p. 35f., by Raimon de Cornet; Jeanroy, *Joies*, no. 20, "Estiuc d'amor," pp. 90–94, by Johan Guombaut.

35. Cf. *Recueil* 1, no. 5, "Quant froidure trait a fin," pp. 28–30; and no. 11, "Quant glace et nois et froidure s'esloigne"; p. 41f.; "Altlothringische Lieder," no. 2, "Quant li dous temps se repaire," pp. 587–92 (cf. n. 52, below); and *Recueil* 2, no. 82, "Quant li russinol se cesse," pp. 74–78.

36. Cf. the famous *estampida* by the troubadour Raimbaut de Vaqueiras, which begins, "Kalenda maya / Ni fuelhs de faya / Ni *chanz d'auzelh* / Ni *flors de glaya* / Non es que·m playa" (First day of May, no leaf of beech, no song of bird, no flower of iris is there that pleases me). Gautier de Coincy, ed. Långfors, no. 33, "Ne flours ne glais," pp. 536–38, stt. 1–2.

37. For Der Heulzing, see Wack., no. 538a; for Muscatbluet, see Eberhard von Groote, ed., *Die Lieder Muscatbluets* (Cologne, 1852), no. 3, "Des meyes zit den anger wit," pp. 7–10; no. 5, "Hort wie der mey gar mancherley," pp. 12–14; and no. 18, "Na lust reit ich da freuwet mich," pp. 52–54; and see Oswald von Wolkenstein (op. cit., note 5, chapter 2), no. 129, "Aller werlde gelegen hat," pp. 317–19. For "Mundi renovacio," see Adam of St. Victor, no. 20, p. 130, or AH 54, no. 148, p. 224f.

38. Brown XIII, no. 54, p. 108f.

39. Cf. Schroeder, chap. 3, sec. 7, p. 149.

40. Davies, no. 71, p. 160f., st. 1 of 2.

41. Cf. Josef Szoevérffy, "L'hymnologie médiévale: recherches et méthodes," *Cahiers de civilisation* 4 (1961): 419.

42. Zumthor, *Essai*, p. 411.

43. Cf. Pitra (op. cit., note 14 above), p. 374; Theodoros Studites, *Iamben*, ed. P. Speck, Supplementa byzantina 1 (Berlin, 1968), no. 17, st. 2; Symeon the New Theologian, *Hymnes*, ed. Johannes Koder and trans. Joseph Paramelle, 3 vols., Sources chrétiennes 156, 174, and 196 (Paris, 1969–73), 1:194, vv. 46–64, for example; Mauropus (op. cit., note 165, chapter 2), no. 7, p. 5ff.; and Prodromos, PG, vol. 133, col. 1205A.

44. John of Howden (op. cit., note 165, chapter 2), stt. 172–74, p. 17.

45. Pagliaresi (op. cit., note 31, chapter 2), "Di, Maria dolce," p. 181, st. 8, ll. 45–50.

46. Cf. Giustinian, item no. 60, "Benedeta virginella madre de dio," pp. [pv^v–pvi^v].

47. G. Scipione Scipioni, "Tre laudi sacre pesaresi," *Giornale storico della letteratura italiana* 6 (1885): 222, l. 4.

48. Cf. Giuseppe Ferraro, *Poesie popolari religiose del secolo xiv*, Scelta di curiosità letterarie, vol. 152 (Bologna, 1877), poem H, p. 58, st. 6, vv. 1–4.

49. A Spanish poem by Juan Alvarez Gato—CC, vol. 1, no. 146, "Vienen de todos lenguaxes," pp. 266–69—is an especially successful example of a love-poem addressed to the Virgin Mary in which the reader is to take fire from the speaker's own passion.

50. Folquet de Marseille (op. cit., note 166, chapter 2), no. 28, "Vers Dieus, e·l vostre nom," p. 110, st. 3, vv. 1–4.

51. Theodoros Studites, (op. cit., note 43 above), no. 97, p. 257.

52. Cf. the passage from John of Howden above. Cf. Richard Otto, "Altlothringische geistliche Lieder," *Romanische Forschungen* 5 (1890): 583–618; no. 3, "A l'oure de meydi, an la plus grant chalour," p. 593, st. 6; and no. 8, "Or m'en irai en sospirant," p. 610, st. 36, vv. 141–44.

53. Cf. Wack., nos. 710, 715, 746, and 750 ("edli sel" [noble soul], the phrase that Heinrich von Laufenberg uses, derives from mystical tradition); cf. Oswald von Wolkenstein (op. cit., note 5, chapter 2), no. 2, pp. 6–9.

54. Cf. Jacopone, no. 53, pp. 146–52 (see also Contini [op. cit., note 42, chapter 1], vol. 2, no. 11, "Jacopone da Todi," pp. 97–104.

55. Cf. Gerard Genette, *Figures* (Paris, 1969), 2:78 (cited in Zumthor, *Essai*, chap. 2, p. 67).

56. Cf. Brown XIII, no. 13, p. 19ff.; *Die Gedichte Christophoros von Mytilene*, ed. Eduard Kurtz (Leipzig, 1903), no. 86, p. 54, v. 1ff.; PL, vol. 171, col. 1425, no. 82; and Abelard, *Hymnarius*, AH 48, no. 119, p. 150, st. 5.

57. Carl Mahn, ed., *Die Gedichte der Troubadours*, 4 vols. (Berlin, 1856–73), vol. 1, no. 196, p. 117, st. 5; the ascription to Guilhem de Sant Desdier is false (see Scheludko [op. cit., note 225, chapter 2], p. 231).

58. Cf. St. Thomas Aquinas, 4 Sent. dist. XV, q. IV, art. 3 ad 2q, nr. 613, 615, 624, on rhetorical figures and sacred literature, in *Scriptorum super libros Sententiarum Magistri Petri Lombardi*, ed. Peter F. Moos, vol. 4 (Paris, 1947), pp. 745–46 (i.e., liber IV, distinctio xv, quaestio iv, art 3 ad 2q, nos. 613 and 615, and ad 3q, no. 624), cited in Wilhelm Breuer, *Die lateinische Eucharistiedichtung des Mittelalters von ihren Anfaengen bis zum Ausgang des 13. Jahrhunderts*, suppl. to Mittellateinisches Jahrbuch 2 (Wuppertal/Kastellaun/Duesseldorf, 1970), p. 299f.

59. Cf. Hildegard von Bingen [op. cit., note 173, chapter 2], no. 76, p. 296.

60. Cf. Grajales, "Clara vírtut / mírall de sancta vída," [pp. 105–7] (fourth from last poem); Riquier, ed. Pfaff, no. 24, "Jhesus Cristz, filh de dieu viu"; Alexis (op. cit., note 37, chapter 2), 2: 58, "Trosne hautain et triclin virginal," st. 1.

61. Cf. Zumthor, *Masque*, p. 166 (citing Alexandre Héron, ed., *Pierre Fabri: le Grand et Vrai Art de pleine rhétorique* [1889/90; reprint, Geneva, 1969], 2:116).

62. Cf. Davies, no. 144, p. 247, st. 1.

63. On the various possible meanings of "we"-forms in medieval religious lyric, see Ohly (op. cit., note 30, chapter 1), "Tu autem," p. 43; on first-person-singular speech and epitaphs, see Georg Misch, *Geschichte der Autobiographie*, 4 vols. in 7 (Frankfurt, 1907–69), 1:224ff., and 2.2:475ff.

64. Cf. AH 50, no. 323, sec. 13, p. 450f., stt. 24, 27–31, and 35f.

65. Pitra (op. cit., note 14 above), Studite no. 10, pp. 355–58, stt. 2, 8, 12f.

66. Cf. Reinmar, sec. 2, no. 6, "Vrôn Êren Dôn," p. 414, vv. 11–12.

67. Cf. Brown XIII, nos. 11a and 11b, p. 18f.

68. Brown XIV, nos. 8 or 10, pp. 9f. and 11f.

69. Brown XIV, no. 30, p. 42, vv. 76–82.

70. The following passages come from *Biblia sacra iuxta vulgatam versionem*, ed. Bonifatius Fischer, et al., vol. 2 (Stuttgart, 1975), and from the *New English Bible* (Oxford, 1976).

> ³benedictus Deus et Pater Domini nostri Iesu Christi
> qui benedixit nos in omni benedictione spiritali in caelestibus in Christo
> ⁴sicut elegit nos in ipso ante mundi constitutionem
> ut essemus sancti et inmaculati in conspectu eius in caritate
> ⁵qui praedestinavit nos in adoptionem
> filiorum per Iesum Christum in ipsum
> secundum propositum voluntatis suae
> ⁶in laudem gloriae gratiae suae
> in qua gratificavit nos in dilecto
> ⁷in quo habemus redemptionem per sanguinem eius
> remissionem peccatorum
> secundum divitias gratiae eius ⁸quae superabundavit in nobis
> in omni sapientia et prudentia
> ⁹ut notum faceret nobis sacramentum voluntatis suae
> secundum bonum placitum eius quod proposuit in eo
> ¹⁰in dispensationem plenitudinis temporum
> instaurare omnia in Christo quae in caelis et quae in terra sunt in ipso
> ¹¹in quo etiam sorte vocati sumus
> praedestinati secundum propositum eius

qui omnia operatur secundum consilium voluntatis suae
¹²ut simus in laudem gloriae eius qui ante speravimus in Christo

(Eph. 1:3-12)

¹   Praise be to the God and Father of
our Lord Jesus Christ, who has be-
stowed on us in Christ every spiritual
⁴blessing in the heavenly realms. In
Christ he chose us before the world was
founded, to be dedicated, to be without
blemish in his sight, to be full of love;
⁵and he destined us—such was his will
and pleasure—to be accepted as his
⁶sons through Jesus Christ, in order that
the glory of his gracious gift, so gra-
ciously bestowed on us in his Beloved,
⁷might redound to his praise. For in
Christ our release is secured and our
sins are forgiven through the shedding
of his blood. Therein lies the richness
⁸of God's free grace lavished upon us,
⁹imparting full wisdom and insight. He
has made known to us his hidden
purpose—such was his will and pleasure
¹⁰determined beforehand in Christ—to
be put into effect when the time was
ripe: namely, that the universe, all in
heaven and on earth, might be brought
into a unity in Christ.
¹¹   In Christ indeed we have been given
our share in the heritage, as was decreed
in his design whose purpose is every-
¹²where at work. For it was his will that
we, who were the first to set our hope
on Christ, should cause his glory to be
praised.

2et vos cum essetis mortui delictis et peccatis vestris
²in quibus aliquando ambulastis secundum saeculum mundi huius
secundum principem potestatis aeris huius
spiritus qui nunc operatur in filios diffidentiae
³in quibus et nos omnes aliquando conversati sumus in desideriis carnis
nostrae
facientes voluntates carnis et cogitationum
et eramus natura filii irae sicut et ceteri
⁴Deus autem qui dives est in misericordia

propter nimiam caritatem suam qua dilexit nos
[5]et cum essemus mortui peccatis convivificavit nos Christo
gratia estis salvati
[6]et conresuscitavit et consedere fecit in caelestibus in Christo Iesu
[7]ut ostenderet in saeculis supervenientibus
abundantes divitias gratiae suae
in bonitate super nos in Christo Iesu
[8]gratia enim estis salvati per fidem et hoc non ex vobis
Dei enim donum est
[9]non ex operibus ut ne quis glorietur
[10]ipsius enim sumus factura
creati in Christo Iesu in operibus bonis
quae praeparavit Deus ut in illis ambulemus

(Eph. 1:1–10)

2 TIME WAS WHEN YOU WERE DEAD IN
[2]your sins and wickedness, when you
followed the evil ways of this present
age, when you obeyed the commander
of the spiritual powers of the air, the
spirit now at work among God's rebel
[3]subjects. We too were once of their
number: we all lived our lives in sen-
suality, and obeyed the promptings of
our own instincts and notions. In our
natural condition we, like the rest, lay
under the dreadful judgement of God.
[4]But God, rich in mercy, for the great
[5]love he bore us, brought us to life with
Christ even when we were dead in our
sins; it is by his grace you are saved.
[6]And in union with Christ Jesus he
raised us up and enthroned us with him
[7]in the heavenly realms, so that he might
display in the ages to come how im-
mense are the resources of his grace,
and how great his kindness to us in
[8]Christ Jesus. For it is by his grace you
are saved, through trusting him; it is
not your own doing. It is God's gift,
[9]not a reward for work done. There is
[10]nothing for anyone to boast of. For
we are God's handiwork, created in
Christ Jesus to devote ourselves to the
good deeds for which God has designed
us.

³benedictus Deus et Pater Domini nostri Iesu Christi
qui secundum magnam misericordiam suam regeneravit nos in spem vivam
per resurrectionem Iesu Christi ex mortuis
⁴in hereditatem incorruptibilem et incontaminatam et inmarcescibilem
conservatam in caelis
in vobis ⁵qui in virtute Dei custodimini per fidem
in salutem paratam revelari in tempore novissimo

(1 Pet. 1:3–5)

³ Praise be to the God and Father of
our Lord Jesus Christ, who in his great
mercy gave us new birth into a living
hope by the resurrection of Jesus Christ
⁴from the dead! The inheritance to
which we are born is one that nothing
can destroy or spoil or wither. It is kept
⁵for you in heaven, and you, because
you put your faith in God, are under
the protection of his power until salvation comes—the salvation which is
even now in readiness and will be
revealed at the end of time.

71. Cf. Reinhard Deichgraeber, "Der Lobpreis in der fruehen Christenheit: Untersuchungen zur Form, Sprache, und Stil der Hymnen der fruehen
Christenheit" (Ph.D. diss., Heidelberg, 1965).

72. PLAC 4.1:330–31.

73. Cf. Mauropus (op. cit., note 165, chapter 2), no. 2.

74. Richard Rolle, *English Writings*, ed. Hope E. Allen (Oxford, 1931),
p. 49f., vv. 9–24 and 33–37.

75. Cf. the Vernon manuscript, e.g., Brown XIV, no. 105, p. 159, vv.
49–72.

76. Scherner (op. cit., note 3, chapter 1), sec. 2.2.c, esp. p. 312.

77. Molinet (op. cit., note 64, chapter 2), no. 14, p. 475, st. 18, vv.
188–91.

78. *Skjaldedigtning* B.2, p. 377, st. 21.1–4.

79. Natalino Sapegno, ed., *Poeti minori del Trecento*, La letteratura
italiana, storia e testi, vol. 10 (Milan/Naples, 1952), "O Cristo, amor diletto, te sguardando," p. 1015.

80. CC, vol. 1, p. 261, st. 9.

81. *Skjaldedigtning* B.2, p. 172, st. 44.

82. R. Bettarini, *Jacopone e il laudario urbinate* (Florence, 1969), vv.
112–13 and 130–35.

83. Menéndez y Pelayo, 4:158, "Andá acá, pastor," st. 6.

84. Ibid., 4:321f., "De quien tomais lengua," stt. 14–15.

85. Ibid., 4:320, st. 7f.

86. Llull (op. cit., note 51, chapter 2), no. 1, pp. 52–68, esp. stt. 9, 14, and 18.

87. In these stanzas, Frauenlob is paraphrasing Revelation 12:1f., 1:12ff., 5:6, and 14:1.

88. Cf. Raby, *Oxford*, no. 262, pp. 398–400; or see AH 50, no. 385, p. 584f. (where the other hymns for Corpus Christi by Aquinas also appear).

89. Cf. Adam of St. Victor, no. 35, "Laetabundi iubilemus," p. 220, stt. 5–6, or no. 26, "Simplex in essentia," p. 168, st. 5; see also Raby, *Oxford*, no. 200, "Versa est in luctum," p. 296, vv. 25ff., by Walter of Châtillon.

90. Cf. John 6:55, and see Ambrose, "Splendor paternae gloriae," in Bulst (op. cit., note 11, chapter 1), p. 40.

91. See the discussion of closure in section iv of chapter 2 above (and especially note 179 on "terminal modification").

92. For an analysis of "Lauda Sion" from the perspective of doctrine, see Breuer (op. cit., note 58 above), pp. 282–300; see also Frederic J. Raby, *A History of Christian-Latin Poetry from the Beginnings to the Close of the Middle Ages*, 2d ed. (Oxford, 1953), pp. 405–8.

93. Jacopone, no. 32, "O Vergen plu ca femena," p. 89, vv. 111–14.

94. Cf. AH 48, no. 263, p. 253, st. 18 and last.

95. Cf. *Menaia tou holou eniautou*, 6 vols. (Rome, 1888–1901), 3: 444 ("theotokion," sec. 2).

96. Cf. *Die Gedichte des Michel Beheims*, ed. Hans Gille and Ingeborg Spriewald, Deutsche Texte des Mittelalters, vols. 60, 64, and 65.1–2 (Berlin, 1968–72), vol. 65.1, no. 435, "O raine magt/Maria, muter Kristi," pp. 240–44.

97. Cf. Brown XIII, no. 3, "Cristes milde moder seynte marie," p. 4, vv. 47–50.

98. Cf. Frances Comper, ed., *The Life of Richard Rolle* (London/New York, 1928), p. 263, st. 10, vv. 7–8.

99. *Bruder Hansens Marienlieder*, ed. Michael Batts, Altdeutsche Textbibliothek 58 (Tuebingen, 1963), p. 181, vv. 4049–64.

100. See Grajales [pp. 9–12, 21, 33, 36, 55, 61, 64, 81, 88, and 99]. Berthomeu Salvador [p. 68] amusingly inverts the topos: "A vos quí nou cors / ha gloríffícada Presente lahors / que may foren fetes . . ." (To you who have glorified our body I present praises that were never made before).

101. Cf. Guittone d'Arezzo, *Le Rime*, ed. Francesco Egidi (Bari, 1940), no. 38, "Beato Francesco, in te laudare," pp. 104 and 107, vv. 25–34 and 135–39; Bianco da Siena, ed. Bini, no. 17, "Udite che m'avvien per Cristo amare," p. 55, st. 100ff., no. 29, "O donna gloriosa," p. 79, st. 30, and no. 30, "O donna gloriosa," p. 81, st. 13; Girolamo Savonarola, *Poesie*, ed.

Mario Martelli (Rome, 1968), sonnet no. 2, "Questa celeste e gloriosa Dona," p. [26], vv. 12–14.

102. Cf. Varanini (op. cit., note 43, chapter 1), p. x.

103. Cf. Liver (op. cit., note 1, chapter 1), p. 231f. (and p. 236, no. 13b); see also Menander, "Peri epideiktikōn," in *Rhetores graeci*, ed. Christian Walz, vol. 9 (Stuttgart/Tuebingen/London/Paris, 1832–36), pp. 127ff. Sometimes, the distinction between classical, literary invocations and a prayer for divine aid in writing is made explicit: cf. Einar Skulason's "Geisli" (cited below, p. 189) or Jorge Manrique's great elegy on the death of his father, "Recuerde el alma dormida," st. 4 (Menéndez y Pelayo 3 : 101f.).

104. *Skjaldedigtning* B.2, p. 404, st. 51.

105. Ibid., p. 427, st. 1., vv. 1–4.

106. PG, vol. 96, col. 1377, st. 1.

107. PLAC 4.1 : 332.

108. Molinet (op. cit., note 64, chapter 2), no. 13, p. 460f., stt. 1–6, vv. 1–96.

109. *Die kleineren Dichtungen Heinrichs von Muegeln*, pt. 1: *Die Spruchsammlung des Goettinger Cod. Philos. 21*, ed. K. Stackmann, 3 vols., Deutsche Texte des Mittelalters 50–52 (Berlin, 1959), 2 : 460ff., stt. 1–6, vv. 1–96.

110. CG, vol. 2, no. 70, "Quién conporná acá en el suelo," p. 334, vv. 4ff., by Bernaldo de la Torre (1540 ed.).

111. Cf. [Eugenio Cecconi] ed., *Laudi di una compagnia fiorentina del secolo xiv fin qui inedite* (Florence, 1870), no. 75, "De la Fede diro in prima," p. 47, l. 29, "novella danza."

112. Gautier de Coincy, ed. Koenig 1 : 37, opening of poem.

113. Ibid., p. 29, "Qui que face rotruenge novele," vv. 1–3.

114. *Recueil* 2, no. 112, p. 139, vv. 1–4.

115. Ibid., no. 104, p. 142, vv. 1–6.

116. Ibid., no. 122, "Qui de la prime florete," p. 160, vv. 52–55.

117. Mazzoni (op. cit., note 223, chapter 2), no. 45, p. 43.

118. Cecconi (op. cit., note 110 above), no. 67, "Santo Agustino dottore," p. 42, vv. 7ff., and no. 69, p. 43, vv. 1–4 (*ripresa*).

119. Adolfo Mussafia, "Monumenti antichi di dialetti italiani," Akademie der Wissenschaft, Vienna, philosophisch-historische Klasse, Sitzungsberichte, vol. 46 (1864), pp. 113–235, esp. 191, poem F, vv. 1–4.

120. Bianco da Siena, ed. Ageno (op. cit., note 149, chapter 2), p. 43, vv. 1–4.

121. Cf. Friedrich von der Hagen, ed., *Minnesinger*, 4 vols. (Leipzig, 1838), 3 : 63, 65, and 67.

122. Helgason 2 : 59, st. 43; Karl Bartsch, ed., *Die Erloesung mit einer Auswahl geistlicher Dichtungen* (Quedlinburg/Leipzig, 1858), p. 224, poem

no. 12, v. 7; and Muscatbluet (op. cit., note 37 above), p. 52, sec. I, no. 21.

123. "Lobgesang auf Maria und Christus von [pseudo-] Gottfried von Strassburg," ed. Moriz Haupt, *Zeitschrift fuer deutsches Altertum und Wissenschaft* 4 (1844): 513–55, esp. p. 541, st. 75, vv. 3ff.

124. von der Hagen (op. cit., note 121 above), 3 : 99, no. 10, st. 1.

125. Cf. the council of Tours (567); see Paul Klopsch, "Anonymitaet und Selbstnennung mittellateinischer Autoren," *Mittellateinisches Jahrbuch* 4 (1967): 15.

126. Ibid., p. 16 n. 22 (Dreves estimated that fewer than 10 percent of the hymns can be securely ascribed).

127. Cf. Peter von Moos, "Gottschalks Gedicht O *mi custos*—eine *confessio*," pt. 1, *Fruehmittelalterliche Studien* 4 (1970): 221f. n. 72.

128. Llull (op. cit., note 51, chapter 2), no. 1, p. 68, st. 32; Mazzoni (op. cit., note 223, chapter 2), nos. 8, 14, 31, and 46; *Recueil* 2, no. 39, "Aymans fins et verais," p. 101, st. 6; Gautier de Coincy, ed. Långfors, no. 31, "Puis que voi la fleur novele," p. 532, vv. 98f. See also Zumthor, *Histoire*, pt. 3, chap. 3, p. 115, concerning the increased frequency of signed work from ca. 1200 on.

129. *Skjaldedigtning* B.2, p. 582, stt. 49 and 51.

130. Konrad von Wuerzburg, *Diu guldîn smide*, ed. Edward Schroeder (Goettingen, 1926), vv. 120f. and 890; Batts (op. cit., note 99 above), p. 166, v. 3675; *Rheinische Marienlob* (op. cit., note 13 above), p. 1, v. 18.

131. Cf. Zumthor, *Langue*, pt. 3, "Autobiographie au Moyen Age?" p. 177; see also Curtius (op. cit., note 201, chapter 2), pp. 515–18, Excursus xvii, "Mention of the author's name in medieval literature."

132. *Cantigas*, nos. 209, 235, and 279; Guittone d'Arezzo (op. cit., note 101 above), no. 32, "O cari frati miei," st. 4; Jacopone, nos. 53, 58 and 67; Lydgate, no. 68; Oswald von Wolkenstein (op. cit., note 5, chapter 2), no. 36 (for example); Bartsch (op. cit., note 44, chapter 2), nos. 31 and 40.

133. Wolfram von den Steinen, *Notker der Dichter und seine geistliche Welt*, 2 vols. (Berne, 1948), 1 : 150, "Ordinis sacri Stephanus honore," st. 10 ("Aeger et balbus . . ."); Gottschalk, "Ut quid iubes," in Raby, *Oxford*, no. 92, pp. 126–28; Froumond, *Die Tegernseer Briefsammlung*, ed. Karl Strecker, Monumenta germaniae historica: Epistulae selectae, vol. 3 (Berlin, 1925), no. 10, pp. 36–38; John the Geometer, PG, vol. 106, nos. 143, 153, 161, "Carmina varia"; John Mauropus, references in Sophronios Eustratiades, "Ioannes ho Mauropous, metropolites Euchaiton," *Enaisima*, ed. Gregorios Papamichael (Athens, 1931), pp. 423–25 (the canon to St. Blaise, PG, vol. 96, cols. 1401–08, is liturgical); Ciro Giannelli, "Tetrastici di Teodoro Prodromo sulle feste fisse e sui santi del calendario bizantino," *Analecta bollandiana* 75 (1957): 229–336, esp. pp. 300–302, and idem,

"Epigrammi di Teodoro Prodromo in onore dei santi megalomartiri Teodoro, Giorgio, e Demetrio," in *Studi in onore di L. Castiglione*, vol. 1 (Florence, 1960), pp. 331–37, esp. p. 168.

134. Cf. the poem by Notker just cited; Raby, *Oxford*, no. 200, "Versa est in luctum," p. 295, st. 1, by Walter of Châtillon; and Audelay, "Lady, helpe! Jesu, mercy!" in Davies, no. 81, p. 170f.

135. Hildegard von Bingen (op. cit., note 59 above), no. 30, p. 246, and PLAC 2:466–68.

136. Pitra (op. cit., note 14 above), Studite no. 12, p. 361, st. 14.

137. Cf. Berceo (op. cit., note 198, chapter 2), "Loores," st. 230; *Baena* (op. cit., note 135, chapter 2), vol. 3, no. 518, "Amigo senor, muy grant piedat," p. 1025, vv. 69–72; Alonso, CG, vol. 2, no. 25, "Tres fieros vestiglos," p. 306, final couplet (1527 ed.).

138. *Cantigas*, prologue, st. 3; no. 10, st. 4; and no. 279 (refrain).

139. Cerveri de Girona (op. cit., note 49, chapter 2), no. 64, "Lo vers de Deu," p. 186, st. 1; François J. M. Raynouard, ed., *Choix des poésies originales des troubadours*, vol. 4 (Paris, 1819), "Domna, dels angels regina," p. 465, by Peire de Corbiac; Riquier, ed. Pfaff, no. 53, "Ben degra de chantar tener"; Mahn (op. cit., note 57 above), Daude de Pradas, vol. 3, no. 1040, "Qui finamen sap cussirar," p. 218, st. 7; *Il Canzoniere di Lanfranco Cigala*, ed. Francesco Branciforti (Florence, 1954), no. 27, "Pensius de cor e marritz," p. 229, st. 1; Noulet/Chabaneau, no. 15, "El mes d'abril," p. 35ff., st. 3 and *tornada*, by Raimon de Cornet.

140. Pero Martines, no. 8, "Singular preu," p. 128, *tornada*; Grajales, pp. [25], st. 5; [27], st. 2; [52], st. 5 and *tornada*.

141. *Recueil* 1, no. 56, p. 144, st. 1.

142. On wasted *toene*, cf. Wack., no. 187, st. 4; on wasted words, Wack., no. 236, st. 39; on rhyme, see no. 199, vv. 257–60; on division into sections, the same text, vv. 67f.

143. Cf. Chenu, chap. 13, "Orientale lumen," pp. 290–98.

144. See Gregory the Great, *Moralia in Job, Libri I–X*, ed. Mark Adriaen, Corpus Christianorum; Series latina, vol. 143 (Turnholt, 1979), "Epistola ad Leandrum," sec. 2, p. 4, "Sacri enim tractator . . ." (ll. 96–105).

145. Chenu, p. 212 n. 1, and p. 361 n. 1.

146. Ibid., p. 161f. and p. 388.

147. See Brinkmann (op. cit., note 8, chapter 1), pp. 37–54.

148. Cf. Chenu, p. 187 n. 12. See also Scherner (op. cit., note 3, chapter 1), p. 68f. (on naming God), after Brinkmann (op. cit., note 8, chapter 1), and pp. 78f. and 147ff.

149. Cf. Alan Gilchrist, "The Perception of Surface Blacks and Whites," *Scientific American* 240, no. 3 (Mar. 1979): 112–24 (bibliography on

p. 174), and Walter Gogel, "The Adjacency Principle in Visual Perception," *Scientific American* 238, no. 5 (May 1978): 126–39 (bibliography on p. 172).

150. Cf. "Reverse English," *Scientific American* 243, no. 1 (July 1980): 76f. (unascribed).

151. Cf. Breyne Moskowitz, "The Acquisition of Language," *Scientific American* 239, no. 3 (Nov. 1978): 92–108, esp. p. 106, on early use of antonyms as synonyms (bibliography on p. 198). Robert Krauss and Sam Glucksberg, "Social and Nonsocial Speech," *Scientific American* 236, no. 2 (Feb. 1977): 100–105, is also relevant to the issue of how metaphor operates; it would seem that one can only learn how to speak a natural language comprehensibly by entering into the viewpoint and the expectations of a language user. Perhaps, then, artistic metaphor offers an ability that we originally developed in our acquisition of language, the opportunity of a new and wonderfully exciting empathy with a consciousness that makes the universe dance to its own tune, in a sense cancelling out the original submission to reality we had to make in learning to speak. Language binds, and language makes free.

152. Cf. Kenneth Burke, *The Rhetoric of Religion*, Studies in Logology (Boston, 1961), in which the author reflects on religion as "words about 'God'" and its terminology as an expression of man's relation to the *word* God. Of particular interest is Burke's concept of "pure persuasion" finding "delight in sheer forms of courtship for their own sake" and of God as "the principle of an ideal audience" for such "persuasion" (see the long footnote beginning on p. 34). On this basis, the close association between courtly and religious poetry, and the courtly and religious ethoses, makes excellent sense.

153. Cf. Zumthor, *Histoire*, chap. 4.

154. Cf. Chenu, p. 171f.

155. The most obvious case of such "conversion" is *contrafactura*.

156. Cf. Zumthor, *Masque*, p. 82.

157. Cf. Hoccleve (op. cit., note 15 above), vol. 1, pt. 2, no. 5, "Syn thow, modir of grace, haast evere in mynde," p. 286, st. 6; and Giustinian, poem no. 8, "Madre che feci quelui chi te feci," pp. [bv^v–bvii], st. 7. See also Galletti, no. 245, "Tu donna sola se' d'amore degna," p. 141, l. 7.

158. Cf. the fourteenth-century Latin Marian panegyric, written in Denmark, printed as item no. 1 in the appendix to Lehmann (op. cit., note 102, chapter 2), pt. 2, "Salve, sancta parens Dei," ll. 73ff., 246, and 248 (and much, much else!).

159. Chenu, pp. 219 and 215. On typology in the later Middle Ages, see also Friedrich Ohly, "Synagoge und Ecclesia—Typologisches in mittelalter-

licher Dichtung," *Miscellanea Medievalia* 4 (Berlin, 1966): 350–69. Among other things, Ohly discusses the spread of typology beyond the purely scriptural zone; Jeffrey, p. 86f., discusses the Franciscan extension of typology to current events and even personal history.

160. Lotman, *Structure*, chap. 8, "The problem of artistic space," touches on the general significance of "open" versus "closed" in literature.

161. Cf. Pietro Damiani, "Paschalis festi gaudium," st. 7, vv. 1–2 (AH 48, no. 55, p. 54): "Brevi sepulcro clauditur, / Qui caelo non capitur" (In a little tomb is shut He who is not contained by the sky). See also Liver (op. cit., note 1, chapter 1), p. 86f., for Latin and Italian examples of "container" metaphors in religious verse. There is of course an analogous use of the motif of the great contained in a small space in epitaphs; the following Spanish verses by Tapia (CC, vol. 2, no. 827, p. 458) are a late medieval version of an old idea:

> Aqui tiene poca tierra
> el que toda la tenia;
> en esto poco se encierra
> el que la paz y la guerra
> del mundo tenia.

(Here a little earth holds him who held all; in this little space is confined he who held [the power of] peace and war for the whole world.)

162. Chief among the antecedents is the sentence from the Office for Christmas Matins, *quem coeli capere non poterant, tuo gremio contulisti* (whom the heavens could not contain, you carried in your womb). Cf. also the early anonymous hymn, "Quem terra, pontus, aethera," which continues "colunt, adorant, praedicant, / trinam regentem machinam / claustrum Mariae baiulat" (Him whom earth, sea, and sky worship, adore, and proclaim, him who rules the threefold mechanism [of the universe] Mary's close carries) (see Raby, *Oxford*, no. 59, st. 1).

163. Cf. Walter of Chatillon, "Dei prudentia, quam pater genuit," st. 5, v. 2, in *Die Lieder Walthers von Châtillon in der Handschrift 311 von St. Omer*, ed. Karl Strecker (Berlin, 1925), p. 11.

164. AH 50, *Mariale*, p. 439, rhythmus 8, st. 34.

165. Reinmar, p. 418, sec. 2, no. 16, vv. 3–6.

166. *Rheinische Marienlob* (op. cit., note 13 above), p. 44f., vv. 1410–17.

167. *Konrad von Wuerzburg: Kleinere Dichtungen*, vol. 3: *Die Klage der Kunst/Leiche Lieder und Sprueche*, ed. Edward Schroeder (1926; reprint, Dublin/Zurich, 1967), Lied no. 1, "Got gewaltec, was du schickest," p. 14, vv. 185–87 and 191–94; see also Lied no. 32, p. 56ff., st. 4, vv. 46–57; and Konrad von Wuerzburg (op. cit., note 130 above), ll. 1256–67.

168. *Recueil* 1, no. 39, "Tant ne me plaist toute phylosophye," p. 78, st. 2.

169. Cf. Gautier de Coincy, ed. Långfors, no. 31, "Puis que voi la fleur novele," p. 531, st. 4.

170. Frauenlob (op. cit., note 6, introduction), p. 64f., st. 14.

171. Nonetheless, Albrecht Lesch (ca. 1420–ca. 1478/79) makes somewhat earlier use of the motif; cf. Wack., no. 546, st. 4, and Leonard Koester, ed., "Albrecht Lesch, Ein Muenchener Meistersinger des 15. Jahrhunderts" (Ph.D., diss., Munich, 1933), poem no. 2, "Ich wil von ainer maget fron," p. 93, st. 12, vv. 1–5.

172. Wack., no. 1431, p. 1154, vv. 7–11.

173. There are exceptions, of course; cf. the outstanding gloss on the Ave Maria, attributed to Fr. Hernando de Talavera, "Oh suma de nuestros bienes," st. 13 ("Tui"), vv. 10–13, in Menéndez y Pelayo 4:331, "Que del [i.e., del vientre tuyo] hizo nido suyo, / Del corto manto que cabe, / A quien mil mundos no cubren" (Who made his nest of your womb, a short cloak to hold him a thousand worlds do not cover), which successfully combines "high" and "low" elements in a synthesis reminiscent of early Gothic art and literature.

174. Galletti, no. 189, "Maria, vergine bella / scala che ascendi e guidi all'alto cielo" (perhaps by Leonardo Giustinian—cf. p. [cviii] of the 1506 collection of his, and others', work). See also Giustinian, "Madre che feci quelui chi te feci / vaso capazo di tanto thesauro," p. [bviᵛ], st. 8; and Galletti, no. 157, "Ave Regina celi, Istella tramontana," p. 71, v. 5, by "Maestro Antonio."

175. Cf. Mauropus's Nativity poem, note 11 above.

176. Cf. Ekkehard IV, *Der Liber Benedictionum . . .* , ed. J. Egli, Mitteilungen zur vaterländischen Geschichte, 1st ser. 31, no. 4, (St. Gallen, 1909), poem no. 24, on the Ascension, "Audiat insomnes celos scandens super omnes," conclusion.

177. Cf. Raby, *Oxford*, no. 200, "Versa est in luctum," p. 295f., vv. 15–24.

178. Cf. Adam of St. Victor, no. 34, "Ecce, dies triumphalis," p. 216, st. 9; and no. 36, "Prunis datum," pp. 228, 230, and 232, stt. 3, 9, and 12. For the mustard-seed metaphors, however (and their application to martyrs), see Gregory the Great (op. cit., note 144 above), "Praefatio," p. 12, sec. 6.

179. AH 50, no. 398, sec. 5, "Cantus ad meridiem," p. 608, st. 70.

180. Reinmar, sec. 2, no. 20, "Vrôn Êren Dôn," p. 420f.

181. Cf. Guittone d'Arezzo (op. cit., note 101 above), no. 35, "O bon Gesú, ov'e core," p. 99, *congedo*; no. 37, "Meraviglioso beato," p. 101, st. 1; no. 28, "O cari frati miei, con mala mente," p. 84, st. 2, vv. 28ff.

182. Cf. Jacopone, no. 27, "O Cristo onipotente, dove site enviato?" pp. 73f.; and no. 79, "O Amor, che mme ami," p. 238, vv. 57–60. See also an anonymous German fifteenth-century poem, Wack., no. 817, in which Jesus is called, more conventionally, "master of arts" (st. 5.4).

183. Cf. Ferraro, *Popolari* (op. cit., note 48 above), poem B, "Or alditi mata pacia," p. 30, st. 2.

184. Cf. Aguiló y Fuster (op. cit., note 40, chapter 1), "Poesies religioses: Les goigs de la gloriosa Mare de Deu de la Concepcio" (the first item in the collection), stt. 1–2 [no pagination].

185. Konrad von Wuerzburg (op. cit., note 130 above), vv. 900ff. Note the effect of reversing the mode of the bestiaries, in which an animal is said to be like Christ; here, Christ is said to be like an animal, and what was magnificative becomes diminishing. Obviously, metaphorical equations are not commutable (i.e., a = b is *not* identical to the equation b = a).

186. Llull (op. cit., note 51, chapter 2), "Lo Desconhort," p. 80, st. 22, vv. 260–62; Ausias March, *Selected Poems*, ed. and trans. Arthur Terry, Edinburgh Bilingual Library, 12 (1976), "Cant espiritual," p. 122, st. 19, v. 147f.; *Cançons nadalenques*, no. 37, "Ou, ou, ou / e tan gran brogit s'ich mou," p. 151, v. 14; Joan Roiç de Corella, *Obras . . .* , ed. Ramón Miguel y Planas (Barcelona, 1913), item 18, "Ans que dels cels," p. 394, st. 6, vv. 44–48, and p. 399, st. 22, l. 172; Pero Martines, no. 3, "Ab quin ale," p. 108, st. 7, v. 52, and no. 10, "Clare Thomas," p. 132, st. 5, and no. 4, "O corredor," p. 111, st. 3, v. 21f.; Grajales, "Sim atreuesch / entrar lescura silua," p. [74], st. 1, by Berthomeu Dímas.

187. Cf. Wack., no. 34, st. 3 (Der junge Spervogel); no. 73 (Der von Kolmar); Anton Schoenbach, ed., *Beitraege zur Erklaerung altdeutscher Dichtwerke: Die Sprueche des Bruder Wernhers*, Sitzungsberichte Akademie der Wissenschaft, Vienna, philosophisch-historische Klasse, 148, no. 7 (1904) and 150, no. 4 (1904–5), pp. 1–90 and 1–106, esp. pt. 2, no. 52, "Diu sêle ist lûter alse ein glas," p. 39, vv. 1–6; Reinmar, no. 189, "Nû seht, wie listic daz er was," p. 504ff.

188. Cf. F. Pfeiffer, "Mariengruesse," *Zeitschrift fuer deutsches Altertum und Wissenschaft* 8 (1851): 289, vv. 474–76; *Rheinische Marienlob* (op. cit., note 13 above), p. 14f., ll. 427ff.; Wack., no. 214, st. 7 (= C. von Kraus, *Deutsche Liederdichter des 13. Jahrhunderts* 1 : 380ff.); *Friedrich von Sonnenburg*, ed. O. Zingerle (Innsbruck, 1878), sec. 4, no. 5e, "Diu welt von rehte wirt," p. 84 [in the *Altdeutsche Textbibliothek* is a new edition of Friedrich that I have not yet seen].

189. Konrad, *Dichtungen* (op. cit., note 167 above), "Leiche Lieder und Sprueche," no. 1, p. 9, vv. 17–20, and no. 32, p. 35, v. 17; von der Hagen (op. cit., note 121 above), 3 : 98, poet no. 24, "Der Misnaere," sec. 8, no. 2,

"Der slange mit spaehen listen," col. 1, and 2:368f., poet no. 136, "Meister Rumzland," sec. 3, no. 2, "Der den zirkel tihte."

190. [Pseudo-]Gottfried (op. cit., note 123 above), pp. 514, 515, 516, 518, and 537, stt. 1, 4, 7, 13, and 64f.

191. Frauenlob (op. cit., note 6, introduction), p. 56f., st. 9; Monk of Salzburg (op. cit., note 11, introduction), G 23, "Die nacht wirt schir des himels gast," p. 224f., st. 1; Batts (op. cit., note 99 above), p. 177, vv. 3945 (solder), p. 180f., v. 4046ff. (brimming vessel), p. 192, vv. 4355–57 (sluice gate), p. 159, v. 3523ff. (puppies), p. 196f., 4475ff. (dogs), p. 207, v. 4774ff. (owls); Heinrich von Muegeln (op. cit., note 109 above), vol. 2, cf. sec. 4, no. 16, (p. 162), 17 (p. 164), 37f. (p. 184); cf. Wack., nos. 1144, 1147, 1148, 1150, and so on.

192. Jacopone, no. 2, "Fugio la croce, ca mme devora," p. 9, v. 61f. (hoop); no. 14, "O amore muto," p. 44, vv. 15–18 (candle); no. 24, "O frate, brig'a De' tornare," p. 66, vv. 51–56 (shoes); no. 25, "Sapete vui novelle de l'Amore," p. 69, vv. 73–76 (quiet house); no. 18, "Amor, diletto Amore," p. 53, vv. 42f. and 34–37 (rich man/merchant); no. 40, "O Francesco povero," p. 118f., vv. 181–88 (fountain); no. 84, "Fede, spen e caritate," p. 257, vv. 185–88, (soul in its ascent); no. 90, "La Fede e la Speranza," p. 292, vv. 89–95 (the soul drowning in God); and "Appendice," no. 4c, "Chi per foco non passa," p. 337, vv. 30–32.

193. Cf. *The English Text of the Ancrene Riwle; from Ms. Corpus Christi College Cambridge 402*, ed. J. R. R. Tolkien, EETS, orig. ser. 249 (London/New York, 1962 for 1960), p. 118f. (= pt. 4, "Temptations," the sixth comfort).

194. Bettarini (op. cit., note 82, above), no. 7, "Oi bella sponsa, no sai," p. 552, vv. 113–16; no. 17, "O Amor pretioso," p. 577, vv. 41–44; no. 18, "Damecte a'ssentire," p. 578f., vv. 32–37 (teasing children); no. 25, "Lamentome cun dolla," p. 596, vv. 15–18 (bad falcon); no. 33, "Tornate a·penetença, peccaturi," p. 611, vv. 7–10 (death on a palfrey); "Recuperi jacoponici," poems 6, "Tornate a·ppenetenca, / ke la sentenca se da," p. 508, vv. 27–30 (flood), and 9, ". . . meravella si dolea" (acephalous), p. 516, vv. 94–98 (water clearing up). Bianco da Siena, ed. Bini, no. 5, "Partito se' da me per mio difetto," p. 29, st. 7.2, col. b (see also Sapegno [op. cit., note 79 above], p. 1132, v. 30), and ed. Gennaro Monti, *Laude mistiche del Bianco da Siena* (Lanciano, 1925), poem 24, "L'Amor m'ha preso, e non so che mi faccia," pp. 107–10, esp. st. 1.

195. Cerveri de Girona (op. cit., note 49, chapter 2), no. 118, "Sermo," p. 368ff., vv. 156–80.

196. Peire d'Alvernha, *Liriche*, ed. Alberto del Monte (Turin, 1955), no. 16, "Cui bon vers agrad' a auzir," p. 161, st. 4; no. 17, "De Dieu non puesc

pauc ben parlar," p. 172, st. 9; and no. 19, "Lauzatz si' Emanuel," p. 194, st. 7 (two cents/narrow field/leap from a hill, respectively). C. Appel, ed. *Der Trobador Cadenet* (Halle in Saale, 1920), "Ben volgra, s'esser pogues," pp. 10–12, esp. the first stanza.

197. Paul Meyer, ed., *Daurel et Beton*, SATF 14 (Paris, 1880), "Lo tractat dels noms de [la] mayre de Dieu," pp. ciii–cvii, vv. 46 (skin/wool), 57–60 (candle), 61–64 (ladder), 262–65 (ground), 282–85 (way).

198. Noulet/Chabaneau, no. 15, p. 35f., vv. 15–18 (Adam), 22–25 (dove), 29–32 (branch), 33f. (fire), and 36–39 (rhymes).

199. Gautier de Coincy, ed. Koenig 3:285, "Mere Dieu, virge senee," st. 7 (chess); v. 1, "Quant ces floretes florir voi," l. 40 (beds); or p. 301, v. 3, "Ma viele," l. 23 (the same); p. 49, v. 1, "Pour conforter mon cuer et mon coraige," ll. 38–40 (milk/table); p. 251, v. 3, "Las! las! las! las! Par grant delit," v. 41f. (old barn); p. 297–99, v. 3, "Ja pour yver, pour noif ne pour gelee," l. 21 (rose), and l. 35 (raspberry), and l. 54f. (Frisia); Gautier de Coincy, ed. Långfors, no. 31, "Puis que voi la fleur novele," p. 532, ll. 68–72 (fish/harvest), and l. 86f. (note).

200. Thibaut de Champagne (op. cit., note 145, chapter 2), no. 58, "Mauves arbres ne peut florir," p. 206, vv. 34–40; no. 60, "De grant travail et de petit esploit," p. 211, v. 7f.; and no. 56, "Deus est ensi conme li pellicanz" pp. 194–97 (child and tree, God behind our backs, and beast-fable, respectively).

201. *Recueil* 1, no. 6, "De la gloriouse fenix," p. 31, ll. 12–15 (sleeping man); no. 12, "Loee tant que loer," p. 43, st. 3 (fish/falcon); no. 21, "Bien est raison, puisque Diex m'a donné," p. 61, ll. 26–28 (King of Tyre); no. 23, "Ja ne verrai le desir acompli," p. 66, ll. 29–32 (rain and wool); no. 27, "De volente desiriere," p. 74, ll. 25–28 (miner); no. 31, "Haute dame, com rose et lis," p. 85, ll. 22–25 (Albigensians); no. 34, "Mere, douce creature," p. 90f., ll. 36–39 (Friday); no. 41, "Douce dame de paradys," p. 107, ll. 53–56 (tomb/womb); no. 42, "Boin fait servir dame ki en greit prant," p. 110, l. 27 (gust of wind); no. 50, "De la mere Jesucrist," p. 126, st. 3 (Christ and mother); no. 51, "Glorieuse virge pucele," p. 128f., st. 3 (spring weather), st. 5.53–5 (tournament), st. 6.56f. (death and frying pan), and st. 7 (coat).

202. Rutebeuf, *Oeuvres complètes*, ed. Edmond Faral and Julia Bastin, vol. 1 (Paris, 1959), poem no. 40, "La mort Rutebeuf: 'Lessier m'estuet le rimoier,'" pp. 575–77, stt. 1 and 5. Paul Meyer, "Les manuscrits français de Cambridge," *Romania* 32 (1901): 22f., st. 3 (anonymous prayer to Jesus Christ).

203. Eduard Bechmann, "Drei Dits de l'ame aus der Handschrift Ms. Gall. Oct. 28 der Koeniglichen Bibliothek zu Berlin," *Zeitschrift fuer romanische Philologie* 13 (1889): 73–77, poem C, "Saves que j'apiel Beghi-

nage?" st. 5.g/k (sword), st. 7.g/k (cord), st. 8.a/d (dye), st. 9a/d (little weight), and st. 16.g (book) (note conceit of "nails of love," hammer, and so on in stt. 13f. as well), Brussels MS, stt. 2–4 (arbalest conceit), p. 79.

204. Concerning religious poetry from Metz, see also Joseph Priebsch, "Drei altlothringische Mariengebete," *Zeitschrift fuer neufranzoesische Sprache und Literatur* 33, no. 1 (1908): 206–13.

205. Richard Otto (op. cit., note 52 above), no. 2, "Quant li dous temps," pp. 589–92, vv. 38f. (meat) (cf. v. 149), 78–84 (harrier), 99–102 (nightingale), and 113–19 (flowers); no. 3, "A l'oure de meydi," pp. 592–95, vv. 15–20 (dressings and pool), 37–40 (spicer/altar/spark), 49–52 (candle), 89–92 (stag), and 104 (feathers); no. 4, "Devant nous sont passeiz hyraulz," pp. 596–98, vv. 25–32 (sea) (cf. poem no. 8, pp. 239–42, for a repetition of vv. 29–32); no. 5, "Ihesus, vergiers d'espices, nostre vie," pp. 599–601, vv. 38–43 (doves); no. 8, "Or m'an irai en sospirant," pp. 606–13, vv. 129–32 (poultice), 169–72 (orchard), and 189–92 (taverns).

206. Jean Brisebarre, "Trois poèmes de Jean Brisebarre le court, de Douai," ed. Amédée Salmon, in *Mélanges de philologie romane dédiés à Carl Wahlund à l'occasion du cinquantième anniversaire de sa naissance* (Macon, 1896), no. 2, "Onques tant n'ama Elaine," p. 222, st. 1 (Helen/ Isaiah); Louis Mourin, "Poésies religieuses française inconnues, dans des manuscrits de Bruxelles et d'Evora," *Scriptorium* 3 (1949): 229, "*Ave* fu dit pour salutation," st. 4.1–4 (grammatical metaphor); *Guillaume de Machaut, Poésies Lyriques*, ed. Vladimir Chichmaref, vol. 2 (Paris, 1909), "Je ne cesse de prier," vv. 55ff. (allegory of fountain, and so on), esp. pp. 127–34 (better at Rome, and so on); Eustace Deschamps, *Oeuvres complètes*, ed. Le Marquis de Queux de Saint-Hilaire and Gaston Raynaud, 3 vols., SATF 16.1–3 (Paris, 1878–91), vol. 1, no. 134, "Secourez moi, douce vierge Marie," p. 258, and no. 125, p. 259; *Oeuvres poétiques de Christine de Pisan*, ed. Maurice Roy, vol. 3, SATF 41.3 (Paris, 1896), "O Vierge pure, incomparable," p. 8, st. 16.

207. *Oeuvres de Georges Chastellain*, ed. Kervyn de Lettenhove, vol. 8 (Brussels, 1866), "Louenge de la tres-glorieuse Vierge," pp. 269–92 (fifty twelve-line stanzas): st. 4 (veins, heart, and so on), st. 16 (apple), st. 25 (grain and straw), and stt. 32–34 (soaring lark). Note also the "container" motif, in modified form, in st. 23: "Qui le hault ciel imperial delite, / Qui neuf coeurs perce et les abymes oeuvre, / Qui part d'une humble ouverture petite / Et tient la terre en rondeur circonstrite" (Who delights the high imperial heaven, who transpierces the nine [angelic] choirs and opens (?) the abysses, who comes forth from a little lowly opening and holds the earth traced out in roundness).

208. Molinet (op. cit., note 64, chapter 2), no. 8, "Quant Terprendreus sa harpe prepara," pp. 447ff. (harp allegory); no. 16, "*Ave*, angelicque sa-

lut," p. 484, l. 18f. (cf. hell as "a castle where Venus is mistress" in A. Keller, *Romvart* [Mannheim/Paris, 1844]), "Un chastel say ou droit fief de l'empire," p. 618, l. 2 (one of twelve "balades de Pasques" in a fifteenth-century manuscript); and no. 15, "A la divine, ardue sapience," p. 478, st. 6.

209. See for instance *Cantigas* no. 260, "Dicede ai trobadores."

210. Cf. *Cantigas* no. 279, "Santa Maria, valed, ai Sennor," st. 3 ("greener than cambric"); no. 246, "A que as portas doleo," refrain (doors); no. 340, "Virgen Madre groriosa, / de Deus filla e esposa" (*alva*). Vicente, no. 5, p. 10.

211. Gonzalo de Berceo, *Obras completas*, ed. Brian Dutton, vol. 2, Colección Tamesis, ser. A, Monographs, 15 (Madrid, 1972), *Milagros*, "Prologue," st. 38.4 and 42 (Domingo / the well); the Marquis of Santillana, "Senor, tu me libra de toda fortuna," in *Poesia religiosa española*, ed. Roque Scarpa, 2d ed. (Santiago de Chile, 1941), p. 49, l. 4 (= no. 25 in Madrid, Real Academia de la Historia 2–7–2 MS 2, to be edited by J. M. Azáceta); *Baena* (op. cit., note 135, chapter 2), vol. 2, no. 317, "Madre de Dios verdadero," p. 692, v. 37f.

212. Nicholas Nunez, "Decidnos, Reyna del ciela / si soys vos," CG, vol. 1, no. 43, pp. 76–78; Frey Gauberte, "Como en salir del rosal," in Scarpa (op. cit., note 211 above), p. 61f. (flower and rosebush). Juan Alvarez Gato, *Obras completas* . . , ed. Jenaro A. Rodriquez, Los Clásicos olvidados 4 (Madrid, 1928), no. 85, "Dy nobis, Maria," p. 150, ll. 19–22 (= CC, vol. 1, no. 118, p. 257) (captain); and CC, vol. 1, no. 116, "Pues tienes libre poder," p. 254, vv. 11f. (pilgrims) (= no. 83, pp. 143–45).

213. Frey Hernando de Talavera (?), "Oh suma de nuestros bienes," in Menéndez y Pelayo 4:325–34, st. 10. 2f. (*In mulieribus*; p. 329, Cerberus); st. 12.7–12 (*Ventris*; p. 330, promised land); st. 13.1–6 (*Tui*; p. 330, chest/vial); st. 14 (*Jesus*, p. 331, hawk and bait); st. 15.4f. (*Sancta*, p. 331, rich cloak) and st. 16 (*Maria*; p. 332, sea).

214. Inigo de Mendoza, CC, vol. 1, "Heres nino y as amor," p. 14, col. a (*romance*); Marquis of Santillana, CC, vol. 1, no. 218, "Virgen, eternal esposa," p. 531, st. 5.4–6; Lucas Fernandez, in J. Peman and M. H. Herrero (op. cit., note 21 above), "Desque Juan le vió llegado," p. 315, st. 6.5f.; Juan Tallante, CC, vol. 2, no. 1087, "Prouidencia diuinal," p. 660, st. 6 (musical metaphor), and no. 1093, "Tu, rogado de ti mismo," p. 670, st. 5.5–8 (Cyrenean).

215. Ambrosio Montesinos, *Coplas a reverencia de San Juan Baptista, y del misterio de la santa Visitacion* . . . , Menéndez y Pelayo 4:278, "Comparacion"; Alonso de Proaza, CC, vol. 2, no. 1115, "El coraçon que llamamos," p. 687, st. 5, col. b.

216. CM, no. 293, "Vos mayor, / Vos mejor, / Vos paristes sin dolor," p. 155, st. 11f., col. b (note container motif in st. 13), by Lope de Baena, is

but one example of these clothing metaphors. CG, vol. 2, no. 66, "Quando el costado divino," p. 330f., stt. 1 and 5, by Andres Quebado (1540 ed.); no. 71 "En aquella eternidad," p. 336, st. 5, by Lazaro Bejarano; no. 72, "Antheo cuando caya," p. 336, stt. 1 and 3, anon. (Antaeus / bread); no. 75, "Resplandeciente luzero," p. 339, stt. 2 and 3, by Ruy García Alleman (Antaeus / bouncing ball); Bartolomeo de Torres Naharro, *Propalladia and Other Works*, ed. Joseph Gillet, 3 vols. (Bryn Mawr, Pa., 1943), vol. 1, "A la Verónica," pp. 209–11 (cf. ll. 4f., 41, 43, 47, 50; see also synonyms such as *estanpar*, ll. 7 and 10).

217. See for instance Brown XV, no. 109, "Brother, a-byde, I the desire and pray," pp. 169–75.

218. *Skjaldedigtning* B.1, "Solarljod" pp. 635–48 (esp. stt. 33–52 and 53–68). Brown XIV, no. 77, "Unkynde man, gif kepe til me," p. 93, ll. 19–21; Brown XV, no. 81, "I syng of a myden," p. 119; and the Corpus Christi carol, Davies, no. 164, p. 272. Davies, "Introduction," p. 23.

219. Helgason 1.2:7, "Rosa," stt. 4 and 7 (fruit/sweat bath), and 1.2: 269, "Fyrirlát mér jungfrúin hreina," st. 2.8 (bright stone). Helgason 2:40, "Maria meïann skiaera," st. 2.4f.

220. *Skjaldedigtning* B.2, "Lilja," p. 414, st. 92.

INDEX OF TITLES, FIRST LINES, AND NAMES

This index includes basic descriptive information about major authors, manuscripts, and texts. Church feast days are listed in the Index of Subjects. The term *medieval religious lyric* is abbreviated throughout as "mrl."

"In dulci jubilo," macaronics in, 113
"In ecclesia" (*cantio*), and stanza linking, 118
Iñigo de Mendoza, Frey (fl. third quarter of fifteenth century; Spanish Franciscan poet): and metaphor, 220; and Spanish mrl, 261
Innocent III, Pope, on risks of typology, 204
"I passed þoru a garden grene," and Chaucerian dream vision, 150
Italy, use of Provençal in, 19

Jacopone da Todi (1230/40–1306; gifted lay author of ca. ninety *laude*): and *aporia*, 186; and "as if there" apostrophe, 137; as author of *laude*, 48; and authorial personality, 128; and autobiographical details, 195; and brevity formula, 134; and dialogue between characters, 145; and diminishing metaphor, 210; and exclamations, 151; "literary" *laude* by, 234; mystical influence on, 201; and mystical mode, 69; and naturalism, 213; and prosopopoeia, 142; and rhetorical questions, 151; and self-apostrophe, 162; and speaker/character(s) dialogue, 143; speaker used as paradigm by, 160; and stanza linking, 119
Jacques de Baisieux, and miniature allegory, 127
Jerusalem: and *kanon*, 80; as a liturgical trendsetter, 32
Joachim of Fiore (twelfth-century Latin writer and prophet), ambivalence of, toward exegesis, 200
João Claro, Friar (1450–1520; Portuguese abbot and religious poet): *horae* by, 62; *prosimetrum* by, 110
Johannes von Rinkenberc, and "container contained" motif, 207–8
John Damascene, St. (ca. 675–ca. 748; major Eastern theologian and religious poet): and *kanon*, 80; trimeters in liturgical poetry by, 78
John Mauropus (ca. 1000–1060/80; leading Byzantine poet): and *aporia*, 187; and "as if there" apostrophe, 137; as author of *kanons*, 81; and authorial personality, 128; and autobiographical details, 196;

and Christmas, 61; and "personal" lyric, 68; and pronoun shifts, 173; and ring composition, 106; use of speaker as paradigm by, 159. *See also* Στόματι πηλίνῳ
John of Howden (d. ca. 1275; outstanding Latin religious poet, author of four-thousand-line *Philomena* and many other poems, mostly Marian): and meditative mode, 67; and mystical mode, 69; and ring composition, 106
John Pecham (d. 1292; Franciscan, Archbishop of Canterbury [1279], and author of *horae*-type *Philomena*, much shorter than John of Howden's, as well as other religious poems): and *horae*, 62; and meditative mode, 67
John the Evangelist, St.: Joys of, 115; and mrl, 60
John [Kyriotes] the Geometer (fl. second half of tenth century; gifted secular and religious poet), and autobiographical details, 196
John XXII, Pope, promulgation of Trinity Sunday by (1334), 40
Jónsson, Abbot Arni (fourteenth century), on violations of rules in religious poetry, 73
Jonsson, Ritva, and *Corpus troporum*, 85
Jordan, Robert, strictures on critical methodology of, 25
Jorge da Silva, *capitolo ternario* by, 98
Josephus [of Sicily, "the Hymnographer"] (ca. 816–886, author of over two hundred *kanons* written at Studios monastery; some poems attributed to him may actually be by Joseph of Thessalonica, Theodore the Studite's brother), and "do as you did" apostrophe (Φαιφρυνέσθω ἡ γῆ), 140
Juan del Encina (1468–1530s; musician and poet, chief literary figure during the reign of Ferdinand and Isabella, playwright and writer of *villancicos*). *See* "Andá acá, pastor"
Juan de Padilla (1468–1518; Carthusian religious poet, imitator of Dante, author of *Retablo de la Vida de Cristo* and *Doce Triunfos de los Apostolos*): and acrostics, 117; and Spanish mrl, 261

(Theodore Prodromos), speaker as paradigm in (epigram), 159

Theodore Prodromos (ca. 1100–1159 or later; prolific writer in prose and verse; first Greek literary figure to incorporate demotic elements into his language): and autobiographical details, 196; and colloquialisms, 199; and dialogue between characters, 146; possible influence of, on Old Norse epigram, 66; and "political" verse, 54; popular influences on, 199, 209; and speaker as paradigm, 159; tetrastichs on Bible by, 66. See also Τῆς ἡμέρας τὸ δόγμα νυκτὶ μανθάνει

Theodore the Studite (ca. 759–826; abbot of the Studion, opponent of iconoclasm, author of iambic poems on monastic duties and of kanons and kontakia): poems by, in trimeters, 66; and references to role of poet, 196. See also Τὸν θείῳ μύρῳ χρισθέντα; Ψυχὴ ταπεινή, δεῦρό μοι, δέξαι λόγον

Theodulf of Orleans, (ca. 760–ca. 821; leading Carolingian court poet), as author of "Gloria laus et honor," 238

Thibaut de Champagne (1201–1253; King of Navarre; outstanding trouvère): and French mrl, 31, 247; and naturalism, 216

Thomas Aquinas, St. (ca. 1225–1274; great Dominican theologian; author of Summa Theologiae; commissioned by Urban IV in 1264 to write hymns and sequence for new feast of Corpus Christi, including Lauda Sion): and Corpus Christi Office, 65; on insinuatio, 164; pronouns and verb forms in Lauda Sion by, 180–85; and regular sequence, 89; and ring composition, 106; views of, on music, 38

Thomas Becket, St. (twelfth century): and Joys of Mary ("Gaude flore virginali"), 114; and vision framework, 149

"þru tidigge us cumet iche dei," as example of pronoun shifts, 171

Τὸν θείῳ μύρῳ χρισθέντα (Theodore the Studite), and poet-speaker in Greek mrl, 168–70

Tornabuoni de' Medici, Lucrezia (1425–1482; mother of Lorenzo the Magnificent; author of some of the best fifteenth-

century laude): as author of laude, 61; contrafactura of May-song by ("Ben vengas Mayo!"), 153

Torres Naharro, Bartolomeo de (d. 1531?; important Spanish poet and dramatist), and metaphor, 222

Toulouse. See in Index of Subjects consistori

"Tout a par moy, affin qu'on ne me voye" (Jean Molinet), pronoun shifts in, 175

Trinity, as subject of mrl, 59

Tripudiati, dancing in streets by, 96

Trisodion, and Byzantine liturgy, 78

"Unkynde man, gif kepe til me," possible influence of ballad tradition on, 222

Valencia: as cultural center, 227; joyas at (1474), 45; poetic competitions at, 227

Vallmanya, Anthoni, and stanza linking, 118

van den Boogaard, N., index to French refrains by, 107

Veles de Guevara, Pero (late fourteenth- or early fifteenth-century Spanish poet), and naturalism, 219

Venantius Fortunatus (540–600; outstanding Christian Latin poet): and hymns, 237; influence of, on mrl rhetoric, 133; and metaphorical repertories, 209; and references to spring ("Tempore florigero"), 153; and trochaic septenarius in, 77

Vergil: influence of, on mrl rhetoric, 133; and medieval education, 134

Vernon manuscript (large fourteenth-century English compendium): character of, 65; moral mode in, 65; naturalism in, 222; refrain-lines in, 96, 107, 108; rhymed Psalter in, 92; ring composition in, 106

Vicente, Gil (ca. 1470?–1536/40; outstanding Portuguese lyric poet and creator of Portuguese drama): and exclamations, 151; and naturalism, 219; and ring composition, 106

Viscardi, Antonio, on liturgical parataxis, 15

Von den Steinen, Wolfgang (Notker der Dichter), on sequence, 82

INDEX OF SUBJECTS

Page numbers in **boldface** indicate the principal discussions of major topics. The term *medieval religious lyric* is abbreviated throughout as "mrl."

canzone: as ancestor of sonnet, 99; in Italian mrl, 48, 233
capitolo ternario, **98–99**; by Bianco da Siena, 193; classical material in, 214; in Italian mrl, 233; by Leonardo Giustinian, 72; and *terza rima*, 46; and verse-tempo, 100
career as poet, feasibility of, in Germany, 50
carmen quadratum: acrostics in, 116; defined, 87. *See also* figure-poem
Carolingian court, and mrl, 238
Carolingian period: contradictory impulses in, 44; and Latinity, 43
Carolingian synthesis of Frankish and Roman, 88
Castilian: as language of lyric, 261; replacement of Catalan by, 227
Catalan mrl, **227–28**; acrostics in, 117; *aporia* in, 186; "as if there" apostrophe in, 137; authorship of, 51; calls to audience in, 157; Christmas lyrics in, 60, 61; didactic mode in, 65; diminishing metaphor in, 210; exclamations in, 151; *goigs* in, 114; inadequacy topos in, 188; indirect prayer in, 165; invocations in, 191; lullabies in, 74; meditative mode in, 67; moral mode in, 65; and mystical mode, 70; naturalism in, 211; *planctus Mariae* in, 61; pronoun shifts in, 171; refrain stanzas in, 107; reverdie in, 153; rhetorical questions in, 151; ring composition in, 106; saints in, 60; self-naming in, 195; self-referentiality in, 197; speaker as paradigm in, 161; speaker/character(s) dialogue in, 143; stanza linking in, 118; "today" motif in, 152; *virelai/virolai* in, 96; visions in, 149
Catalan poetry, earliest, 2
catechetical structure, use of, in mrl, 107
caudae, in *conductus*, 90
Celtic tradition, persistence of, 252
centralism, Byzantine, effects of, 9
change: Byzantine resistance to, 54; and mrl, 225; medieval view of, 7; resistance to, in late Middle Ages, 87
change, historical, 3; and genres in West, 74
change from below: and liturgy, 35, 38; and Western Church, 200
chanson d'amour: and *alba*, 26; analysis of, by Zumthor, 27; contrasted to mrl, 29;

influence of, on Western mrl rhetoric, 133; language of, in mrl, 72; and meditative and mystical lyric, 133; and pronouns in French mrl, 171; self-referentiality in, 197
chanson d'aventure, **148–50**; fashion for, 155; and Middle English mrl, 244; and *pastourelle*, 149; religious versions of, 73–74. *See also* *pastourelle*
chansonniers: recording of French mrl in, 248; recording of Provençal mrl in, 257
chansons avec des refrains, defined, 107
chant royal: and "aureate" diction, 166; number of stanzas in, 116; at *puys*, 96, 248; and refrain, 108
charité, defined, 46
chiasmus, example of, 184
Christian Latin, influence of, on mrl rhetoric, 133
Christian poetry, and new forms, 76
Christmas: and "as if there" apostrophe, 137; and Catalan mrl, 60; and *conductus*, 91; and "do as you did" apostrophe, 140; evolution of, 39; in *joyas*, 61; in *laude*, 47; and macaronics, 113; Marian lyrics for, 61; "popular" character of lyrics concerning, 60; shift in focus of, 41; as subject of mrl, 60–61; as subject of Middle English mrl, 244; and trope, 86; and vision framework, 150
Christmas carols, 244; "as if there" apostrophe in, 137; calls to audience in, 157; and *conductus*, 91; exclamations in, 151; Latin in, 112, 113; naturalism in, 222–23; possible origin of, in dance-song, 74; rhetorical questions in, 151; and Friar James Ryman, 244; "today" motif in, 152; as *zejel*-form, 96
Christmas hymns, paradoxes in, 199
Christmas poetry, exclamations and rhetorical questions in, 151
Christological feasts, evolution of, into Marian feasts, 41
Christ on Cross, and Passion lyrics, 62
church-year: ahistorical cyclicity of, 135; and *laude*, 46, 47; and sequence cycles, 84
citation of hymn incipits, as contrastive structure, 109, 110
classical material: in late mrl, 214, 218, 220, 221; and Jean Molinet, 218

51–52; *capitolo ternario* in, 98; count of years in, 155; dialogue between characters in, 145; "do as you did" apostrophe in, 140; epigrammatic mode in, 66; exclamations in, 152; form, prominence of, in, 247; inadequacy topos in, 188–89; invocations in, 191; Joys/Sorrows of Mary in, 115; lack of aurality in, 100; Latin in, 111, 112; moral mode in, 65; mystical mode in (fifteenth century), 70; naturalism in, 213; and "new song," 193; octosyllabic couplet in, 99; refrains in, 107; religious May songs in, 74; reverdie in, 153; rhetorical questions in, 152; ring composition in, 106; "today" motif in, 152; tripartite stanza in, 93; visions in, 149. See also *capitolo ternario*; *laude*

Italian poetry: earliest, 2; influence of, on Catalan, 227

iubilus, and sequence, 82–83

jeux floraux. See *consistori*

Joachism, and mystical mode, 69

joyas (Valencia, 1474): defined, 45; exclamations in, 151; inadequacy topos in, 188; and indirect prayer, 165; naturalism in, 211; rhetorical questions in, 151; self-referentiality in, 197; stanza linking in, 118

Joys of Mary, 114; and high style in Portuguese, 254; in Provençal, 257; in Spanish mrl, 261

Joys of the Just, 115

kanon, 80–81; acrostics in, 117; autobiographical details in, 196; compared to *kontakion*, 81; form of, 80; history of, 231, 232; origin of, 80; and panegyric, 133; parts of, 81; responsion in, 79; and saints, 60

Kirchenlied, appearance of, 230

kontakion: acrostics in, 117; compared to sequence, 84; debt of, to Syriac hymnody, 80; decline of, 80; dialogue between characters in, 146; *ephymnion* (refrain) in, 107; form of, 79; history of, 231; moral mode in, 66; and panegyric, 133; as part of *kanon*, 81; refrain in, 94; responsion in, 79; and Romanos, 79; and saints, 60; Syriac origins of, 32, 79

lai, 96–98; and French art-lyric, 248; Marian, by Gautier de Coincy ("Ne flours ne glais"), 154; ring composition in, 106. See also *leich*

laity, estrangement of, from clergy, 44, 46

laity as authors: of Catalan mrl, 51; of German mrl, 50; of Greek mrl, 53; of mrl, 49; of Portuguese mrl, 51; of Provençal mrl, 50; of Spanish mrl, 51

language: choice of, in Iberian poetry, 18; choice of, in lyric poetry, 19; choice of, in medieval literature, 18; and differences in style or subject, 19; social standing of, and poetry, 50; written, in Middle Ages, 8

Latinity, evolution of, in Middle Ages, 43

Latin language: incomprehensibility of, in Middle Ages, 43, 270n.35; position of, in Western Middle Ages, 10; shift in status of, 49; use of, in Middle Ages, 19; and vernaculars, 76, 111–12

Latin mrl, 237–39; acrostics in, 117; *aporia* in, 187; "as if there" apostrophe in, 137; audience for, 49; authorship of, 48–49; autobiographical details in, 196; calls to audience in, 157; Christmas in, 61; chronological limits of, 1; citation of hymn incipits in, 110; colloquialism in, 199; compared to Greek mrl, 4; creation of forms in, 75; details from "life" in, 199; dialogue between characters in, 145, 146; didactic mode in, 65; "do as you did" apostrophe in, 140; epic rhetoric in, 134; epigrammatic mode in scriptural paraphrase in, 66; epiphrasis in, 163; exclamations in, 151, 152; indirect prayer in, 164; invocations in, 189–90; macaronics in, 110, 111, 112, 113; major authors of, 239; Mary-Psalters in, 92; meditative mode in, 67; metaphor in (pre-1200), 209; metaphor, impact of nontraditional, on, 203; moral mode in, 65; and Old Norse epigram, 66; *pastourelle* in, 149; penitential mode in, 195; pronoun shifts in, 167–68, 172–73, 175; references to occasion or performance of poem in, 196; refrains in, 107; reverdie in, 74; rhetorical questions in, 151, 152; ring composition in, 106; and seasons, 153; self-apostrophe in, 162;

Designer: Lisa Mirski
Compositor: G & S Typesetters, Inc.
Printer: Thomson-Shore, Inc.
Binder: John H. Dekker & Sons
Text: 10/12 Sabon
Display: Solemnis, Sabon